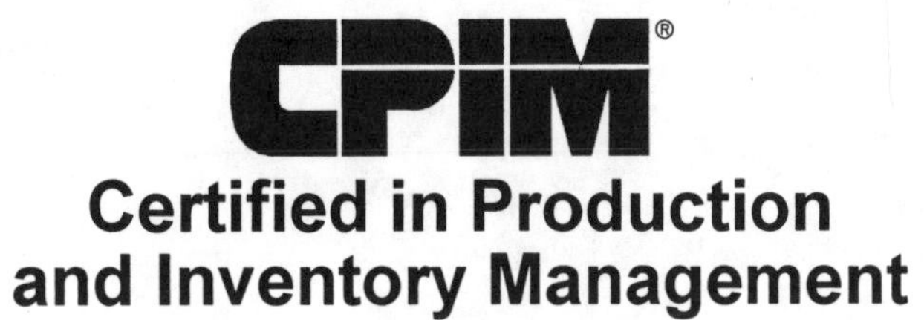

Certified in Production and Inventory Management

Inventory Management Reprints

Revised 1998

Articles selected by the Inventory Management Committee of the APICS Curricula and Certification Council

© 1998 APICS—The Educational Society for Resource Management

ISBN: 1-55822-136-0

Library of Congress Number: 97-74539

No portion of this publication may be reproduced by any means without prior permission from APICS. Contact society headquarters at the address below for information concerning reprint policies.

The society will not be responsible for any statements, beliefs, or opinions expressed by individuals in this publication. The views expressed are solely those of the individuals and do not necessarily reflect endorsement by the society.

APICS — The Educational Society for Resource Management
5301 Shawnee Road
Alexandria, VA 22312-2317
(703) 354-8851

Printed in the U.S.A.
Stock #05010, 8/98

Contents

Objectives and Policies

Inventory Systems

Techniques

Distribution Inventory Planning and Control

Preface

As in the past, the articles in this publication were selected by the Inventory Management CPIM Committee based on relevancy and content: relevancy from the viewpoint of belonging to one of our four main topic areas, content from the viewpoint of confirming and perhaps challenging our existing body of knowledge.

Reprints are the committee's vehicle to validate inventory management's role as a viable element in the APICS CPIM curriculum. Additionally, the reprints give the committee an opportunity to quickly cover topics that spotlight state-of-the-art inventory management practices and processes.

We encourage candidates to be familiar with this material and see the reprints as one of our "key" resources. The committee uses these reprints to document new trends and confirm existing concepts in a timely manner.

New for this version, in addition to bringing in 12 new articles, we have reorganized the articles so that all are contained within their appropriate subject area:

- Objectives and Policies
- Inventory Systems
- Techniques
- Distribution Inventory Planning and Control.

Please use this text to augment your studies in the area of inventory management, and share your feedback with us and your peers. We welcome your comments and recommendations for the future.

APICS Inventory Management CPIM Committee

David L. Rivers, CFPIM, CIRM, Committee Chair
Sharon M. Dow, CPIM, CIRM
Jim Greathouse, CPIM
William Leedale, CFPIM, CIRM
Paul Pittman, Ph.D., CFPIM
James W. Rice, Ph.D., CFPIM
Angel Sosa, CFPIM
Joan Walsh, CPIM, CIRM
Mark K. Williams, CFPIM

Reprinted from APICS 1987 *Conference Proceedings.*

How to Use Inventory Turns to Stimulate Productivity Improvements

Roger Ahrens

Productivity and inventory turns seem like very different animals. This presentation will examine the correlation between the two and also show how this knowledge can be utilized to stimulate and measure productivity improvements at all levels of the organization.

Productivity

Loosely defined, productivity means getting more with less. Managers and supervisors have traditionally thought of productivity gains in terms of worker efficiency. Workers have thought of productivity improvements as having to work harder. Consequently, over the decades an adversarial relationship has developed which has fostered a negative association with the word productivity.

The lack of significant productivity improvements did not pose a big problem for North American industry because the market for our goods grew at a faster rate than we could produce them. This left us in the enviable position to pass the increased cost of doing business to the customers. Many people affectionately refer to this period as the glory years. Out of this has developed several generations of managers, technicians and workers who have never really understood the concept of productivity and why it is necessary for the long term survival of the organization. Enter into the scene overseas competition. Our first line of defense was unbelief and a barrage of reasons why this competition was unfair. Many industries have demanded protective measures from our governmental agencies. In fact, it hasn't been until the last couple of years that some industry leaders have admitted that the real enemy is ourselves. Over the long run, complacency caused by prosperous times provided an opportunity for our competitors. They could provide better product for less in the market place.

To remain in business a manufacturing organization must be relentless in its continual search to be more productive. What must be done to become more productive? To be more productive a manufacturing unit must find ways to *move material to, through, and out of the plant to the customer with minimum wasted material, labor, overhead, and elapsed time.* Productivity gains can be realized when everyone in the organization understands and believes in this principle and is also motivated and committed to pull together as a team to accomplish this end.

Productivity improvement is a team activity. Team work must be a partnership between management and workers. Teamwork between management and the workers is a partnership that has to do with direction, objectives and motivation. Teamwork throughout the staff elements of the organization must be mutually supportive. Outstanding individual player contributions rarely make a winning team. Likewise with productivity, the individual efforts or the efforts of the various operating units often do not contribute to productivity gains of the entire organization. The players that are motivated and play well together as a team are the winners.

Because the spirit of productivity team work is not well understood, many manufacturing organizations are vulnerable to the productivity trap. In their zest and sometimes desperation to make productivity improvements they are willing to buy solutions without a clear understanding of what needs to be fixed. There are a multitude of remedies available on the market which claim to increase productivity. Some of these remedies may yield improvement for one or more areas of the organization. But, no matter how well intended, these solutions are a waste of resources and time if they do not contribute to the increased productivity of the entire organization. Remember, we don't succeed unless we pull together as a team.

Productivity Measurements

How do we determine if productivity improvements are being attained? On the surface this seems fairly straight forward. Productivity is the relationship between inputs and outputs.

$$\text{Productivity} = \frac{\text{Output}}{\text{Input}}$$

To use this ratio there needs to be a common unit of measure (i.e., pieces, pounds, feet, sheets, boxes, tanks, etc.). The numerator, output measurements, are application dependent. From a micro view of the manufacturing process, the output is the amount of product completed by a work center, cell, or department. From a macro view of the organization, output is shipments. Regardless of the perspective, outputs can quite easily conform to these units of measure. The input denominator is somewhat more complex. The inputs of a manufacturing process can be categorized as labor, burden, and material. These inputs do conform to the above listed units of measure. The only obvious common unit of measure for these inputs is cost. Therefore the common unit of measure for both inputs and outputs is cost. Provided cost is used as the common unit of measure, then the cost of output is really the more familiar COGS (Cost of Goods Sold).

What does the productivity ratio tell us? The productivity ratio measures the relationship between production inputs and outputs which is in effect the rate of flow. It is generally assumed that a manufacturing process can not yield more output than what was originally input. This is because every manufacturing process produces waste in the form of wasted material, labor, time, administration, etc. This would seem to indicate the productivity ratio should always be less than one. If it were not for inventory this would be true. This dimension of the productivity model deals with the resident amount of inventory that is in process. If this inventory is decreased, then the productivity ratio can exceed one for the period of time the inventory is actually decreasing. Understanding this, it becomes evident that the productivity ratio changes from one measurement period to another really reflect the changes in waste and inventory.

Relationship between Productivity and Inventory Turns

From the Japanese we have learned that much of inventory is the result of mistakes and is a coping mechanism to compensate for production disruptions. The concept of JIT—make what you need (no more) when you need it (no sooner)—clearly identifies inventory as accumulated waste. Inventory hides mistakes and problems. This is why the Japanese believe that inventory is evil. Therefore inventory must be the inverse of productivity and represents the accumulation of nonproductive activities.

Inventory is a static evaluation which measures the accumulative amount of waste at a point in time. The amount of inventory is not as significant as how often the inventory is used. Therefore it is desirable to express inventory as a factor of volume. This measurement is known as the inventory turn ratio:

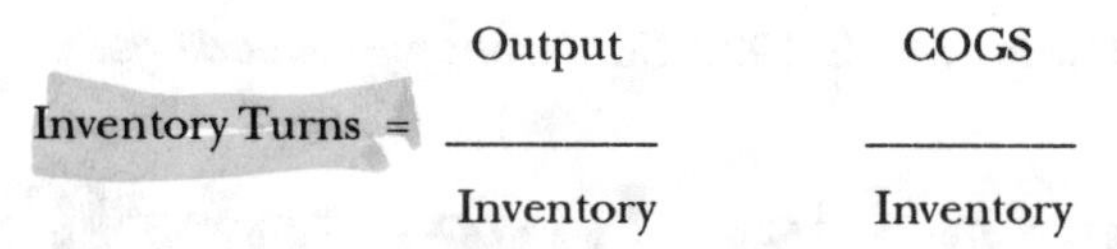

$$\text{Inventory Turns} = \frac{\text{Output}}{\text{Inventory}} \qquad \frac{\text{COGS}}{\text{Inventory}}$$

In many ways the inventory turn ratio is a better barometer of productivity than the productivity ratio. Ed Heard claims that the inventory turn ratio is an under-rated measurement that might be the singular best indicator of productivity improvements. Although the productivity ratio is a good measurement it is an intangible measurement which is abstract for most people. The input portion of the productivity ratio is a value that is not normally readily available or tracked by most companies. Conversely, inventory is a commodity that people can see, touch, and sometimes smell. The values required to compute the ratio are readily available. Business people relate to inventory and many are familiar with the traditional inventory turns measurement or ratio.

Even though the familiarity with inventory and the inventory turns ratio is an advantage it can also work as a disadvantage. Many of the people who are acquainted with inventory turns know that traditionally the inventory turn ratio has been used as an aggregate financial measurement to measure how efficiently an operating unit's inventory is utilized. They also recognize that rarely has this financial measurement stimulated much meaningful improvement activity. This is because most companies have a misalignment between the responsibility for inventory management and the authority to make decisions that impact inventory. Usually the material management types are saddled with the responsibility for inventory management. Even though they are the experts on inventory management, they are not the people that make most of the operational decisions, establish the company objectives, and formulate the procedures and policies that establish the amount of inventory required. For example lot sizes and leadtimes clearly appear to be a P&IC responsibility. Closer examination reveals that the parameters that drive the lot size are the manufacturing process and equipment, the assignment of setup and run cost, the forecasted volume, and the replenishment policy.

Likewise, the parameters that drive leadtime are the lot size, the manufacturing methods (batch or flow), the definition of the work day, manning policies, experienced absentee rate, and the scheduling rules. Clearly the responsibility for inventory is a team activity and extends well beyond the scope to materials management. Instead of one aggregate financial measurement of inventory there needs to be inventory objectives that are localized to specific management responsibility areas. If inventory is viewed as the accumulation of waste and the responsibility and accountability for inventory is localized, then the inventory turn measurement can be a very effective productivity tool.

Cascading Inventory Turn Responsibilities

Inventory turn is a good barometer of productivity but turn objectives and measurements must be localized to yield results. This means that turn objectives need to be developed starting with the general Manager and cascade down through the organization becoming more and more specific as these objectives are driven deeper into the organization. For example, the V.P. and General Manager can break the company inventory turn objective down to his/her subordinates.

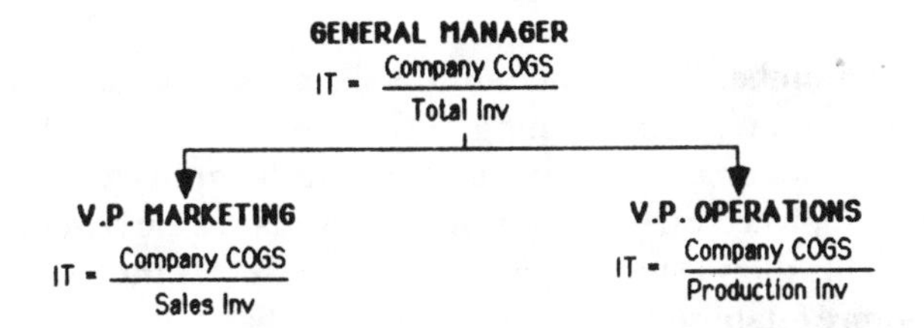

Notice that all three positions have the same COGS (Cost of Goods Sold). If the inventory was equally divided between Marketing and Operations, the inventory turn objective would be twice as large for the V. P.'s of Marketing and Operations than for the company as a whole. This upsets some people because the measurement counts the sale of the same goods twice. Remember this is not a financial measurement but a tool to communicate the inventory turns performance expected lower in the organization. This type of scheme is logical if you view Marketing as a distributor and Operations as a vendor for the Marketing organization. Instead of using the COGS it would be better if the Operation's equation used the COGPP (Cost of Goods Produced and Purchased) if that information is available. To make this type of system work you must be creative. For starters, use the existing information available until enough confidence is gained to create better information.

To be effective, the inventory turn objectives still must be driven deeper into the organization. For example, the V.P. of Marketing can in turn break the sales inventory turn objective down to his/her subordinate.

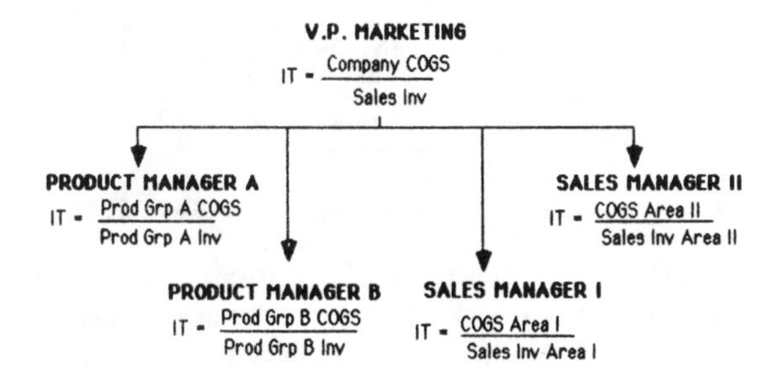

At this level of management it is desirable to match the numerator and the denominator of the turns equation if the information is available. Notice that for Product Manager A the COGS for Product Group A is matched with the inventory for Product Group A. The equation for Product Manager A is not specific about inventory. This inventory can include all the Product Group A inventory or just Product Group A Sales inventory. Which option is selected is dependent upon the information available and the responsibility and authority of Product Manager A. Make the measurement and object fit the situation and the personalities involved.

On the Operation/Manufacturing side of the organization the inventory turn objective also needs to be broken out.

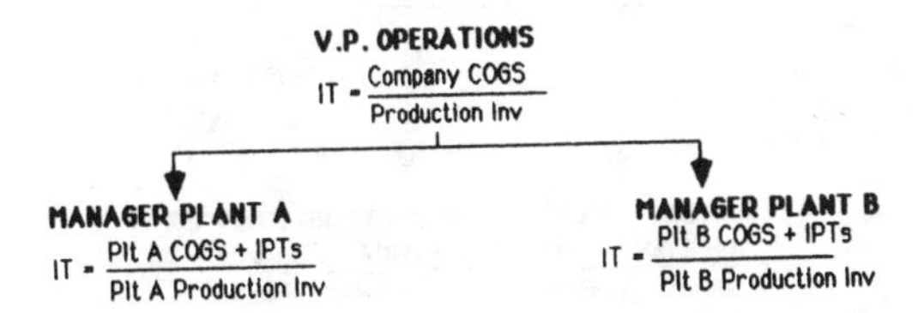

In this example, the V.P. of Operations creates inventory turn performance objectives for each of the plants. The numerator or output side of the equation needs to include all the plants customers. These customers could be sales/marketing, other plants within the company using the IPTs (Inter Plant Transfers) system, or contract work done for others. It would be a cleaner measurement for the plants to use the COGPP (Cost of Goods Produced and Purchased) instead of the Plant COGS plus the IPTs if this information is available.

In turn the Plant Manager should develop inventory turn objectives for his/her staff. At this level of management functional organizations are more prevalent. In functional organizations responsibilities are compartmentalized by specialty area (i.e., P&IC, M.E., Purchasing, Shop Departments, etc.). The establishment of meaningful turn objectives at this level requires some creativity. In many organizations inventories are categorized (i.e., raw materials, semi-finished goods, WIP, purchased parts inventories, manufacturing inventories, supplies, etc.) Although there is not a cost of good sold for each inventory category, inventory turn objectives can be calculated for each inventory category using the overall cost of good sold for the operating unit or plant. This is very similar to what was done at the general management level except that in a functional organization responsibilities overlap. More than one manager can be responsible for each inventory category. To view this relationship clearly, a matrix of responsibilities and inventory categories needs to be created.

RESPONSIBILITY / INVENTORY CATEGORY MATRIX

	Raw Matls	WIP	Pur Parts	Manf Parts	Supplies
P&IC	X	X	X	X	
M.E.		X		X	
Purchasing	X		X		X
Production		X		X	X
Maintenance		X			

Striving for joint goal achievement should encourage managers with overlapping responsibilities to work together as a team to exceed the goal. Using this information inventory turn goals can be developed for each management responsibility area.

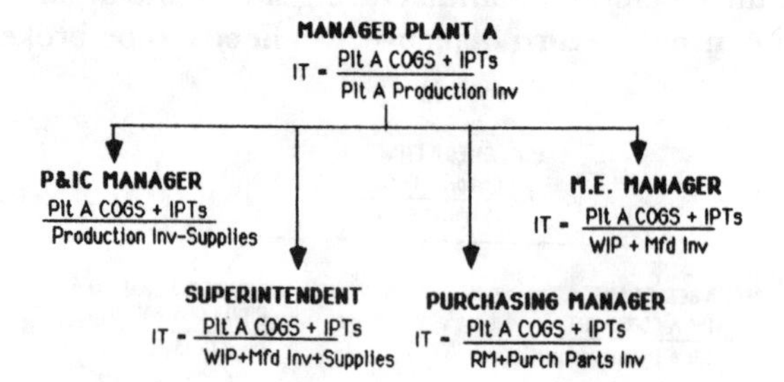

It is conceivable that this system of cascading inventory turns can be extended to production lines and work cells. Using the JIT focused factory concept combined with the small group improvement activities, it is very desirable to establish inventory turn objectives at this level. The inventory turn objective can be used to communicate the commitment that must be made to reduce waste or nonproductive activities in all levels of the organization. Remember the goal is to encourage improvements relative to volume, not necessarily to make financially precise measurements.

Inventory Turn Performance Measurements

The inventory turn performance objectives are to be a mutual agreement between the individual with the responsibility and their supervisor. The establishment of this objective should take into consideration historical performance, long range direction of the company, and current and up-coming year operational plans. Point inventory measurements such as year-end and quarter-end encourage extra ordinary actions toward the end of the measurement period to make the measurement look good. To encourage improved performance over the long haul I recommend setting objectives using year average inventory values as a basis.

Once the inventory turn objectives have been established, a performance monitoring system needs to be developed. The purpose of this system is to track actual performance to the inventory turn objectives on a regular basis. There are several methods of tracking actual inventory turns:

YEAR-TO-DATE (Y-T-D) ANNUALIZED

$$\text{Inventory Turns} = \frac{\dfrac{\text{Y-T-D COGS} \times 12}{\text{n mos}}}{\dfrac{\Sigma\ \text{Inv} \ldots \text{n mos}}{\text{n mos}}}$$

The number "n" is the months since the beginning of the fiscal year. A shortcoming of this measurement is that it places unequal weight on each month's input. A lot of weight is placed on each month's performance early in the year. This diminishes as the year progresses. If the objectives were established using a year average basis, at year-end the basis for both the objective and the actual performance will be in synchronization.

CURRENT MONTH

$$\text{Inventory Turns} = \frac{\text{Current mo COGS} \times 12}{\text{Current mo Inv}}$$

This measurement is very dynamic, fluctuating considerably from month to month.

THREE MONTH ROLLING AVERAGE

$$\text{Inventory Turns} = \frac{\text{Past 3 mos COGS} \times 4}{\text{Current mo Inv}}$$

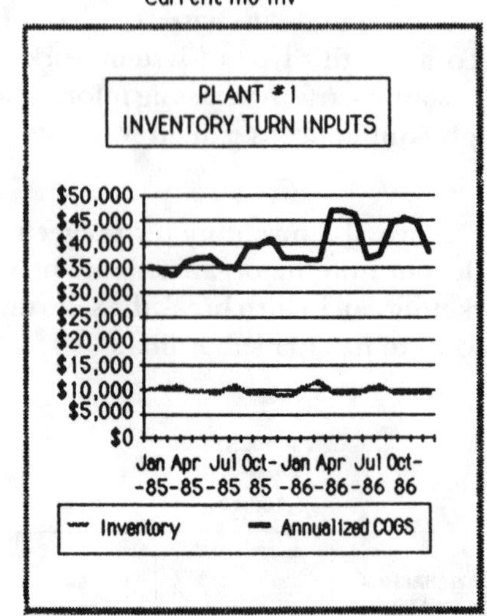

This is the performance tracking measurement that I recommend. It is smoothed but yet dynamic enough to react to significant business trends. Also, it is easy to understand.

 © APICS

To be useful as a management tool these performance measurements need to be made on a timely basis and must be made frequently. I recommend once per month. Quarterly is not frequent enough. A picture is worth a thousand words. Therefore it is very desirable to use graphs to chart monthly performance to plan. This is an excellent application for a personal computer. A typical performance chart might look like the graphs below. These graphs are shown in pairs to show the effect inputs (inventory and COGS) have on the inventory turn ratio. Notice that in this example the annualized COGS, which is about 3.5 times larger than inventory, has a much greater impact on inventory turns.

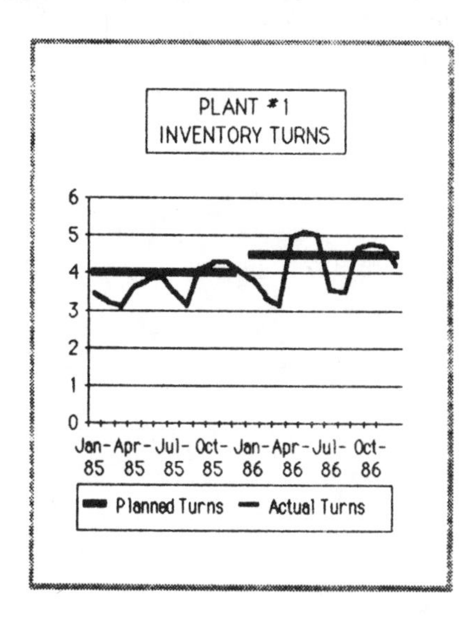

Implementation

This concept can be effective, but like all good ideas it needs a champion to carry the flag. A material management type of individual is in an excellent position to be a champion for this project in your organization. As we noted previously, material management types have the responsibility and accountability for inventory but lack the authority to make the critical decisions required to significantly increase inventory turns. Maybe this is because we have misinterpreted our charge. Top management is not necessarily asking us or our staff to reduce inventory. They want us to use our expertise to coordinate or lead the efforts of the organization to gain the desired results.

Imagine yourself in the role of champion for this cause. First you must experiment to determine how this concept will work in your organization. Start with the inventory turn objective listed in the Annual Operating Plan. If this is not available, determine the actual inventory turns for last year and increase it by 10% as an objective for the upcoming 12 months. Using this as a starting point start to break out the inventory by major responsibility area. Then compute the inventory turn objective for each responsibility area. When this is finished do the same thing for the next tier of management. Keep repeating until you have driven the responsibility for turns as low as possible in the organization. Once you have convinced yourself that this will work in your organization and you can explain exactly how it will work, you should be then prepared to sell this concept to your boss. Remember, that when making management level presentations it is important to be able to make your point concisely and quickly. Charts and graphs are much more effective than stacks of data. If you can sell this to your boss you must be prepared to assist him to sell it to his boss.

Even though this concept was introduced to the organization by you it is important that when it is implemented, it is implemented and fully embraced from the top of the organization. These turn objectives must become an integrated part of the performance evaluation of all those who directly or indirectly have inventory responsibility. Objectives are always taken more seriously when coupled with the financial compensation package. The goal is getting the total organization to rally around productivity improvements by using inventory turns as a barometer of progress.

Once the concept is approved, the maintenance of the objectives and measurement data becomes an issue. Although this type of management information is a natural for the accounting function, I recommend that it be done by the P&IC function. This recommendation is made because it takes some creative manipulation of the information available to make it work. Also, it is important that this information be distributed as timely as possible. Month-end is always a very busy time for accountants. Obviously this will not carry the same priority with them as it would if it were done by the materials management function.

Conclusion

Productivity means getting more with less. Improved productivity means eliminating all kinds of waste. Inventory is the result of mistakes and is a coping mechanism to compensate for production disruptions. Reducing inventory reveals the obstacles to productivity improvement. Therefore inventory and productivity are linked. Inventory is the barometer that gauges productivity improvements. To be effective, inventory turn objectives must be localized to individual management responsibility area. Integrated company inventory turn objectives can be developed to cascade through every management area that directly or indirectly has inventory responsibility. When backed up with a performance measurement system the inventory turn becomes a powerful tool. Inventory turns objectives gain the attention of each management responsibility, because they are individualized. In turn they promote teamwork; to meet these objectives managers must work together to resolve the problems which cause inventory. The result is improved productivity for the entire organization.

About the author

Roger Ahrens is Manager of Manufacturing of the OTC Tool & Equipment Division of Sealed Power Corporation, located in Owatonna, Minnesota. He has 17 years manufacturing management experience. He graduated from Mankato State University with a B.A. degree. He has participated in the APICS Certification Program and is certified at the Fellow level.

Roger was Chairman of the 1986 APICS International Conference and Technical Exhibit held in St. Louis. He has served on the APICS Board of Directors as Region V Vice President and was also President of the Twin Cities Chapter of APICS. He was influential in forming the Small Manufacturing Special Interest Group of APICS. He has made many technical presentations at APICS chapter and regional events. He presented papers at APICS International Conferences and Seminars.

Reprinted from APICS 1986 *Conference Proceedings.*

Inventory Ratios—Reader Beware

R.A. Bonsack

I. Introduction

Ratios and ratio analysis is generally a subject for statisticians or financial analysts. Why then should be interested in inventory ratios? Several thoughts come to mind in addition to the idea that a good inventory controller must be part statistician and financier:

1. Ratios are the most commonly used management control tools—used for goal setting, trend monitoring, and performance measurement. They are easy to compute; they graph nicely; they become a common language between divisions, groups, departments. Ratios put large and small groups on a common basis, and the fact that ratios are non-accounting oriented rids them of the bookkeepers stigma.

2. Ratios are frequently misused due to lack of understanding. Because they appear conceptually simple, the reader does not concern himself with the elements that make up the ratio.

3. Understanding the elements and their characteristics, and thereby the use of ratios from which to draw operating conclusions, can be a very powerful management tool.

II. Overview of the Primary Ratio: Inventory Turnover

To the warehouse manager, "inventory turnover" is an expression of how many times per year a warehouse-full of inventory is physically moved in and out. Mathematically, it is expressed as a ratio between sales (at cost) and average inventory investment. Both are correct and have their places. The accepted formula is:

$$\frac{\text{Cost of Sales}}{\text{Average Inventory}} = \text{Inventory Turnover or Turns}$$

Why Cost of Sales and not Sales? Sales (gross or net) for a given number of units of product over a period of time will vary depending on discount practices, commissions, returns and allowances, etc. It is an inconsistent number for our purposes. The standard cost of those same products, however, does not vary. Sales volume, therefore, for purposes of expressing how much product flowed through the warehouse, is expressed in terms of the standard cost of those products sold. This volume of sales activity can then be compared to the value of inventory normally found in the warehouse, also expressed at standard cost value. The formula, more completely stated, is:

$$\frac{\text{Annual Cost of Sales (at standard)}}{\text{Average Inventory Cost (at standard)}}$$

Various other factors are occasionally used to compute turnover rates that appear in business publications and technical papers from time to time. A word of caution and an example or two seem appropriate. "Sales" can be expressed as gross sales, net sales, sales at standard cost, or sales at actual cost. Industry-wide studies such as those published by Dun and Bradstreet usually use net sales since that is the only sales-related figure available on the published financial statements. Cost of sales at standard is not generally shown on these financial statements.

Variable Sales Cost	
Gross Sales	$120
Net Sales	100
Actual Cost of Sales	85
Standard Cost of Sales @ 80%	
- Using $100	80
- Using 120	96
Average Inventory	20

Note that there are three possible figures, $80 standard cost based on Net Sales, $85 actual cost, and $96 standard cost based on gross sales, which could be used in the turnover computation.

(1) $\frac{85}{20} = 4.25$ Turns

(2) $\frac{80}{20} = 4.00$ Turns

(3) $\frac{96}{20} = 4.80$ Turns

Furthermore, "average inventory" can be a difficult number to agree on. Generally, this is an annual average. If the year being analyzed has been completed, this could be computed by taking the average of the beginning and ending inventory levels for the year or by averaging the monthly averages throughout the year. It could be an average of month-end figures. It could simply be the year-end balance, assuming it typified the year.

If you are in the middle of a year and are annualizing monthly or year-to-date data, even wilder numbers can be calculated. This will be illustrated later. Another example, holding sales cost constant but varying inventory value:

Variable Inventory

Beginning Inventory	$ 18
Ending Inventory	20
Annual Average Based on Actual Monthly Average Balances	22

(1) $\frac{80}{18}$ = 4.4 Turns

(2) $\frac{80}{20}$ = 4.0 Turns

(3) $\frac{80}{22}$ = 3.6 Turns

Preliminary conclusion: There are numerous ways to compute the inventory turn ratio or to express the elements of the ratio. Therefore, further exploration of what should be considered should prove interesting and provide some insight as to how best to present and use inventory ratios.

III. Case Studies: Turnover and Other Ratio Analysis

The Case Company

Statement of Operations

($000 Omitted)

Sales - Gross		$120
Discounts - Allow.		20
Sales - Net		$100
Cost of Sales -		
Labor - @ Std.	$20	
Mat'l - @ Std.	40	
Overhead	20	
Cost @ Std.	$80	
Variances	5	
Actual Cost of Sales		85
Gross Profit		$ 15

Balance Sheet

(Inventories Only)

Raw Material	$ 10
Work in Process	3
Finished Goods	7
Total Inventories	$ 20

Over-all ratios are as dangerous as averages. They hide a great deal that may be of significance. Often responsibility for the various segments of inventory — raw material, work-in-process, and finished goods— is divided organizationally, and an inventory turnover ratio that combines all three is of questionable value. No one is accountable for performance and management action cannot be properly directed. Structure your ratio analysis and performance reporting according to at least two criteria:

1. Inventory accountability (organization)
2. Availability of data from the accounting system

The second point reflects the fact that not all companies account for inventories in the same manner. Companies with high throughput rates or low work-in-process often recognize only raw material and finished goods. Non-manufacturing companies have only finished goods. Notice how turn rates vary when dealing with selected segments of the inventory:

Case A

(1) Turn = $\frac{80}{20}$ = 4.0

(2) Finished Goods Turn = $\frac{80}{7}$ = 11.4

(3) Raw Material Turn = $\frac{80 \times (\text{\% of Mat'l in Product})}{10}$ = $\frac{80 \times 50\%}{10}$ = 4.0

What impact would result if raw material turnover increased 100% — from 4.0 to 8.0?

Reduce Raw Material to	$ 5
Work in Process	3
Finished Goods	7
	$15

Turn = $\frac{80}{15}$ = 5.33 - only 30% higher than above

Conclusion A: Pinpoint inventory responsibility and structure your ratio analysis accordingly.

Case B

The financial reporting practices and methodology, in addition to basic segmentation illustrated above, will cause changes in the turn numbers:

	Was	Is
Raw Material	$10	$ 9)
Work in Process	3	3) = 22
Finished Goods	7	10)
Supplies		1
Reserves		(3)
	$20	$20

(1) Turn = $\frac{80}{22}$ = 3.64, Not 4.0

The method of Cost Accounting can change Cost of Sales. Direct Costing, whereby only the variable portion of product cost is included in cost of sales, yields a lower figure the Absorption Costing where all factory-related costs (both fixed and variable) are included in Cost of Sales.

Direct Material	$40
Direct Labor	20
Total Direct Cost	$60
Fixed Mfg. Cost	20
Total Cost of Sales	$80

(2) Turn = $\frac{60}{20}$ = 3.0, Not 4.0

A further caution regarding accounting treatment is to be aware of inventory reevaluation (cost standard adjustments and physical inventory adjustments) that can impact turn statistics.

Conclusion B: Get to know your accountant and the system they use. The accounting methods as it relates to cost accounting data versus general ledger (balance sheet) data can distort ratio reporting.

Case C

If significant product line differences exist or your management is product-line oriented, additional stratification may be necessary and desirable. Often inherent with this situation, however, is the fact that a significant portion of raw materials are common to more than one product line. Computation of turns for raw material by product line may be impractical at best arbitrary since portions of the total raw material inventory would have to be assigned or allocated to product line categories on a basis that is itself arbitrary.

A practical solution to this dilemma is to control raw material as a total and to monitor finished goods by product line. Work-in-process should be handled based on the ease of segregation by product line. In the example below it is handled as is raw material and is not segregated.

	Total	Prod. A	Prod. B
Raw Material	$10	-	-
Work in Process	3	-	-
Finished Goods	7	4	3
	$20		

To compute turns, Cost of Sales must also be broken down by product line. Product line management should set turnover goals based on the characteristics of the market they serve — response time, service levels, standard products verus specials— are some considerations.

Cost of Sales: Prod. A.	$30
Prod. B.	50
	$80

Fin. Goods Turn (A) = $\frac{30}{4}$ = 7.5

Fin. Goods Turn (B) = $\frac{50}{3}$ = 16.5

Conclusion C: If ratios are product oriented, to be sure line management understands the differences between product lines and how raw materials and work-in-process are handled.

Case D

Closely related to the example above as it relates to finished goods inventory management, is the situation that can arise in a multi-warehouse environment. Warehouse managers usually have inventory responsibility, and it is important to set attainable and realistic goals for turn at their location. Care must be taken to assure that the Cost of Sales used in the turn computation relates properly to the goods moving through the subject warehouse. If a significant portion of the merchandise sold is drop shipped from the factory and never appears as part of the warehouse inventory, the turn figures for that warehouse may be misleading. A comparable warehouse with the same cost of sales base but no drop shipment activity will have a much higher inventory and will appear to be doing a poorer job. Plant-warehouse location and distribution strategy can have a significant impact on turnover performance. Across-the-board turn goals are dangerous.

Conclusion D: Proper use of ratios for field warehouse management will require analysis of each situation and specialized training efforts.

Case E

Perhaps the most dramatic distortions of turnover data occur when mid-year cost data is annualized to provide a basis for comparison to average inventory. Monthly and fiscal year time intervals are really quite arbitrary and are primarily for the convenience of the accountant, so we must be careful not to let them distort the data.

If monthly data is annualized, several factors have been at work on those figures:

- Seasonality
- A four-week or five-week month
- 18 to 25 days
- Holidays
- Demand fluctuations
- Strikes

To compute an annualized Cost of Sales using any one month's Cost of Sales figure can result in distortions of turnover rates of several hundred percent.

Conclusion E: When computing an annual Cost of Sales figure, use one of the following:

- Year end (full year actual) total
- Rolling average of at least 6 months
- Year to date cumulative average, annualized (at least 3 months—ignore fiscal year)

Other Ratios

Even though turnover is the most commonly used ratio for measuring inventory performance, there are several others that have appeal under the right circumstances.

Inventory to Current Assets — A rule of thumb frequently used to argue the significance of inventory investment is that it represents 50% of current assets. For a "typical" manufacturing firm, this is often true. The three major assets included in Current Assets are cash, accounts receivable, and inventories. Inventory in the most cases the largest of these and receivables the next largest. Ratios expressing the percent inventories represent of the whole must be tempered by the makeup of the whole since it can vary dramatically from one accounting period to the next or as seasonality and economics affect cash and receivables.

Inventory to Total Assets: — This ratio is an extension of the first and includes fixed assets in addition to current. The major item here is plant and equipment. In some firms "Gross Operating Assets" consisting of receivables, inventories, and plant and equipment, are combined to compute a "Return of Assets" ratio by comparing these to profits.

Number of Months' Supply — The amount of inventory available, particularly raw materials, can be expressed in terms of the number of months' worth based on current sales or production rates. Operating personnel often relate better to this way of expressing turnover. If raw material turns 4 times per year, the average amount on hand is 3 months' worth.

Number of Days' Sales — It is similar to the above and often used for finished goods. this provides a good yardstick for expressing current inventory balances in a manner quite clear to sales and marketing people.

Inventory to Net Working Capital—"Net Working Capital" is the difference between Current Assets and Current Liabilities. It is a measure of the basic health of the company. A comparison of inventory investment to net working capital is an indication of liquidity of the company; that is, the makeup of net working capital in terms of short-term available cash. If the total amount of net working capital is equal to or less than the value of inventories, inventories are probably too high in relation to cash and receivables. This ratio should be less than 1.0 to be comfortable. Some portion of net working capital should be in the form of cash or receivables that can be quickly converted to cash.

IV. Conclusions—Managing with Ratios

Though several conclusions have been drawn along the way, it will be helpful to summarize. Several steps may be necessary to improve the usefulness and accuracy of inventory ratios. And do not be impatient. Depending on how "tuned in" your management has been to this subject over the years, a fair amount of "undoing" and education may be necessary.

In order to be able to use ratios to manage inventories your must first develop sound and acceptable ratios. I suggest an approach such as the following:

* If ratios are a regular part of current reporting practices, learn all there is to know about them

-Who prepares them

-What are the formulae

-Who reads them

-How are they used

* Enlist the assistance of the accounting department to analyze the availability of data and the structure of the cost accounting system.

* Profile the inventory and define each manageable segment

-Natural inventory groupings

-Product lines

-Warehouse locations

-Organizations — accountability.

* Interview key managers about how they use ratios and about other data they might find helpful. You may have to do some education in this area to make it meaningful.

* Develop a recommendation to incorporate changes that appear meaningful and a plan for their implementation. This may include training sessions at various levels in the sales, warehousing, and general management areas.

Managing better using ratios is a function of several considerations. You will have to judge for yourself what best fits your organization.

* If financial and operational reporting dominated by a strong controller with little input from line management?

* Is the chief financial person creative and operations-oriented? Is he or she empathetic to line management needs?

* Is the inventory accountability clearly stated and understood? Is it clear enough that inventory performance is tied to personal income?

* Is line management capable of using ratio data effectively in their day-to- day decision making? Do they understand?

Some of the ideas I want to leave you with are implicit in the above points. The following decisions would be made easier if the inventory data and relate ratios provided a clear definition of inventory makeup and activity.

* What is an acceptable composite turnover rate for my division (company, product line) for business planning (budgeting) purposes?

* What turnover goals should be established for each warehouse in the system, considering local market factors, distribution strategies, and composition of local warehouse stocks?-

* What is the best inventory strategy: Should most inventory be kept in the raw state and finished goods kept low at the sacrifice of delivery response time? Can raw material be kept low by more frequent buying but with a sacrifice of price discounts? In our earlier case study a shift of inventory from finished goods to raw material by delaying production, considering the 50% labor and overhead content, would change turnover as follows:

	Case A	Revised
Raw Material	$10	$12
Work in Process	3	2
Finished Goods	7	4
	$20	$18
Turnover (on cost @ $80)	4.0	4.5

The foregoing was intended to illustrate the point made in the title of this paper — "Reader Beware." Inventory ratios come in an endless variety of sizes and shapes. If you and your department's performance are being measured with ratios, you had better by fully aware of their makeup and implications.

About the Author

ROBERT BONSACK is Director, Operations Planning, Corrosion Control Division of Ameron in Brea, California. He holds a Master's degree in Production Management from U.C.L.A. Bob spent 5 years in production control and production management and was a consultant in production control and cost accounting for 12 years. He has been active in APICS since 1964, and held offices, including: President, Los Angeles Chapter; Region VII Vice President; National Vice President, Education; and National Executive Vice President in 1973. He is a frequent speaker on the subjects of production and inventory control and cost accounting.

Reprinted from the 1990 APICS *Conference Proceedings.*

Setting and Implementing Inventory Management Objectives in the 1990's: Their Effects on Service Level and ROI

Laura B. Casteel

How much inventory is "enough" to support a given service level goal? This is the fundamental question confronting most manufacturing and distribution operations. As corporations move into the 1990s, they are faced with the realization that service level is being used with increased frequency as a competitive weapon. Price advantages and quality/technology superiority are only part of the reason a customer purchases product from a given vendor. Service, including shorter, guaranteed delivery lead times, is growing in importance as customers evaluate vendors. The challenge is how to maintain a competitive service level at the lowest possible cost. Optimizing the costs associated with achieving a given service level is one of a corporation's single greatest opportunities to increase the bottom line ROI. The proper setting of inventory management objectives is the critical path for most corporations trying to meet this challenge.

Reasons for Inventory

In the past, inventory has been reluctantly accepted as a cost of doing business. During the 1980s, published works discussing the concepts of "Zero Inventory Management" and "Just-in-Time" (JIT) have increased corporations' awareness of proven methods to reduce lead times, improve the flow of materials and increase the ability to react to changes in demand. But the reality is, inventories still exist in most corporations.

Some of the basic reasons inventory exists are:

1) Forecast Error - Managing forecast error to ensure that service level goals are maintained in an environment where there is the potential for unknown demand variability through replenishment lead time.

2) Capacity Constraints - Managing capacity constraints to ensure the right product is available when the customer needs it in environments that do not have the luxury of unlimited capacity availability (ex. seasonal products).

3) Economic Opportunities - Taking advantage of economic opportunities to ensure that all the costs associated with replenishing inventory are optimized in environments where there are price advantages associated with quantity buys, cost advantages associated with set-up costs vs. run/lot sizes, and transportation cost savings opportunities (especially in a distribution oriented environment).

4) Supply Variances - Managing supply variances to ensure that the firm production schedule is met in environments where potential quality variance and yield considerations (ex. semiconductor manufacturing) are prevalent.

Corporations need to consider these four reasons for inventory when setting their inventory management objectives and creating their inventory replenishment plan. This plan is the driver of work support systems such as MRP II. Finely tuned MRP II systems enable a corporation to precisely execute a plan. An MRP II system without a stable front end plan is like a finely tuned race car without a skilled driver.

The Uncertainty Factor

Corporations have made significant investments in the creation of policies and procedures and in the implementation of computerized systems to ensure the accuracy of on hand inventory balances, lead times, costs, customer orders and replenishment orders (e.g. purchase orders, manufacturing orders, master production schedules). The next challenge lies in improving a corporation's ability to manage "the uncertainty factor" while considering its impact on service levels and inventory replenishment costs. The primary cause of the uncertainty factor is forecast error.

It is difficult to quantify the hard dollar improvements that result from improving forecast accuracy unless management of the error inherent in the forecast process is addressed properly.

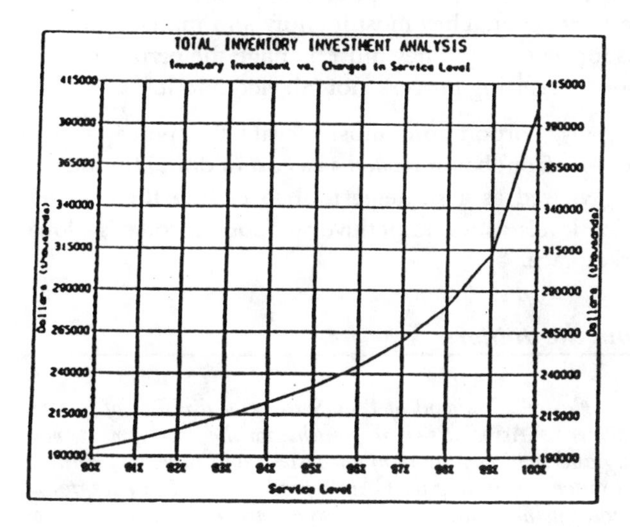

Figure 1

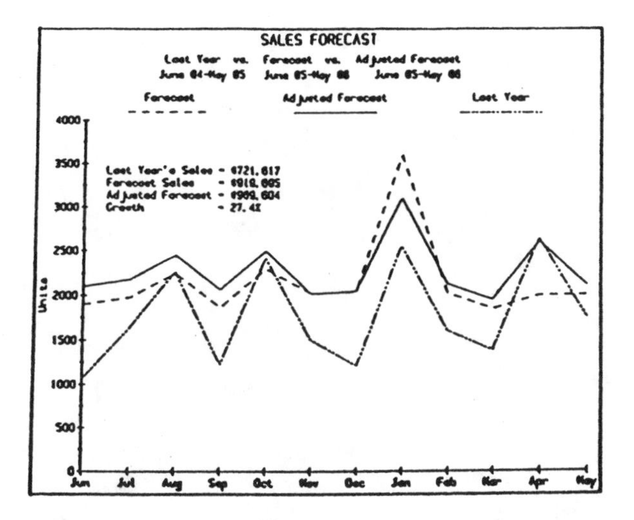

Figure 2

Managing Forecast Error

A key component in managing the error inherent in the forecast process is the setting of proper inventory management parameters.

The setting of a "service" stock that is part of the inventory replenishment plan is critical. "Service" stock calculations must consider:

1) Forecast Error Through Replenishment Lead Time

2) The Service Level Desired

3) The Optimal Replenishment Size

4) Accurate Lead Times

Consideration of Forecast Error when setting service stock is intuitively straightforward, however, unless the service level desired and the optimal replenishment size are considered, corporations will not be able to become less reactive and more proactive. The cost associated with expediting will continue and service levels will not be able to be met at the lowest annual cost, therefore, negatively affecting ROI.

Setting Service Levels

Consideration of service levels is key when setting inventory management objectives. Determination of service levels requires the involvement of many parts of an organization. Organizations should specifically decide 1) what service level is required in their given marketplace to maintain a competitive advantage, and 2) how much inventory can a corporation afford based upon their ROI objectives.

If a service level objective that is affordable is less than 100% (a goal theoretically impossible) then an organization must accept the fact that they will stockout. If they set a service level goal of 90% then they should feel they are meeting their objectives if they stockout 10% of the time.

If an organization finds it needs to maintain a higher service level at the same level of investment, they need to address reducing the cost associated with replenishing inventories, reducing the replenishment lead times and reducing the forecast error.

The Five Projections

The setting of inventory management objectives (service level/inventory investment) is a challenge that is statistical in nature because of the interrelationship of multiple variables. If it is done properly, service levels can be met at the lowest annual cost and corporations will become more proactive vs. reactive.

Five projections are required to support this process. These projections must be calculated as accurately as possible. They include:

1) Projection of demand for every item by location.

2) Projection of optimum inventory levels needed for every item by location to meet the specified service level goals.

3) Projection of a time-phased forecast of suggested replenishments needed for every item by location up to fifty-two weeks by week to meet the desired service levels and inventory investment goals for each item.

4) Projection of inventory levels through time given the current replenishment schedules for up to fifty-two weeks by week.

5) Projection of cost optimal replenishment order sizes for every item by location based upon the lowest total annual cost to procure, manufacture, and distribute that item and meet desired service levels.

Projections 2-4 are required to assist corporations in the proper management of the forecast error.

Summary

As we move into the 1990s, corporations are encountering increased global competition. They are realizing that the environment in which they have learned to operate is changing and that they must become more proactive in nature, identifying new opportunities and challenges before they occur. They must identify and manage the reasons for inventory. They must manage the error inherent in the forecasting process, not fall victim to it.

Finally, corporations must elevate the perception of inventory from being viewed as a cost of doing business to being viewed as a strategic tool to enable them to use service levels as a competitive weapon in today's global marketplace.

About the author

Laura Casteel, President of BSA Systems, a division of Benton, Schneider & Associates, is responsible for the development, marketing and implementation of forecasting and inventory management systems including the GAINS product line. Her background includes business and consulting experience in management information systems, manufacturing, distribution, and business requirements planning.

Ms. Casteel has degrees from Southern Methodist University in Applied Mathematics and English. She is an active member and has served on the board of directors of several professional organizations including the American Production and Inventory Control Society, Purchasing Managers Association and DPMA. She is a frequent speaker and advisor for business groups and professional societies.

Reprinted with permission of the *Journal of Cost Management*, Winter 1996, © RIA Group, Boston, Massachusetts.

Problems with Existing Manufacturing Performance Measures

Dileep G. Dhavale

Performance measurements, evaluation systems, and reward systems are indispensable management tools. They can help motivate employees to work toward fulfilling the organization's strategic objectives. By contrast, poorly designed or poorly implemented performance measurement systems can encourage dysfunctional and suboptimal behavior throughout an organization.

Recent developments in manufacturing—e.g., Just-in-Time production and the focused factory—and technology (e.g., computer-integrated manufacturing systems) have led many managers to reconsider the appropriateness of traditional performance measures to the new manufacturing environment. Not surprisingly, many traditional performance measures (along with their associated procedures and assumptions) have proven to be unsuitable or even counterproductive.

The Problems

The sections that follow discuss problems resulting from the use of traditional performance measurement and evaluation systems in advanced manufacturing environments. In particular, later sections discuss the problems of using standard costs and variances as performance measures.

Financial performance measures inappropriate at operations level. Many performance measurement systems use financial measurements that are too abstract because they are too hard to relate to activities taking place on the shop floor. Financial measurements often fail to provide information that is useful for decision making.

For example, managers may want to know how often a machine breaks down because of a certain critical part, but that information is usually unavailable because the company's information system collects only financial information. Unless the maintenance department collects data about repairs and develops an appropriate database, this information is simply unavailable. Although most companies develop and maintain financial databases well, few keep nonfinancial information with the same degree of accuracy and detail. As a result, financial performance measures are developed even when they are inappropriate simply because the information is available.

Inclusion of nonmanufacturing, allocated, or noncontrollable costs. Performance measures that include nonmanufacturing, allocated, or noncontrollable costs are distorted. A manager cannot judge the effectiveness of new initiatives and improvements because of the impact of these costs. Allocated costs create an additional problem. Changes in allocation methods change performance measures without any change in performance itself. Nevertheless, many companies continue to include allocated costs in their performance measures. The reasons for such a policy include:

- To inform lower-level managers about the additional costs so they realize the need to generate adequate revenues to cover all the costs;
- To determine "full" product costs; and
- To create an adversarial situation between staff and line managers so that line managers will exert influence to control nonmanufacturing costs.

Excessive reliance on financial measures

An excessive reliance on financial measures encourages suboptimal behavior among managers. Inordinate emphasis on financial measures can tempt managers at the cell and focused-factory levels to improve the performance of their subunits at the expense of long-term benefits to the organization. Such suboptimal actions include:

- Pushing partially completed units just beyond the point where percentage completions are measured;
- Starting units just before the end of a period; or
- Completing high-margin or large orders before the end of a period and ahead of their scheduled dates.

All these actions can improve the contribution margins for a cell or factory while hurting the company as a whole.

No linkage between performance measures and strategic objectives. Performance measures used to evaluate managers and employees at different levels in an organization must support its strategic objectives. Without such a linkage, the managers and employees may behave suboptimally by acting to improve performance measures that are not linked to company goals.

For example, if raises in a supervisor's salary depend on meeting production quotas, then production quotas will understandably be that supervisor's number-one objective—not improving quality or customer service, as the company's strategic objectives may require.

But, for one reason or another, organizations—from non-profit universities to for-profit companies—fail to establish these linkages. For one thing, establishing performance evaluation and reward systems is time consuming. It is difficult to change the system to reflect changing strategic objectives, then fine-tune it until it truly reflects and supports those objectives.

Moreover, few organizations have invested adequately in nonfinancial databases that will support organization-wide operational performance measures. Budgetary and other financial measures cannot adequately reflect corporate priorities.

Some organizations even resort to slogans, jingles, speeches, and campaigns in the hope that they will induce the desired response from employees. This may work in the short run, but for a lasting impact there is no substitute for having a linkage between strategic objectives and the measures used to evaluate employees.

Checks and balances among performance measures. Many complex factors and variables interact with each other in manufacturing, either implicitly or explicitly. It is often possible to show improvement in the performance of one aspect of a manufacturing system at the expense of another. To avoid suboptimization of this sort, the set of performance measures used in evaluations must provide checks and balance on each other so that a manager cannot ignore one aspect of the production process without affecting at least one of the measures.

Too few performance measures. Suboptimization also occurs when organizations put excessive emphasis on just one or two performance measures in the hope that emphasizing performance of those components will improve the performance of the system as a whole. The favorite candidates for these one or two chosen performance measures often are machine and labor use. But machine and labor utilization does not necessarily improve the performance of the system as a whole as measured by such important indicators as cycle time, customer satisfaction or on-time delivery rate. On the contrary, utilization simply increases the inventory of goods that nobody ordered.

Too few performance measures. In some companies, managers face a reverse problem. Instead of too few performance measures, they have too many. In such a situation, managers lose sight of the main objectives; they do not know which measures are important and need to be acted upon. Having the right level of detail is more important and useful than just having more details.

Irrelevant measures displayed. The problem of too many performance measures often results from inclusion of irrelevant measures. Performance measures are irrelevant if they are not used on a continuing basis. Not all performance measures should be reported routinely, because some only distract managers' attention from what is important. Nonetheless some performance measures may be useful even if they aren't provided routinely. For example, data about frequency and cost of machinery breakdowns can be useful in negotiating purchase of new equipment and demanding higher reliability or lower prices even if this information is not provided in regular, routine reports to all managers.

Communication of performance measures. Organizations also need to find the best way to communicate performance measures to intended users. Reports and printouts work well at high levels of management or shop-floor employees.

Visual communication techniques (e.g., graphs, charts, flags of different colors, flashing lights, spaces with painted outline of the intended item or equipment) often prove very effective. Employees can also be taught to use simple keystrokes on terminals to gain access to graphical representations of the current status of any performance measure.

Use of total production. Many current performance measures use total production or totals produced in their computations—i.e., both good and defective units in performance measures done so as to encourage efforts to improve quality: The emphasis is placed on production of *good* units. Such dysfunctional behavior is especially detrimental in Just-in-Time and continuous improvement manufacturing environments.

Measurement of performance and evaluation. Performance measurement is the first step, but it is not enough simply to measure performance. Performance must also be analyzed and evaluated. Evaluation of performance measures induces the desired result and behavior from employees; the mere act of measurement does not. Beyond the evaluation phase, mechanisms must be in place to check whether required actions have been taken. As straightforward as this sounds, this process is often not followed to its culmination. As a result, companies fail to reap the benefit of their performance measurements.

Use of Standard Costs and Variances

Standard cost and variances are the most widely available financial measures for shop-floor activities; they are also perhaps the most widely misused.

Standard cost systems were developed in the 1920s and were widely used during World War II. They were developed for a manufacturing system drastically different from today's manufacturing environments of cells, focused factories, and computer-integrated manufacturing.

Formerly, production occurred in large batches, and direct labor was a major component of the manufacturing cost. Since automation was minimal, production rates were determined by how efficiently labor completed its task.

Consequently, the major focus was on improving labor efficiency by using time and motion studies and other industrial engineering techniques. Standard time and the resulting standard costs were more than adequate as performance measures for that manufacturing environment.

In today's manufacturing systems, however, direct labor is not a significant component of total manufacturing cost. Speed of operation is not determined by how fast an operator can work, but by the type of automation and manufacturing system used. The sections that follow discuss specific problems with standard cost and variance systems that make them unsuitable for cellular manufacturing environments and focused factories.

Continuous improvement. According to a recent survey of cell manufacturing and focused factory systems, adoption of continuous improvement programs is one of the reasons for impressive performance. In a continuous improvement program, a process is continually improved to obtain better cycle times, quality, and efficiency. As a result, an established standard time becomes invalid as soon as the first improvement is implemented, yet—in many companies—it takes up to six months for a new standard to be put in place. Standard time is a static concept. In a continuous improvement environment, therefore, it is of limited use.

Learning curve disturbances. The learning curve phenomenon makes use of standard times even more questionable. The rate of learning is higher just after an improvement is implemented. The rate continues to drop over time until a plateau is reached, when rate changes become small.

In older manufacturing systems, it was possible to wait till the plateau phase to perform the time studies to obtain stable time standards. But because of continuous improvements in today's manufacturing environment, instead of a smooth learning curve and an eventual plateau, discontinuous learning curves occur with drops in the production rates when the new improvements are implemented. The plateau is never reached because of constant improvements, so there are no stable time standards.

Lack of timely information. Standard cost information is not timely. Variances are available only a week or ten days after month-end closings (unless the information is available on-line.) This time lag makes it impossible to take any corrective action as a batch is actually being made. In a dynamic manufacturing environment, what happened last month is ancient history.

Too much aggregation of data. Variances are generally computed for all batches completed during a time period. But a cell manager needs information by batch or by product so that problems can be pinpointed. An aggregate variance fails to inform a manager whether a problem occurred with all batches or just some.

Built-in inefficiencies. Standards have built-in inefficiencies. A standard material cost includes the cost of making defective units and the costs of scrap and waste. A standard labor cost includes allowances for such subjective factors as skill, effort, condition, and consistency. Furthermore, labor standards allow for job fatigue, learning time, unavoidable delays, personal needs, setups, and preparation time.

Adherence to budgets. Many organizations emphasize adherence to budgets based on standard costs. To avoid either favorable or unfavorable variances, managers sometimes resort to dysfunctional behavior such as:

- Running a plant or a machine center to absorb manufacturing overhead when there is no immediate demand for the products being made;
- Misclassifying direct and indirect labor to manipulate manufacturing overhead and avoid labor-related variances;
- Purchasing low-cost, low-quality materials, or purchasing in huge lots to take advantage of volume discounts.

These actions may improve the budget-related performance of the managers, but they hurt the performance of the company as a whole.

Direct labor emphasis. Many standard cost systems analyze direct labor costs in great detail, then compute various ratios using that cost. This is a holdover from the days when labor costs constituted a large percentage of the manufacturing cost. In today's environment, direct labor costs do not warrant such minute attention. Continued use of performance measures based on direct labor sends a confusing signal to managers at the cell and factory level.

In traditional cost accounting systems where direct labor is used to allocate manufacturing overhead, analysis of overhead often does not vary according to direct labor, so changes in direct labor use cannot explain overhead spending problems. Activity based costing has pointed this out.

Popularity of standard costs. Despite these problems, many corporations continue using standard costs and variances. Some possible explanations for this follow.

In many companies, standard costs are used for inventory valuation purposes, so the computation of variances from those data is relatively easy and inexpensive.

For some companies, it may be the only set of performance measures that could be computed for all products and departments because databases are unavailable to develop operational performance measures on an organization-wide scale.

Standard costs have been around a long time, so many middle and top managers are used to variances, which have provided a frame of reference developed over many years. It is difficult for these managers to give up something they understand (or misunderstand).

Standard cost and variance calculations are an integral part of many accounting software packages, so collection and routine processing of data to get standard cost and variance information is no added burden.

Given all the problems with standard costs and variances, however, standard cost analysis should not occur for cell manufacturing and focused factory systems. An alternative is target costs.

Different Performance Measures for Different Levels of Management

Performance measures differ substantially according to the different levels of management for which they are intended. Top management generally prefers performance measures that are finance oriented (e.g., net income, earnings per share, and return on investment.) Lower levels of management such as shop foremen, supervisors, and cell managers prefer nonfinancial, operational measures (e.g., number of idle machine and cycle times.) Shop -level managers use performance measures that cover longer periods, such as a month, a quarter, or even a year.

Between these management extremes are other levels of management—e.g., focused factory heads, department heads, and plant managers—whose needs and requirements for performance measures fall somewhere between the extremes. Middle-level managers may use both financial and operational measures. For example, they may be interested in financial measures (e.g., contribution margin of products or payback times for cells) and also operational measures (e.g., defect rates of different cells). Exactly what kind of performance measures a middle-level manager needs depends on his responsibilities and the corporate structure.

Multidimensional performance measures. Performance measures for top management are multidimensional; they tend to summarize many functions or activities into a single measure, such as net income. Lower levels of management, on the other hand, need one-dimensional performance measures (e.g., number of defects or number of late orders.)

Performance measures used by top management are affected by many external factors, including the economy and the marketplace, whereas performance measures at lower levels mainly reflect the effect of internal changes that will show a significant impact on specific performance measures over many cells, focused factories, or plants so that changes in one cell are hardly noticeable.

Unrelated financial decisions often obscure the impact of operational changes. Savings from substantial decreases in inventories resulting from implementation of Just-in-Time programs can be overshadowed by additional taxes resulting from depletion of last-in-first-out (LIFO) inventory. The impact of improvements in operations is generally gradual and continuing; it usually takes several periods to become noticeable. Financial changes, such as changes in bad debt and pension expense, make a larger and more immediate impact on the bottom line.

Desired Properties of Performance Measures

Here is a list of properties that performance measures should have (many of which are general enough to be useful in any manufacturing system, and even in nonmanufacturing settings):

Make performance measures understandable: Performance measures should be easy to understand.

Be clear about what is being measured: Performance measures should clearly indicate what they measure (i.e., if the goal is to measure on-time delivery, the goal should not be obscured by some generic name like "customer satisfaction index," of which on-time delivery is only a part.)

Ensure that data can be collected: Data for performance measures should be easy to collect.

Make the performance measures timely: Performance measures should be available on a timely basis so that corrective action can be taken.

Link the performance measures to strategy: Performance measures should have linkages to strategic objectives.

Tailor performance measures for different levels of management: Performance measures should be appropriate for different levels of management.

Avoid allocations: Performance measures should not use allocated costs.

Encourage the good of all: Performance measures should not encourage dysfunctional or suboptimal behavior.

Make performance measures relevant: Only performance measures that an entity is responsible for should be included in its report. Avoid irrelevant and insignificant measures.

Improve communication: If budgets are used as the main communication tool, include nonfinancial performance measures in the budget.

Stress teamwork: Use performance measures for groups rather than for individual workers.

Avoid proxies and surrogates: Surrogate performance measures should be avoided unless they have very good correlations with the characteristics to be measured.

Shoot high: Performance measures and their targets should be based on external benchmarks rather than just internal standards.

Act rather than react: Performance measures should be active—i.e., designed to avoid expected problems and difficulties in the future.

Reprinted from 1988 APICS *Conference Proceedings.*

Use of the Inventory Turnover Measurement

Martin P. Edelman

This presentation will fully explain how to use inventory statistics to determine how well your company/division is managing inventories compared to similar companies. If your inventory turnover is not in the upper quartile of similar companies, focusing resources on improvement should bring about savings and the competitive advantage truly needed. The session should have applicability for general management as well as inventory/distribution/purchasing/financial management. The agenda is presented as Figure 1.

Use of the Inventory Measurement

AGENDA

- Inventory Turnover Defined
- Sources Of Comparison
- Potential Inventory Reduction Development
- Sample-potential Inventory Reduction Calculation
- Sample-inventory Carrying Cost Savings Calculation

Figure 1

INVENTORY TURNOVER DEFINED

DEFINITION

- THE NUMBER OF TIMES THAT AN INVENTORY "TURNS OVER" OR CYCLES DURING THE YEAR
- A MEASURE OF HOW WELL YOUR INVENTORY INVESTMENT IS WORKING FOR YOU

FORMULA

$$\text{TURNS} = \frac{\text{ANNUAL COST OF SALES}}{\text{AVERAGE INVENTORY}}$$

Where AVERAGE INVENTORY IS CALCULATED

- AS AN AVERAGE OF DAILY VALUES; ← BEST
- AS AN AVERAGE OF MONTHLY VALUES; ← OK
- AS THE PHYSICAL INVENTORY; ← WORST

Figure 2

Introduction

Have you ever wondered if inventory is really an asset? It appears on the Asset side of a Balance Sheet. It's critical for distributors and necessary for manufacturers. Yet, too often a company looks for financing for expansion and goes to great effort, and expense, to borrow from a bank when monies are available in liquid assets called inventory.

Inventory Turnover Defined

It is appropriate here to provide several definitions of the term Inventory Turnover (see Figure 2). It is:

- The number of times that an inventory "turns over" or cycles during the year; or
- A measure of how well your inventory investment is working for you.

  - As an example, if you average 30 model Al radios in inventory to support sales of 300 for the year, you turned your inventory over 10 times. If you average 30 in inventory to support sales of 600, you leveraged your investment 20 times. Clearly, the higher the turns, the better your leverage; or
- The ratio of Annual Cost of Sales to Average (Cost of) Inventory

  - Cost of Sales is used rather than Sales so that we're comparing costs, sales costs to inventory costs, and not including company profits, allocated overhead, etc.

  - Average Inventory is normally a calculated figure and should be developed by the best possible and practical means. It's usually the sum of the extension of item quantity times unit cost.

  .. Best calculation—an average of daily values (such as those developed in the financial community.)

  .. Acceptable calculation—an average of monthly values. This is usually most practical and cost effective and does average the peaks and valleys of the business year's investment in inventory.

  .. Worst calculation — the value of the physical inventory. This biases the turns since a physical taken during a valley period would indicate high turns and vice-versa.

SOURCES OF COMPARISON

- DUN & BRADSTREET (D&B)

  "INDUSTRY NORMS AND KEY BUSINESS RATIOS"
  (AN ANNUAL) PROVIDES BY SIC:
  SALES TO INVENTORY RATIO
  QUARTILE FIGURES

- ROBERT MORRIS ASSOCIATES (RMA)

  "ANNUAL STATEMENT STUDIES"
  PROVIDES BY SIC:
  COST OF SALES TO INVENTORY RATIO
  QUARTILE FIGURES

Figure 3

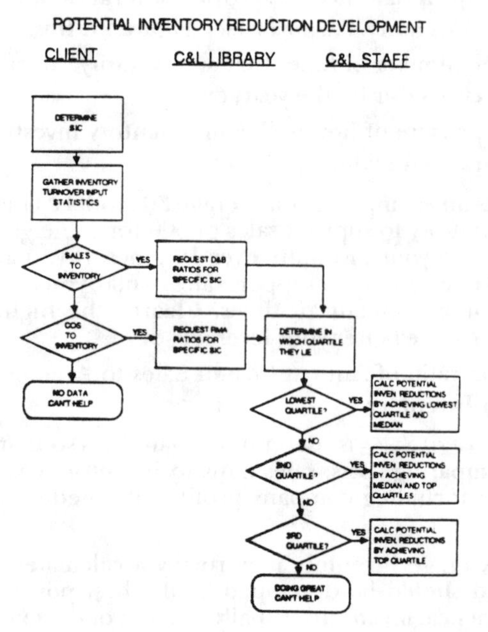

Figure 4

Sources Of Comparison

There are two major sources of comparison statistics, Dun & Bradstreet (D&B) and Robert Morris Associates (RMA). (See Figure 3.) D&B provides data including sales statistics while RMA provides data including cost of sales statistics. The reason for this difference appears to be that some companies prefer not to provide cost of sales figures since it is an indicator of their profits.

SAMPLE-POTENTIAL INVENTORY REDUCTION CALCULATION

DATA COLLECTION FROM COMPANY

SIC: 5122

TURNS=COS/INVENTORY=$16MILLION/$10MILLION= 1.6

RMA REPORTS FOR SIC 5122

HIGHEST QUARTILE DIVISION	8.1
MEDIAN	5.5
LOWEST QUARTILE DIVISION	3.8

CALCULATION

- TO IMPROVE FROM 1.6 TO 3.8, THE LOWEST QUARTILE
  PROJ. INVENTORY=COS/PROJ. TURNS
  =$16MM/3.8=$4.2MM

INVEN. REDUCTION POTENTIAL=OLD INVEN.-PROJ. INVEN.
=$10MM-4.2MM=$5.8MM(58%)

- TO IMPROVE FROM 1.6 TO 5.5, THE MEDIAN
  PROJ. INVENTORY=COS/PROJ. TURNS
  =$16MM/5.5=$2.9MM

INVEN. REDUCTION POTENTIAL=OLD INVEN.-PROJ INVEN.
=$10MM-2.9MM=$7.1MM(71%)

Figure 5

Both collect data from thousands of companies and sort it by SIC code. The SIC code is a U.S. government Standard Industrial Classification code dividing all economic activity into 10 major divisions comprising approximately 900 different descriptions. Thus, every business activity is classified into one of approximately 900 SIC codes. It is from this sort that we can obtain a myriad of data and in particular the ratios of "sales to inventory" and "cost of sales to inventory." Both sources rank the companies in ascending turns sequence and provide this data by quartile.

(As a refresher, each quartile represents 25% of the reporting companies. Thus the lower quartile indicates the "turns" achieved by the worst 25% of the companies. The middle quartile (median) indicates that 50% of the companies are below and 50% are above the "turns" specified. The upper quartile indicates that only 25% of the companies are achieving the "turns" reported.)

Potential Inventory Reduction Development

A great deal has been written lately on so-called "expert" systems. I maintain that this is not a new concept, but a new phrase to explain and perhaps exploit an old concept.

Remember in high school mathematics and science we learned about theorems. These theorems about the relationships between the three sides of a triangle (Pythagoras), or energy and matter were developed by

SAMPLE-INVENTORY CARRYING COST SAVINGS CALCULATION

WHEN AN INVENTORY REDUCTION IS ACHIEVED,THE COST OF ACQUIRING AND TAKING CARE OF THAT INVENTORY IS REDUCED BY NOT HAVING TO FINANCE IT, WAREHOUSE IT, INSURE IT, PHYSICALLY COUNT IT, ETC.

INVENTORY CARRYING COST (ICC) ELEMENTS	
INTEREST (FINANCE)	10-20%
OPPORTUNITY	3-10%
HANDLING	1-2%
SPACE	1-3%
DAMAGE	1-2%
SHRINKAGE	0-2%
TAXES	0-2%
INSURANCE	0-2%
PHYSICAL INVENTORY	1-2%
GENERAL AND ADMIN.	1-2%
TOTAL	18-47%

IN THE PREVIOUS EXAMPLE, IF A 20% ICC IS USED

	ANNUAL RECURRING SAVINGS
$5.8MM X 20%=	$1,160,000
$7.1MM X 20%=	$1,420,000

Figure 6

"experts" in their field. Thus a2 + $b^2 = c^2$ represented an expert system. Giving any value of a and any value of b we could always correctly calculate c.

Similarly, a proven methodology with formulae can be considered an expert system. Let's look at Figure 4, Potential Inventory Reduction Development. We determine the SIC code of the company in question and calculate its recent "turns" (inventory turnover). We then compare it to our comparison sources. Thus, if we could only obtain sales statistics we would use D&B ratios for the specific SIC code; and if we were able to obtain Cost of Sales statistics, we'd use Robert Morris Associates ratios. By simple plotting we can determine in which quartile they lie and thus how good they are doing compared to similar companies.

If their turns are in the lowest quartile, we should calculate the potential inventory reduction by achieving the lowest quartile and then the potential inventory reduction by achieving the median. The logic here is to expect a modest improvement rather than a quantum leap to the top quartile.

If the company's turns is in the second quartile, we should calculate potential inventory reductions by achieving the median and then the top quartile.

Similarly if the company is in the third quartile, we should calculate potential inventory reduction by achieving the top quartile.

Finally, if their turns is in the fourth quartile, they are doing great and should be teaching others how they achieved their excellent inventory turns.

At this point, I'd like to address those companies where their SIC code is in one of the categories designated as "n.e.c." (not elsewhere classified). Approximately 10% of the 900 SIC codes are catch-alls, thus grouping several diverse businesses; e.g., there are 3,597 Fabricated Metal Products Companies, n.e.c. In these cases the approach should be to develop inventory turnover ratios for the company's last three years. If their progress is upward, then encourage them to the same percentage increase. If their progress is downward, then motivate them to achieve the turns they had once achieved. And, if their turns are flat, then encourage them to a small improvement.

Sample—Potential Inventory Reduction Calculation

Let's take an example to show how to develop the potential inventory reduction. (See Figure 5.) Our sample company distributes drugs and proprietaries, SIC 5122. Their Cost of Sales last year was $16 million and their Average Inventory was $10 million. Thus their Turns = 1.6 calculated by Cost of Sales + Inventory = $16 million + $10 million. When we consult Robert Morris Associates' Inventory Turns ratios for SIC 5122 we find the highest quartile to be 8.1, the median 5.5 and the lowest quartile 3.8.

We can see that this company falls into the bottom quartile. Using our "expert system" we then calculate the projected inventory by achieving turns at the lowest quartile division, i.e., turns of 3.8. So, Projected Inventory = Cost of Sales + Projected Turns = $16 million + 3.8 = $ 4.2 million

Thus, the Inventory Reduction Potential

= Old Inventory — Projected Inventory

= $10 million — $4.2 million

= $ 5.8 million, a 58% reduction.

We can then project inventory reduction by improving to achieve turns at the median level, i.e., turns of 5.5

Projected Inventory = Cost of Sales + Projected Turns

= $16 million + 5.5

= $ 2.9 million

Thus, the Inventory Reduction Potential

= Old Inventory — Projected Inventory

= $10 million — $2.9 million

= $ 7.1 million, a 71% reduction.

If your company needs cash to invest in its future by providing new facilities or equipment, R&D, marketing, advertising or personnel, why not finance it by better management of inventories?

Sample—Inventory Carrying Cost Savings Calculation

Reduction of inventory is not the only benefit by achieving higher turns. When you reduce inventories you also reduce inventory carrying costs and these savings recur every year. Let me explain. When an inventory reduction is achieved, the cost of acquiring and taking care of that inventory is reduced by not having to finance it, not having to warehouse it, insure it, physically count it, etc.

The inventory carrying cost elements with estimated annual rates are listed in Figure 6. It shows the main element to be the cost of money, i.e., interest or finance charges which is often 10-20% per year. The next biggest element is that of opportunity, estimated at 3-10%. This includes investments in launching new products or opening new markets. Other inventory carrying cost elements include the cost of handling, 1-2% per year; space, 1-3%; damage, 1-2%; shrinkage, 0-2%; taxes, 0-2%, depending upon state; insurance, 0-2%; physical inventory, 1-2%; and general and administrative costs of 1-2% per year. Thus, for most companies, inventory carrying costs is 18-47% per year. This means that maintaining the asset called inventory is costing most companies approximately one-fifth to one-half of what the inventory is worth, each year!

In the previous example we identified the inventory reduction potentials for a company in the 5122 SIC code. If we were to assume a conservative inventory carrying cost of only 20%, our annual recurring savings would be as follows:

Achieving Turns at	Inventory Reduction	Annual Recurring Savings
Lowest Quartile (3.8)	$5.8 million	$1,160,000
Median (5.5)	$7.1 million	$1,420,000

These are additional monies generated from improving control of liquid assets which can be used to gain competitive advantages, open new markets, hire needed skills, provide additional profits or dividends.

Conclusion

Without visiting a company or investigating how it goes about its business and what efforts it uses to control its inventories, we have a technique to measure its effectiveness. This technique involves the inventory turnover ratio (turns) and its comparison to turns achieved by similar companies.

The next logical step, once we've determined that there are apparent opportunities for inventory reduction, is to analyze what can be done to effect that reduction. But that's the topic of another lesson.

About the author

MARTIN P. EDELMAN CMC, CFPIM, Senior Consultant, Coopers & Lybrand, New York City, has served APICS as an elected Society Director and Vice President for four years as well as President of his home chapter, Northern New Jersey. He is the author of the APICS "Practical Forecasting Training Aid" (1985) and the editor of the APICS "Make Vs Buy Decision Training Aid"(1988). Martin has spoken at the last seven Conferences and at numerous APICS chapters. He received a B.S. in mathematics from the Polytechnic University in New York in 1962, earned CPIM status in 1978, CMC (Certified Management Consultant) in 1986, and CFPIM in 1988.

Reprinted from 1990 APICS *Conference Proceedings.*

Excess Inventory: A Roadblock to World-Class Manufacturing

Jim Mottern

The development of World Class Manufacturing has clearly entered the age of American industrial supremacy. The new manufacturing philosophies and practices evolving out of Japanese automotive and electronic producers in the mid 1960's destroyed America's competitive advantage and set the agenda for the rest of this century and beyond. Our global manufacturing competitors revolutionized operations with a focus on continuous improvement to eliminate waste. Effective inventory management is one of the critical processes world class manufacturers have mastered as they continuously improved their operations.

What is Inventory?

Inventory is usually classified as raw material, work in process, finished goods and spares or service inventory. From a total manufacturing viewpoint, inventory can also include company owned tooling, fixtures and production supplies. Inventory can also be considered both an asset and a liability.

Inventory is an asset because it has physical value that can be exchanged for money. However until this exchange is made, inventory truly acts as a liability requiring investment in material, labor and overhead costs. Inventory drains business capital and cash flow away from other productive uses such as investment in technology and new products. Inventory reduces profit, until it is sold.

Inventory Level Definitions

The amount of inventory can best be measured by product cycle time. Excess inventory is usually defined by accounting as the quantity over twelve or eighteen months of usage. Many companies sell or scrap excess inventory as inventory carrying costs exceed the present value of the asset. A high inventory level is usually defined as a quantity greater than that required for several production cycles usually translating to a six month or larger supply which equates to two or fewer inventory turns. An optimum inventory level is the minimum quantity needed to effectively support the production process and deliveries expected by customers. World Class Manufacturers consider any quantity over the optimum level as waste and always seek to eliminate this unneeded quantity. Optimum inventory can be measured by "spins" in a World Class Manufacturer as it turns ten or more times a year.

Causes of Excess and High Inventory

Inventory levels above optimum quantities are caused by a number of different but often interrelated problems. The effectiveness of a manufacturer's philosophies, practices and systems determines the conditions that exist and the impact they have on inventory. A partial list of the conditions causing inventory include:

- Inventory at an optimum level supporting production and distribution
- Risk inventory purchased in anticipation of additional sales
- Inventory lot size (EOQ) or minimum buy quantities
- Inaccurate (too long) lead times
- Inaccurate bills of material
- Inaccurate/overstated master production schedule
- Inaccurate yield quantities (too high) when materials levels are primarily managed by shortages
- Inaccurate stores or WIP records
- Excessive kit modification activity when unused items are not managed
- Unmanaged engineering change activity

These conditions are especially troublesome when the manufactured product has a deep bill of material, a long cumulative lead time and many options.

Traditional Role of Inventory

Inventory traditionally has been considered a needed asset to meet customer service goals and to keep the plant operating efficiently. High customer service requires increased finished goods and sometimes semi-finished goods inventories. This is especially true if the product has a long manufacturing lead time. Inventory traditionally has been used to balance production bottlenecks and to keep operators and machines at a high utilization level. Inventory also has commonly been used to buffer the manufacturing process against unplanned demand and supply. Fluctuation in demand was generally handled by safety stock at the finished goods level or at strategic points in the bill of material. Fluctuation in supply was also handled with safety stock plus scrap allowance on assemblies and individual part numbers. Often a difficult part to manufacture had safety stock at many levels in its bill of material as machine downtime, scrap, rework and vendor delays were considered a normal part of the production process and had to be compensated with inventory buffers.

Role of Inventory in World Class Manufacturing

World Class Manufacturers consider inventory as a liability to be avoided whenever possible. Inventory beyond optimum levels is considered waste and there is constant effort to reduce it to a theoretical goal of one unit. Inventory also masks unacceptable quality and therefore should be reduced to identify problems needing correction.

Roadblocks to World Class Manufacturing

Inventory, in addition to being waste itself, hides waste in the production process created by machine downtime, scrap, rework and unbalanced lines/bottlenecks. Until inventory is reduced to expose these problems they will generally continue to add unnecessary cost to the product. A company cannot become a World Class Manufacturer until it addresses these problems successfully. High inventory levels also indirectly affect overhead costs by increasing the number of people needed to manage and control material, the total required warehouse/stores space, and the amount and type of material handling equipment. Engineering change activity is more difficult with high inventory quantities. Not only does high inventory often make effective engineering change management more time consuming, frequently parts are missed in the change process requiring them to be reworked later at a higher cost or scrapped if the rework costs are too high. Also, high inventory levels challenge the materials management function to avoid obsolescence costs. When high inventory levels create large production lot sizes, production control often has to manually intervene in the production process to expedite parts and break setups. This effort is waste in itself and disrupts a continuous flow of material.

World Class Inventory Management Checklist

World Class Manufacturers' continuous focus on eliminating waste can be translated into the following inventory management attributes:

- Management commitment to continually work on reducing inventory to an absolute minimum.
- Raw material to the optimum level to support a continuous flow production environment.
- WIP quantities to a lot size of one.
- Minimum or no finished good inventory (supported by very short production cycle times).
- Management understanding that inventory can be reduced below certain levels only when manufacturing processes are improved. This translates into a commitment to improve the processes along with and in support of inventory reduction.
- Clear understanding of the relationship between production cycle time, inventory level and cash flow by product or product line.
- Class A MRP II user status to manage purchasing activities, raw materials and finished goods.
- Streamlined production process using JIT or other pull processes.
- Minimal use of EOQ and minimum buy quantities.
- Measurement of manufacturing in units produced rather than measurement of personnel or machine efficiencies.
- Effective engineering change management.
- Use of concurrent engineering concepts.
- Quantification of the average engineering Change Order cost.
- Reporting and minimizing Engineering Change Order volume.

Steps to Achieve World Class Inventory Management

Most North American manufacturing companies are just beginning their programs which contain the following action items:

Develop and publish the management commitment to reduce inventories to an absolute minimum. Establish inventory goals and managements in:

- Inventory spins

- Inventory investment by product line

Embark on an aggressive Total Quality Management (TQM) program to improve processes that will in turn support significant inventory reduction.

Conduct an objective inventory management assessment using company personnel from corporate and/or other divisions or experienced consultants.

This assessment should include:

- Material management and control policies and practices
- MRP II system utilization
- EOQ/minimum buy quantities
- Safety stock
- Scrap allowance factors
- Record accuracy (BOM, inventory, master production schedule lead time)

Schedule field trips to the best inventory management companies.

Chart and publish current inventory levels compared with industry averages and World Class inventory managers.

Summary

World Class Manufacturers excel at inventory management because they consider inventory a waste to be avoided. World Class Manufacturers believe that inventory hides quality problems that add to product cost and therefore must be reduced to expose these problems for correction. This is in contrast to the traditional view of inventory as an asset to be managed and necessary to buffer demand and supply fluctuations. Management commitment, effective policies and practices, capable systems and a successful TQM program are all needed to achieve a World Class Inventory Management.

About the author

JIM MOTTERN is a Partner in the West Coast Manufacturing Consulting Practice of Ernst & Young. He specializes in assisting companies along the path to World Class Manufacturing. Jim is certified as a CPIM, CMA and CPA. He is a former president of the San Diego APICS chapter and is a frequent speaker to national and regional manufacturing industry groups.

Reprinted from *Production and Inventory Management Journal*, Fourth Quarter, 1991.

Inventory Management—The Big Picture

R. Natarajan, Ph.D.

During the last decade, the thinking on the proper role of inventories in organizations has undergone a drastic change. Needless to say, the adoption of Just-in-Time (JIT) principles (which have proved to be quite effective) has been the catalyst bringing about this change. Though it is still classified as an asset from an accounting and financial standpoint, inventories have come to be viewed in operations as evil, albeit a necessary evil, required to sustain the various activities. Some, like Shigeo Shingo [5], have pronounced them an absolute evil.

As a natural consequence, in the profession there has been a rethinking concerning the approaches to managing inventories. Inventory management is no longer viewed as a narrow discipline associated with topics such as lot sizing or cycle counting. Increasingly, it is being acknowledged that the body of knowledge needed for managing inventories has to be broader than it has been in the past. (It is worth noting here that in a related development, APICS will offer a certification program in integrated resource management (CIRM). Changes in the existing certification curriculum are also being proposed.)

There is some evidence concerning the transformation in thinking among practitioners and academics. An analysis of the articles that appeared in this journal during the last five years reveals that the number of articles in the lot-sizing area is experiencing a decline, while the number in JIT and zero inventories is increasing. This cannot be just a coincidence. The shortcomings of focusing on lot-sizing problems and, in particular, on EOQ models, have been exposed. For instance, Eliott Weiss [7] and Burnham and Mohanty [1] have argued that a systems view is necessary while dealing with inventory issues. Lot sizing covers only one aspect and leads to sub-optimization. Gene Woolsey [8] has called for a requiem for EOQ.

This article attempts to highlight the integrative aspects of inventory management. Through a cause-and-effect diagram and a new interpretation of the familiar inventory river-flow analogy, the systemic nature of inventory management is brought out. The linkages between inventory management and competitive advantages are also discussed.

The River-Flow Analogy

The now-familiar river-flow analogy (see, for instance, Hall [3] and Chase and Aquilano [2]) has been used to illustrate the idea that higher inventory levels are evil. They cover up problems in manufacturing—among others, those relating to quality, maintenance, absenteeism, and suppliers—like the water covering the rocks. Reducing the water level exposes the rocks which can be cleared away, thus allowing a smoother flow. Similarly, inventory reduction can be used to confront the various problems. This is the rationale behind JIT, sometimes referred to as forced problem solving. Now we can add other twists to this analogy. The depth of the stream is associated with the level of inventories, but what about the width and the length? The width can be associated with the variety of parts while the length represents the material-flow distances from the suppliers to customers (see Figure 1). To complete the analogy, the flow rate of the water can be likened to the velocity of the transformation of raw materials into finished goods. This velocity is just the reciprocal of the throughput time.

Such an interpretation brings into focus the integration of strategic and competitive factors with inventory management. The firms compete on the basis of cost, delivery, and quality. They are under constant pressure to produce their products cheaper, quicker, and with better quality. Reducing the throughput time by faster value addition to the materials clearly would lead to a competitive edge. This also would lead to advantage on the cost front—inventory costs are reduced as materials now spend less time in the system. This brings out another point: inventory costs are determined not only by the level, but also by the duration of time the materials spend in the system. A better indicator of inventory costs is "dollar days." Westinghouse, for example, uses a model called OPTIM [6] to track and measure the cost buildup over time as the value gets added to the materials. Such a model can be used as a diagnostic tool for identifying opportunities for shrinking the time as well as inventory levels.

Product variety can be enhanced by having more options for the product, but this would also increase inventory costs. This brings the design dimension into inventory management. From this perspective, increasing commonality of parts clearly makes sense. Flow distances are also

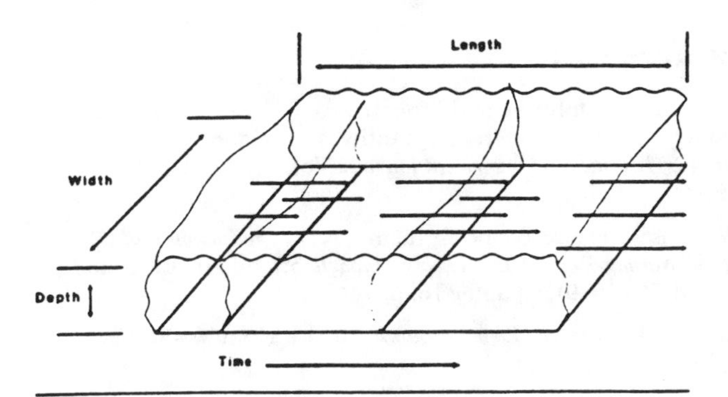

Figure 1 *Inventory River Flow*

affected by strategic considerations. In this context, it is not just the plant layout that is important; location decisions are equally important. It is common in electronics or even in textile industries to send the components and semi-finished materials all over the globe for completion of certain operations. Such globe girdling simply adds to inventory costs. In summary, we can express the total inventory costs to the firm as: total level of inventory (value in $) times carrying-cost percentage times total time spent in the system, where the summation is over all the parts used in the transformation. Total time spent in the system will be a function of the flow distances as well as the product velocity. Thus, the modified river-flow analogy provides a more complete picture of the inventory costs.

Cause-and-Effect Analysis

The cause-and-effect diagram shown in figure 2 can be used to organize all of the information about the various

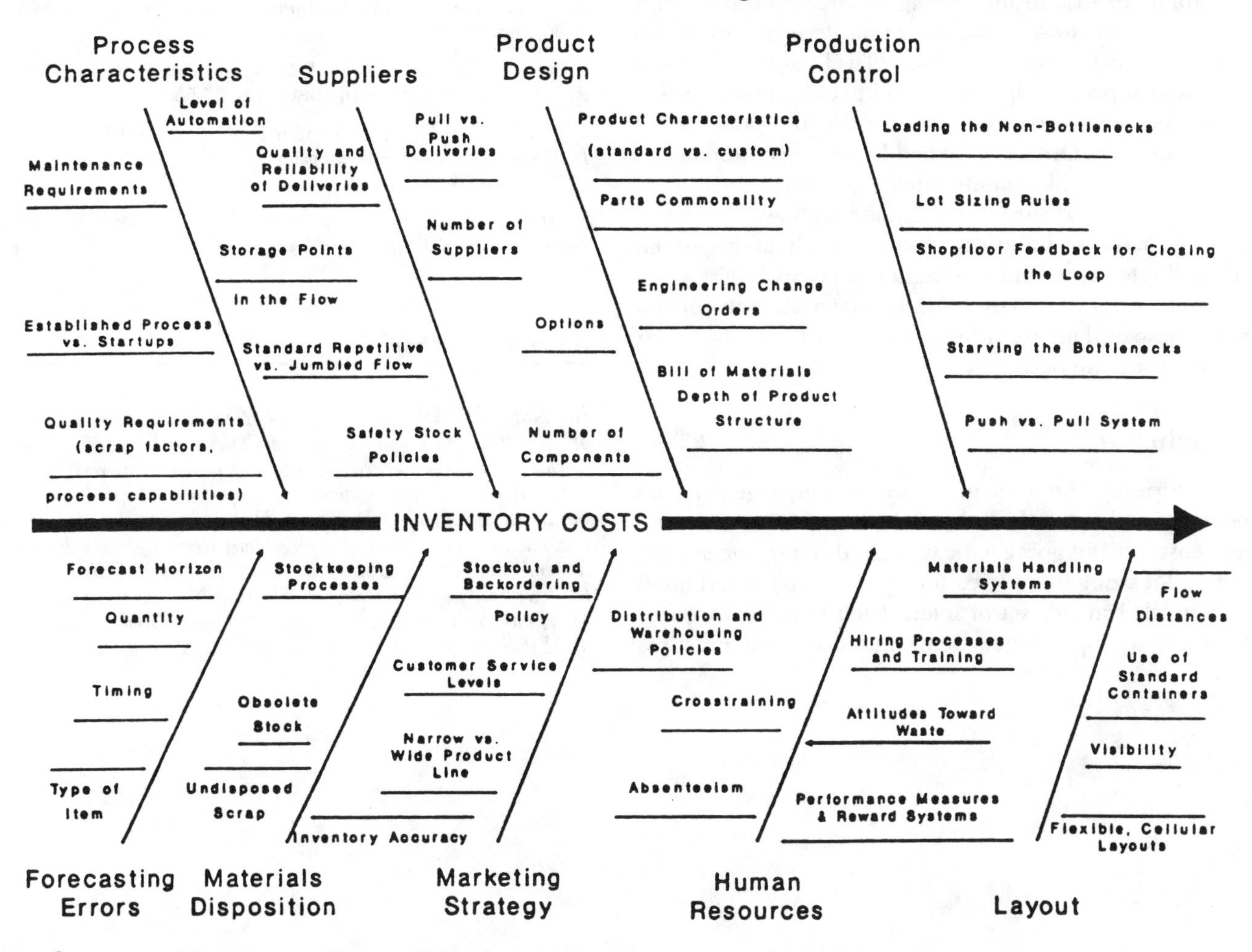

Figure 2 *Cause-Effect diagram of factors contributing to inventory costs*

factors that influence inventory costs. It complements the river-flow analogy because it identifies and isolates in greater detail the variables that influence the height, length, width, and rate of flow of the inventory river. Though some of the branches in the fishbone diagram appear independent, there is interaction between them and it is important that such interactions be understood. As Hal Mather [4] points out in an article that addresses the interaction between bill-of-materials structuring, product design, and forecasting, design considerations greatly influence the production lead time as well as the inventory levels required at the end-item level to provide customer service.

For many of these factors, their relationship to inventory costs is rather obvious, but for some it is not readily apparent. For example, training given to employees affects inventory accuracy in terms of following correct procedures. Cross training is important particularly in labor constrained operations. Availability of multiple skills provides the ability to sustain the adding of value even if there is machine breakdown or absenteeism. Performance measures can greatly impact inventory levels, although this is not often appreciated. Using machine utilization rates as a measure of performance is an incentive to produce more than is needed. On the other hand, stressing customer-oriented measures like on-time delivery would promote behavior that would speed up the material flow. The use of bigger materials-handling systems, such as high-tech AS/AR systems, encourages higher inventory levels as well as a longer duration period for the materials in the operation compared to pushcarts or standard containers for transporting the parts.

Conclusion

Historically, the domain of inventory management has been defined narrowly. It should be recognized that inventory costs are not going to be brought down by concentrating on lot sizing or cycle counting alone. It is determined by a much broader set of interrelated factors. Before attempting to implement systemic manufacturing practices such as JIT, it is important to understand what constitutes the "big picture" in inventory management. This article has proposed the use of some simple tools to accomplish that.

References

1. Burnham, John M. and Mohanty, B. B., "Requiem for EOQ—But Unified Order Quantity is Alive and Well," *Production & Inventory Management Journal*, Vol. 31, No. 1 (1990), pp. 80-83.

2. Chase, Richard B. and Aquilano, N. J., *Production and Operations Management: A Life Cycle Approach*, 5th ed., Irwin. Homewood, IL (1989), Chapter 16, p. 744.

3. Hall, Robert W., *Zero Inventories*, Irwin. Homewood. IL (1983), Chapter 1, p. 13.

4. Mather, Hal F., "Design, Bills of Materials, and Forecasting—The Inseparable Threesome," *Production & Inventory Management*, Vol. 27, No. 1 (1986), pp. 90-107.

5. Robinson, Alan, *Modern Approaches to Manufacturing Improvements: The Shingo System*, Productivity Press, Cambridge, MA (1990), pp. 41-43.

6. Sullivan, Edward, "OPTIM: Linking Cost, Time and Quality," *Quality Progress* (April 1986), pp. 52-55.

7. Weiss, Elliott N., "Lot Sizing is Dead: Long Live Lot Sizing," *Production & Inventory Management Journal*, Vol. 31, No. 1 (1990), pp. 76-79.

8. Woolsey, G., "A Requiem for the EOQ: An Editorial," *Production & Inventory Management Journal*, Vol. 29, No. 3 (1988), pp. 68-72.

About the author

R. "Nat" NATARAJAN, Ph.D., CPIM, is an associate professor of operations management at the College of Business, Tennessee Technological University. His current research interests are in the areas of Just-in-Time systems, management of quality, and the management of new technologies. Dr. Natarajan has published in this journal, Operations Management Review, and others. He is a member of APICS, DSI, and TIMS. He received his Ph.D. from the University of Kansas and MS from Northwestern University. He is currently academic liaison for Upper Cumberland Chapter of APICS and has also served as its VP of Education.

Reprinted from APICS 1988 *Conference Proceedings*.

Field Inventory: Do You Really Need It?

David K. Nelson

As companies strive to reduce inventories through Just-in-Time (JIT) principles, many are treating field stock as a necessary evil, with service requirements and transportation cost tradeoffs driving finished goods deployment decisions. The growing use of distribution requirements/resource planning (DRP) systems has improved the quality of the field stocking decisions and execution, but the underlying question remains: Is field inventory really necessary? This paper presents several alternatives to field inventory that may be cost-effectively used to meet today's increasing service standards.

Field Inventory Defined

The term "field inventory" can only be defined with respect to each company's outbound distribution network. For purposes of this paper we assume a make-to-stock environment with manufacturing plants supplying plant warehouses that, in turn, replenish regional or local distribution centers (DC's). Field inventory consists of finished goods (or replacement parts) that are stocked in distribution centers that are not physically "connected" to the facilities in which they were manufactured (i.e., not plant warehouse inventory. This distinction is important, since this paper does not make a case for higher or lower total finished goods inventory. Rather, it addresses the question of when and why inventory, which would otherwise remain in a plant warehouse, should be deployed to remote locations, and vice versa.

Why Field Inventory Exists

The placement of part of a company's inventory in field DC's has traditionally been in response to one of more of the following: Customer order cycle time and completeness requirements, transportation costs, plant warehouse capacity, and marketing strategy.

The issue of order cycle time can be summed up in one statement: "I want it yesterday!" Before we had sophisticated inventory management systems, speed of delivery was paramount, often because orders were placed at the last moment, or when stockouts had already occurred. Since cycle time includes not only the shipment transit time, but also the time required to "process the paperwork," it can commonly take several days before the order is even released to the DC for shipment. If the order is too small to fill a truckload, yet too large to go via express delivery, a shipper may find himself slave to his carrier's less-than-truckload (LTL) terminal network. Prior to deregulation of the trucking industry, this often meant several days to a week to go just a few hundred miles. Establishing remote stocking locations in close proximity to customers is one way to reduce outbound transit time, theoretically by having to go through fewer LTL terminals between origin and destination. Although carriers have made significant improvements in LTL transit time (out of competitive necessity), and new order processing systems help reduce "paperwork" delays, LTL delivery time is still a concern to many logistics managers.

Order completeness simply means a single shipment per order , as opposed to split shipments from different source points. For now we assume that all of the line items requested are in stock somewhere in the distribution network. Aside from the obvious need that a customer has to replenish his inventory or keep his line running in a JIT environment, the desire for a complete shipment also stems from the added complexity involved in handling two or more shipments for a single purchase order. Not only are there additional handling costs, but many purchasing systems have problems dealing with multiple receipts per order. Thus, a field stocking location may be used as a way of consolidating all of the requested items into a single shipment.

Perhaps the major reason companies have chosen to maintain field inventory is the freight cost structures that exist today. Although freight rates have generally come down since deregulation, it can still be relatively expensive to ship many small orders individually over several hundred miles, and recent LTL rate increases have not helped. Since LTL rates are based upon weight, freight classification, and distance (and subject to minimum charges), there is a point at which it becomes less costly to move products in truck load quantities for most of the distance, stock it in a DC and then ship it out LTL or UPS to fill customer orders.

Plant warehouse capacity can also force remote deployment of inventory. If you do not have room for it at the factory, and have to move it anyway, why not move it closer to the customer? Finally there is the issue of marketing strategy. This is closely related to the transit time issue, in that companies may use local inventory presence as a selling point with buyers who may be skeptical as to delivery time. The idea works in theory, as long as the local DC remains properly stocked with all items that buyers want. Yet, even with DRP, there is always the need to expedite a shipment from the factory direct to the customer, due to local stockouts.

There are, of course, other reasons why companies may choose to deploy inventory to the field. High frequency of customer pickup, ultra-short lead time requirements (e.g., in hours instead of days), poor service coverage by non-local carriers, etc., may all warrant a remote DC. But the issue can usually be distilled down to delivery time, and transportation cost.

Alternatives to Field Inventory

With interest rates creeping up again, a steady reduction in unemployment (and the corresponding increase in labor costs), and an overall greater emphasis on total logistics management, the time is right to evaluate alternatives to a network of remote DC's stuffed with inventory. The six approaches presented here are pool distribution, multiple-stop truckload shipments, dedicated equipment, backhaul scheduling, continuous route moves, and stockless warehouses. Each represents a shift from inventory assets to distribution resources as a means of meeting service needs in the most cost-effective manner.

Pool Distribution

The concept of pool distribution has been around for a long time. Generally, it means using a third party to provide local or regional distribution of product. It differs from public warehousing and distribution in that the product is not stocked, but merely cross-docked from a truckload shipment. It works especially well in markets that have a high concentration of customers who order frequently (i.e., metropolitan areas). Consumer products manufacturers are often major users of pool distribution, since their customers have been steadily increasing the number of direct-store-deliveries and reducing the volume that flows through inbound distribution centers.

The mechanics of pool distribution are fairly simple. It is based on the reality that it costs considerably less to ship in truckload quantities than in the smaller quantities that make up individual orders. For example, a detergent manufacturer may have orders from ten customers in the Detroit area, with each order representing 4000 pounds of product. If the manufacturer's factory is in Little Rock, and the customers want delivery in 3-4 days, he faces a dilemma. Unless he has local stock, he would have to ship 10 orders of 4000 pounds each via an LTL carrier. Even though LTL rates per pound decrease as the shipment size increases, it will nearly always be greater than a corresponding truckload rate per pound. In addition, it may not be possible to meet the delivery requirement if the product must move through several of the carrier's LTL terminals enroute to Detroit.

Under pool distribution, the manufacturer "buys" a truckload move for 40,000 pounds from his plant in Little Rock to a distribution agent in Detroit. Not only does this move (the line-haul) take a minimum amount of time, since it can travel non-stop, but the transportation cost per pound is considerably lower over the majority of the distance, versus LTL rates. Once in Detroit the product is shipped from the trailer, cross-docked, and loaded and shipped using a local fleet. What is sacrificed here, compared to using a local DC, is the time it takes to run the line-haul.

The cost structure of pool distribution is similar to that of a distribution center network. The cost of the line-haul exists in both environments, since DC's must be replenished anyway. The local delivery cost will be comparable as well. However, the difference is in the handling cost at the distribution agent. Generally pool distributors will quote a "distribution rate" which includes the handling at their warehouse, as well as local distribution. In theory this should be less than it otherwise costs the manufacturer to receive, put away, store, pick, and ship the product at a local DC. However, it tends to be most economical with larger LTL orders that can be handled by distribution agents at lower costs per pound. Note also though, that pool distribution can be accomplished using a company's own facilities. The key is to avoid stocking the product locally (and all of the associated cost).

Clearly the biggest stumbling block to pool distribution is the timing issue. Whereas a local DC can deliver next-day (or potentially even same-day), the line-haul component of pool distribution typically increases delivery time by at least a day. Most companies have solved this problem by incorporating a scheduled delivery program into their pool distribution environment. By specifying one or two days in a week as the scheduled delivery days for a certain geographic area, and requiring a minimum order lead time, shippers have been able to meet customer expectations and lower their costs at the same time.

The scheduled delivery program has several advantages. From the shipper's standpoint, it increases the likelihood that he will have enough volume to fill out a truckload for the line-haul, since he ships to a particular area only once or twice per week instead of every day. By properly grouping geographic areas into days, he can also smooth out his distribution workload. From the customer's standpoint, fill rates will likely be higher, since inventory levels at the plant warehouses are not as volatile as at a local DC. Also by working with suppliers and the local distribution agent, a customer can conceivably reduce the number of individual shipments to be received. If multiple suppliers use the same distribution agent, and the same delivery day, the cost of receiving each order can be reduced by combining products from multiple suppliers on a single local delivery. Thus, pooling can also be used to improve inbound logistics as well. The flip side of this issue is the increased coordination required for a supplier to ensure that line-hauls from various plants (containing different items) arrive at the distribution agent at the same time for consolidation and outbound shipment—a process that should ideally be transparent to the customer.

Multiple-Stop Truckload Shipments

For customers who place orders that are relatively large, yet not truckload size, shipment can often be made from plant warehouses on a multiple-stop truckload. Let's assume customers in Cincinnati, Columbus, and Cleveland each order 13,000 pounds of product that can either be shipped LTL from a DC in Pittsburgh, or direct from the factory in Dallas. In a multi-stop truckload scenario, the factory "buys" a truckload move from Dallas to Cleveland and pays an additional charge for 2 stops. Depending on the freight rates, this alternative may be cheaper than separate LTL shipments from Dallas or even from Pittsburgh. Transit time is still an issue, but the difference is probably no more than 1-2 days.

The use of multiple-stop truckload moves is not a complete alternative to field inventory, since few companies have customers that all order in large quantities. Also, the customers should be relatively close to one another, to maximize the distance in which the trailer moves fully-loaded. Finally, depending on the size of the individual orders and the amount of the stop-off charge, there is a point (e.g., 2 stops) above which a pool shipment or straight LTL is cheapest and quickest. What multiple-stop LTL moves do allow, however, is a reduction in field inventory at remote DC's, since large orders need not even go through the local facility.

Dedicated Equipment

Another alternative to local stocking and LTL shipping is the use of dedicated equipment. Under this arrangement a shipper contracts with a carrier to effectively "lease" the services of a driver and vehicle over a period of time. It is similar to operating a private fleet, without all of the fleet maintenance hassles. Dedicated equipment may be used to make multiple, large deliveries that might otherwise be too expensive for multiple-drop TL or local LTL shipment. Again, the benefit is not complete elimination of field inventory, but a further reduction, since a greater number of large orders are not being shipped from a remote DC. Dedicated fleet arrangements also dovetail quite well with pool distribution systems on the line-haul portion (to the distribution agent).

Continuous Route Moves

Continuous route moves provide a means of shipping large quantities at rates that are even below those of a full truckload. The primary requirement for a continuous route move is an inbound truckload shipment. Instead of "concluding the transaction" with the truckload carrier on receipt of the inbound freight, the shipper arranges for an extension of the move.

For example, say that our Little Rock detergent manufacturer has a truckload of raw material coming in from Salt Lake City, and has a large order to be shipped to a customer in Birmingham. Instead of shipping the customer order LTL from Little Rock (or LTL from a remote DC in say, Atlanta), the incoming trailer is loaded with the outbound goods and sent on its way. The carrier has a nominal charge for the stop in Little Rock, and bills the manufacturer as if he moves a full truckload from Salt Lake City to Birmingham.

Such moves are used when the incremental cost to move the truckload the additional distance is minimal. Of course, the carrier must have a good reason for doing so as well. Often this is the case if the carrier can minimize non-revenue miles as a result. Continuous route moves tend to work best when the outbound shipment is one that occurs on a regular basis, thus permitting the shipper and carrier to plan in advance for the additional move. Again, by providing a cost-effective means of getting product to the customer in the same amount of time as it would take from a field DC, this approach can help further reduce a company's dependence on field inventory.

Backhaul Scheduling

One offshoot of JIT is the desire for customers to have greater control over their inbound logistics. This is especially true in situations where the customer maintains his own fleet for re-distribution. Grocery chains, mass merchandisers, and manufacturers with heavy interplant material flows are a few examples. By working with the customer's fleet dispatcher, it may be possible to service him from a plant warehouse, rather than a local facility by letting his own vehicles carry the shipment.

Retail chains are particularly receptive to this idea. Even with a great deal of direct-store-delivery there will always be a need for a consolidated shipment from the chain's own distribution center. Quite often the trucks return to the DC empty, much to the dismay of the distribution manager. If a manufacturer has a facility near one of the chain's stores, and also has an order to be sent to the chain's DC, the opportunity is clear. Because retail chains typically send a truck to each store at least once weekly, there is the possibility of serving most of their inbound needs in this manner, completely avoiding local inventory requirements for this customer.

It should also be noted that backhaul scheduling can be done with third-party carriers as well; and several non-transportation companies that operate large private fleets also solicit backhaul freight to improve their cost-effectiveness.

Stockless Warehouses

This final approach can mean a lot of things, but in this context it refers to a distribution point with no building (e.g., a fenced trailer yard). One group that has considered this concept is the beverage industry. A major complexity within this industry is the return of empty bottles and/or cans to a bottler. This, combined with a marketplace requiring high-volume local delivery using specialized equipment, has somewhat forced the industry to use multi-stop distribution. It simply is not possible to service 30 retail outlets 150 miles away from the bottling operation in a single day. Therefore, the company must either sell through distributors or set up their own field warehouses.

One way around this is to reposition delivery vehicles in strategic market areas, and use separate equipment to transfer trailers with the next day's deliveries to the local area. The trailer is dropped in a fenced yard, and the tractor picks up the local trailer full of empty bottles for the return trip. Thus, the company uses its trailers as "moving warehouses." The savings here are in DC operating cost, or distributor profit margin.

Choosing An Alternative Approach

The six approaches that have been discussed are not mutually exclusive. That is, several can be used either separately or in conjunction to address certain pieces of a company's business. The overall goal is to service the customer without having to put inventory all over the country, and using distribution resources to achieve JIT performance. Choosing an approach to use begins with one simple step: Identifying and rationalizing (if you can) each SKU of field inventory.

Wait a minute—that is not as simple as it sounds, especially in a sales/marketing-driven company. But before giving in to all of the doomsday stories of lost sales due to no local stock, first investigate the service time and cost associated with the current system. Then simulate the use of some of these alternative approaches for all or part of the customer base serviced by a given field DC. Incidentally, do not hesitate to enlist the assistance of carriers in this analysis. Of course, get your own transportation/distribution people involved. If you find a scenario that appears realistic, make arrangements with the customer to try it on a pilot basis, perhaps passing along some of the savings.

Summary

This paper has raised the issue of why companies deploy their inventory to remote locations. Several alternative approaches for getting product to the customer without having to use field stock have been presented. Even the strongest proponents of Zero Inventory and JIT will confess that there will always be the need for some inventory. Given this fact, it only makes sense that inventory should be kept in as few "piles" as possible for maximum flexibility and minimum "safety" stock. So do you really need field inventory?

About the author

David K. Nelson CPIM CDP is the Manager of Logistics Planning at North American Philips Corporation in New York, a multi-billion dollar manufacturer of consumer electronics, small appliances, lighting products, and electrical components. Prior to joining NAPC, he was a management consultant both with his own firm and with Cleveland Consulting Associates. He has also held materials management positions with Dow Corning Corp. His professional emphasis is on manufacturing/logistics integration, as well as strategies and systems for distribution and customer service.

Currently a member of the Mid-Hudson Valley APICS Chapter, Mr. Nelson has been both a speaker and reviewer at previous international conferences and has also spoken at regional seminars and chapter meetings. He holds a BS in Industrial Management and a MBA in Management Information Systems from Indiana University and is a member of the Council of Logistics Management and the International Customer Service Association.

Reprinted from APICS 1985 *Conference Proceedings.*

Dollar Days

G. Guy Sorrell and M. L. Srikanth, Ph.D.

Introduction

The spectacular success of Japanese repetitive manufacturers has led U. S. Industry to make a fundamental reexamination of manufacturing practices, including a challenge to our traditional ways of thinking about the value of inventories. A strong movement has begun in the United States to displace "Just-in-Case" production with Just-in-Time production. Corporations are placing greater emphasis on controlling and monitoring inventory levels and manufacturing managers are being required to reduce inventories quickly and drastically. Massive investments in plant and product design are being undertaken to achieve this goal.

It is generally recognized that one of the major contributors to the Japanese success is their emphasis on operating, without work stoppage, with extremely low inventories. Inventory is considered to be more than just unnecessary. It is a waste and as such has to be eliminated.

In spite of this recognition of the crucial role of inventory, traditional financial and accounting systems and practices are not designed to recognize the full economic value of minimizing inventories. This paper describes how inventories are treated in the traditional accounting system and the role of inventory as a competitive factor. An approach is presented by which inventory can be evaluated financially so that the full performance contribution of inventory reductions in a manufacturing plant can be determined. Finally, the use of dollar days is presented as a means to monitor the effectiveness of the management of inventory levels.

Measures of Operating Performance

Three traditional key financial measures of a company's operating performance are:

- Net Profit
- Return on Assets
- Cash Flow

For analytical purposes, these financial measures may be represented by three equivalent operational measures:

- Throughput
- Inventory
- Operational Expense

Inventories impact traditional financial measures in two ways:

1. DIRECT IMPACT: Any reduction in inventory will free funds that were tied up in inventory and if freed cash is paid out, total assets are reduced and return on assets is increased.

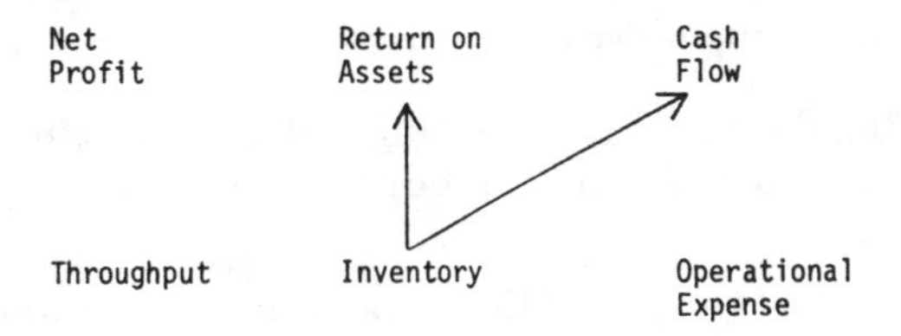

2. INDIRECT IMPACT: Inventories influence the traditional financial measures through the cost of carrying inventory, an operating expense. Carrying cost is more than just the interest charge on the capital tied up in inventory. It includes a host of other charges or costs incurred in the holding of inventory such as handling, storage, taxes, obsolescence, scrap, product damage leading to rework or quality losses, etc. Today, the number generally used for computing carrying cost is in excess of 30 percent and variable carrying costs are considered to be in the 20 percent range.

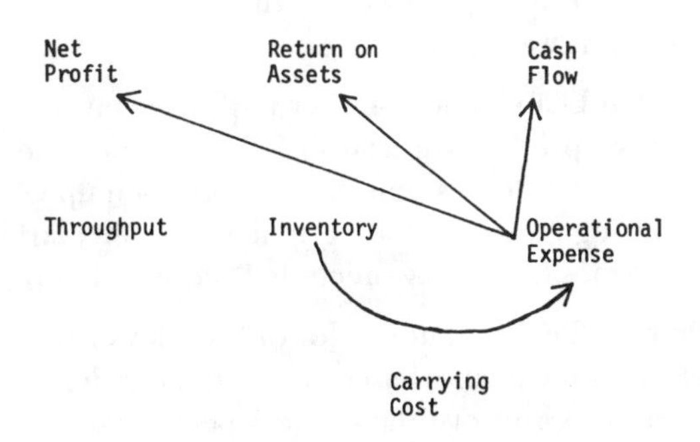

The effect of reducing operational expense through inventory carrying cost reduction is an improvement in all three traditional financial measures.

The net effect of inventory reduction can be seen by considering the following example:

Total Sales	= $100 million
Total Assets	= $ 50 million
Inventory (60% Material Value)	= $ 20 million
Net Profit (10%)	= $ 10 million
Return on Assets	= 20%
Sales Margin on Materials	= 50%

Competitive Advantage Through Inventory Reduction

Inventory reduction provides a competitive edge—a key lesson learned these past few years. The impact of inventory on the competitive posture is primarily in three areas:

1. The Product the Company Offers: The effect of inventory reductions on the product offered by a company is two-fold.

(a) Product Quality—The favorable impact of inventory reductions on product quality is well-known and documented.

(b) Engineering Improvements—The lower the inventory, the more rapidly new products can be introduced and improvements made to current products. The benefits to this are more than the cost of avoiding obsolescence. In a fiercely competitive market, ability to keep pace with the competition in product improvement may be vital. Being able to introduce changes readily and at low cost may turn out to be the best competitive edge in such a market place. Huge profits may be realized while the competition is catching up.

2. Responsiveness to the Market: In addition to new products, inventory impacts a company's ability to respond to the market in two ways:

(a) Quoted Lead Times—Lower in-process inventories means shorter production lead times and hence shorter delivery lead times to customers. This can open up whole new market segments, including make-to-order markets, where lead times previously precluded successful entry.

(b) Delivery Performance—Not only do lower production lead times mean shorter customer delivery lead time quotes, they also improve the delivery performance. This almost counter-intuitive result is due to two main effects. First, as the production lead time shrinks, less production is based on forecast and more on firm orders. Second, short production lead time improves the ability of the company to react to unforeseen events—production problems or demand shifts. A company with a short production lead time can serve a larger market segment with less disruption from both inside and outside disturbances.

3. Price Competitiveness: Reduced operating expense, improved quality and improved delivery of the product enable a plant to be more flexible on price. The product can be sold for a lower price without reducing profitability. On the other hand, the market may be willing to pay an even higher price in return for a superior product with more dependable delivery.

The combined effect of all these factors is a greater competitive edge. Thus, inventory improvements not only affect the operating expenses of a company (through the carrying cost) but they also affect the throughput.

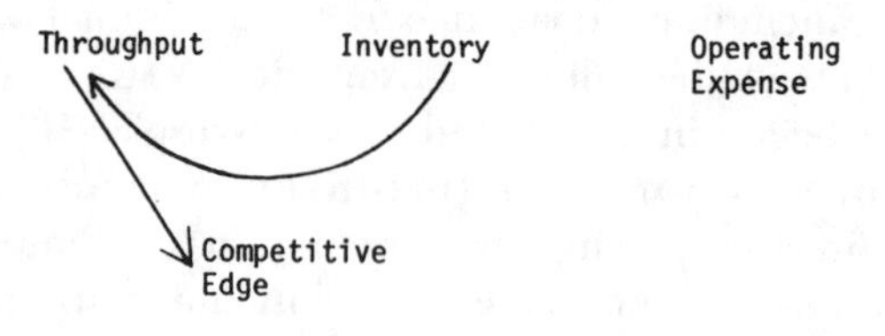

The improved throughput will then have significance to the financial performance of the plant.

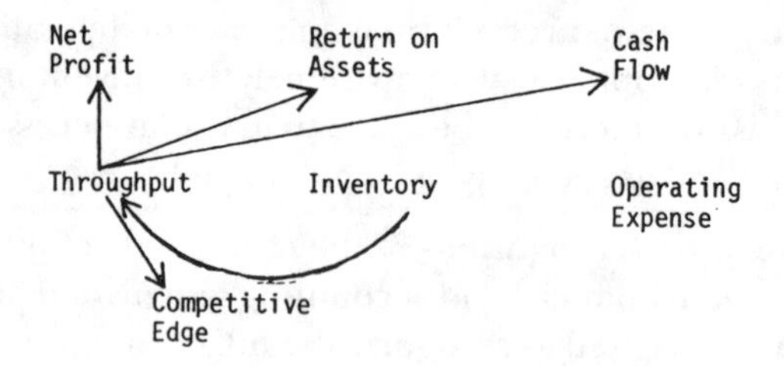

If we reduce inventories by 50 percent to $10 million, cash is increased by $6 million (assuming that only purchased material cost is eliminated) and the asset base is reduced to $46 million ($50 million, less $10 million inventory plus $6 million freed cash). Operational expense drops by $2 million ($10 million inventory reduction variable carrying cost of 20%). This, likewise, increases profit $2 million and assets to $48 million. The net effects on the traditional financial measures are:

Inventory Reduction	= $10 million
Increase in Net Profit	= $ 2 million
Increase in ROTA (using end of year assets of $48 million)	= 5% (to 25%)
Increase in Cash	= $ 8 million

Beyond Traditional Measures

The value of inventory reductions as seen by the traditional accounting practices depends on the cost of inventory reduced. Accordingly, companies reach a point at which further inventory reductions appear to have little significant financial value—at least when only traditional accounting data are considered. In the example used before, if inventory were $2 million (50 turns) and total assets were $32 million (ROTA = 31.25%), a 50% reduction in inventory would have the following impact on the traditional key financial measures:

Inventory Reduction= $1.0 million

Increase in Net Profit = $ .2 million

Increase in ROTA = 0.825%

Increase in Cash = $ .8 million

Compare the benefits of a 50% inventory reduction when inventory turns were at 5 and a 50% inventory improvement when turns are at 50 and the ROTA performance improvement hardly seems worth the effort (our second example). We can conclude then, that the traditional measure of economic impact of any percentage reduction in inventory is a function of the value of inventory relative to the value of total assets. We can further conclude that under traditional performance measures, economic analysis computes the ROTA increase of a percentage reduction in inventory that varies inversely with the number of inventory turns.

Nevertheless, as exemplified by the Zero Inventory crusade, there continues a very concerted effort to reduce inventories well below what can be justified using such traditional cost analysis. This is not because of the manufacturing community's perversity to invest beyond the point of reasonable return, but because of an understanding that the true value of inventory reduction goes beyond the traditional "cost reductions" assigned to inventory reductions. As inventories are reduced, the ability of the organization to react to external and internal factors is greatly increased. As inventories are reduced, the company's competitive position improves.

In our second example, if the 50% inventory reduction could be accompanied by an increased sales level of 10% without an increase in the cost of manufacturing, results would be as follows:

Increased Sales = $10 million

Increase in Net Profit = $ 5.2 million

Increase in ROTA = 10.05%

Increase in Cash Flow = $ 5.8 million

In this case, the effect of inventory improvements due to throughput increase completely dominates the effect of Operational Expense reductions. This is indicative of the financial impact of what may be referred to as a competitive edge .

Dollar Days—An Approach To Measuring The Management Of Inventory

Once all dimensions of the impact of inventories on operating performance are accepted, the next major step is to determine how well a company is managing this crucial asset. This should be followed by a detailed analysis to determine how improvements can be made.

To evaluate a company's inventory performance, two things are necessary:

- Measurement of the level of inventory.
- Establishment of a basis for evaluation.

Keeping in mind that the role of inventory is to support and maintain the throughput of the company, let us see how we can approach these questions in a systematic fashion.

In raising the question of measurement, we are not attempting to determine which among the traditional accounting alternatives—LIFO, FIFO, various ways of absorbing overhead costs, etc.—is better. Neither are we addressing inventory costing for tax or other regulatory objectives. Our focus is the operating unit and how to measure inventory in such a way as to provide both a performance measure and a diagnostic tool.

When a manufacturing organization operates efficiently, material flows through the plant in a smooth, synchronized fashion. Lead times are short and the plant can respond quickly to both internal and external events. The converse is true of a poorly managed operation. Material moves in an uncoordinated and erratic fashion, staying in large quantities for extended periods of time in the plant.

To properly evaluate the level of inventory, it is necessary to know not only how much material is in the plant but also how long it is going to remain in the plant. The true measure of inventory management is a combination of how much material there is and how long before it can be converted to throughput. This is the basis for the concept of dollar days .

Inventory Dollar days = Material value of inventory x Number of days before it can be sold

All elements of inventory are valued the same way whether raw material, work-in-process or finished goods. The total inventory dollar days of the plant is the sum of the inventory dollar days of each physical piece of material.

Total Inventory Dollar Days = Sum of inventory dollar days of each component or in-process item

For example, if a produce-to-order plant has an inventory of $10 million and a production lead time of 5 days (for simplicity - assume one product, one component, fixed demand and fixed lead time) then:

Total Dollar Days inventory =
($10 million) x (5 days) = $50 million

The dollar days measure of inventory places emphasis not only on the material value of the inventory but also on how long it is likely to stay in the plant. Thus, both expensive materials and slow-moving inventory can be identified as opportunities for performance improvement. Most often, it is slow-moving inventory that, on closer analysis, reveals the causes for poor plant performance.

It is not enough to know the value of what is on the floor. It is necessary that these values be compared to the value of what should be on the floor. The inventory that should be on the floor is the inventory that is required to support the throughput of the plant. We refer to this part of the plant inventory as the relevant inventory. Inventory that does not serve to support the throughput we refer to as excess inventory. Let us look at these components.

1. Relevant Inventory: Inventory that is required to support the throughput of the plant. This consists of material that is being processed at various resources and is required for meeting the current demand. If there were no disruptions, no additional inventory is needed. To protect the throughput of the plant from disruptions, it is necessary to provide appropriate buffer inventories at strategic locations. Buffer inventories are required in front of bottlenecks and in front of assembly operations.

2. Excess Inventory: Inventory in the plant not relevant to meeting the throughput objectives. Excess inventory is not obsolete inventory. Obsolete inventory is not inventory at all, it is equivalent to waste and is identified as such. The material that is identified as excess is needed to satisfy market demand; however, it was purchased and may have been put into production ahead of when it was absolutely necessary.

The very definition of relevant inventory requires the plant to have a valid schedule. Without a valid schedule, it is impossible to determine what should be in the buffers. Excess inventory represents investment that is unnecessary, and it exists as a result of inventory management policies and practices that are inappropriate and counterproductive. Measuring a shop supervisor's performance on the level of direct labor utilization, and the use of cost-based lot sizing rules have been demonstrated as counterproductive policies.

Applying the dollar day measure to the excess inventory helps to quantify the opportunities for performance improvement.

As a quantitative measure, dollar day enables plant management to prioritize the various actions required to eliminate excess inventories. Reduction of excess inventories does not require investments, but a new way of looking at the manufacturing operation is required. All of the factors that make it necessary to have more than "zero" inventory, such as large set-up times, poor yields, downtime on machines, and unreliable vendors must be, and have been, considered in determining the buffer size. Some of the actions that can help reduce excess inventories are:

- Activate workers only as needed
- Reduce lot sizes on non-critical resources
- Use transfer batches to split and overlap production operations.

Buffers of relevant inventory consist of materials in the quantities required by the detailed plant schedule. The time that these materials are planned to spend in the buffers is determined by the reliability of the preceding operations and replenishment lead times. Improvements to these operations, will impact the time protection element of inventory buffers, since the more reliable an operation the less safety time is needed in the schedule. The dollar day measure of inventory helps to quantify these buffer inventories. The impact of improvements in non-critical operations can be quantified and priorities for productivity improvements can be set based on their impact to the plant as a whole. Actions that help reduce relevant inventories include:

- Reduce set-up times
- Improve yield and quality of operations
- Cross-train workers to do different jobs and set-ups
- Improve vendor reliability.

The dollar day measure of inventory places emphasis on both the dollar element of inventory and the time element of inventory. As an analytic tool, dollar day is used to identify the real opportunities for improvement.

To fully exploit the dollar day concept as a productivity tool, it is necessary to have a valid plant schedule. Inventory in the plant can then be separated into relevant inventory and excess inventory and the causes for excess inventory can be identified.

As we have observed, management policies based on traditional cost accounting principles can obscure the existence of excessive inventories. A new set of management policies will help identify excess inventories and facilitate elimination.

Once the excess inventory has been eliminated, management can analyze the relevant inventory, starting with the component that has the highest dollar day contribution, and initiate actions through which inventory buffers can be systematically reduced. Thus, the dollar day measure, along with a valid schedule, provides a measurement of the level of inventory and a diagnostic tool at the same time.

Productivity improvement activities should include elimination of excess inventories and reduction of relevant inventories. Just as carrying costs assign a value to inventory reductions, dollar day serves to connect the value of inventory reductions to the competitive edge of the plant. A next step may be to quantify this link

Summary

The impacts of inventory improvements are far greater than what is recognized in traditional accounting and financial measurement systems. Once inventory "fat" has been eliminated, improvements in inventory management performance contribute directly to the competitive posture of the company. This is the result of a favorable impact on the product the company offers, responsiveness to the market and improved cost competitiveness.

Measures for evaluating inventory performance that recognize the role of inventory are needed. The dollar day concept is such a measure. Together with a valid schedule, dollar days serves as both a measure of the value of inventory and a diagnostic tool. With this measure, the performance of a plant in managing its inventory assets can be evaluated relative to the capabilities of that plant.

Through dollar days analysis, opportunities for improving inventory management can be identified and improvements made. Furthermore, dollar days provides a rational basis for measuring and evaluating programs for inventory reductions.

About the authors

G. GUY SORRELL, CPA, CPIM, is a Partner in Deloitte Haskins & Sells, an international firm providing consulting and accounting services to a variety of industries. He serves his firm as National Industry Coordinator for consulting services to Textile and Apparel companies and is National Lead Industry Specialist for manufacturing consulting engagements. Mr. Sorrell has an office in Greensboro, NC.

Mr. Sorrell is Past President of The Piedmont Triad Chapter of APICS. He presently is Chairman of the Steering Committee of the APICS Special Interest Group for Textiles and Apparel and is a member of the Manufacturers Association.

Guy is a business school graduate of the University of South Carolina and received an MBA from Georgia State University.

Dr. M. L. SRIKANTH is the Director for Operations for Creative Output, Inc. He received his Bachelors and Masters Degrees in Science from Mysore University and his Doctorate from Boston University. Prior to joining Creative Output, he was an Assistant Professor at Boston University.

Since joining the firm, he has led the installation of OPT (Optimized Production Technology) at major U.S. companies including General Electric, Ford, General Motors, Schovill and John Deere. He has been instrumental in effecting major improvements in the materials management activities of a number of companies.

He is an accomplished speaker and gave major presentations at Region I's 1980 and 1983 seminars. He is a frequent lecturer at Creative Output's educational seminars and has published articles in a number of leading scientific journals. Dr. Srikanth is a member of APICS.

Reprinted from *Production and Inventory Management.* Third Quarter, 1988.

Excess Capacity Versus Finished Goods Safety Stock

John B. South, Ph.D., and Ralph Hixson

A number of writers have pointed out that excess capacity can significantly reduce the level of queue work-in-process inventory [2, 3, 4, 6]. It has been shown that in some situations the cost of increasing capacity when the input rate is held constant can be more than offset by the reduced costs resulting from the reduction in work-in-process inventory. In addition to reducing work-in-process inventory, there is another benefit of excess capacity; the safety stock requirements are not as great when there is excess capacity available to respond to fluctuations in demand.

Responding to a temporary reduction in demand, Kustom Electronics reduced their production output rate but did not reduce the labor force level proportionately to the reduction in output rate, resulting in excess capacity. While operating with excess capacity, Kustom Electronics found they could maintain essentially the same level of service with less finished goods Inventory. Part of this was due to the reduced manufacturing cycle time resulting from reduced WIP inventories, but part was due to the flexibility that is provided by excess capacity. This flexibility experienced by Kustom Electronics is consistent with Plossl's comments on excess capacity: "Adequate capacity is essential to executing any plan correctly; excess capacity is the primary requisite for flexibility. This is worth everything it costs if you want fast reaction to changes and upsets [4]."

Comparing Costs

Direct labor is often a small fraction of the total cost of finished product; a unit of finished goods inventory contains materials and overhead costs in addition. If the equipment is available, then excess capacity is attained by paying for additional direct labor. The cost of excess capacity is equal to a percentage of the cost of an additional unit of finished goods safety stock. On the surface it would appear that it is much cheaper to pay for direct labor excess capacity than to pay for finished goods safety stock. The problem is that direct labor is an expense item and safety stock is an asset. This asset does cost money in the form of carrying and holding costs, but it is a fraction of the value of the asset, for example, 20% per unit of inventory per year.

If we assume that direct labor cost is 15% of the cost of a finished unit, then the annual cost for one unit of excess capacity per year is equal to 15% of the cost of one unit of finished goods safety stock. It would appear that we should substitute the unit of excess capacity for the unit of safety stock which costs 20% of a unit annually. The question is: is sufficient excess capacity to produce one more unit of final product per year adequate to respond to the fluctuations in demand for which the unit of safety stock is being held? The answer is yes if demand is fairly uniform over the year and the order cycle is one year. In this case, the safety stock is used to cover yearly fluctuations in demand. If the order cycle is one month, then one unit of capacity per year is not sufficient to respond to fluctuations in demand at the end of the order cycle. The unit of safety stock that can be used to respond to a unit increase in monthly demand requires a unit of monthly excess capacity to replace it. That is, sufficient additional direct labor must be hired to be able to produce an extra unit per month. Thus, the annual cost of excess capacity is the same as the direct labor cost of 12 finished units, which is equivalent to (12)(0.15) = 1.8 units of cost. This is considerably more than the 0.2 unit cost of one unit of finished goods inventory. Note that it isn't necessary to have sufficient excess capacity to produce an extra unit every day. If lead time is a month, then the one more unit is produced in the months where an extra unit is demanded. If lead time is less than a month, the extra unit is produced the next month with a few days back-order time. This becomes clearer in the discussion of the hypothetical model considered next.

A Simple Model

If more than one product is produced, then the excess capacity can substitute for several units of safety stock and the desirability of the excess capacity is increased. Consider the following model. Each of four products produced by the firm has the following probability distribution for demand:

Demand	Probability
2	0.05
3	0.90
4	0.05

 © APICS

TABLE 1: Probability Distribution for Total Demand

Total Demand	*Probability*
9	0.0005
10	0.0122
11	0.1471
12	0.6804
13	0.1471
14	0.0122
15	0.0005

Table 1 *Probability Distribution for Total Demand*

The average demand for each product is three units. The average total demand for all four products is 12 units. The probability distribution for total demand is given in Table 1. If production capacity is equal to the average demand, 12 units, the probability that demand will exceed production capacity is 0.1598 (0.1471 + 0.0122 + 0.0005 from Table 1) or almost 16%.

To avoid a stockout, we could carry one unit of each item in safety stock. The alternative to the safety stock method is to add sufficient direct labor so that production capacity equals 13 units. This will permit the production of an extra unit when total demand exceeds the average demand of 12 units. There is still a small probability that demand will exceed 13 units, resulting in a stockout. This probability (that demand is 14 or more units) is 0.0127, less than 1.3%, so customer service is approximately the same with one unit of excess capacity as with four units of safety stock.

As mentioned earlier, the comparative cost of the two options depends on the length of the time period to which the assumed demand (and thus production) is applicable. If we are talking about quarterly, then the average demand is 12 units per quarter and the excess capacity is one unit per quarter. Thus, the annual excess capacity direct labor cost is (0.15 units/ unit)x(4 quarters/year) = 0.6 units. This is less than the cost of holding the four units of safety stock: (0.2 units/unit)x(4 units) = 0.8 units per year. In this case, the excess capacity could be justified solely on the reduction in the finished goods safety stock required to maintain a satisfactory level of customer service. If the total demand in Table 1 is monthly demand or weekly demand, then the annual cost of excess capacity (1.8 units if monthly, 7.8 units if weekly) would be considerably more than the holding cost of the safety stock it would replace.

An Example with Excess Capacity

The example in Table 2 suggests one way production might be scheduled when there is excess capacity. It is assumed that the order cycle is four weeks and that demand for the four products is fairly uniform and has the probability distribution in Table 1. That is, average demand for each of the products over a four week period is three units with average total demand equal to 12 units. The amounts demanded in Part (a) of Table 2 require the production of 13 units in the first four-week cycle: 3 units of A, four units of B, three units of C, and three units of D, i.e., (3, 4, 3, 3). For the second, third, and fourth four-week cycles, the production amounts required to meet demand are (3, 3, 2, 4), (3, 2, 3, 3), and (3, 3, 3, 3), respectively. The latter demand pattern is the one we would expect to see most frequently. The total units demanded for the four four-week cycles are 13,12,11, and 12, respectively. Thus we have a high demand period and low demand period compared with two average demand periods.

Sufficient capacity to produce 13 units is scheduled for each four-week period. Thus, Parts (b) and (c) of Table 2 show 3 1/4 units produced each week, except in those weeks where idle time equivalent to one unit of capacity is incurred. It is important to note that it is not necessary to have excess capacity of one unit per week or per day to respond to fluctuations in demand. It is only necessary to have one unit of capacity for the complete time period to which the model in Table 1 is assumed to be applicable. For the example in Table 2, the excess capacity of one unit for the four week time period is spread uniformly throughout the four weeks with 1/4 unit of excess capacity per week.

The basic scheduling rule that is being applied in Table 2 is to schedule all 3 1/4 units of capacity every week until idle capacity sufficient to produce one unit can be incurred, i.e., when production is planned for the week, idle capacity equivalent to one unit's production can be scheduled and all requirements based on current knowledge of demand can be met. Partial units of idle capacity are not allowed in any given week's production schedule. Thus, in week 1 after the three units of A are produced, the additional 1/4 unit of capacity is used to start producing the next item, B. This is done even though it is not known until the beginning of week 2 that the demand for item B will be for 4 units during weeks 2 through 5. In Part (b) it is assumed that customer lead time is four weeks, so demand is known for the next four weeks when production is planned at the beginning of week 2. Four units of B are scheduled with some overlap into week 3. Three units of C and of D are scheduled, making a total of 13 units produced during weeks 1 through 4. This is in-response to demand requirements (3, 4, 3, 3). This same rule applied

TABLE 2: Scheduling with Excess Capacity

(a) DEMAND

WEEK																		
1	*2*	*3*	*4*	*5*	*6*	*7*	*8*	*9*	*10*	*11*	*12*	*13*	*14*	*15*	*16*	*17*	*18*	*19*
A	A		A |	A	A	A	|	A		A	A |	A	A	A	|			
	B	B	B	B |	B	B		B |	B			B |	B		B	B |		
		C	C	C	|		C		C |	C	C		C |		C	C	C |	
			D		D	D |	D	D	D	D |	D	D		D |	D		D	D |

(b) PRODUCTION (Customer lead time = 4 weeks)

WEEK															
1	*2*	*3*	*4*	*5*	*6*	*7*	*8*	*9*	*10*	*11*	*12*	*13*	*14*	*15*	*16*
A	¾B	½B	¼C	A	¾B	½C	¼D	A	¾B	½C	¼D	A	¾B	½C	¼D
A	B	C	D	A	B	C	D	A	B	C	D	A	B	C	D
A	B	C	D	A	B	I[a]	D	A	I[a]	C	D	A	B	C	D
¼B	½B	¾C	D	¼B	½C	¾D	D	¼B	½C	¾D	I[a]	¼B	½C	¾D	I[a]

(c) PRODUCTION (Customer lead time = 1 week)

WEEK															
1	*2*	*3*	*4*	*5*	*6*	*7*	*8*	*9*	*10*	*11*	*12*	*13*	*14*	*15*	*16*
A	¾B	½C	¼D	A	¾B	½B	¼C	A	¾B	½C	¼D	A	¾B	½C	D
A	B	C	D	A	B	C	D	A	B	C	D	A	B	C	D
A	B	C	D	A	B	C	D	A	B	I[a]	D	A	I[a]	C	D
¼B	½C	¾D	I[a]	¼B	½B	¾C	D	¼B	½C	¾D	D	¼B	½C	¾D	I[a]

[a] I = one unit of idle capacity.

Table 2 *Scheduling with Excess Capacity*

in week 6. After item B production is completed in week 6, the 1/2 unit of remaining capacity is applied to item C production. By the beginning of week 7 it is known that demand for Item C is only for two units during the next four weeks, so one unit of idle capacity is scheduled in week 7. For weeks 12 and 16, demand for item D can be met with 2 1/4 units of capacity, allowing a full unit of excess capacity to be scheduled for those weeks.

Shorter Customer Lead Time

In Part (c) of Table 2 it is assumed that customer lead time is only one week. Thus, when production is scheduled for an item, the demand for that item for the next four weeks is not known. This necessitates additional scheduling rules. Production is scheduled to meet forecasted demand of three units unless (1) the demand for that item was for four units during the previous four weeks, i.e., there is a back order for that unit or (2) the demand for that item was for only two units during the previous four weeks, i.e., there is a unit of the item in inventory carried over from the previous production run.

If there is a back order for an item, four units of production are scheduled; the one unit back-ordered demand plus the forecasted demand of three units for actual demand information results in a production pattern similar to Part (b), but offset by one four-week cycle. Weeks 5-8 of Part (c) have the same production schedule as weeks 1 through 4 of Part (b), and so forth.

In week 2 of Part (b) it is known that four units of item B will be required for the next four weeks, so the production run of item B is not stopped until four units are produced. In week 2 of Part (c) the demand for part B is not known, so the forecasted or average demand amount of three units is produced. This results in a shortage or back order in week 5. The response to the back order is to keep the production run of item B in week 6 going until 4 units of B are produced. A similar comparison can be made between week 7 of Part (b) and week 11 of Part (c). Production is ended after two units of C are produced in week 7 of Part (b) because it is known that only two units will be required during the next four weeks. Only two units of C are completed in week 11 of Part (c) because of the three units produced during the previous production run of item C was not sold during the previous four weeks.

The shorter customer lead time case does have occasional back orders and extra units of inventory carried over into the next production cycle. However, the back orders are for no longer than a week and the occasional extra unit of inventory is offset by the fact that whenever a production run of four units is made it is in response to a back order, so the extra (fourth) unit does not go into cycle stock inventory as it does in the longer-lead-time case.

The safety stock method would also be affected by the difference in customer lead times. Safety stock is available to respond to fluctuations in demand. In our model, the four-week production rate would be equal to the average forecasted demand, 12 units, when the safety stock method is used. Thus, whenever demand is greater than 12 units during a four-week time period, safety stock is consumed, and whenever demand is less than 12 units, safety stock is replenished or built up, i.e., the average level of safety stock is four units but at any point in time it could be more or less than four units. The response to using the capacity available from a deficiency in demand in one item to replenish a deficiency in safety stock of a different item is delayed in the short-lead-time case relative to the long-lead-time case. For example, if the demand, for item A for the next four weeks is for only two units and it is known, then we would produce two units of A and one unit of B this week, two units of B and one of C next week, and three units of C the third week, resulting in an extra unit of C produced to replenish C's safety stock. This scheduling pattern would be delayed four weeks in the short-lead-time case. Forecasted demand of three units of A would be produced this week; four weeks later it would be observed that demand was only for two units during the previous four-week period, resulting in an extra unit of item A safety stock. The response to two units of item A safety stock would be to produce only two units of A and so on.

An Example with More Products

The simple example in Table I is easier to visualize than an example using the normal distribution, but the probability calculation difficulty increases as the number of products increases. Using the normal distribution permits us to quickly look at the implications of excess capacity with regard to finished goods safety stock when dealing with a large number of products. If average demand for each product is 50 per time period with a standard deviation of 6 units and it is desired to satisfy at least 95% of the demand for any given time period, then the safety stock for each product would be (1.65) (6) = 9.9 or (rounded) 10 units for each product [1]. If we have 25 products, then the total safety stock required is 250 units.

If we wanted to respond to variation in demand with excess capacity, we would not need a full 250 units excess capacity. The use of excess capacity permits us to use the capacity freed up from a product that has less than average demand for the time period of interest to produce more of a product that has more than average demand for that particular time period. This fact is reflected in the results of statistical theory which states that if the demands are independent, the standard deviation of the sum of the demands is equal to the square root of the sum of the individual squared standard deviations. Thus, we have standard deviation of the sum

If we want to cover 95% of total demand for any given time period, 1.65(30) = 49.5 or (rounded) 50 units of excess production capacity are required. If the time period of interest is quarters, then the direct labor cost in units of finished goods of excess capacity is 4(50) (0.15) = 30 units cost (assuming direct labor is 15% of cost) versus the finished goods inventory cost of 250(0.20) = 50 units cost. This would make the excess capacity cheaper than safety stock. On the other hand, if the time period of interest is months, then the direct labor cost of excess capacity is 12(50) (0.15) = 90 units, which is more than the cost of safety stock.

If the number of products in the above example is increased tenfold from 25 to 250, then the total safety stock required is 250(10) = 2500 units. The equivalent excess capacity requirement is found by multiplying the standard deviation of total demand for 250 products, $6(250)^{1/2} = 95$, by the standard normal factor 1.65, resulting in 157 units of excess capacity. The annual cost of the safety stock is 2500(0.20) = 500 units. The annual cost of the excess capacity if the period of interest is quarters is 157(4) (0.15) = 94.2 units. If the period of interest is months, then the cost of excess capacity is 157(12) (0.15) = 282.6 units, which is also less than the cost of safety stock. If the time period of interest is weeks, then the cost of excess capacity, (157) (52) (0.15)=1225 units, would be greater than the cost of safety stock.

Summary

The examples in this article suggest how one might evaluate the trade-off between excess capacity and finished goods safety stock. (They are given for insight and not as models that consider all ramifications, therefore they cannot be used to make a definitive statement about the exact point at which excess capacity should be substituted for finished goods safety stock.) The examples do suggest, however, that when excess capacity exists, a reduction in finished goods safety stock may be possible, and in some cases the inventory reduction may be sufficient to offset the cost of the excess capacity. Excess capacity may occur for various reasons: keeping trained workers when there is a temporary reduction in demand; "lumpiness" of resources, i.e., it isn't possible to buy half of a machine or hire 3/10 of a worker; or it may be deliberately employed to control work-in-process inventory as suggested in the references cited at the end of this article. Whenever there is excess capacity, for whatever reason, the opportunity it may provide to reduce finished goods safety stock should not be overlooked.

References

1. Fogarty, Donald W. and Hoffman, Thomas R., *Production and Inventory Management*, South-Western Publishing Co., Cincinnati, OH (1983), p. 217.

2. Fox, Robert E., "MRP, KANBAN, and OPT—What's Best?" American Production and Inventory Control Society 25th Annual International Conference Proceedings (1982), p. 484.

3. Gue, Frank S., *Increased Profits through Better Control of Work in Process*, Reston Publishing Co., Inc., Reston, VA (1980), pp. 56-57.

4. Kanet, John J., "Toward Understanding Lead Times in MRP Systems," *Production and Inventory Management*, Third Quarter (1982), p. 9.

5. Plossl, George W., "How Times Have Changed. Have Your People Adjusted?", *News Note* 51, George Plossl Educational Services, Inc. Atlanta, GA (January 1984) .

6. South, John B., "Continuous Excess Capacity Versus Intermittent Extra Capacity to Control Average Queue Size in a Random Environment," *Production and Inventory Management*, First Quarter (1985), pp. 103-110.

About the Authors

JOHN B. SOUTH, PhD, is Vice-president of Manufacturing at Politron, Inc., Pittsburg, KS. He has taught production management at Western Carolina University, NC, and Pittsburg State University, KS. John received his Ph.D. from the University of Utah. Prior to teaching, he worked professionally in cost accounting and business planning. He is a member of the Southeast Kansas Chapter of APICS.

RALPH HIXSON, CFPIM is Vice-president of Manufacturing Operations at Kustom Electronics, Chanute, KS, a manufacturer of traffic safety radar, voice, and digital communication systems. He has worked as a line foreman, general foreman, production control manager, materials manager, and production manager for a store fixture manufacturer and an electronics manufacturer. He has a BBA and an MBA from California Pacific University. Ralph is currently active in the Southeast Kansas Chapter of APICS, serving on the Board of Directors.

© APICS

Reprinted from the *1996 APICS International Conference Proceedings.*

Eliminate (Don't Automate) Inventory Tracking

Robert A. Stahl, CPIM

Being competitive in today's global markets is not easy, nor does it happen by accident. As a result, most companies are investing heavily in upgrading their competitive posture through the implementation of advanced methodologies, which are now becoming affordable to even the smallest of companies.

It is also true that this newly affordable technology is advancing more rapidly than most organizations can absorb and effectively implement it. We've learned that technology alone is insufficient to improve competitiveness... and when done improperly it adds cost with very little advantage.

We have further learned that the effective implementation of technology must be rooted in a foundation of common sense, accompanied by a fundamental shift in traditional thinking. How we manage and track inventory is one of those very fundamental shifts in thinking that must take place to effectively benefit from much of the new methodologies. This paper addresses changing the mind-set about properly managing and tracking inventory.

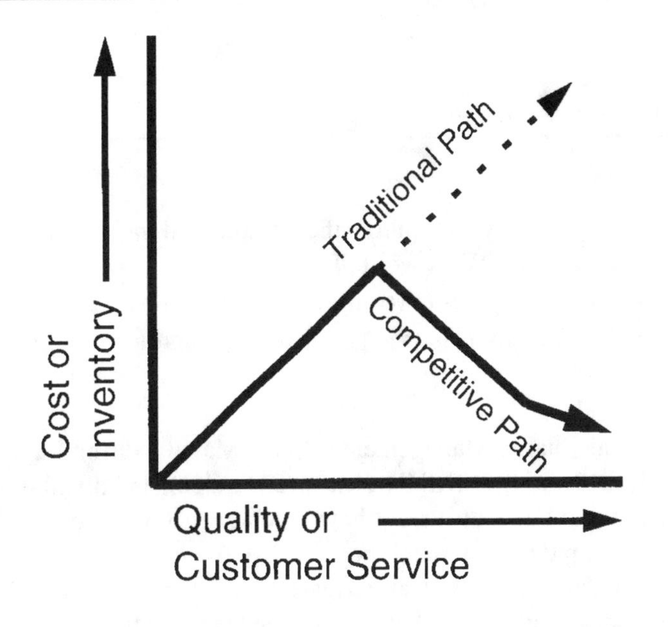

Figure 1. *Muted trade-offs*

Manufacturing Mission

Today we have come to understand that the objective of a manufacturing company is more than simply making a profit. While making a profit is certainly an imperative, it cannot be done in sustainable fashion without also satisfying customers and employees as well.

Some rather high profile companies have been late to realize that **owners** (profit), **customers** (service), and **employees** (work processes) are equally important. Some have waited until they lost much of their competitive advantage and a considerable market share before they learned this tough lesson, and have begun to downsize. Sustainable competitive advantage only happens when all of these constituencies enter into a mutually beneficial partnership.

Acknowledging that equally serving these three constituencies is essential, but the real challenge is... *how do you do that?* Traditional mind-set has said that the way to achieve competitive advantage is to weigh one constituency against another, looking for the optimum point of trade-off. In recent years, however, through the implementation of improved technology and understanding, this trade-off type thinking has become obsolete and is becoming a serious liability to making change and improvement.

A proper manufacturing mission must be geared at satisfying all of the constituencies. Such a mission might be stated as follows:

Achieve superior performance in your ability to—

1. Satisfy the expectations of the customer (**high quality**),

and

2. Improve work processes (**low cost**), and
3. Be quick to change direction (**quick response, flexibility**).

Obviously, this presents the same trade-off notion as does the playing of one constituency against another. This trade-off type thinking is destructive and unnecessary with proper understanding and a changed mind-set. **Figure 1** depicts what we've learned about the advantages of learning how to mute these trade-offs.

The old mind-set asked the questions, "how much quality can we afford?"... or "how much do we have to raise the inventory to get better customer service." Today, there is a wealth of information that has enabled us to gain under-

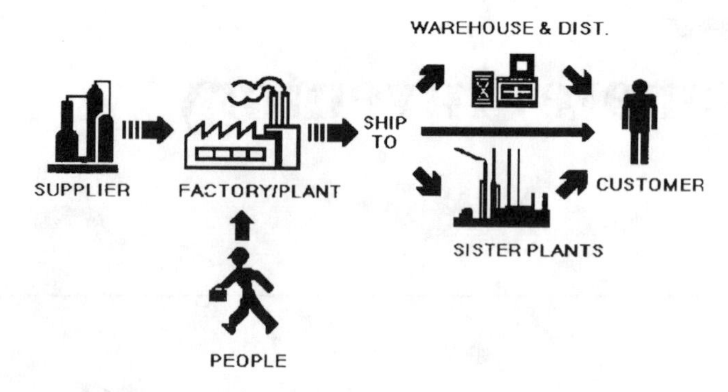

Figure 2. *Value-adding supply chain*

standing in a way that muting these traditional trade-offs is indeed possible. What we'd like to do is:

- Have high quality (conformance) and low cost
- Have quick response (good service) and low inventory (cost)
- and so on...

Total Quality Management (TQM), Manufacturing Resource Planning (MRP II), Just-in-Time (JIT), and the like have taught us that it's not how much quality you can afford but rather how much poor quality (nonconformance) can you afford. We've learned that sitting inventory is product that was produced that was not needed in the timeframe that it was produced... This should be eliminated by producing something that is needed. As we begin to gain the capability to do both, we gain the competitive advantage of a "double-edged sword."

Traditional Manufacturing and Inventory Tracking

Relative to inventory management, the overall objective of a manufacturing company was best stated by George Bevis (Late Executive V.P. of the Tennant Company) when he said, " ...the objective of a manufacturing company is to manage the flow of inventory to satisfy customers' needs." He further stated, "...do this well, and the profits will come in the mail."

The operative word here is ***flow***. That means ...without stopping. A manufacturing process involves a series of steps (often called a *Supply Chain*) that add value to purchased parts and materials that are in economic demand by customers. This is graphically depicted in **Figure 2**.

Traditional mind-set *disconnects* the individual steps of a manufacturing operation by placing inventory as a buffer between each step in the sequence. This inventory would supposedly allow each operation to run at its own rate, gaining economies through the independent efficiency of each operation. Additionally, this disconnect was made more dramatic by large lot sizes that were geared at gaining economies of scale. We have learned that both of these tend to be false economies.

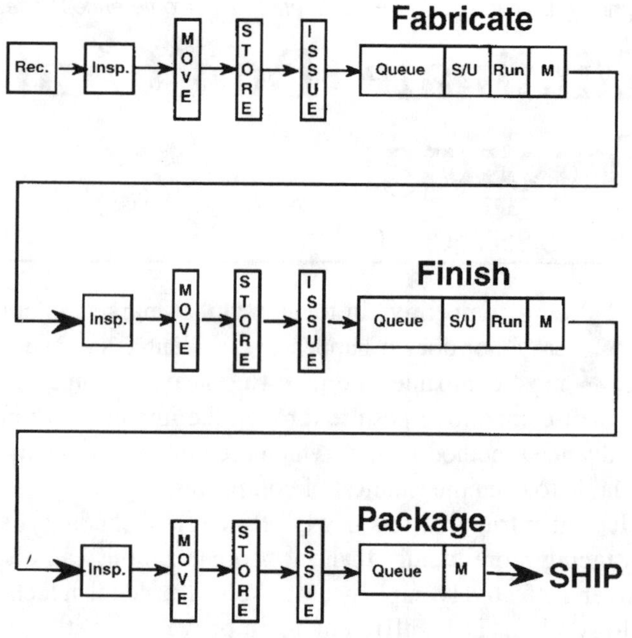

Figure 3. *Traditional manufacturing process*

Figure 3 shows the detail of the many activities that a product would go through during this *typical* production process. It is certain that each and every one of these activities add cost, but only the actual *run time* adds true value.

On top of these costs is the tracking of inventory that is necessary as material is received, stored, issued, added to WIP, and then received through each of these manufacturing cycles. All of this made the manufacturing process the opposite of the objective, resulting in Low Quality, High Cost, and Slow Response.

For some period of time we focused in inventory management on how to handle the inventory tracking activities more efficiently. We added *Automatic Storage & Retrieval* devices (ASRs); we then automated the relief of component inventory by the use of *backflushing*; we then added *bar coding* to make recording more efficient; and most recently we've added *Radio Frequency* transmission (RF) units. Under traditional conditions, these things seemed to help, but in fact were treating the symptom...too much inventory.

In recent years, there has been a lot said and done about gaining a synchronous flow to all manufacturing processes, linking together the various steps of a manufacturing operation...creating the *flow* that George Bevis referred to. The most popular term for this notion is *Just-in-Time*; meaning in a specific sense to have inventory only when it is needed…not sooner…not later…not more…not less…but…*just in time* at every step of this operation.

Inventory: An Asset or An Expense

One of the reasons we have failed, until recently, to focus on the elimination of inventory, rather than on efficient handling, is that our primary performance measure didn't recognize inventory for what it truly is—an expense (cost) not an asset. Traditional inventory accounting adds all inventory to the balance sheet as an asset, taking it to *cost of sales* (an expense) only when it is sold, rather than when it is produced.

From a traditional accounting standpoint this would be displayed in the financial statements as seen in **Figure 4,** with inventory shown as a line item in the asset column, and cost of sales (material, labor, and overhead) as an expense on the income side. With this type of financial reporting, if manufacturing produced or received more inventory than was needed (clearly something that is not the ideal), this would not be seen as an adverse condition.

For example, what would happen if inventory goes up by 20! **Figure 5** displays how this would be reflected in these traditional financial statements: Inventory would increase from 30 to 50, while Current Liabilities (Accounts Payable) would also increase from 30 to 50, causing Net Worth and Net Profit to remain unchanged.

In other words, with traditional accounting the financial statements would not reflect that something undesirable had occurred—that is, you produced or received more inventory than was needed. Not a "proper" reflection of a problem!

As an alternative, just suppose that all inventory was considered an expense (cost of sales), how would this look? As can be seen in **Figure 6**, Cost of Sales would increase by 20, increasing total expenses form 95 to 115, and Current Liabilities (Accounts Payable) would increase by the same 20, from 30 to 50, causing Total Liabilities to raise to 60. In this case Net Worth would drop from 50 to 30, and Net Profit (Loss) would drop from 5 to (15)…clearly reflecting the unfavorable condition that took place, until the excess inventory was indeed sold, when this affect would be reversed. This would gain some attention to the problem!

The net result…when things are not done as you'd like, it is properly reflected in the financial statements (performance measures) at the time it happened. In traditional manufacturing environments where inventory does rise and fall regularly and sharply, reporting such swings externally would not necessarily be wise. This should, however, be no reason to report internally with this same misdirecting information.

ASSETS:		**INCOME:**	
Cash	10	Sales	100
A/C Rec	10		
Inventory	***30***		
Plant/ Equip	35		
Other	5		
TOTAL	90	TOTAL	100
Less:		*Less:*	
Cur. liab.	(30)	***Mat'l.***	***(30)***
Debt	(10)	***Labor***	***(5)***
		O/H	***(15)***
		G&A	(40)
		Tax	(5)
TOTAL	(40)	TOTAL	(95)
Net Worth	**50**	**Net Profit**	**5**

Figure 4. *Traditional financial statements—inventory as an asset*

ASSETS:		**INCOME:**	
Cash	10	Sales	100
A/C Rec	10		
Inventory	~~30~~ ***50***		
Plant/ Equip	35		
Other	5		
TOTAL	~~90~~ ***110***	TOTAL	100
Less:		*Less:*	
Cur. liab.	~~(30)~~ ***(50)***	Mat'l.	(30)
Debt	(10)	Labor	(5)
		O/H	(15)
		G&A	(40)
		Tax	(5)
TOTAL	~~(40)~~ ***(60)***	TOTAL	(95)
Net Worth	**50**	**Net Profit**	**5**

Figure 5. *Inventory as an asset—inventory increased by +20*

If this more accurate financial reporting were done as part of performance reporting, it would hasten progress on those things that would enable the elimination of excess inventory. Doing the right things is often a function of performance measurements. In other words, performance measurements must align with desired performance, and traditional financial reports simply do not properly align in this regard.

Ideal Manufacturing Process

Having established the need to have performance measurements which reward movement toward the ideal performance, we must recognize that understanding, desire, and performance measurements alone do not make the ideal process possible. We must be sure to not try and live in the ideal vision of the future, but rather we must live in the reality of the present. That reality is that we have not eliminated all of the obstacles that make inventory unnecessary. At the same time, it is important to keep a focus on the ideal.

The ideal flow in a manufacturing company is to receive and produce today only what is needed by customers today. If this ideal were to be pictured, most of the non-value-adding "boxes" of Figure 3 would be eliminated. This is more than a wish, but a lot of hard work eliminating some very specific constraints, such as setup time, lot sizing, process reliability, and the like.

Under these circumstances, whether you treat inventory as an asset or an expense is a moot point, because you would never receive more inventory than was needed in any given time period, thereby bring to cost of sales all inventory as an expense, regardless of the accounting method. Clearly not the case in most circumstances, however.

Generally speaking, tracking of inventory through its various stages of manufacturing (stock rooms and WIP) is done for two reasons: inventory valuation (financial reporting) and to support proper planning and scheduling. In the ideal environment, tracking inventory is also a moot point because all inventory received would make its way to cost of sales within the same day . . . eliminating the need to track for either valuation nor planning and scheduling. In other words, there is so little inventory, there is no need to worry about it, nor track it.

How to Begin the Journey

Someone once said, "a long journey begins with a single step." Indeed the achievement of a zero inventory manufacturing environment for most companies is a long way off. The journey toward that objective, however, is not a leap of faith but a set of logical and iterative steps, beginning with a first one.

ASSETS:		INCOME:	
Cash	10	Sales	100
A/C Rec	10		
Inventory	30		
Plant/ Equip	35		
Other	5		
TOTAL	90	TOTAL	100
Less:		*Less:*	
Cur. liab.	~~(30)~~ ***(50)***	***Mat'l.***	~~(30)~~ ***(50)***
Debt	(10)	Labor	(5)
		O/H	(15)
		G&A	(40)
		Tax	(5)
TOTAL	~~(40)~~ ***(60)***	***TOTAL***	~~(95)~~ ***(115)***
Net Worth	~~50~~ ***30***	***Net Profit***	~~5~~ ***(15)***

Figure 6. *Inventory as an expense—inventory increased by +20*

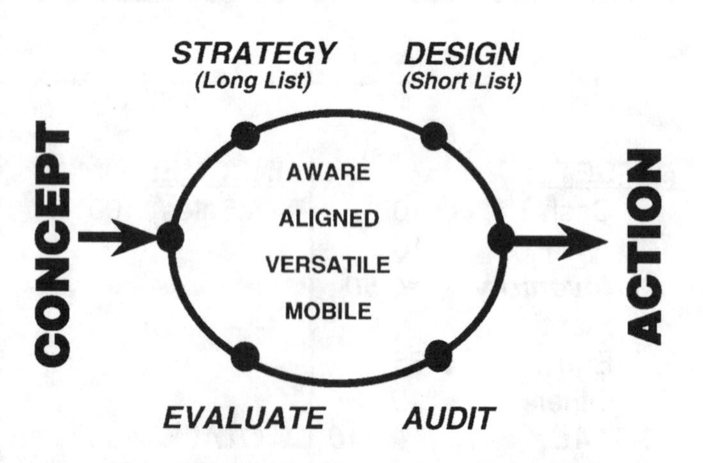

Figure 7. *Logic loop*

While action is the clear objective of getting started with any project, action is not the first step. Gaining a consensus in concept by the leadership function is. This logical progression is shown in **Figure 7**.

Gaining a consensus in *concept* means coming to an agreement on "how you would like thing to be in the future." Obviously, one indication of a change in mind-set is a willingness to create internal financial reporting (performance measurement) to reflect inventory as an expense rather than an asset. If an agreement in concept cannot be reached, no actions will be successful, but rather create

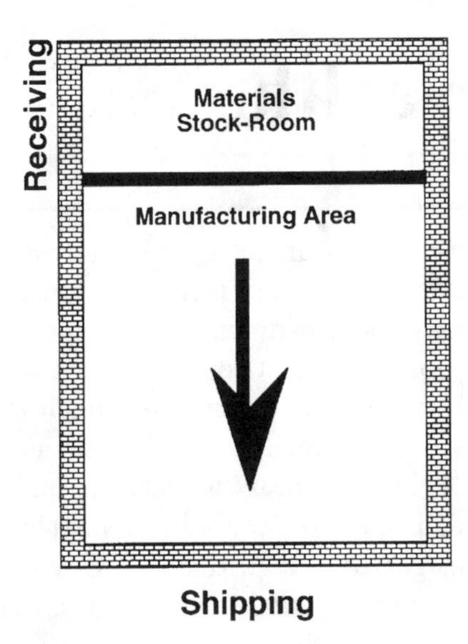

Figure 8. *Materials*

conflicts and frustration, from which behavior problems are likely to result.

Once a consensus in concept is reached, then it must be identified what are all of the things that need to be put in place to make it so. This *strategy* (the long list) is likely to be larger than the available time and the resources. It is therefore then necessary to prioritize this list to come up with "how and in what order will you begin work" (the short list). Only then will the energy of an organization be aligned so that consistent and rapid progress toward the ideal can be achieved.

Once actions begin to take place, then the result of those actions must be audited and evaluated in order to assure consistent support of the original concept being sought after. It is very possible that once taking actions, the organization will be smarter, such that a revision to the initial concept and action list will be made. This is normal and necessary for successful progress.

General Strategy about a Pilot

A "cold turkey" implementation of this notion is not likely, nor desirable. The creation of a pilot area is normally part of a successful path forward. To do otherwise, often will create more trauma than an organization can handle—inside and outside. This is because you cannot totally consider inventory as an expense until there is very little of it, which is not the case as you begin.

This pilot type of thinking needs to "isolate" an area that will be treated with this new mind-set and new performance measurements. In **Figure 8**, the area shown as the "Manufacturing Area" would be a typical isolated pilot.

This area, by policy, would "receive" inventory from the stockroom only in amounts that they were going to immediately consume. This "received" quantity would, by policy, be expensed as it was delivered. This would *force* the necessary improvement to material handling practices for "incoming" materials to make them more effective and efficient. This would then evolve to the outside suppliers also learning how to handle smaller and smaller quantities of materials, so that they could deliver directly to "point of use," resulting in the elimination of the stockroom itself.

Some organizations have foolishly eliminated inventory control and discipline before they eliminated inventory. This is a mistake! As long as there is lots of inventory, it must be controlled and disciplined with traditional methods—cycle counting and the like. The real payoff comes when inventory has been substantially eliminated, which gives the sustainable double-edged advantage of high quality (conformance), low cost (inventory), and quick response (flexibility).

Summary

In today's highly competitive global marketplace, it is more important than ever to seek out sustainable competitive advantage. New technologies and methodologies provide a real source for doing this. It is only those, however, that recognize that it is not the technology itself that gives the competitive advantage, but rather the proper understanding and application of that technology.

Relative to inventory tracking and management, the best way to do this well is to not do it at all. That is... get rid of the inventory without trade-off in customer service, quality, or response. This begins with a change in mind-set which takes inventory off the balance sheet as an asset, and begins to call it the expense that it is.

About the Author

Robert Stahl, CPIM, is the President of the R.A. Stahl Company in Attleboro, Massachusetts, and is a Senior Partner in the education and consulting firm Partners for Excellence. *His 16 years of consulting experience are complemented by his highly successful contributions while in manufacturing line management. He has helped numerous companies in varied environments improve their competitiveness.*

Mr. Stahl, graduated from Villanova University and is listed in Who's Who in America. *He is also a member of the Association for Manufacturing Excellence (AME) and the Operations Management Association (OMA). He is a frequent speaker at professional society events, and his articles are published in many trade journals.*

Reprinted from *Fortune* ©1993 Time Inc. All rights reserved.

The Real Key to Creating Wealth

Shawn Tully

What if you could look at almost any business operation and see immediately whether it was becoming more valuable or less? What if you as a manager could use this measure to make sure your operation—however large or small—was increasing in value? What if you as an investor could use it to spot stocks that were far likelier than most to rise high? What if using this measure would give you a marked competitive advantage, since most managers and investors aren't using it?

There is such a measure—but you'll have to move fast to seize your competitive advantage, because it is catching on quick. It goes by several names, depending on which user or consulting firm you talk to; McKinsey and others do a lively trade teaching it. The preeminent popularizer of the concept is Stern Stewart & Co. of New York City, which calls it economic value added, or EVA. It is today's hottest financial idea and getting hotter.

Seeing why is easy. Managers who run their businesses according to the precepts of EVA have hugely increased the value of their companies. Investors who know about EVA, and know which companies are employing it, have grown rich. Little wonder that highly regarded major corporations—Coca-Cola, AT&T, Quaker Oats, Briggs & Stratton, CSX, and many others—are flocking to the concept. "EVA played a significant role" in AT&T's recent decision to buy McCaw Cellular for $12.6 billion, says William H. Kurtz, an AT&T financial executive. AT&T this year will make EVA the *primary* measure of business units' and managers' performance. Explains Quaker CEO William Smithburg: "EVA makes managers act like shareholders. It's the true corporate faith for the 1990s."

So what is it? Simply stated, EVA is just a way of measuring an operation's real profitability. What makes it so revealing is that it takes into account a factor no conventional measure includes: the total cost of the operation's capital. The capital is all the money tied up in such things as heavy equipment, real estate, computers, and other stuff that's expected to be productive for a while after it has been purchased, plus so-called working capital, mainly cash, inventories, and receivables. EVA is simply after-tax operating profit, a widely used measure, minus the total annual cost of capital.

Here's how Coca-Cola CEO Roberto Goizueta, a champion wealth creator, explains it: "We raise capital to make concentrate, and sell it at an operating profit. Then we pay the cost of that capital. Shareholders pocket the difference." This turns out to be profound. Incredibly, most corporate groups, divisions, and departments have no idea how much capital they tie up or what it costs. True, the cost of borrowed capital shows up in a company's interest expense. But the cost of equity capital, which the shareholders have contributed, typically appears nowhere in any financial statements—and equity is extraordinarily expensive capital. Until managers figure all this out, they can't know whether they're covering *all* their costs and value to a company.

Understand that while EVA is easily today's leading idea in corporate finance and one of the most talked about in business, it is far from the newest. On the contrary: Earning more than the cost of capital is about the oldest idea in enterprise. But just as Greece's glories were forgotten in the Dark Ages, to be rediscovered in the Renaissance, so the idea behind EVA has often been lost in ever darker muddles of accounting. Managers and investors who come upon it act as if they have seen a revelation.

You'd act that way too if you had been at CSX for the past five years. "EVA is anything but theoretical," says CEO John Snow, who introduced the concept at his company in 1988. "How we use capital determines market value." Snow has lots of capital to worry about, a mammoth fleet of locomotives, containers, and railcars. His stiffest challenge came in the fast-growing but low-margin CSX Intermodal business, where trains speed freight to waiting trucks or cargo ships. Figuring in all its capital costs, Intermodal lost $70 million in 1988. In other words, its EVA was negative $70 million. Snow issued an ultimatum: Get that EVA up to breakeven by 1993 or be sold.

Freight volume has since swelled 25%, yet the number of containers and trailers—representing a lot of capital—has dropped from 18,000 to 14,000. They used to sit in terminals for two weeks between runs, but once CSX managers started seeing them as expensive, idle capital, they figured out ways to return them to the rails in five days. This is hardly rocket science. But before EVA, no one had done it; no one had had enough incentive to do it.

The company is also making do with a locomotive fleet of 100 instead of 150, a $70 million reduction in capital. How? On the route from New Orleans to Jacksonville, Florida, four locomotives used to power trains at 28 mph. But the trains arrived at midnight, long before they were unloaded onto trucks or freighters. Spurred by the EVA imperative, CSX decided to run the trains at 25 mph with only three locomotives and arrive three hours later, still in plenty of time to be unloaded at 4 or 5 a.m. The three locomotives also use some 25% less fuel than four. Slower trains and surging productivity met Snow's challenge. Intermodal's EVA was $10 million last year and is on track to triple in 1993. Wall Street has noticed: CSX stock was at $28 when Snow introduced the EVA program and was recently at $75.

It's a similar story in another capital-intensive business, making gasoline engines. Before introducing EVA in 1990, Briggs & Stratton was a rigid hierarchy. The company had no profit centers in the engine business below the corporate level—like most companies, it had no idea of each division's EVA—and it took macho pride in making almost all components in-house.

Today headquarters grants a wide berth to five divisions that make engines for lawn mowers, pumps, and other products. Each knows its EVA, and that knowledge has led to big savings from outsourcing. The company is phasing out production of the largest engines for pumps and generators, freeing the capital that had been unprofitably tied up in making them. Says John Shiely, the executive in charge of engineering: "EVA's discipline caused us to make the right decision." Now it buys premium engines, at a lower cost, from Mitsubishi. Molded plastics and other components, once made in small batches in-house, flow from suppliers that produce huge quantities.

Briggs & Stratton struggled with a miserable 7.7% return on capital in 1990, way below the capital's 12% cost. By focusing on that hurdle, the company has just cleared it, and the stock market is applauding: The share price has jumped from $20 in 1990 to $80 recently.

One of EVA's most powerful properties is its strong link to stock prices. The two numbers show a remarkable tendency to move up and down together. Says James Meenan, chief financial officer of AT&T's long-distance business: "We calculated our EVA back to 1984 and found an almost perfect correlation with stock price." Stock prices track EVA far more closely than they track such popular measures as earnings per share or operating margins or return on equity. That's because EVA shows what investors really care about— the net cash return on their capital—rather than some other type of performance viewed through the often distorting lens of accounting rules. For example, IBM's cash flow per share and book value per share increased smartly between 1984 and 1989. But anyone looking at the company's EVA in that period (see chart) had a far better idea what was happening.

For this reason, investors understandably favor companies committed to increasing EVA. Eugene Vesell, senior vice president of Oppenheimer Capital, which manages $26 billion, says, "We like to invest in companies that use EVA and similar measures. Making higher returns than the cost of capital is how we look at the world." Oppenheimer has earned 17% annually on average over the past decade, well above the S&P 500.

EVA is not just for industrial companies. In general, it works fine in service businesses as well. A few types of companies require special adaptations of basic EVA analysis. Examples: natural resource and land companies and others with assets that appreciate rather than depreciate.

At AT&T, Chief Executive Robert Allen is breaking the ultimate corporate monolith into lean operating units. The driving tool is EVA. Until recently AT&T provided balance sheets for only a half-dozen huge groups, such as long-distance services and telephone equipment. But dozens of units sold products and services ranging from telephone sets to toll-free 800 numbers. The capital used by each of the myriad long-distance services was lumped together at the group level. Since no individual service knew how much capital it used, none had any idea if it was beating its cost of capital and thus adding value to AT&T.

Allen's solution: Starting last year he encouraged managers to divide their businesses into profit centers resembling independent companies. The long-distance group now consists of 40 units selling such services as 800 numbers, telemarketing, and public telephone calls. All the capital each one uses, from switching equipment to new-product development, goes on its balance sheet. "The effect is staggering," says Meenan. "'Good' is no longer positive operating earnings. It's only when you beat the cost of capital." Some businesses found they had been posting negative EVAs for years. Now they're on a tough timetable to make the hurdle.

One of America's most enthusiastic proponents of EVA is Coca-Cola's Goizueta, who extolled return on capital long before formally introducing EVA companywide in 1987. "I'm a great returns man," says Goizueta, seated in his antique-filled Atlanta office sipping steaming espresso from a red Coca-Cola cup. He has included a clear and persuasive description of EVA in Coke's latest annual report. On weekends Goizueta scours other companies' annual reports for impressive rates of return, reclining on pillow embroidered with a favorite slogan, *THE ONE WITH THE BIGGEST CASH FLOW WINS*. He uses simple metaphors to distill EVA: "When I played golf regularly, my average score was 90, so every hole was par 5. I look at EVA like I look at breaking par. At Coca-Cola, we are way under par and adding a lot of value."

To get there, Goizueta used a double strategy. First he concentrated capital in the hugely profitable soft drink business: "As Willy Sutton used to say about banks, that's where the money is." He dumped a motley of businesses that made pasta, instant tea, plastic cutlery, desalinization equipment, and wine. All posted returns on investment of 7% or 8%, far below their cost of capital. Soft drinks earn much, much more, so that Coke last year earned 29.4% on capital, almost 2 1/2 times its cost.

Second, Goizueta focused on raising returns far faster than the bill for capital. One tool is leverage. In the early 1980s Coke was practically debt-free. To Coke's costly equity—it was much costlier in those high inflation days—Goizueta added less expensive borrowings, lowering the average cost of capital from 16% to 12%.

At the same time, he coaxed the business into doing more with the capital it had—or with less. The company produces more concentrate with 40 plants now than it produced with 52 in 1982. "We've even replaced expensive metal containers for concentrate with inexpensive plastic ones," says Coke CFO Jack Stahl, another gung ho EVA advocate.

Result of all this: Coke's EVA has surged an average of 27% annually for the past five years. Coke stock is up from $3 to $43 since Goezueta took over 12 years ago.

To see how EVA can change a company's attitude and behavior from top to bottom, look at Quaker Oats. Until Quaker adopted the concept in 1991, its businesses had one overriding goal—increasing quarterly earnings. To do it, they guzzled capital. They offered sharp price discounts at the end of each quarter, so plants ran overtime turning out huge shipments of Gatorade, Rice-A-Roni, 100% Natural Cereal, and other products. Managers led the late rush, since their bonuses depended on raising operating profits each quarter.

This is the pernicious practice known as trade loading (because it loads up the trade, or retailers, with product), and many consumer products companies are finally admitting it damages long-term returns. An important reason is that it demands so much capital. Pumping up sales requires many warehouses (capital) to hold vast temporary inventories (more capital). But who cared? Quaker's operating businesses paid no charge for capital in internal accounting, so they barely noticed. It took EVA to spotlight the problem.

The evangelist is William Smithburg. A smooth extrovert who sports striped suspenders and flamboyant ties. Smithburg, 55, became Quaker's CEO in 1981 at age 43. He is a physical-fitness buff and fierce competitor who plays handball and pumps iron.

Smithburg is using EVA to pursue a lofty goal: transforming Quaker from a journeyman into one of the food industry's most profitable companies alongside Kellogg and General Mills. Says he: "Our biggest problem was using too much capital."

Quaker employs a version of EVA it calls controllable earnings, which is yielding big savings at a sprawling plant in Danville, Illinois, that makes breakfast cereals and snacks. Until last year the plant operated at a slack pace early in each quarter and planned purchases, production, and deliveries for the big bulge at the quarter's end. Near the start of each quarter the plant would start filling warehouses with two- to three-month supplies of boxes and plastic wrappers as well as ingredients like granola and chocolate chips. It needed huge stocks because it turned out most of its products in a six-week surge. As products rolled out, Quaker packed 15 warehouses with finished goods. Corporate headquarters absorbed the costs of those inventories and encouraged managers to keep big, comfortable stocks. Says Steven Brunner, the strapping, mustachiod plant manager: "I used to treat inventories like they were free."

To smooth out the bumps—and save capital—Quaker ended the trade-loading madness in the fiscal year ended June 30, 1992, canceling the usual year-end promotions. Predictably, the stock plunged—temporarily. Free from the quarterly scramble, the Danville plant is whittling away at working capital and pays a stiff capital charge in the internal accounts for stocks of raw materials and finished goods. Result: The plant has trimmed inventories from $15 million to $9 million, even though it is producing much more, and Quaker has closed five of the 15 warehouses, saving $6 million a year in salaries and capital costs. Says Brunner: "Controllable earnings makes me act like an entrepreneur."

As Smithburg forecast, the long-term strategy is paying off. "We knew the customers would come back," he says. "But when they did, our capital costs were much lower." Controllable earnings have flourished. Most important, the stock is up 30%, to a recent $65.

Since EVA measures value creation and can be figured at levels well down in the company, it is an ideal basis for many managers' compensation. It provides a startling new view of a familiar process.

Most companies determine bonuses by how an executive performs against a budget; the most common target is a percentage rise in operating earnings. But the budget benchmark has a glaring flaw: Managers have an incentive to negotiate a target that's easy to beat. "The negotiation process is long and difficult," says Derek Smith, executive vice president of Atlanta's Equifax, an information services company that now bases compensation on EVA. "Instead of reaching for the stars, managers have an incentive to aim low." Most plans also rein in managers by imposing caps. For example, Harnischfeger Industries of Brookfield, Wisconsin, limited bonuses to 40% of base pay for all but a half-dozen top executives. It's switching to an EVA compensation plan in November.

Such a plan typically consists of two familiar parts, a bonus and stock incentives, applied in new ways. Bonus targets are established automatically each year as a percentage gain in EVA, determined by averaging last year's target, say 10% with last year's result, say 20%. That would fix this year's goal at 15%. Bonuses have no limits. But what if a manager gets lucky, earning a handsome bonus because of a swing in the business cycle? Companies generally put some part of an exceptional bonus in a "bank" and pay it out over the following three years. The manager's "bank balance" shrinks if he or she fails to keep meeting targets.

Some EVA companies object to setting goals by formula. Coca-Cola and Quaker negotiate EVA targets with their managers. "There are too many variables, " says Philip Marineau, Quaker's president. "Some businesses, for example, are just starting out with heavy investments and need a special timetable to reach a positive EVA." Marineau, however, says that it's far easier to set challenging targets than under the old system: "The compensation system is driving managers to reach higher."

Pay component No. 2, a stock incentive program, is also unusual. Instead of receiving stock options, a no-lose arrangement by definition, managers risk real money. CSX's plan shows how the program works. In mid-1991, 160 managers accepted a company offer to sell them shares at the market price of $48.325. They paid 5% cash; the company lent them the balance at 7.9% interest. The program ends next July, when the managers can cash in their shares. If the price stands above $69, CSX will forgive the loans' interest and 25% of the principal. If it doesn't, they'll have to pay the interest on their loans; they could even lose money. But with the stock recently at $75, that looks unlikely. Shareholders won't complain.

EVA is powerful and widely applicable because in the end it doesn't prescribe doing anything. If it tried, it would inevitably run aground in certain unforeseen situations. Instead it is a method of seeing and understanding what is really happening to the performance of a business. Using it, many managers and investors see important facts for the first time. And in general, they validate EVA's basic premise: If you understand what's really happening, you'll know what to do.

Ways to Raise Eva

There's nothing fancy or complicated about how to make economic value added (EVA) go up. It is a fundamental measure of return on capital, and there are just three ways to increase it:

- **Earn more profit without using more capital.** You probably spend much of your time thinking of ways to do this; cost cutting is today's favorite method. Nothing wrong with that. But focusing on it often blinds companies to the other ways of raising EVA.
- **Use less capital.** In practice, this is often the method that companies adopting EVA find most effective. Coke uses plastic containers for concentrate instead of costlier metal ones. CSX figures out how to operate with 100 locomotives instead of 150. Quaker reschedules production to require fewer warehouses. What to do with the capital saved? Companies can return it to shareholders through higher dividends or stock buybacks, or can....
- **Invest capital in high-return projects.** This is what growth is all about. Just make sure you expect these projects to earn more than the *total* cost of the capital they require.

Reprinted from *PURCHASING MAGAZINE*, May 7, 1987. © Cahners Publishing Company.

The Old World Opens Up

Production goods may be the fuel of American manufacturing, but maintenance, repair, and operating (MRO) items are the muscle that holds each enterprise together.

But for a long time MRO was the "third world" of industrial purchasing. Not much happened for two reasons:

1. MRO wasn't considered worth the effort when compared with opportunities in production goods. Most purchasing departments chose to handle MRO as a service function with most attention on minimizing user complaints.
2. Few tools existed that could be used by buying pros to overcome the obstacles presented by large numbers of items needed in relatively small quantities.

But that's all changing now as better trained buyers with better tools come on the scene. A new breed of purchasing professional is keying in on making the MRO buy more cost effective and on broadening the definition of its MRO responsibilities. At the same time, suppliers are starting to sell more intelligently in this newly sophisticated market environment. In a nutshell, MRO buying has entered a golden age of opportunity.

What kind of items fall within the purview of MRO? They make up a medley. According to a recent *PURCHASING* survey, 'Most important' buys for industrial companies include bearings, motors, hydraulics, forms, electronics, lubricants, materials handling gear, safety supplies, numerical-control tooling—and everything else from abrasives to zinc.

The world of MRO, in other words, is very much an *omnium gatherum*. And it was to bring that diversity into sharper perspective—to identify MRO practices and opportunities as they exist today—that we made our survey. Here's the story, with key points charted for ready reference:

1. Pareto's Law may not be broken, but the twin tables and charts here show that at least some purchasing execs are putting a bend in it—to their advantage.

It's Pareto's Law, you'll remember, that says 80% of the orders go for 20% of the dollars. That's at the "C" end of the ABC spectrum, where MRO items are supposedly nuts-and-bolts, penny-ante items. (The big bucks, conversely, go for just a handful of high-cost production goods.)

Well, maybe so. But the current average percentage of purchase dollars spent on MRO is now 17%, and the average percentage of orders issued is 36%. That's still a bit more than a 2:1 orders-to-dollars ratio, but it's a lot less than the 4:1 of 80/20. And it means that more and more smart buyers are getting out from under the enormous paperwork burden that pyramids when MRO is handled on a one item, one order basis.

Take a look at the two pie charts, comparing dollar percentages and order percentages with those of five years ago. Both have gone up for about 30% of the survey respondents. For roughly 50 to 60% of the buyers, there's been no change. But only 9% report decreases in dollars while 23% report declines in orders.

1. Twin views of MRO's scope

What percentage of purchase dollars are MRO?

MRO as % of purchase $	% respondents
1-5%	19%
6-10%	24%
11-25%	36%
More than 25%	21%

Versus five years ago

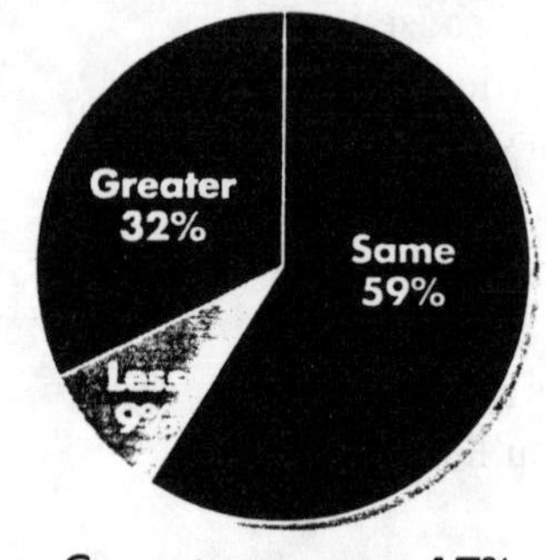

Current average = 17%

What percentage of purchase orders are MRO?

MRO as % of POs	% respondents
1-5%	6%
6-10%	23%
11-25%	32%
More than 25%	39%

Versus five years ago

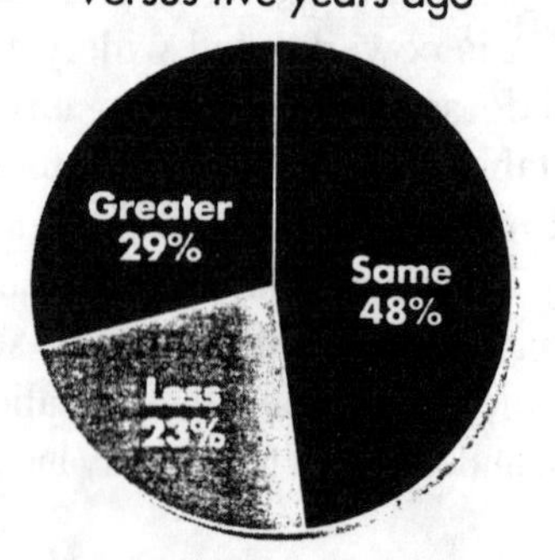

Current average = 36%

 © APICS

Consolidation, as we'll see, is the magic word. And it's a necessary one, given the pervasive, into-every-corner-of-the-plant nature of the MRO purchase. That means sorting, and maybe commodity coding (more about that later, too). Remember that there are five major categories into one of which even the most exotic MRO item will probably fit:

(1) Consumables, such as lubricants, solvents, and tooling, that regularly have to be replaced to keep the end-product going out the back door; (2) spare parts and repair items that may be needed for routine maintenance or in a big hurry; (3) miscellaneous supplies needed for specific tasks; (4) items required for end-products but not physically incorporated into them, such as inner and outer cartons, labels, instruction booklets; and (5) minor capital equipment, along with jigs and fixtures.

2. More than three out of four of your colleagues recognize that "substantial" savings are possible through better MRO buying. They say that means reductions in total costs, not just initial price. Sure, price reductions are important and bankable, especially when they result from efficiencies in the supplier's operation (possibly thanks to some customer action). But, by and large, price may be just the tip of a cost iceberg that also includes:

- **Inventory.** Despite recent downturns in interest rates the cost of money is still significant. It's pointless to have unneeded stocks on hand as long as there are other options.
- **Transportation.** Movement of goods is a cost that automatically stretches with distance. That's why a lot of your peers are moving to local sourcing.
- **Paperwork.** As noted in the preceding section, the administrative costs of pushing out orders and logging goods in are beginning to pop like Day-Glo ink on many firms' financial books.
- **Operation.** Function is the key here, as PMs strive to find top quality MRO items that will last longer, provide more consistent yields, offer higher reliability, guarantee compliance with EPA, OSHA, and other regulations, and satisfy individual workers.

"We want the best quality and the best service and *then* we want the price," says George R.A. Milne, PM, Delta Faucet, and chairman of NAPM's MRO committee. At his firm, he adds that one of the major goals for all plant managers is to reduce indirect labor costs. One way to track the savings that come from better quality MRO goods, he says, is to relate it to the frequency of downtime.

At Herman Miller, Inc., Zeeland, Mich., says manager of procurement administration Jim Heisingh, standardization on particular brands—of sanding papers, stretch wraps, and masking and filament tapes—has already been pegged to the functional use of those items.

A next step, Heisingh continues, will be folding MRO suppliers into a vendor rating plan that's already in effect for 17 different categories of production-goods suppliers. It's part of a deliberate effort to "slim down" the vendor base—one in which top performers are invited in to receive awards from Herman Miller's top brass, and hear about future plans.

Such involvement of the executive suite—and of others in the buying firm—is a must for buying quality goods that save dollars over the long term, say survey respondents.

"You've got to educate using departments and involve higher management," says a North Carolina PM.

"Get engineers involved with purchasing and maintenance," counsels a Wisconsin PM. "Don't let them be isolated dreamers in an ivory tower."

3. Only 17% of purchasing departments running material requirements planning (MRP) programs include MRO items in such computerized scheduling.

Where it exists, the inclusion is generally of fairly recent vintage: say a year or two. Other PMs have plans to go on-stream. "Not yet, but we will soon," says Terry Neal, buyer with Shaw-Barton Co., Coshocton, Ohio.

Because MRP systems are by nature driven by marketing's sales forecasts, many of the MRO/MRP setups are limited to quasi-production items that have to accompany finished products.

As an Indiana PM notes: "Every product we ship requires a particular styrofoam insert and a carton; every 12 require an outer shipping container and so many square feet of shrink wrap."

On the other hand, says Thomas W. Dickson, there is a real place for computerization of maintenance scheduling and the purchase and issuance of repair items can be linked to it. Dickson is a consultant in Greenville, S.C., and also owns several manufacturing firms specializing in materials for Detroit's auto-makers.

On purchased items such as belts, bearings, pulleys, and couplings, Dickson says, the part numbers in his firm include a commodity code. And he is making extensive use of bar coding to process such information. For example, tool crib attendants use a bar code wand to read item descriptions as they issue items from stock. The data go right into computer memory, and the computer automatically reorders (subject only to a quick human once over in purchasing) at pre-set reorder points.

4. Three quarters of the survey respondents say they are deliberately pulling their MRO requirements together into chunks of business that are more attractive to suppliers—and more efficient for vendors and customers alike.

Terminology varies: from contract, to systems contract, to price agreement, to blanket order. But nomenclature matters less than how real consolidation is; even a sexy name won't save a setup where purchases are still balkanized and fragmented. This means firmer arrangements with fewer sources.

"We're setting up contract agreements for extended periods," says John J. Castelli, materials manager, Micro Computer Access, Inc., Los Angeles.

"We have gone to systems contracting, and reduced the number of suppliers from more than 25 to only three," says Stoelting, Inc.'s PM Phil Parsche in Kiel, Wis.

There are variances in the percentages of MRO items under "growing" plans, as compared to all MRO purchases. But the overall average percentage is a healthy 36%, and even more significant is the pattern of changes over the past five years.

Specifically, 58% of your colleagues say they have increased the percentage of MRO contract buys. Another 38% report no change. Only a puny 4% say they have cut back on contract buying in the MRO area.

Some multi-plant PMs say they are holding back on corporate contracting because they don't have a workable commodity code. Indeed, many of them fume over this lack, and also gripe that corporate computer mavens tend to drag their feet in developing purchasing systems.

Other purchasing execs are turning to consultants to develop codes for them, or to already existing codes. "We have as many systems as we have clients," says William Hyde, president, Brisch Birn and Partners, Ltd., Ft. Lauderdale, Fla., which specializes in numbering systems that provide hierarchical classification of parts and commodities.

General Electric purchasing's own goods and services code (GEGS), for its part, has already been licensed to several other firms. The GEGS code covers some 25,000 commodity classifications, with nice touches such as cross-links between synonyms. (Example: "box" and "carton.")

So far, the GEGS code for GE's own use has been maintained in a mainframe computer. But recently, using an Emerald Systems Corp. disk drive, GE staffer Steve Schumaker proved the feasibility of storing the code in personal computers, and having buyers throughout GE use their PCs to find out who else is buying what, where. "The technology is there," says Schumaker, noting that the individual PCs, just as the mainframe is now, could be updated quarterly on actual purchases by GE's operating units.

"The PC's advantage is access time," says corporate sourcing's Dave Bonnot, who oversaw Schumaker's project. "You're contending only with yourself, and you can analyze the data any way you want."

5. The industrial distributor is still the king of the hill when it comes to getting customers' MRO business. The percentage of MRO requirements going to distributors marches steadily upward.

Overall, the average is 70%. The median—the point where half the respondents report higher percentages and half report lower ones—is an even stronger 80%.

Compared to five years ago, in fact, 37% of your colleagues say they are giving a bigger share of the MRO business to distributors. No one is giving a smaller share; the other 63% report an unchanged picture.

"We are reducing the distributor base by going to distributors that are computerizing their systems to better manage their businesses," says Tom Sheperd, Greenfield Industries, Augusta, Ga.

Federal-Mogul Corp., says PM Doug Rossman at Detroit HQ, now has a pilot program at four plants to evaluate a commodity-code system for item consolidation. If it proves out, it will be expanded to some 20 plants. Meanwhile, Federal-Mogul has learned a lot about the efficacy of regional field purchasing councils for pooling requirements.

At one time, says Rossman, such councils grouped together plants making similar products. "But now we're taking a geographic approach and it's working a lot better, because different plants can use the same distributors."

6. When your colleagues tab their distributor gripes on a 1-10 (good to bad) scale, it's obvious that distributors are seen as earning their keep. "Competitive pricing" gets a healthy 2, as a rounded average.

"Quality does almost as well, posting a 3. But "inventory" gets a 4, and "technical backup" gets a 5.

How do these scores stack up versus five years ago? The biggest improvement has been in pricing. The biggest fall-off has been in inventory. And some PMs think distributors may be relying too much on computers in lightening their inventory burden.

"More distributors are depending on computer inventory from several branches to back up [local] stocks," says Park R. Johns of ICI Americas, Inc., "and that means a longer delivery time from some other area."

7. As seen from the customers' side of things, distributors' stocking policies are pretty much in a state of flux. Some distributors are taking on new lines. But almost twice as many are trying to consolidate. And the upshot is additional unhappiness over the breadth and depth of distributors' local (immediately available) inventory. Comments:

- Distributors' inventory is our number-one problem. They are cutting back and forcing us to go to manufacturers, whose delivery is just as good."
- "They seem to carry more lines but less inventory in each."

- "Fewer items carried mean longer lead time for us."
- "There are many cases where distributors have to fill up a quota to accumulate enough orders for the factory to manufacture the item."

When MRO items require some customizing, PMs say, it's especially important for buyers to share requirement forecasts. Indeed, such sharing is always a good idea, even where strictly shelf-items are involved." Accurate forecasting of company needs," says Chris Principe, purchasing agent for Sonicor Instrument Corp., Copiague, N.Y., is one of the most important steps in improving MRO buying.

8. If there's one thing that makes a distributor steam, it's being viewed as nothing but a " middleman." So they often speak of value-added services—and no less than 42% of your colleagues say distributors are offering more such services.

Some of these services relate to production, or semi-customizing of the goods themselves. "Many have added secondary processing or will subcontract it," says L.H. Decker, purchasing agent, Wisco Industries, Inc., Oregon, Wis.

Metal service centers have for years offered some bending, forming, and other operations in addition to cutting and shearing. Chemical distributors are now increasingly getting into processes such as blending, while electronic outfits offer niceties such as board stuffing and sorting of components into kits for assembly.

To many of your purchasing colleagues, however, there's also a lot of value added when distributors live up to their unique position as 24-hour minutemen.

Key comment from an Illinois PM: "We are asking for more such services, and we're getting them. Perhaps they have always been available, but we are asking somewhat louder these days."

Reprinted from *PURCHASING MAGAZINE*, May 21, 1992. © Cahners Publishing Company.

A Simple Idea Saves $8 Million a Year

Sometimes the simplest concept can be the most efficient and cost effective, says Larry Brandt, senior supervisor of purchasing and material control at Bethlehem Steel's Burns Harbor plant in Chesterton, Ind.

Brandt credits an MRO buying plan, set up around a single-sourced bin-stocking concept, with saving Burns Harbor more than $29 million since 1984. For 1991 alone, he expects a savings of more than $8 million on the 21 "supplier agreements" written against about 80% of the Burns Harbor MRO bill.

The system is simple. The supplier comes in once a week and takes stock, makes up an order based on predetermined stocking levels, and files a release order. New stocks usually come in within two days and the materials are put away.

The fundamental concept behind the system is single sourcing—with a twist. Once a supplier is chosen for a particular commodity, that supplier provides all products used by Bethlehem in that product line. The other twist is "cost plus" pricing. A profit margin is agreed upon for every product during the negotiation of the contract. The result, according to Brandt, is an "average price of materials 5-10% lower than we used to pay."

Bethlehem has spent the past eight years refining the program and learning as it goes. The first supplier in the program underwent little evaluation, and went out of business four months later. As a result the evaluation process is now intense and can take anywhere from six months to a year.

The selected supplier meets with Brandt and other Bethlehem employees to establish how the program will be implemented and monitored. The lynch pin of the program is a three-part "snap set" invoice that also serves as the initial order, packing list, proof of delivery, and the invoice to Bethlehem's accounts payable office at corporate headquarters in Pennsylvania. "This form eliminates all the rest of the paperwork done by Bethlehem employees. We don't have to keep anything on our computers because the supplier keeps all the records," says Brandt.

The evaluation process doesn't stop when the supplier is chosen. The Burns Harbor team has developed an intensive monitoring and measuring program. Brandt has monthly meetings with each supplier to chart implementation of the program. Monitoring is done on several levels:

- **Audits.** Buyers conduct mini-audits yearly and suppliers must submit financial statements. Suppliers are audited by Bethlehem's internal audit department every five or six years. Invoices and prices are checked as well as determining whether all Bethlehem procedures have been followed correctly. Bethlehem has audited three suppliers in the past eight years and all have been successful.
- **Management reports.** Bethlehem requires three levels of usage reports. The first is a report of all products used at specific mill locations for the current month and for the current year. The second is a report of all products used for the whole mill—total volume. The third is a report of each item used throughout the plant—this helps the supplier standardize items.
- **Delivery performance.** Suppliers must give reports on their delivery performance. One result of the use of the bin-stocking system is there are no partial orders—whatever isn't delivered is added into the next week's order. Brandt estimates that delivery performance is 98% within two days, compared with 50% within a week before the supplier contracts were put into place.
- **Service.** Bethlehem requires all suppliers to document cost savings as a result of problem-solving and cost-cutting ideas suggested by their supplier representatives.

Benefits of the program have been far-reaching. Brandt began collecting data on the cost savings after the first year when he realized its magnitude. Here's a look at his scorecard:

- Inventory reduction: Between 1984 and 1990 Bethlehem held a $15.4 million inventory of MRO products. At the end of 1990 it had $7.8 million in inventory, a 56% reduction, which created a $7.5 million savings. The inventory turnover rate also has been slashed from eight months of supply in 1985 to just 4.6 months in 1990.
- Delivery performance: The average delivery performance is 95- 99% within two days, while the lowest is 90%. Three suppliers have reached 100% on-time delivery.
- Cost-saving ideas: Because of single-source contracts, suppliers have been highly cooperative in sharing new ideas and expertise.
- Administration: Brandt places the cost of processing a purchase order at $30 prior to the supplier agreements. He claims it now costs the Burns Harbor plant just $4 to process the three-part form. With 41,000 orders in 1990, Brandt estimates Bethlehem has saved at least $1 million a year in the administration of orders.

- Product savings: Brandt states that Bethlehem has paid about 5% less for materials since the start of the "cost-plus" program, resulting in a $1.3 million savings per year.
- Cost avoidance: Brandt asserts Bethlehem has saved approximately $800,000 per year on unnecessary materials. "Our suppliers can only order what we have agreed upon and have covered under the contracts. This eliminates discretionary items, incorrect parts, and overstocking," says Brandt.
- Reduced search time: Based on surveys taken throughout the mill, Brandt estimates that the time spent looking for materials has been cut by 95% since the bin- stocking methods have been employed, thus saving Bethlehem $3.5 million in 1990.

Brandt says there are also results that can't have a dollar figure placed upon them. He points to the changing roles of buyers and sales representatives. "Before, buyers spent 50-60% of their time listening to salesmen. Now that the selling is done up front the buyer can concentrate on sourcing the proper materials. The focus has shifted from distributor and manufacturer as allies to buyer and distributor as allies. It has come to 'you make what I need.' Our buyers are actually getting involved in the negotiations with the manufacturer for the prices to the distributor."

"By working together to standardize equipment and find more uses for products, many distributors have increased their sales volume discounts from their suppliers."

Reprinted from *Industrial Engineering Magazine*, November 1989. Copyright 1989. Institute of Industrial Engineers, 25 Technology Park/Atlanta, Norcross, Georgia 30092.

The Carrying Cost Paradox: How Do You Manage It?

Paul Bernard

The concept of carrying cost is one of the foundation principles of materials management. It is based on the fact that procuring and carrying inventory involves overhead costs which should be reflected somehow in materials management decisions. The longer a part is carried and the greater its value, the higher its "carrying cost." It is generally agreed that part costs are minimized at the point where carrying cost matches reordering cost. The biggest problem companies have though, is figuring out what these costs really are and whether optimizing individual part costs will optimize or sub-optimize total part costs.

Carrying cost is so fundamental to materials management that companies forget that it is only an accounting construct. It isn't a "cost" at all, but an aggregation of inversely related cost-of-money and operating costs allocated in some manner to individual parts. Since it is not necessarily a true measure of the cost to carry a specific plan because of the aggregation process, it may be erroneous as a decision element at an individual part level.

The cost-of-money element is a function of both the level of inventory as calculated from part price and the length of time it is owned. This is the portion of carrying cost which is easiest to determine since it is related to directly measurable financial factors. It basically consists of the company's cost of capital as well as factors for taxes, insurance and other financial elements. It is also the one intuitively targeted for reduction by more frequent and smaller receipts when companies consider ways to reduce "carrying cost."

Conversely, operating cost such as processing and handling tend to be a function of level of effort. Processing costs are correlated with the number of orders and receipts and include ordering, planning, quality assurance, stores, MIS, accounting and related expenses. The more orders, receipts, issues and transactions there are, the higher the processing costs. Processing costs can be thought of as "non-touch" materials-related costs.

Similarly, receiving more frequently will reduce the per load quantity but may actually increase the number of loads and related effort, and therefore, the handling cost. This is especially true with unit-loads such as pallets, wire baskets or metal bins which incur the same basic per load handling cost whether they are 95% full or 95% empty.

A decision to reduce carrying cost by receiving materials more frequently has the potential for significant cost reductions. However, it may have just the opposite effect in actual practice, especially for companies which receive in unit-loads. If the reduction in "cost to finance inventory" (defined as the cost-of-money component of carrying cost) is more than offset by increased operating costs for processing and handling, actual costs will increase.

The minimum cost for a part is at the point where the cost to finance it matches the cost to process and handle it as illustrated in Figure 1. This point may be different for each part and identifying it requires an understanding of the various elements of carrying cost. This carrying cost curve differs from that in an EOQ (Economic Order Quantity) equation since it is not in all instances upward sloping. It recognizes that cost-of-money is not the only consideration in determining how to manage and reduce materials-related overhead "carrying" costs.

The minimum cost point is not fixed. It can be identified through a structured analysis and managed by the company through programs designed to reduce costs in each of the carrying cost categories. The intent though is not to individually optimize each part. Cost inter-relationships among parts must be accounted for as well. Companies seeking to minimize *total* operating costs must do so by identifying the optimal trade-offs among each individual part.

Carrying Cost Paradox

It is difficult to determine how much time the purchasing manager, or indeed anyone, spends on each part. It is much easier to determine all of the departmental costs associated with each functional area. Because of this, carrying costs tend to be more accurate on an aggregate inventory basis and less accurate on an individual part basis.

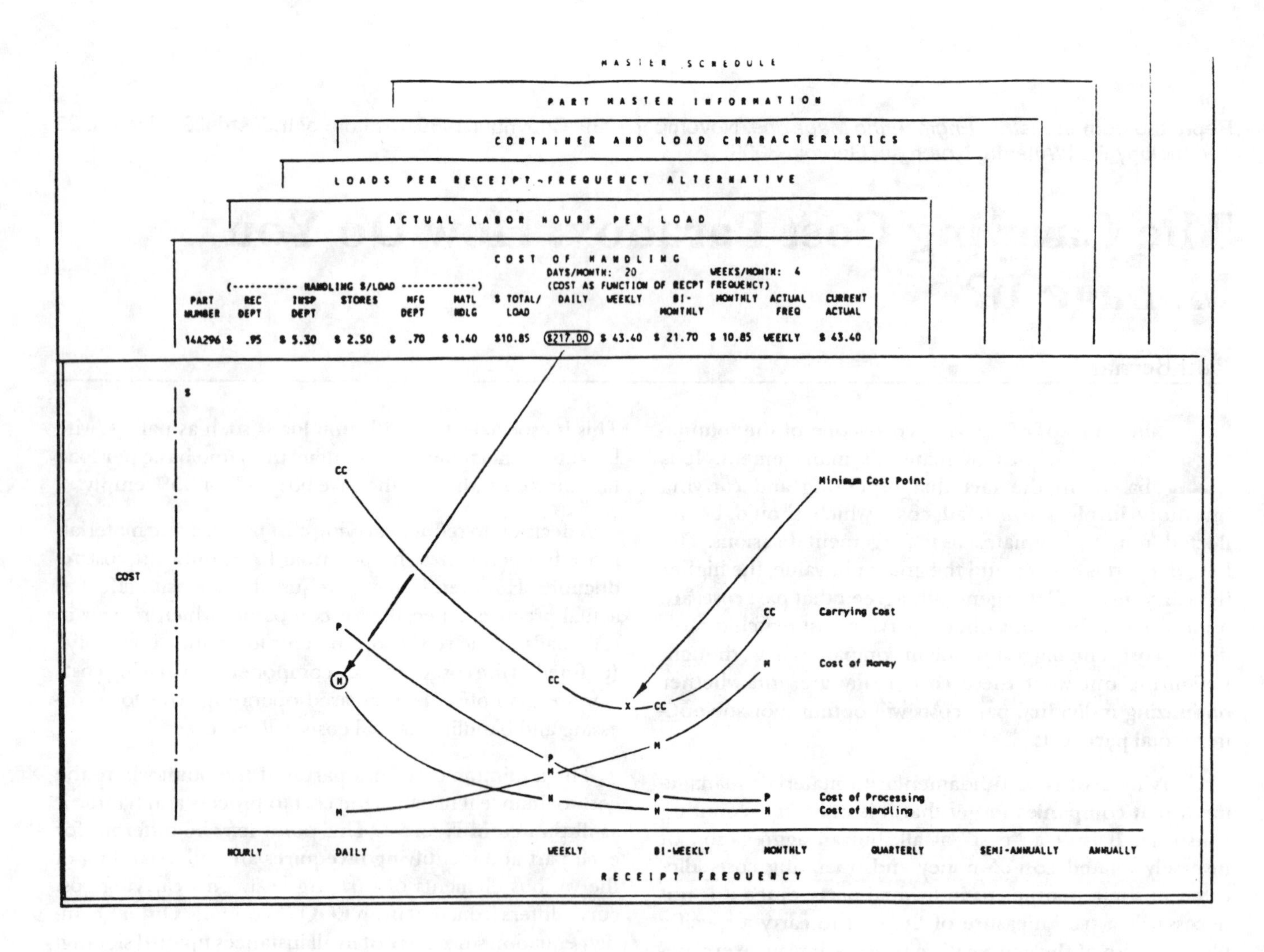

Figure 1 *Materials-related Costs*

The adequacy of this type of top down aggregate approach is being questioned by more and more companies. The very assumptions used to simplify the cost allocation process make it difficult or impossible to identify actual overhead costs at part or employee levels of detail. Yet, this is where carrying cost is supposed to assist management in making materials-related operating decisions.

The problem is not with the idea of a carrying cost per se. It does cost money to plan, order, receive, store, move, scrap, track, inspect, count, pay for and insure inventory. The problem is with the idea that all relevant materials-related overhead costs can be accurately allocated through an aggregate carrying cost formula to all parts based on their price. Price is not necessarily an indicator of materials-related overhead requirements.

Even operating conditions can change costs for the same part at different points in time. Consider the cost differential between a routine replenishment order and a critical stockout requiring expediting, premium pricing and air shipment. Glossing over actual operating or timing differences among parts due to the aggregation process reduces the company's ability to manage and reduce actual costs for individual parts and therefore, actual costs in general.

It is not uncommon to use a 24% per year carrying cost factor since 24% divides evenly into 2% per month. However, 24% by definition includes more than the cost of money since many companies have a cost of funds in the 7-12% annual range. Companies which apply such a standard carrying cost multiplier to all parts based on unit price are implicitly assuming that all carrying cost elements are price sensitive. No one would argue that financial factors such as inventory investment, insurance and taxes fall into this category. However, a multiplier has the effect of assuming that processing and handling costs are based on the price of the part as well. Therein lies the paradox: *Carrying cost is not reduced as receipt frequency increases where it costs more to process and handle the part than the savings in the cost-of-money.*

Allocating all materials-related overhead costs based on part price falsely assumes that:

- Expensive parts require *proportionally* more planning, procurement, expediting, inspection, accounting, MIS and related "overhead" resources than less expensive parts (since overhead is allocated based on material price).
- **Carrying cost is an accounting-generated value for evaluating decisions on the basis of their effect on materials-related overhead costs. It incorporates assumptions which may make it inappropriate as a basis for certain types of materials management decisions.**
- Expensive parts move proportionally further than less expensive parts (since move cost per foot is equal).
- Expensive parts require *proportionally* more handling than less expensive parts, or . . .
- . . . Expensive parts are handled by personnel with higher job classifications and more expensive equipment than who handle less expensive parts (since handling cost per load is based on physical, not price, characteristics).
- Expensive parts require *proportionally* more storage and handling space than less expensive parts (since price per square or cubic foot is a constant).
- Reducing any of the above factors *saves more money* for expensive parts than for inexpensive ones (since carrying cost is price sensitive).
- Finally, if any of the above factors are not true, *it doesn't affect the carrying cost* (i.e., if traditional methods are still used to determine carrying cost in spite of all of the above factors, it must be because the "time value of money" is the dominant factor).

If assumptions such as those listed above are not reasonable for specific parts, then the carrying cost allocated to them probably isn't correct either if it includes processing and handling costs in addition to the cost-of-money. If the carrying cost isn't accurate, then the savings attributed to carrying cost as a result of inventory reductions aren't accurate either.

Underlying Problem

The underlying problem is one of information availability. Company decision-makers frequently do not have access to information which defines the relationship between receipt frequency, container type, cost-of-money and cost of processing and handling for each part. In such situations, decisions may be justified simply on cost-of-money savings alone. Managers may not even be aware of any adverse effects to processing and handling costs. They may continue to believe that total costs are decreasing when in fact they may not be.

To maximize savings, decisions should be based on operating at the point where the sum of financial, processing and handling costs across all *parts is minimized.*

Managers can obtain the information they need to define this point through a Materials Management Analysis. Such an analysis allows decision-makers to assess the effect of alternative operating scenarios on *actual* processing, handling and money costs for each part before a change is implemented.

The basic premise behind such an analysis is that overhead costs can be determined for each part based on actual operating conditions. This requires an analysis by part and person and results in a fairly comprehensive data base of information. There are two major differences with this approach compared to traditional carrying cost allocations:

1. "Fixed" overhead costs which represent unused capacity are not allocated to the cost of parts under review. Unused machine time or floor space, for example, are separated from costs to be assigned to parts since they are not part of those part's cost structure. These types of costs should only be charged at product or higher levels to maintain their visibility. Consider a $52,000/year machine used 10 hours per week to produce 10 pieces of a single part. If the machine will not be sold if the part is eliminated or outsourced, it can be considered as fixed overhead and the part should not be charged for the extra 30 hours/week of available capacity (and neither should any other part). Machine cost per part would be $25 ($1000/week/40 hours/week), the rate for 1 machine hour at full utilization. The balance of the machine cost should be allocated to a management "opportunity cost" budget.

Variable costs, however, are fully chargeable. This includes manpower, machines and floorspace if their costs will be eliminated if the parts under consideration no longer require them. If the machine in the above example will be sold for $52,000 if the part is eliminated, the part should pick up full costs for it at a machine rate of $100 per part because the only reason it exists is to process these 10 pieces/week.

Resolving this question of variable and fixed costs is crucial to the outcome of the analysis. Basing calculations on IE standards may not identify the benefits of alternative operating decisions. In the above variable cost example, costing the part at $25 per hour compares favorably to a $40 purchased price. However, it fails to identify the actual $60 savings potential per part due to outsourcing the part and selling the machine. Also, spreading the additional $75 per part in unabsorbed cost over the rest of the inven-

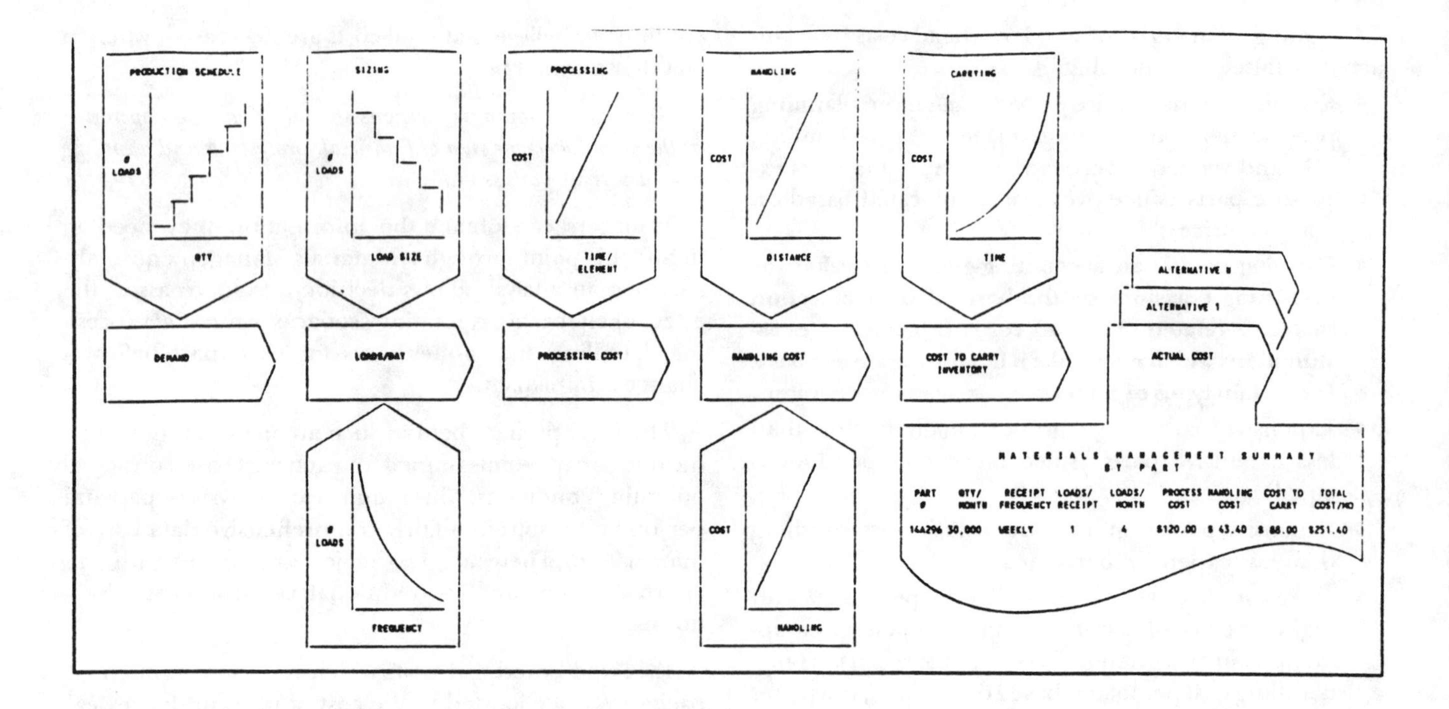

Figure 2 *Materials Management Analysis*

tory through an overhead cost formula makes it appear that:

- Other parts are more expensive than they really are.
- This $75 per part can be recouped by reducing the overhead cost of these other parts. This is an obvious fallacy since it has nothing to do with them at all.

2. The other major difference with traditional carrying cost allocations is that the level of detail is sufficient to establish specific improvement programs for each part and person as part of some larger Just-in-Time or cost improvement program. This cannot be done accurately with traditional carrying costs based on averages and allocations. These individualized programs can then be integrated so as to balance processing, handling and cost-of-money components for every part in ways which optimize *total* operating costs.

Analysis groundrules

Based on the preceding discussion, there are some rules to follow in performing a Materials Management Analysis. They ensure that only controllable costs are assigned to each part:

Rule 1: Cost categories only include portions of cost that realistically cease to exist if the category is eliminated.

Cost categories must be broken into functional groupings. Within Purchasing, such groupings might include negotiating, order processing, expediting, change order processing and file maintenance. Supplies and MIS types of overhead are included within each function in addition to labor hours spent per part. However, overhead excludes floorspace and managers' salaries if neither will be eliminated if the company eliminates individual functions or portions thereof.

Costs which can't be reasonably assigned and managed at the part level belong at the product or some higher level.

Rule 2: Costs are based on actual costs paid, not on some type of standard which allows for less than 100% utilization.

For a material handler, per load cost is a function of utilization level. The hourly rate is calculated on productive hours only, not on normal shift hours (i.e., the fewer the number of loads moved, the higher the cost per load). This encourages the company to either assign additional work to the handler to improve utilization level and reduce per load costs, or reassign or eliminate his or her work in order to achieve a full headcount reduction.

"Paper" cost savings are not recognized by the analysis. They merely act as an indicator of improvement for evaluation purposes, not as an end in and of themselves.

Rule 3: Costs for the analysis do not have to be "exact."

The intent is to isolate those parts which deviate from the norm. Parts with low costs will be identified as such, while those with excessive costs can be targeted for special action (thus increasing their cost even further in the short term). Using averages for normal functions such as purchase order processing and invoice matching is acceptable as long as exceptions are properly identified and treated accordingly.

Materials management analysis

The analysis itself consists of six basic steps. Each one generally requires setting one or more variables to define the controllable aspects of the operating environment. Results are then used in one or more of the remaining steps to calculate cost per part. This is illustrated in Figure 2 and discussed below:

1. Part Demand—Total quantity per time is a function of the production schedule and product structure. It may be factored upwards by applying scrap and service parts factors as well.

2. Loads/Day—Total quantity from Step 1 divided by quantity per container defines the number of loads (rounded up) to be received over the time period selected. Actual supplier carton or load sizes may be used, or a standard size may be selected for evaluation. Dividing by the receipt frequency determines the loads per receipt. These values can then be allocated to specific days based on each part's receiving policy (hourly, daily, weekly, biweekly, monthly, quarterly, etc.).

3. Processing Cost—Overhead cost areas must be broken down to a part level of detail to determine processing cost. They might include Purchasing, Stores, Accounting, MIS, and Quality Assurance. Each of these areas is then further broken down by function, with costs assigned based on the cost per operation and number of occurrences. For example, expediting a part each week is costed at the rate for one expedite activity times the number of weeks in the period. Incoming inspection is costed at the rate for one inspection activity times the number of receipts from step 2 for the period.

4. Handling Cost—Variables for determining handling cost include handling scenario, distance and move time. Handling scenario refers to the actual handling process and personnel involved. This requires time-studying the various handling activities involved such as load, move, unload, stack, etc. and costing them at the rate for the individual doing the work. This rate is a function of the utilization level and may be different for different handlers or even different handling scenarios. Distance may be varied to determine the effect of relocating the dock, storage area or point-of-use. Time associated with distance may vary based on type of material handling equipment used and load carrying capacity.

5. Cost to Carry Inventory—The cost-of-money element of carrying cost is dependent on factors such as the cost of borrowing money, the opportunity cost associated with using the company's money, purchase and discount terms for the part, transportation charge, setup cost, special charges and minimum purchase order charges, to name a few. Some of these amounts are assigned on a per order basis from Step 3. The rest are based on average inventory level which may be a function of receipt frequency and quantity from Step 2, and normal stocking level based on part value or day's supply considerations.

6. Actual Cost—Processing cost, handling cost and cost to carry inventory are then summed. The result is a calculation of actual cost for each part, as opposed to an average cost based on all parts. By varying the operating factors in Steps 1-5, management can determine the specific degree and area of change required to obtain actual cost reductions for individual parts while assessing the effect on inventory in general. For example, while it is advantageous to incrementally reduce handling costs across all parts, no actual savings can be obtained until headcount is reduced. It may be better to forego global incremental "paper" savings in favor of focused actions which eliminate specific material handlers. Companies don't have to rely on generic carrying costs for decision-making if they *know* what the actual costs are.

Companies—especially those in unit-load material handling environments—which justify inventory reduction or capital investment programs based on reducing carrying cost may actually increase actual costs if carrying cost is not properly understood.

On the one hand. . .

Two points are important to keep in mind:

1. "Paper" cost reductions are a way to keep score for the company's continuous improvement program. However, the score is only meaningful if costs are accurately represented. Traditional carrying costs may not be accurate at a part level, so anticipated savings may be achievable by implementing specific part strategies.

2. Incremental "paper" cost reductions are not real. Carrying cost savings commonly stated as a percentage of unit price which result from more frequent receipts cannot include processing, handling and other non-financial fac-

tors unless manpower reductions or other cost savings are achieved as well.

Receiving parts more frequently is a legitimate way to reduce the "cost to carry inventory." It may or may not be a legitimate way to reduce "carrying cost."

About the author

Paul Bernard, CFPIM, PCMM is a senior systems engineer/project manager with Litton Industrial Automation. He is responsible for developing strategic integration programs designed to continually improve the competitiveness of client manufacturing operations. These programs require a balanced business and technical perspective which Paul provides from 13 years of manufacturing and systems engineering, materials management and MRP II system design experience.

Paul has published a number of articles and technical papers on materials, project and performance management topics. He obtained a BSMIE from Clarkson University and an MBA from Canisius College.

Reprinted from *Production and Inventory Management*, Third Quarter, 1988.

Inventory Management in the JIT Age

Henry H. Jordan

In its April 20,1987 special report on U.S. manufacturing, *Business Week* stated:

> Paper entrepreneurialism, the juggling of financial assets by legions of MBAs and lawyers, must be replaced by a new commitment to keeping manufacturing in America. To do that, business must invest in production methods that can respond to rapidly changing markets.

A number of companies have already made a commitment to just-in-time production. Many others are on the verge of doing so. It is generally recognized that effective implementation of Just-in-Time will result in a significant reduction of inventories. As a matter of fact, inventory levels are key indicators for measuring just-in-time performance.

The Just-in-Time philosophy on inventory management is simple:

- Strive for a level of zero inventories.
- Produce items at the rate required by the customer.
- Eliminate all unnecessary lead times.
- Reduce setup costs to achieve the smallest economical lot size—ideally, a quantity of one.
- Optimize material flow from suppliers through the production process to the point of sale of the finished product, so that inventories are minimized.
- Ensure high quality and dependable just-in-time delivery from suppliers.
- Implement a Total Quality Control (TQC) program which will minimize scrap, rework, and resultant delays in production.
- Minimize safety stocks.

While the Just-in-Time inventory management philosophy is simple, execution is not.

Inventory Classification

To manage inventories effectively, we should have a clear understanding of what we are controlling.

What are the different item types? These should be classified by inventory segment. Typically, these are: raw materials, purchased components, manufactured component, manufactured subassemblies (frequently referred to as intermediates in the chemical and other process industries), work in process, packaging materials, and finished goods (which may be further subdivided to reflect stocks at the manufacturing plant and at distribution centers and branch warehouses).

How many different items are there in each inventory segment? This provides information as to the magnitude and complexity of the inventory management effort; a small number of different items is easier to manage than a large number.

What is the unit cost of each item? Since the cost of inventory investment is a major consideration in making decisions regarding order quantities and safety stocks, the cost of each item should be available to the inventory manager.

Even under the most ideal Just-in-Time conditions of minimum lead times and minimum setup or ordering costs, inventory investment is an important factor which must be considered by the inventory manager.

What is the anticipated annual demand for each item? If there are more than a few items in each inventory segment, an ABC analysis of each inventory segment will be of significant help in establishing controls and setting priorities for effective management of all items.

Purchased Items

In a Just-in-Time environment, raw materials and other purchased items should be delivered by the supplier when they are needed. A blanket purchase order or other suitable form of a basic agreement should cover the terms and conditions for procurement. Delivery of the item should be direct to the point of use in the manufacturing plant; any double handling of material should be avoided.

The supplier should ensure a smooth flow of material to support production. This requires optimum communication and coordination between the manufacturing plant and the supplier.

A direct relationship between the Production Control Department of the manufacturing plant and that of the supplier is effective. The supplier should be considered by the manufacturing company as an extension of the plant and should be included in all planning activities which involve his products. Purchasing should authorize specific individuals in production to represent the company on matters pertaining to schedules and delivery quantities.

Several techniques exist for controlling the flow of material from the supplier to the manufacturing company. The specific technique should be selected which will best suit the implementation of the Just-in-Time concept for the particular item being purchased. Automatic inventory replenishment by vendor is a technique where the supplier determines the need for required materials based on frequent deliveries to the plant. Depending on the nature of the production process as well as the material involved, this could range from many times a day to a less frequent interval. Visual review of existing inventory by the supplier will determine how much to deliver.

This method of inventory control is not foreign to U.S. commerce and industry; visit a supermarket and see how the bakery driver delivers his goods. He replenishes the baked goods based on a visual review of what is on the shelves. The same is true for soda and candy vending machines. Those using oil to heat their homes are certainly familiar with this type of inventory system; the driver comes by the house periodically and fills up the tank.

Another technique is verbal ordering by production. This is an approach instituted in 1972 at Copeland Corporation for corrugated cartons, where the shift foreman would phone the supplier's local warehouse and order materials for the next shift. Of course, the buyer-supplier relationship must be one of mutual trust and confidence. Under the Just-in-Time concept, the pipeline is kept lean. Shortages as well as overages in quantities delivered will be noted quickly.

There should be no need for incoming Quality Control inspection. The vendor's quality must be such that incoming inspection of materials can be eliminated. Where required, as in the pharmaceutical industry, lot integrity should be maintained by the identification of each lot by the vendor and continued traceability through the manufacturing process.

Inventory Accounting

With the possible exception of high-dollar-value items usually identified by individual serial number, such as aircraft engines or computers, inventory records can be posted by backflushing.

This is a method for automatic calculation of component usage by bill-of-material explosion of the end item for the quantity completed. It can be applied to a flow process as well as a batch process manufacturing operation. It is particularly well suited to a Just-in-Time manufacturing operation, where the production cycle time is short.

For low-unit-cost items, such as fasteners and labels, the inventory record posting requirement can be eliminated altogether. Such items can be expensed when delivered and invoiced by the vendor. Visual controls usually suffice for reordering.

Inventory Policy Code

In addition to the inventory segment (item type) classification and the ABC code, each item should be identified by an inventory policy code. This code is used to designate the specific method of inventory management to be applied to the item, such as automatic inventory replenishment by vendor, vendor delivery based on verbal order, or vendor delivery based on written order. For each of these methods, the technique to be used for triggering the inventory replenishment action must be established and identified by the inventory policy code.

The code must also define the requirement for transaction reporting and the degree of inventory record keeping. These may include one or more of the following options: (1) transaction reporting of receipts, (2) transaction reporting of issues, (3) transaction reporting of serial number items, (4) transaction reporting of scrap and rework, (5) transaction reporting of returns to vendor, (6) receipt and issue calculation based on backflushing, or (7) no transaction reporting nor perpetual balance in the inventory record.

The inventory policy code states how each item is to be managed. Both the people and the computer system need to know how to use this code for effective implementation of inventory management in a Just-in-Time environment.

Transportation Methods

Implementing Just-in-Time may result in increased transportation costs due to smaller lot sizes and more frequent deliveries. However, in some industries such as chemicals there are significant trade-offs between the economy of longer lead time and less flexible rail shipments versus more frequent tanker truckloads. Each of these cases must be examined on its own merits and on a continuing basis to determine the optimum solution.

Interplant Transfers

The methods of inventory control of materials and components from vendors apply equally well to those obtained from a feeder plant in the company. It is of utmost importance to have excellent communications between the plants to ensure timely and balanced material flow.

Material Requirements Planning

Just-in-Time requires flow of material in the exact quantity required and at the exact time; the key word is "exact." Regardless of the specific method used to achieve this exact material flow, there must be advance planning to ensure that material is available when needed. Material requirements planning is the best technique to accomplish this.

MRP provides the basic logic for determining not only future material requirements but also manufacturing capacity requirements. State-of-the-art MRP II computer systems provide the user with on-line, real-time simulation capabilities to explore a broad horizon of "what if?" situations. While Just-in-Time strives for the smallest economical lot sizes, there may be valid reasons for acquiring larger inventories of certain items. Two examples:

A crop which is harvested only once or twice a year.

Infrequent and small quantity demand of an item where the cost of delivery of such small quantities would be prohibitive. While it can be argued that this would be a case for value engineering and manufacturing methods improvement, the overall demand value of the item may not warrant the expenditure of such an effort.

MRP with its "look ahead" capability allows us to make sound decisions for purchasing, as well as manufacturing resources planning. The latter includes manpower, plant facilities, equipment, and tooling. This powerful technique provides essential information which helps suppliers plan their production for Just-in-Time delivery.

Implementation

The basic steps required for implementation of inventory management in a Just-in-Time environment can be summarized as follows:

- Review segmentation of the inventory by item type; ensure that all items have been properly classified.
- Ensure that the unit cost is stated for each item.
- Establish the anticipated annual demand quantity for each item.
- Run an ABC analysis for each inventory segment.
- Assign appropriate ABC code to each item.
- Establish blanket purchase orders, purchasing agreement, or contract for selected items with qualified vendors.
- Authorize individuals in production to release vendor delivery quantities against blanket purchase orders, purchasing agreement, or contract.
- Establish inventory policy code for each item based on the method of inventory control and the method of transaction reporting and recording.
- Review and establish minimum economical order quantities and safety stocks required by Just-in-Time production.
- Measure inventory performance to determine effectiveness of Just-in-Time production and inventory management.

Conclusion

Just-in-Time will change our conventional thinking concerning the management of inventories and streamline our methods for inventory control. Proper selection and implementation of these methods will yield substantial benefits by improving customer service, shortening delivery lead times, and significantly reducing inventory investment. It does not, however, eliminate the need for sound inventory planning.

About the author

HENRY H. JORDAN, CMC, CFPIM, is chairman of the Center for Inventory Management. He has served on the APICS Curricula and Certification Council and as chairman of its Inventory Management Committee and its Just-In-Time Committee. Hank is currently chairman of the APICS Curricula and Certification Council. He is also a member of the Institute of Management Consultants and the International Society for Inventory Research, and a senior member of the Institute of Industrial Engineers. Hank is an editor of the Production and Inventory Control Handbook and author of the System Implementation Handbook, the APICS Training Aid on Cycle Counting for Record Accuracy, and numerous articles. He serves on the Editorial Review Board of P&IM Journal. Hank has had 20 years' experience as vice-president of manufacturing, production and inventory control manager, director of procurement, and director of quality assurance and field service engineering. As project and government contracting officer, he was responsible for guidance and control systems for the government's missile and space program.

Reprinted from the APICS 1990 *Conference Proceedings.*

The Importance of Making Just Enough

George W. Plossl

Manufacturing is characterized by over—or underproduction—making too much or too little. The problems associated with each are all too familiar; overproduction generates excess inventory and underproduction makes customers wait and starves workers and machinery. Most executives in manufacturing companies believe that they must choose the lesser evil in these two bad situations, not knowing there is another alternative. Most choose to "run a lean operation" on the assumption the idle workers and low machine utilization are worse than excess inventory and some disappointed customers.

In this presentation I want to identify the serious problems, many of which are poorly understood, of both overloading and underloading; outline the hierarchy of plans needed for tight control of resources; show how the needed resources can be evaluated simply; examine the roles of the major functional groups in sound planning and effective execution; and illustrate the correct solutions of some common problems.

Today's Most Common Problem

Here is the sequence of activities set into motion when a large customer order is imposed on a plant which does not have and cannot get adequate capacity to handle it together with all existing orders. Plant workcenters will fall into one of two categories; those which have adequate capacity and those which do not (the bottlenecks). The former will make all of its components needed to produce all orders but the latter will not be able to do this.

In the conventional plant, the resulting shortages of parts and subassemblies will prevent completion of many products and will initiate many crisis-fixing actions. Expensive substitute materials and alternate processing operations will be employed, order batches will be split and small quantities for important orders hand carried through remaining operations. Overtime will be worked, especially in final assembly and test.

The final results are inevitable; three of the most important objectives of any manufacturing firm—high customer satisfaction, low costs and small inventories—will not be achieved. Quality will probably suffer too. No computer-based system, however powerful, even when operated by competent people, will change this scenario. Attempting to execute a plan without adequate resources is fatal to plants attempting to be competitive.

Imposing a plan which requires less than a plant's capabilities is almost as bad but the resulting problems are different. Here the formal system cannot generate enough work to keep facilities busy. The compulsion to avoid idle workers and to keep machines operating, especially expensive ones, will take over and orders "forced" out of the system early. Material flow becomes unbalanced, Work-in-Process builds, lead times lengthen, raw materials and purchased parts are made into specific items too soon and flexibility in their use is lost.

The problems caused by long lead times are very serious but are not usually recognized by those unfamiliar with the way manufacturing operations should be run. This includes many managers and executives with experience in industry who think they understand but who do not. Such amateurs are extremely dangerous to their companies and to American industry.

Plans based on long lead times are invalid; too many things will change—delivery times and quantities, product designs, processing methods and work priorities, for example—between planning and execution. Many crises will affect quality, costs and deliveries. Supplier deliveries will not be timely. Inventories will be unbalanced and too high, particularly Work-in-Process. Obsolescence losses will be high when designs change. Overhead costs will be excessive from attempts to cope with upsets. Plants will be oversized, machine capacity wasted and operations will be inflexible. No company operating with these handicaps can be successful in today's worldwide competitive economy.

Once the full effects of overloading and underloading are understood the conclusion is inescapable: there is no valid alternative to making just enough.

Understanding Manufacturing

Manufacturing is a process consisting of two flows; materials and information. Materials flow from suppliers through a company's plant to its customers. Information flows in three looped systems, out associated with suppliers, one with customers and the third with internal company activities. Another system, with which we are not concerned here, accepts input from and provides information to

 © APICS

people outside the firm—stockholders, government and the like.

Two fundamental questions must be answered: "Are we making enough in aggregate output?" and "Are we working on the right things today?" The quality of the answers will determine the quality of the performance of the operations. The first, the capacity question, is more important than the second relating to priority.

Three important activities must be handled: planning, execution and control. Planning assigns numbers to future events. Execution converts plans to reality. Control measures deviations from plans, sporting the significant from the trivial an reporting the former to those responsible for taking corrective actions.

While planning and execution activities overlap and go on simultaneously, they have very different purposes. Planning defines all the resources needed to produce what has been planned. Execution applies the resources available to produce what customers need now.

Understanding this difference is essential to knowing how to produce just enough. Since plans are projections of expected or desired future occurrences, they will never be exact statements of what will be executed. Because of this uncertainty, forecasts, budgets and other types of plans should be stated in two or three figures—maximum and minimum, optimistic and pessimistic, best and worst scenario are terms describing the high and low limits; the expected value is equally useful, particularly if it is not in the center between the other two.

Plans are needed in a hierarchy:

Strategic—long range plans, focusing on the future direction of the company, attempting to answer these questions:

What business are we in now?

What business do we want to be in? When?

What actions are needed now in Engineering, Marketing, Production,

Finance?

Do the strategies of these functions match?

This last question is most important. In one client company, marketing people saw fast response to new products and orders, more product varieties, quicker and on-time deliveries and low costs as essential to being competitive. Production was measured primarily on high direct labor efficiency and machine utilization and low costs; they wanted good forecasts, stable operations, fewer models, longer time to change and higher selling prices. It is obvious that different strategies were being followed. No wonder marketing referred to their plant operations as "A millstone around our necks."

Business—long range plans concentrating on the company's products, involving answers to such questions as:

Which of our products are now mature?

Which are still growing?

Which are declining and should be dropped?

What new products are needed now? Later?

What products are competitors bringing out?

Business plans are concerned primarily with product families and the markets they will serve. They translate strategic plans into more specific statements of hardware and services.

Our interest in making just enough utilizes data in strategic and business planning only to evaluate the uncertainty and magnitude of possible changes in the more specific production plans and master production schedules. These are the third and fourth sets of plans in the hierarchy and cover short term future actions.

Production—plans for facilities required to produce product families defined in the front end of the business plans. The questions are:

What resources are now just adequate?

Which are surplus to our needs?

Which are now overloaded?

What new technologies are coming? When?

What new people skills are needed? When?

What new capital equipment is needed? When?

What other sources of resources are available outside our own facilities?

Production planning determines the specific mission of each facility (variety of production, focused factory, R & D and prototypes, etc.) and aims at maximum use and benefits from each. It includes new plant construction and acquisition of additional facilities.

Master production schedules (MPS's)—these very detailed plans make the transition from aggregate data on product families and facilities to specific products and resources. Each MPS is a statement of what should be produced to support the higher level strategic and business plans. Each covers a specific configuration of product defined by a bill of materials. In their development, consideration is given to sales forecasts, existing customer orders, market opportunities and needed inventory changes.

The MPS's attempt to balance customer needs against available resources defined in production plans. This crucial step determines whether the plans are realistic or not, meaning that resources are now or can be available in time to make all that is planned. Data in the formal planning and control system translate production quantities into required resources of people, machines, tooling, test equipment, purchased materials and services and other resources. All deficiencies must be made up or the MPS changed!

MPS's are planning data. Execution of plans begins for long lead time activities, like procuring machinery, equipment and some purchased materials, before customers' needs are defined. Well-run companies, now called world class, keep internal lead times short to avoid committing flexible resources to specific items until such needs have been defined by specific orders. Although few do it, it is a rare company that could not hold off starting final assembly until after such orders were in.

World class companies make every attempt to match orders to their plans where this can be done without jeopardizing the real needs of customers. This minimizes the changes needed to execute plans. Inevitably, however, some customer will require something different from what has been planned.

Formal computer-based systems make it easy to test available materials, capacity and other resources to detect any deficiencies preventing making what customers really need. Fast, flexible operations will overcome most deficiencies in time to meet customers desires. The best proof that this is possible is the success of expediting efforts in most companies today!

The obvious response to this statement is that expediting is expensive, destructive of quality and most undesirable. It certainly is when it is practiced frequently and is the only method of getting some orders completed quickly. In the environment characterized by better communication with suppliers and customers, sound plans, adequate capacity, flexible resources and few surprise upsets, the last moment actions to get needed work done is both feasible and preferable to other alternatives.

How Much Is Enough?

As stated earlier, capacity questions are much more important than those relating to priority. Ironically, common practice is exactly opposite. The great bulk of effort is aimed at getting specific schedules and sequences of orders completed promptly. Material requirements planning is overworked to produce detailed schedules for each component and individual work orders and purchase orders are tracked diligently through all operations to completion.

Capacity requirements planning, however, and its companion function input/output control, are conspicuous by their absence in too many firms. The lead time to process any order, purchased or manufactured, is the sum of the lead times of the various operations, paperwork and physical, needed to process it. Obviously a few orders can be moved quickly through any plant by giving them high priority so that they are not delayed sitting in queues of work. This is why expediting works. Equally obviously, the size of the queue (the amount of Work-in-Process) determines the average lead time of orders passing through any workcenter. Good control of the priority of all orders requires that average lead times be short, requiring low Work-in-Process levels.

All inventories, including Work-in-Process, can be controlled only by balancing input and output rates. Short, dependable lead times on individual orders result only when workcenters have small queues and this is possible only when flow rates of work to and from them are smooth and swift. There is no magic! Priority plans are futile fiction unless capacity planning and control are effective.

Two basic methods of capacity requirements planning are available. The most popular is the classic bottom-up approach using the profile of both released and planned orders from material requirements planning. Each order is scheduled through needed operations (using estimates of setup, processing, move and queue times), the work content at each operation is calculated from setup and processing standards and the total load resulting from all orders scheduled to be in the workcenter in each time period is added up. Practically every software package labels this a "Capacity Requirements Plan."

This technique is highly precise but of very dubious accuracy and usefulness because:

*Load and capacity are very different. Load is the depth of water in a tub; capacity is the rate the water is running in (input) and out (output). Input and output can be adequate and balanced with any level of water in the tub. Equating load to capacity requirements assumes that all work in workcenters is to be cleared through and no Work-in-Process will be left!

*Calculated loads are almost invariably erratic, due to different sized batches. Capacity is difficult, often impossible, to vary much from week to week. Only the average load, easy to calculate directly, has much meaning.

*Few companies have accurate work standards and even fewer have complete coverage of all work. More rapid future changes will make complete coverage impracticable.

*Any relation of actual work times to standards is all too often coincidental.

*Unplanned demands are not included. These result from unexpected customer orders, scrap, rework, record errors and added operations. While these should be eliminated, they are facts of life yet in most plants.

*Capacity data are needed over fairly long horizons; it takes time to hire and train workers and to buy, install and get new machines running, even longer to build new plants. Over a horizon of several weeks or months, the profile of orders in any material requirements plan is very unlikely to be valid. Design and methods changes, use of substitute materials and alternate routings, varying subcontract work and many other factors will insure that what is planned now is not what will be executed later.

In well disciplined plants, use of detailed data on specific orders and workcenters is very useful in detecting potential problems a few days in advance using techniques called finite loading, operation sequencing and operational analysis. However, as techniques to use for capacity planning and control they are useless and are very expensive compared to alternatives.

Practicable, workable approaches to capacity planning are top-down. They use product family requirements from the production plan or master production schedules and estimates of work content for groups of similar parts. Typical of product data in a production plan are:

	Jan	Feb	Mar	Apr	May	Jun
Family #1	120	130	140	140	150	150
" #2	55	55	55	55	55	55
.						
.		etc.				
.						

Shown are quantities of families of similar products to be made in the next six months. The number of different models in each family is not important. Estimates are made for the amount of work needed to make all the components for each family processed in the important (not all) workcenters. These are set up in a bill of labor, so called because of its resemblance to a bill of material. The estimates should be carefully made and should include allowances for the kind of unplanned work experienced in the recent past. Their accuracy is not vital to the process as will be explained later.

Product Family	#1	#2	. . . .
Work Center	Estim Hours	Estim Hours	
102	10	9	
105	8	12	
106	14	18	
108	22	20	
.	.	.	
.	.	.	

The total hours needed in each month to process the components for each family are then calculated for each workcenter by multiplying the number of units to be made by the hours required to make them in each workcenter. Here are January's data, now in estimated hours:

Work Center	Product Families #1	#2	. . .	Jan Total Month
102	1200	495	. . .	7,495
105	960	660	. . .	6,630
106	1680	990	. . .	9,220
108	2640	1100	. . .	13,455
.	.	.		.
.	.	.		.

The final step is to tabulate the data for each workcenter for as far out in the future as is needed to provide information to those responsible for having adequate capacity. This could be from two months for hiring some types of workers to two years or longer for new plant design and construction. A column is then added showing the actual hours of output from each workcenter in the recent past, called demonstrated capacity, as shown here:

Work Center	Demon Capac	Capacity Requirements Jan	Feb	Mar	Apr
102	7,540	7,495	7,650	7,725	7,860
105	7,750	6,630	6,770	6,900	7,070
106	8,330	9,220	9,220	9,220	9,220
108	13,535	13,455	13,620	13,790	13,945
.	.	.	.	.	.
.	.	.	.	.	.

This simple, rough-cut technique has been used very effectively in many companies making a wide variety of products. Although the calculations can be made manually, most companies using the technique prefer to use personal computers with spreadsheet programs. These enable them to play "What if?" and simulate the effects of changes in product demands, mix, methods, and worker productivity improvements. Experienced companies keep working to improve the accuracy of the estimates, add or delete workcenters, develop plans for more resources and find other uses for the plans.

From this example, comparing existing demonstrated capacity with requirements, it appears that workcenter #105 has been producing too much and #106 too little, The differences of over 10% in both cases are too great to ignore; differences within 5% would be no concern. The first thing to do is check the time estimates for significant errors. If none are found, the workcenter capacities should be changed.

The example shown for internal workcenters is equally applicable to suppliers and subcontractors and also to other resource needs such as energy, testing, tooling, and even clerical work. All that is needed is to add to the bill of labor some measure of the amount of each resource required to produce each product family.

After getting started and testing for gross error, the capacity data should be used in input/output reports to achieve more level release of work to starting workcenters and smoother flows between them and to insure that adequate capacity is maintained. Close monitoring of the actual amount of work in queues will provide a sensitive early warning signal (rising or falling queues) when input and output rates get out of step. Adequate capacity to handle the total throughput required is essential; any company not making enough in total will never make the right items on time.

Primary Roles of the Functions

Computer hardware and software are now available in practically every company to do the data processing associated with sound planning. The capacity planning, input/output control and material availability analyses techniques are simple and are covered well in planning and control literature. We know how to do the job.

It is not a task for one department or group, however; each major department must become part of the team insuring that their company makes just enough of the right things. The conventional views of the roles of each function must be challenged and revised.

Marketing is traditionally believed to be responsible for recommending new products and markets and developing advertising programs. These are important activities, of course, but two other activities, often low on their priority list, are even more important in sound planning. Recommending products to be discontinued can free up resources for more beneficial use. Identifying potential new customers for existing products can permit plans to be made to meet any special requirements of fast delivery or unique features they may require. Such contingency plans can pay off in high profit margin business. Today's emphasis on partnerships of suppliers and customers carries great potential benefits for those suppliers who become the single source for the customer. Marketing is the best group to target customers for developing such relations.

The conventional role of sales is getting orders, often with little concern for profits, growth or impact on operations. Their primary role, providing intelligence on all aspects of customer relations so that sound, stable plans can be made, is neglected. "The customer is always right" is the excuse for lack of information on the true situation. Customers express their "wants" by placing orders; their real "needs" can be quite different. The proof lies in the few real problems generated by the many poor deliveries customers get. Sales should be measured on the number of "surprises" triggered by unexpected customer changes or new orders. They should investigate customer changes to find the reasons and prevent future occurrences.

Design engineering is correctly assigned the task of developing new and improved products. Product designs determine the bulk of material costs and processing; there is little others can do to cut costs and improve these. More important even is the effect on flexibility and fast response to customers' needs when unique features are built into products in early stages of manufacture. Design engineering must add flexibility, modularity, manufacturability and standardization to their list of criteria.

Production usually carries responsibility for getting high labor efficiency and machine utilization and keeping costs low. Theirs is expected to be a "lean and mean" operation in which they follow instructions of supervisors, methods engineers, quality control experts and safety specialists. Making just enough will be traumatic for them; little Work-in-Process, small lots, quick changeovers and constant attention to improving every aspect of their work will be an entirely new way of life. Their new role will be "Make just enough total product, make the right ones today, make them fast and make them right the first time; while you are dong this, think of better ways."

Finance and cost accounting raise and manage capital, report company performance to interested outsiders, prepare and administer budgets, audit operations and report findings to management, provide cost data to anyone needing them and handle financial transactions with customers and suppliers. Their plates are full. Their great change will come from increased concern for value as opposed to cost. Traditional cost accounting practices record the costs of everything but the value of nothing. Data on production machinery are typical. The costs of existing and new equipment, desired return on investment, current book values, present utilization levels and assigned overhead charges are readily available. No recognition is given, however, to the value of unused capacity, to permit faster, more flexible operations and to capture new business as it becomes

 © APICS

available. Their roles must change from passive, punitive overseers to active partners in the business growth.

Top management is expected to provide strategic leadership, strong direction and good public relations. Many have become obsessed with financial manipulations in which manufacturing companies are treated just like stocks and bonds in a portfolio. Knowing "how to read the numbers" is seen by many as enough to qualify for the job. To reverse the decline of American industry, top managers must learn a new role. This will require understanding how manufacturing really works (the two flows, making enough and making the right ones) and stimulating improvements through challenging goals on higher quality, faster and more flexible operations, teamwork among functions and refusal to admit that problems cannot be solved.

The Right Choices

Manufacturing is a game of least worst choices. In problem situations, and these occur frequently, it seems that there are never good alternatives. Problem solving involves defining the available alternatives and selecting the least worst. It is very important to see all of the alternatives; this is not easy, particularly when the manufacturing process itself is not well understood. It is not easy either to identify all the relevant factors to be considered in selecting one alternative. To illustrate, let's consider three problems.

Problem #1—The Big New Order: A fine, large order has just been received for quick delivery. Unfortunately, it will overload the plant in the periods in which it will be processed. What choices are available?

*Refuse to accept it—this is a non-alternative which no management will consider.

*Accept it and release it for production. Implicitly this denies the validity of data indicating overloads and expresses blind faith that all will be well. This is the most common choice, resulting in all the serious problems described in the beginning of this paper.

*Analyze the overloads and get additional resources needed. This will require overtime, adding workers, subcontracting work or using alternative (less efficient) operations. Lots of data must be available for quick analysis.

*Trade off with other customers orders for the same of very similar equipment, delaying them until resources are available later. If these customers' current real needs permit the delay, the problem goes away. If not, the problem devolves into selecting which customers' delayed delivery will do the least harm.

*Use a combination of the last two choices to minimize the number of delayed shipment and also the extra cost of adding resources.

The Right Choice—This will attempt to avoid or at least minimize the need to change plans by significant amounts. Knowledge of customers' present real needs is essential; this will usually be different from those perceived when orders are placed well in advance. Successful companies will be flexible and fast to adjust to customers' real needs. This requires ready sources of needed resources, including contingency plans made in advance of need, unused capacity in critical machines, additional (temporary?) workers and willing subcontractors. Very important are accurate data and a system to access pertinent records easily and quickly.

Problem #2—The Tortoise Syndrome: It is taking too long to deliver products after receipt of customers' orders, jeopardizing competitive position. What are the alternative actions available to management?

*Advertise other product and service features better than competitors. If strong advantages are available, this might attract many customers but certainly not all.

*Cut prices to offset slow deliveries, reducing profit margins unless costs can be cut. Competitors may match the price cuts. Even if they do not, some customers may still be lost.

*Reduce delivery times by attacking all delays in information and material processing. The time taken and costs incurred must be balanced against the benefits. The first actions taken should get the most benefits for the least efforts. In-depth knowledge of the manufacturing process is required to carry this off.

The Right Choice—The last alternative is the least worst for both the short and long term. Fast delivery is now and will continue to be as important to customers as price, quality and other product and service features. Other choices at best simply postpone the inevitable loss of market share. The starting points are unnecessary delays. In paperwork processing, these can be eliminated quickly by small employee teams finding and fixing bottlenecks and unbalanced flows and speeding processing through use of computer and data handling equipment. In material flow, excess Work-in-Process can be cut out quickly by input/output control based on rough-cut capacity planning. Long storage times can be trimmed by changing planning lead times. Benefits will come fast and will include capital freed up, higher worker productivity, lower overhead costs, less obsolescence and more on-time deliveries to customers.

The Critical Machine: A major piece of plant equipment has become heavily loaded and a new machine is both expensive and has long delivery. What are the available choices?

*Transfer part of the load to other machines or to subcontractors with the same equipment. This will raise costs.

*Implement a computer scheduling program to optimize the use of the machine. At best, this is an expensive, temporary fix unless the overload is caused solely by poor scheduling.

*Eliminate delays in machine use due to trivial causes, including poor maintenance, tool troubles, work-holding fixture problems and lack of materials and operators.

*Cut setup and changeover times to reduce idle machine time. The cost of tooling redesign and work station reorganization will be a factor and this approach may take time.

*Redesign the products to avoid components machined on this equipment. This will involve busy design engineers, may increase costs and take a long time to implement the changes.

The Right Choice—First, eliminate all wastes of running time from trivial causes; this commonly overlooked action achieves significant benefits at little or no cost. Next, reduce setup times by separating internal elements (must be done with machine stopped) from external (can be made with machine running), converting internal elements to external, organizing tool, fixture and material layout and retraining workers to get the job done quickly. Setup cuts from hours to minutes can be achieved quickly at minimum expense and can increase machine capacity by 25% or more. Study product redesign for long term benefits, not stopgap measures.

Conclusion

Choosing between making too much and making too little seems the only alternative to managers who lack understanding of the manufacturing process. The only proper choice is to make just enough to satisfy current customers' real needs.

Material shortages and threatened late deliveries of products to customers focus attention on priority planning and control techniques. These are very often only symptoms of inadequate capacity. Capacity planning and control, insuring the ability to make enough in total, is a prerequisite to making the right items. Most companies neglect this function.

Rough-cut capacity planning techniques are simple and effective. When they are linked to input/output control, material flow can be smoothed out and speeded up. The benefits include less capital in Work-in-Process, shorter cycle times, more valid plans, lower costs and improved delivery to customers.

Teamwork among all major organizational groups is necessary to make the best plans and execute them quickly and well. The process of identifying all available alternatives in problem situations and choosing the least worst is essential. Companies who know how to do this well can make just enough, meaning only what customers need now.

About the author

George W. Plossl, CFPIM, is founder and president of G. W. Plossl & Company in Atlanta, Georgia. He is the only pioneer still active in this field of manufacturing planning and control. His work over three decades for APICS, including leading the initial six years of the Certification Program, organizing and working in the MRP Crusade, preparing special reports, editing bibliographies and chapters in the Handbook, was recognized by Honorary Membership in APICS and life membership in the Atlanta Chapter.

His counseling clients have included practically all of the Fortune 500 firms. Counseling, seminars and speaking assignments have taken him to every industrial country in the Western world. He is famous for clear, dynamic, practical and humorous treatment of his subjects.

His book, Production & Inventory Control: Principles & Techniques, is often called the Bible of the field. His other published works, including five books and numerous articles, are acclaimed as thorough, practical and useful to both educational and operational people at all levels in manufacturing organizations.

Reprinted from the APICS 1991 *Conference Proceedings.*

Throughput: The Key to JIT

Nicholas M. Testa Jr.

Introduction

In the late 1970's American business began to recognize the great advances in manufacturing technique that were being practiced in Japan. Visit after visit was made to Japan by management experts to learn the secret. Various elements of the Japanese experience were brought back and touted as the reason for their success. Quality circles, Kanban, SPC, Zero Inventory, the Japanese work ethic, and others were among these. Each of these had its followers. Dr. William Ochi wrote a book, Theory Z, comparing and analyzing the differences between the two societies and how a unique American approach was developing. Dr. Demming, who taught the Japanese Statistical Process Control, has his 14 Points and Crosby, who wrote Quality is Free and other management classics, has his 14 Steps. What is the underlying thread that makes these things work as an integrated whole?

Throughput is the answer. The goal of throughput is getting the product through the entire process in the least amount of time. In a recent newspaper article, new software was discussed that would allow the design of clothes from thread to finished product in one integrated step. The advantage was the ability to respond more quickly to the constantly changing directions in style. The important element is that the process is now faster and that is called throughput improvement, Throughput improvement means meeting the customers needs with a smaller amount of resources, time, and inventory.

We shall review the traditional thinking and why it heads us in the wrong direction. We shall examine the concepts of throughput, its use as a measuring tool, and its optimization.

Lot Sizing and Setup

In the first half of this century the concepts of manufacturing engineering evolved. Time and motion studies became popular. They focused on the elements of work. This gave rise to management thinking that the way to reduce costs was to eliminate these work elements and "engineer" a faster way to get the job done. Cost accounting was called upon to provide management with measures of these operations. Managements attention was directed to achieving the lowest piece price. Cost accounting's job was to collect these individual minimum cost elements and total them into product costs. No attention was paid to the direct or indirect cost of the unused material.

Production and Materials were charged with making product at the lowest cost. This focused Production on long continuous production runs. Production was encouraged to spend money on capital equipment that would enable them to make product at very small piece costs. This led to more and more complex machines. These were invariably designed to call for longer and longer setups but that was considered the price that had to be paid to get the piece cost down as low as possible. Longer setup times called for longer production runs to amortize the setup cost over larger quantities. A truly vicious circle was created.

The similar thinking in Material was embodied in the EOQ formula. EOQ calls on the Material staff to place purchases for the quantities that will be the best balance between ordering and carrying costs. Since the vendors were using price breaks to encourage larger buys to keep those setups amortized, this provided further encouragement in purchasing to buy larger lots of material.

Having the Right Items

What these analyses assume is that all the inventory is of equal value or worth over time and that the company will not be constrained in meeting its customer desires even if those desired are different from the "on hands" inventory. This is easily solved in traditional systems by carrying inventory of various products. That way product is always available no matter what the customer wants. Marketing is happy but inventory is skyrocketing.

I was recently in a plant where each supervisor was allowed to plan departmental production to meet what the "customer," the next department, might need. There was no communication of need. The supervisors just made their own guesses. Many of the departments had significant capital equipment and they were sure to make the runs as economical as possible. Management helped this along by measuring piece cost and evaluating each supervisor on it. Although the product took minutes to manufacture, it took weeks to get through the factory. The actual production areas were hard to find in the factory due to the nearly 20 foot high walls of inventory creating a maze on the factory floor. Each operation was running at its economical best, but the factory was very inefficient. The plant was closed and the workers discharged. This was an extreme example of suboptimiztion.

MRP and JIT

Most companies today use MRP systems to coordinate their internal department activities. They allow themselves the indulgence of buffer stocks, safety stocks, and other inventory excesses to cover up their problems. Zero Inventory programs start by working on the symptom, not the cause of the problems. To be effective these programs must attack the reason why the inventory was created. If a company is not careful, Zero Inventory can become a dangerous brut force game. It calls for navigating the company's ship around the business inventory lake while avoiding the rocks that pop up. As you drain the inventory out of the system more and more rocks and problems, appear.

Traditional techniques are not wrong. They are not looking at a broad enough perspective. For example, for many years there was a debate as to the compatibility of MRP and JIT. The two systems seemed to differ and call for different actions. MRP is more tolerant of management and planning errors. It provides a means of blanketing problem areas with inventory. Taken to its limiting case of a lot size of one, no safety stocks, no setup time, and no queue time the MRP results are identical to JIT.

MRP is the time phasing of material requirements. Since both MRP and JIT are similar when stripped of their inventories causing padding, we can examine the elements in the previous paragraph to better understand throughput

Time to Produce and Throughput

Most manufacturing systems have cost accounting modules that collect and report the time it take to make the product. In other cases the factory will have to be relied upon to know how long it takes to make the product. If neither of those methods work, an engineer can conduct a time and motion study or a sample product can be timed. In any case, the direct labor put into the product can be identified. To this one must add any time that the product must spend in nonlabor processes. Examples of these are drying time, burn in time, or curing time. These processes continue without labor but the product must spend time in them in addition to the time when labor is being applied. The combination of this labor time and process time is the "time to produce" the product.

In most companies this is a relatively small length of time compared to the time the product takes to transit the factory from the purchase of raw material to the shipment of finished goods. This longer time is the current throughput time. If the time to produce is accurate in reflecting the amount of time that it actually takes to produce one product, then any time between that and the current throughput time is potentially waste and should be a target for elimination.

If one asks the senior Production Control or Master Scheduling staff of a company how quickly they could get a rush order through the factory with no compromise in quality in an emergency, they will probably answer with some pride that is would take much less than the normal lead time. Their pride is in the knowledge that they can get the product around all the delays (times when the product is not being worked on but is sitting idle). Those very delays should be removed from the regular production to get all the product out in the shorter time. Each additional second that product is in the factory represents money that has to be spent in carrying costs, material movement, and expediting. It also presents an opportunity for people to spend money on it unnecessarily. Examples would be conveyors to handle queues, racks and shelves to neatly store waiting material, packaging for storage, counting, and sorting good from bad.

If there is a defined need for one item and two are built as a lot to satisfy some lot size rule, the throughput time will be about double the time to produce. Think about how this can be multiplied if one applies EOQ to every part in the factory in an attempt to reduce the per piece costs of setups. As the bill of material is stepped through and each process or order is optimized to the EOQ quantity, the next one in line will optimize to an even higher quantity. Keep in mind that the EOQ logic is by definition a "round-up" process never a "round-down." Throughput time will lengthen as the factory has to deal with this inventory that is "economically" produced but not needed. Each level or process step will compound the quantity.

Safety stock, which most MRP's put before first period demand, is product for which there is no need. It is insurance against unforeseen demand or supply variations. Any time spent working on this product, before product with real demand, is pure waste. This wasted time must be added to the time needed to make the correct product and this total time is the current throughput time for the product. It increases the difference between the time to produce and the throughput.

Then there are the queue and wait times that are handled so nicely by MRP systems. These are "cop-out" inventories. Someone, probably management, has not done their job in getting the process in balance. Inventory pools have been created to cover up this shortcoming. Balance the line, synchronize the process and get rid of this inventory as soon as possible.

It does not take many of these examples to bring home the message. A lot of the things we have been doing for years in the name of efficiency and making the individual processes more efficient are at the expense of throughput. It takes longer and longer to produce the product by lengthening the time it takes to get the product through the entire process.

I was once asked to settle a debate between a master scheduler and production control manager over the merits of using safety lead time instead of safety stock. Time and inventory are directly related. The relating factor is the planned or actual production rate. The longer the product is in the factory, the higher the inventory will be. Conversely, reducing throughput will reduce inventory.

Using the Throughput Key

To begin the process, obtain the time to produce and the present throughput time for the product or products to be improved. The difference between these is the easiest and quickest place to make progress. It is an excellent idea to post this data and keep track of improvement as time progresses. A chart of this information will serve as the measurement of the progress on the program. Applying Pareto's Law to the elements of the difference will focus attention on the largest contributing elements.

Once material enters the plant it should never rest. Each employee should work on the product and pass it to the next employee who will do the next task. If the product is resting anywhere (not being worked on), then waste exists and can be eliminated. JIT's Kanban system as modified by Hewlett Packard to Kanban Squares is an excellent means of synchronizing the internal operations.

Keeping these things in mind, a multilevel approach can get things going quickly. Top management must address system simplification and quality without compromise. Middle management and the technical experts will have to attack the setup design, lead and queue time removal. The workers and their immediate supervisors can improve ways they are doing the task from simple changes in positioning to new tools or procedure changes.

The single unifying idea on which all of these groups must focus is "How can we reduce the throughput time?" This applies to each step, operation, and interoperational activity in the plant.

Top Management Tasks

Top Management must do all of those familiar things, such as involvement, commitment, support, and providing resources, which are required for a successful project. In addition they must pursue three major project areas. First, they must be willing to give up the traditional cost accounting driven concepts of efficiency based upon piece cost minimization in each process. Secondly, they must look at company systems, procedures, and computer programs with the goal of simplifying them by answering the question: "How can we reduce the throughput time?" Thirdly, Top Management must also insist on quality without compromise. This is not asking for ultimate perfection but an unswerving commitment to conform to the customer's expectations or stated specifications. A solid quality program must be in place to insure that the waste of rework and short cuts that reduce product quality are avoided.

Middle Management & Technical Experts

This group will be involved in implementation of the projects of the Top Management group. In addition they will have the responsibility of designing the changes needed in set up processes. The Japanese call this Single Minute Exchange of Dies, SMED. It is necessary to reduce setup everywhere, not just in "die" operations. The concepts, though, are the same. The shorter the setup time and the less costly the setup, the smaller the number of units over which the setup must be spread. Even is EOQ formulas are used, the recommended order quantity will go toward one as the cost to order (setup cost) goes to zero.

Managers and Experts who form this group must also change the processes to eliminate the queue times and any other "sitting around" that the product may do. This may include a campaign to remove shelving. Most shelving is only a place to collect excess inventory. Conveyor systems may serve exactly the same purpose. There must be a valid value adding reason to move product on a conveyor. If not, the conveyer is merely a very expensive shelf. This group of people is the closest to the design and management of the systems and processes and can find and eliminate wasted time in these areas.

Workers and Their Immediate Supervisors

There is a vast opportunity at this level for improvement. In most companies this group is not empowered to seek out and make any improvements. This has to be changed. They must be encouraged to look for both large and small opportunities. That same question must be asked: "How can we reduce the throughput time?" This can take the form of changing the way the work is done in a work center. It could be the addition of new or specialized tools or aids to do the job better, faster, or in a higher quality fashion.

Measurement

Measurement should be as simple as possible and should be from receiving dock to shipping dock. One of the easiest methods is to use the time to produce. It can be set as the goal and the throughput can be reduced until it reaches the time to produce. Some of the waste elimination projects will also reduce the time to produce so even this target will tend to decrease as the improvements are made.

Another method is to insert a test or marked unit in the production run and time its completion of the process. In one factory I simply chalked numbers on the side of truck bodies as they passed down a production line. If you use these sampling techniques they should be applied in regular daily or weekly increments. If your company has sophisticated systems for collecting data, these can provide outputs to monitor. In all cases, plot the results in a visible location so everyone can take part of the ownership in the results.

A Simple Action Plan

When each of us managers walks around the factory floor, through the office areas, or even do our own jobs at our desks, each task should bring a question. The question should be: "How can we reduce the throughput time?" We must ask that question of our subordinates, our peers and ourselves. Everything we do in MRP, JIT, SPC, TQC, and Zero Inventory should be measured by improving throughput. Throughput crosses all of these boundaries and is a good measure in all of these systems.

About the author

NICHOLAS M. TESTA, JR.

Nick has twenty-nine years of manufacturing experience. He holds a BS in Physics from the University of Santa Clara, an MBA from the University of Southern California, teaching credentials in Business and Electronics and a Certificate in Production and Inventory Control from California State University at Fullerton. He is certified at the Fellow level by APICS. He has served as an instructor in management at California State University at Fullerton. Nick is an internationally known speaker on such topics as JIT, TQC, SPC, inventory levels, service parts, production control interfaces and careers in materials management. He was Chairman of the 1984 APICS 27th Annual International Conference.

Nick held various engineering and management positions at North American Aviation, now part of Rockwell International, Becton Dickenson, Endevco Division, Xerox Corporation, and Sargent Industries. As Manufacturing Planning and Control Manager at the Gar Wood Division of Sargent, his duties included the development and implementation of their MRP system. Nick joined the American Edwards Laboratories Division of American Hospital Supply Corporation as Manufacturing Control Systems Project Manager and then served as Materials Manager. He led the design and implementation of the manufacturing system including MRP and sophisticated job and operational based cost accounting. Nick also served as Manufacturing Manager before leaving to join Newport Electronics as Vice President of Operations. He was responsible for all production, quality, manufacturing engineering, material and related functions for Newport. Nick moved Newport into the world of JIT (Just-in-Time) manufacturing. Nick operated his own consulting business, Manufacturing Solutions, which specialized in Management, Materials, and Systems consulting. He is currently the Director of Operations at Checks in the Mail.

Reprinted from APICS 1990 *Conference Proceedings.*

Using Push and Pull Strategies in Combination to Manage a High-Volume, Repetitive Operation

Al Webber

The purpose of this paper is to present the effective implementation and use of a push manufacturing strategy used in combination with a pull manufacturing strategy for a high-volume, repetitive operation. The effects of this combination on material planning, production scheduling, and inventory control will be explored. The information maintenance requirements to efficiently manage these combined strategies will also be discussed. Lastly, the potential benefits from this project will be presented.

Business Background

The Safety Products Business of the E-A-R Division of Cabot Corporation, headquartered in Indianapolis, Indiana, manufactures a variety of hearing protection products for use in the industrial and consumer market places. Demand for these products is world-wide.

A make-to-stock manufacturing strategy is employed by the Safety Products business. The sales strategy used is to ship orders within 24 hours of receipt. The processes in place are high-volume repetitive.

Because of an increase in demand for current products and a significant growth in new products, a business decision was made to move the Safety Products operations from the facility it jointly occupied with another of the E-A-R Division's businesses into a new facility. Just-in-Time manufacturing practices were designed into the operations at the new facility. A plan was also put together to implement a formal MRP system to support the manufacturing operations.

Material Flow

In the new plant, much effort went into coming up with a layout that minimized the number of times material was handled. Some of this was accomplished by establishing process flows for product lines and reducing the number of times material was handled as well as the travel distances. The overall material flow into and out of the plant was also considered and a resulting material flow that was short, simple and organized was established. See Figure 1.

In order to eliminate "material congestion," incoming materials are received into three different locations in the new plant rather than 1 as in the old facility. As they come in, materials are located near the equipment that will be using them. This eliminates extra handling steps. Interplant material is handled only once after it is produced and is also located near the equipment that will use it. Again, extra handling steps are avoided.

Lastly, all finished goods that are produced flow into one finished goods area in the plant from two different directions. Shipments are made from this finished goods area through dock doors that are used only for shipments since all receiving is done at three different locations in the plant. The net result of all this activity is a short, simple and well organized material flow with a minimum number of handling operations.

Overall Material Control Strategies

Both Push and Pull strategies are being used to control production and materials in E-A-R Safety Products operations. An overall layout of these strategies is illustrated in Figure 2. According to the APICS dictionary, a push system in production refers to the manufacturing of items at the times required by a schedule that was planned in advance. For materials, a push system refers to the issue of material according to a given schedule.

A pull system in production refers to the producing of items only as demanded for use or to replace those taken for use. In material control, it refers to the withdrawal of inventory as demanded by the using operation.

At E-A-R, push strategies are implemented using both Master Production Scheduling and Material Requirements Planning. Pull strategies use the pick list for customer orders, rate schedules for continuously-run products, and Kanban as the means to effectively control production and materials. Each of these strategies will be explored in more detail.

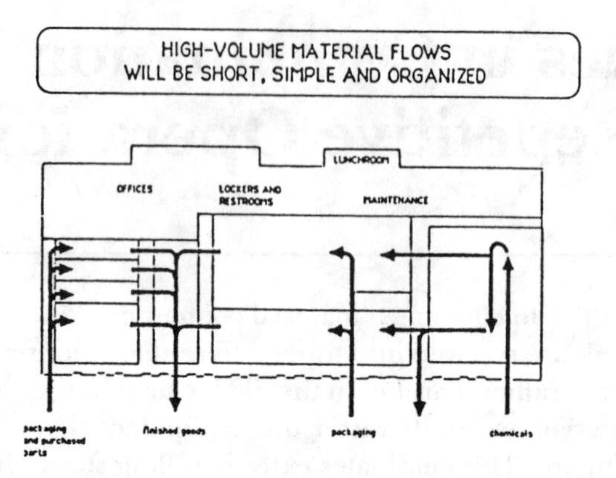

Figure 1

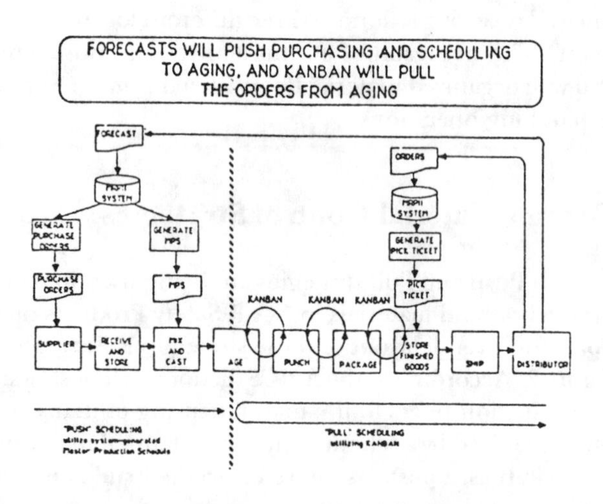

Figure 2

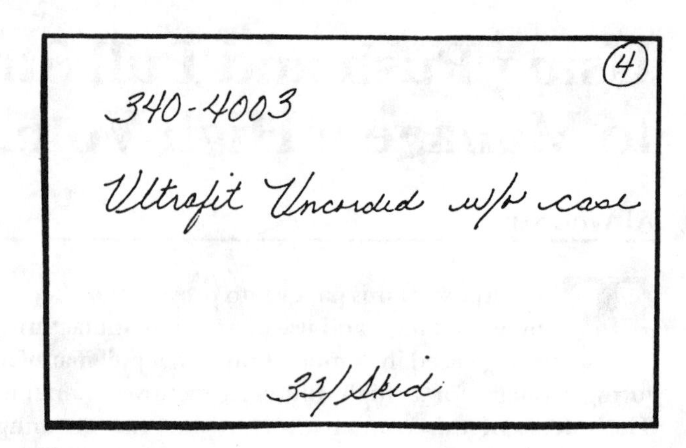

Figure 3

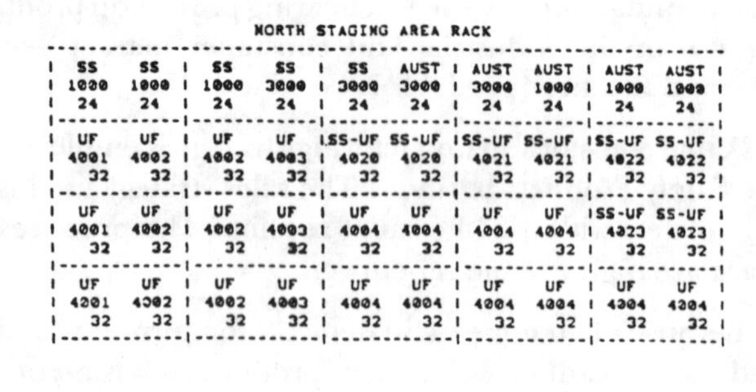

NORTH STAGING AREA RACK

SS 1000 24	SS 1000 24	SS 1000 24	SS 3000 24	SS 3000 24	AUST 3000 24	AUST 3000 24	AUST 1000 24	AUST 1000 24	AUST 1000 24
UF 4001 32	UF 4002 32	UF 4002 32	UF 4003 32	SS-UF 4020 32	SS-UF 4020 32	SS-UF 4021 32	SS-UF 4021 32	SS-UF 4022 32	SS-UF 4022 32
UF 4001 32	UF 4002 32	UF 4002 32	UF 4003 32	UF 4004 32	UF 4004 32	UF 4004 32	UF 4004 32	SS-UF 4023 32	SS-UF 4023 32
UF 4201 32	UF 4302 32	UF 4002 32	UF 4003 32	UF 4004 32	UF 4004 32	UF 4004 32	UF 4004 32	UF 4304 32	UF 4204 32

Figure 4

Pick Lists Used To Pull Finished Goods

In a make-to-stock environment, products are manufactured before the receipt of customer orders and are shipped "off the shelf" after the customer orders are received. In most organizations, orders from customers are entered into an order entry system and a pick list is generated. The finished goods as specified in the pick list are then PULLED from inventory and shipped to meet the customer requirements.

Kanban Used To Pull WIP

Kanban is a method of Just-in-Time production control which uses standard containers, locations or locations with a single card assigned to each. When the container or location is empty, Kanban signals production or a vendor to manufacture the item to replenish stock.

Kanban Cards

At E-A-R, Kanban cards are used to schedule most non-continuously-run finished goods. Figure 3 shows a sample

PARAMETER	TIMING
Safety stocks	6 mos.
FG Kanban levels	3 mos.
WIP Kanban levels	3 mos.
WIP inventory levels	1 mos.
MRP order quantities	As Req'd
Rate schedules	Weekly
Master schedules	Weekly
MRP runs	Weekly
Kanban card checks	Daily
Kanban area checks	Daily
Kanban container checks	Continuous

Figure 5

Kanban card. A Kanban card is assigned to a location in the finished goods rack area. All locations in the finished goods area racks are assigned to different products (see Figure 4). The number of racks assigned to each finished goods item is based on past sales history, forecasted sales, and the manufacturing or purchasing lead time.

The number of locations designated for each item is set so that inventory is always available for shipping while new stock is being produced. Each item is assigned a minimum of two locations so that when one location is empty and being replenished, the other location is available for shipments. All items are reviewed quarterly and the number of locations adjusted accordingly.

Kanban Areas

While every attempt was made to eliminate the need for sub-assemblies in our Just-in-Time manufacturing processes, a small number of work-in-process items were identified. Some of these items are needed in the production of several end products. Others have a long manufacturing lead time. To minimize the number of finished goods locations needed to meet customer requirements and to minimize overall inventory investment, a few WIP items do exist.

Kanban areas are used to control a number of WIP items. In one instance, one 50-foot row in the finished goods area is divided in half. When one half of the row is empty, this visually signals to production to make more product and fill it up again.

In another instance, several small 10-foot rows along a wall in the production room are identified for another WIP item. Whenever any of the rows are empty, production again is visually signalled to start up manufacturing to replenish the stock. In most instances this WIP item is continuously manufactured. In the past though, it would frequently be over-made and excess inventory would start accumulating. This condition will no longer occur using a Kanban area.

Kanban Containers

Several purchased parts and a number of manufactured WIP items are controlled using a fixed number of containers for each item. When a container is emptied in manufacturing, it is either sent back to the manufacturing point in the plant or sent back to the appropriate vendor to be refilled. The item number of the part to be produced, description of the part, and quantity to be produced are on each container. The number of containers assigned to each part is based on usage. Each item is reviewed at least quarterly to insure that not too many or too few containers are in use. Containers are also reviewed whenever the master schedules for the products using the containerized materials are changed.

Rate Scheduling Used To Pull Raw Materials

Only a few items make up the bulk of the items sold and manufactured. Because of this fact and the high volume that these products represent, these items are run continuously. Rate schedules exist for all continuously-run products. These rates are based on forecasts of demand and finished goods inventory levels, and the capacity available to build the products. The rates are checked weekly but are only modified whenever there is a significant change in demand, finished goods inventory forecasts, or available capacity.

The rate schedules for continuously-run products are fed directly into MRP to schedule materials. Materials are then pulled to meet the rates set for these continuously-run products. Since the rates change infrequently, many opportunities exist to control inventory levels to a minimum and to take advantage of volume discounts and blanket orders more frequently. When the rates do require modification, only small changes are usually felt by MRP.

Master Scheduling/MRP Used to Push Materials

A number of items used in the manufacture of several end products are capacity-constrained in their manufacture or require an aging time before they can be used. Because of these factors and the desire to NEVER run out of these materials, each has its own master schedule.These master schedules are based on forecasted customer demands and WIP inventory levels. These master schedules are then exploded into MRP to push materials into inventory. Either rate schedules or Kanban will use these materials in the production of other products.

WIP inventory levels for master scheduled items are set based on forecasted peak demand. A safety stock is also set that is equal to the amount of material that would be needed to run the down-line operations at full capacity. Normally, this level equals 7-day production less 5-day production times the delivery lead time. This safety stock is needed because Kanban could call for full capacity during peak times.

Maintenance Requirements

In order for a combined push/pull system to operate effectively, certain operating parameters need to be checked and updated on a periodic basis. A summary of some of these parameters and review periods are:

IN THE LONG-TERM, THE NUMBER OF INVENTORY TRANSACTION LOCATIONS COULD BE CUT BY MORE THAN HALF

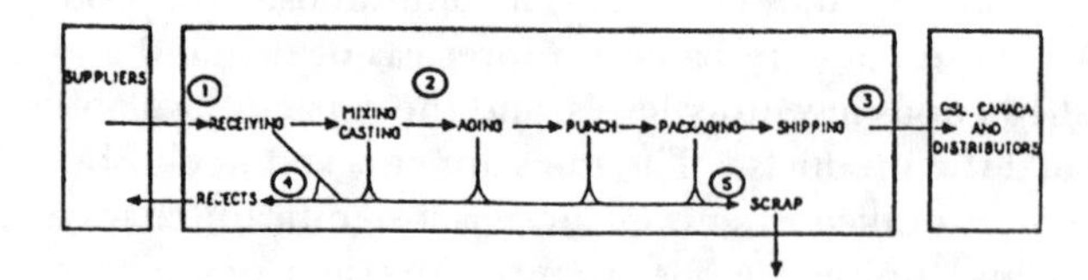

Of course, whenever other significant changes occur, it may necessitate changing parameters more frequently. Examples of significant changes include:

Master schedule changes

Vendor delivery problems

Increased/decreased customer demand

Loss of manufacturing capacity

Excess scrap

Too efficient manufacturing

Whenever possible, parameter changes should be kept to a minimum or avoided when the changes are small. Minimizing changes, just as ignoring small, frequent MRP messages, leads to better delivery performance from manufacturing and vendors.

Benefits

Several benefits resulted from using the different push/pull systems that were implemented at E-A-R. Some of these include:

1. On-time shipments improved from 67% to 100%.
2. Backorders were reduced from 33% of monthly shipment volume to 0.
3. Only 5 inventory points are required for inventory control (see figure 5).
4. Bill-of-Materials are very flat.
5. Scheduling is simplified.
6. MRP runs are much less complicated.

Summary

Push and Pull systems can be used in combination with each other in managing a high-volume, repetitive operation. In fact, they can be used with each other in managing most types of operations. The single most important rule in trying to determine the best method in which to control a manufacturing operation is to break the entire process down into the smallest steps possible, then to control each individual step with the best system for that function. Too many times, a solution is identified for an entire process, then the same solution is applied to all down-stream operations. This may be efficient in not having to implement more than a single system, but is not very effective in optimizing the total operation. Also, the implementation and use of several simple systems is often much easier to manage than a larger system that is set up to handle several different requirements.

About the author

Al Webber is Materials Manager for the E-A-R Division of Cabot Corporation in Indianapolis, Indiana. Prior to joining Cabot, he held positions in Materials, Engineering and Systems for Corning Glass Works and The Wickes Company.

Mr. Webber has a BS in Aeronautical Engineering and an MS in Industrial Engineering from Purdue University. He has participated in several MRP II implementations from both the functional and systems areas. He has taught classes on Manufacturing Resource Planning (MRP II), Forecasting and the Implementation of Systems. He has also taught business, statistics and data processing courses for the University of South Carolina and Pepperdine University.

Mr. Webber is certified in Production and Inventory Control (CPIM) by APICS, has been an APICS member for the past 13 years and a past APICS Chapter President, Vice President of Programs and Vice President of Seminars. He is also a speaker at APICS chapter meetings, seminars and conferences.

Reprinted from *APICS—The Performance Advantage,* April 1995.

Inventory—Asset or Liability?

Richard E. Crandall, CPIM, CIRM

Accounting calls inventory an asset. However, some production and operations management (POM) authorities call inventory a liability, or at least not an asset (Sharma 1993). Is one right and the other wrong, or are they talking about different things? This article describes these apparent differences and explains how the positions between accounting and POM should be reconciled if a company is to manage its inventory effectively. It addresses the specific questions of:

- Why is inventory called an asset by accounting and never a liability?
- When is inventory considered an asset by POM? a liability?
- What is excess inventory? What are the causes of excess inventory?
- How can excess inventory be disposed of? prevented?
- What changes in management practices will be needed?

Managers who understand both the accounting and operations viewpoint of inventory will do a better job of inventory management for their company.

Background

Accounting views an asset as something a company owns, and a liability as something a company owes; therefore, inventory will always be considered as an asset by accounting. For POM purposes, an asset is something that has greater value than its cost, and is able to generate income for the company.

If inventory were always an asset, in both the accounting and POM sense, there would not be a difference in viewpoints. This ideal situation exists when finished goods inventory is readily salable and moves quickly through the distribution steps from the manufacturer to the customer. Agreement also exists when the work-in-process inventory is moving steadily through the manufacturing process without undue delays, such as in a Just-in-Time environment. Finally, both parties believe that a raw materials inventory that is compatible with the needs of manufacturing is also an asset. In essence, inventory is an asset when it includes the right quantities of the right goods at the right place at the right time.

Conversely, for POM, a liability is something that has greater potential cost than value, or its presence prevents sales of other products, thereby causing it to generate a loss of income for the company. When and how can inventory become a liability in the POM sense? A simple answer is when a company has excess inventory at any point along the value chain from raw materials to customer shipment. Rosenfield (1993) defines excess inventory as existing when "the potential value of excess stock, less the expected storage costs, does not match the salvage value." If excess inventory is viewed as a liability, there is a need to determine which inventory is excess and what can be done about it. Often a company doesn't recognize that they have excess inventory because the management reporting system (usually a part of the accounting system), does not adequately identify where and how much excess inventory exists.

Causes of Excess Inventory

How does a company end up with excess inventory? What, or who, produces it? The following examples are representative, but not exhaustive, of the causes of excess inventory.

- Marketing—Marketing may want to have inventory available for a fast response to the customer, or simply to have product available for immediate sale. To do this, they must forecast demand for a variety of items and, no matter how diligent they are and methodologically sound their forecast method, the resultant forecasts are never perfect. Consequently, some finished goods inventory does not move as expected and eventually becomes unnecessary, or excess. Another possibility is that new products replace existing products, making obsolete the inventory of the replaced products. With the increasing emphasis on customer service and shorter lead times, it will be difficult for marketing to avoid generating excess inventories. Marketing decisions generally affect finished goods inventories.
- Production—Production may want to avoid unfavorable labor variances or to improve their labor efficiencies and machine utilizations. This can be done by producing at a level capacity load that also avoids fluctuations in the work force; however, it also produces excess inventories at times. Excess inventories also result when the manufacturing process produces good, but out-of-spec, products that can be sold only if a customer is found who can use them. The temptation is to keep and value these products even with no known customer. Finally, some processes require starting a quantity of parts higher than the order quantity to allow for process defects and assure having enough good units to ship. This often results in an excess of units that

may not be shippable but are good units. Again, the inclination is to hold these units in expectation that a repeat order will make them shippable; often, however, they end up as slow-moving, or excess, inventory. Production decisions can affect both work-in-process and finished goods inventory.

• Purchasing—Purchasing may want to buy a larger quantity to get a price discount; this can easily result in excess inventory at the raw materials or purchased parts stage. While this approach may look good in the short term, with favorable purchase price variances, it can generate excess inventories that will be costly in the long term.

• Production planning—Production planning may want to utilize available capacity in the shop. To do so, they schedule the production of standard products that are in constant demand. Eventually, some of these standard products become nonstandard, and excess inventory results. Another possible scenario is that a customer requests a manufacturer to produce and hold a certain amount of inventory, at any stage in the process, for that customer's exclusive use. While this situation implies that the manufacturer will not end up holding this special inventory, sometimes they do. Decisions by production planning can affect inventory at any stage of completion: raw materials, work-in-process, or finished goods.

The conditions described above, and others, can lead to excess inventories. Often, the different functions within an organization are in conflict about how much inventory to have. Top management may have to choose a compromise position with respect to inventory levels and product mix. Obviously, nobody wants excess inventory or sets out to create it. But what are the reasons behind its creation?

Why is Excess Inventory Created?

Sometimes, the performance measures used in a company cause the buildup of inventory to be attractive. For example, most companies use income, or costs, as a measure of performance, especially for production managers, purchasing agents and marketing managers. These groups tend to focus more attention on the income statement than on the balance sheet. If the level of inventory does not change, there is no effect on income. An increase in the level of inventory often increases income because it reduces the unfavorable labor and overhead variances that occur when there is erratic or less-than-ideal capacity levels of production. Conversely, a reduction in the level of inventory often causes a reduction in income by introducing variable work loads and unused capacity, causing unfavorable labor and overhead variances. Fry (1992) provides an excellent explanation of this effect.

While the increase in inventories generates income, it has the opposite effect on cash flows by decreasing available cash. A reduction in inventories has the reverse effect—a positive cash flow. This presents a conflict in that managers in most companies use income more as a measure of performance than cash flow. However, the ultimate measure of a company's value is its cash flow—a position that accounting understands but does not always communicate to the rest of the organization.

Another cause of excess inventories is the mistaken idea that having inventory on hand is always desirable. Most persons view assets as something good, and liabilities as something bad. A better way is to view inventory as stored costs that will eventually be charged to the income statement. Inventory buildup, then, is a way of postponing the reporting of costs until those costs are, in theory, matched against the sales to which they belong. The Accounting Review Board Ruling 43 says that: "In accounting for the goods in the inventory at any point of time, the major objective is the matching of appropriate costs against revenues in order that there may be a proper determination of the realized income."

The present methods used to value inventory are limited in helping us to deal with excess inventories.

How is Inventory Valued?

Two questions need to be addressed in deciding how to value inventory: (1) Is the individual unit of inventory correctly valued, or has excess cost been assigned to each unit? and (2) Does the inventory contain excess units that should have less than full value? The latter question involves evaluating the probability that the unit will be sold and when it will be sold.

These questions require a way to assign an initial value to the unit, and some way to revalue the units as the units remain in inventory unsold.

Initial Valuation

Accounting provides two ways of valuing inventory: cost or market value, whichever is lower. The lower value purports to provide a conservative value for the company and its reported income. While conservatism is the objective, it may not be the result. As pointed out below, full absorption costing is the least conservative way of valuing inventory of the methods described, yet it is the only one generally accepted by accounting practice.

Market value—Market value is not a practical way to value inventory, in most cases. It not only requires a way to determine the market value of inventory but also a way of adjusting the value of inventory as the market value fluctuates. Trying to develop a dynamic (adjusted through time) estimate of this factor is beyond the capability of most accounting departments. As a result, most companies do not attempt to use market value of inventory as an ongoing valuation method.

Cost value—One of the key decisions in valuing inventory is to decide which costs should be stored. These costs include direct materials, direct labor, and fixed and variable overhead expenses. Historically, accounting practice required that all of the above elements be assigned to the product and stored in inventory until the product is sold. In recent years, several alternative viewpoints have been proposed: activity-based costing (ABC), direct costing and theory of constraints (TOC).

- **Activity-based costing (ABC).** This supports the traditional approach of assigning all overhead costs to the product and storing them in inventory; however, it questions the methods of allocating the overhead expenses to the products. This approach allocates the overhead expenses differently, and goes beyond just cost allocation to emphasize a closer analysis of overhead to eliminate the non-value-added portion as unnecessary.
- **Direct costing.** Many management accountants like this costing method for use in planning, analysis and control; however, financial accountants have never accepted it as a method for valuing inventory. It advocates the assignment of fixed overhead expenses to the period in which they were incurred, and not to be stored in inventory as a product cost. This means that inventory has a lower cost value, and therefore, less impact on the income statement. It also more clearly identifies overhead elements, offering greater opportunities to reduce them.
- **Theory of constraints (TOC).** As with direct costing, this approach advocates that all overhead should be a period expense. They go further to say that even direct labor is more fixed than variable in today's manufacturing environments and should be a period expense. This means that only direct material purchase cost would be stored as costs in inventory, resulting in even lower inventory values than for direct costs. TOC also promotes the idea that only sold product that is sold (throughput) should be recognized as inventory (8).

Note: Although valuing inventory at the cost of materials may initially appear to be a very conservative valuation, it may not be. As manufacturers move more toward being final assemblers and increase their purchases of subassemblies or fabricated parts, the direct materials portion increases to a point where it represents 60-70 percent of the cost of sales (2). However, accounting practices can be misleading. Material costs to a final assembler are material, labor and overhead to a subassembler; material costs to a subassembler are material, labor and overhead to a fabricator; and material costs to a fabricator are material, labor and overhead to a materials processor. Figure 1 shows how the cumulative effect of this sequence could be to reduce the direct material content to a very low portion if one considers only the materials cost of the materials processor. The most conservative way to value inventory is at the scrap value of the raw materials used.

Each of the above positions is different from the traditional method of full absorption costing that assigns the maximum amount of cost to the product. The traditional approach stores the greatest amount of costs to be "matched" against subsequent revenue; the more recently proposed approaches store less for future release against revenue and, as a result, cause less distortion of the income statement during inventory buildup and reduction. Even more important, the three approaches listed above actively promote the analysis of overhead costs and the elimination of costs that are unnecessary. The full absorption method disguises overhead and discourages careful analysis; it is a financial accounting tool, not a management accounting tool.

The current thinking of many managers, including some accountants, is to store less costs in inventory and reduce the impact of inventory changes on the income statement.

Revaluation of Inventory

Most companies use full absorption costing to value inventory. This does not present a problem if inventories are low and goods are moving smoothly through the manufacturing and distribution process. In this situation, the overhead costs are not stored in inventory very long and do not seriously affect the income statement.

However, when inventories build up and become excess to the needs of the business (when the probability that they will be sold at a price higher than their accumulated cost is low), they become liabilities and the inventory valuation should reflect this through some reevaluation process. Inventories that do not sell promptly fall into this category. However, most companies do not discriminate among inventories when assigning an initial value; they assume that all product will be sold, no matter why it was created.

Auditors attempt to assess such factors as age, potential obsolescence, damage and other degradation of inventory in assigning an overall reduction in the inventory value. However, they usually do this only during the annual audit and seldom do it in a way that would be of benefit to inventory managers in identifying the causes of excess inventory that could lead to preventing or reducing the buildup of excess inventory.

There is a need to develop a way to adjust, usually reduce, inventory values as time passes and the probability

FUNCTION	REASONS TO INCREASE	REASONS TO DECREASE
Marketing Finished goods	• Increase sales through immediate delivery • Reduce lead time to customers	• Change mix to have salable items available • Make cash available for other programs
Production Work-in-process	• Fill in low load periods to level production • Increase labor efficiency and machine utilization	• Reduce congestion on shop floor • Reduce lead times to provide faster service
Purchasing Raw materials	• Obtain quantity (volume) discounts • Reduce number of purchase orders required	• Shift emphasis from cost to quality and delivery • Reduce number of vendors to be dealt with
Production planning	• Reduce the number of late shipments to customers • Ship more from stock to meet shorter due dates • Reduce number of production orders	• Keep production capacity open for customer orders • Shorten due dates by wait times in the process • Increase flexibility to respond to customers
Accounting	• Reduce overhead volume variances • Increase working capital	• Reduce physical inventory task • Reduce cash requirements

Table 1. *Incentives to increase/decrease inventory*

of sale diminishes. While this is logical, there are practical problems that must be faced, and most companies do not have a formal way of adjusting inventory values.

A more desirable solution is to prevent the accumulation of excess inventories, i.e., prevent the problem, not find a better way to report it. How can this be done? A company must first identify which inventory is excess; then it must sell or otherwise dispose of the excess inventory; and, finally, it must establish practices that prevent the recurrence of excess inventory. Rosenfield (1993) offers a way in which excess inventory can be identified, and White (1989) describes several ways in which a company can dispose of excess inventory.

Changes Required

To reduce existing excess inventory and prevent its recurrence, a company requires changes in attitudes, objectives, performance measures, operating methods and accounting practices. It also requires the integration of various functions within the organization.

Changes in Attitudes About Inventory

Managers need to change their thinking about the desirability of having inventory versus the desirability of not having inventory. Table 1 contains a comparison of the reasons for having inventory (the traditional perspective) and the reasons for not having inventory (the contemporary perspective).

These changes in attitude come from the realization that today's competitive environment requires attention on customer service, product flexibility and product quality, as well as product cost. White (1989) describes how customer service can be improved by removing the slow-moving inventory ("sludge") from the inventory base. Beddingfield (1992) also points out the competitive advantages of improved inventory management.

Changes in Objectives

Transition from the traditional way of thinking to the contemporary requires a combination of rethinking strategic objectives and changes in the performance measurement system. Both topics are important and several authors have discussed these issues, especially Dixon et al (1990) and Vollman et al (1993). Part of this change process involves establishing global objectives that can be translated into local objectives for each organizational function, such as marketing, production, materials management and accounting. As previously mentioned, the choice of inventory level and product mix may present conflicts among functions and requires a holistic approach to reach a common objective.

Changes in Performance Measures

It is necessary for the local (functional) performance measures to be closely related to the general financial performance measures, such as income and return on investment. As previously mentioned, building inventory is a way to show improved performance in income, which is used directly, or in some related form, as a measure of performance for functional areas such as marketing, production and purchasing. If other performance measures were used, such as customer service levels, the practice of building inventories, especially the less-salable inventories, would probably decrease.

Changes in Operating Practices

Marketing, production and purchasing have to effect the needed changes to eliminate existing excess inventories and minimize the buildup of future excess inventories. To do this, they need help from the accounting function in identifying and measuring the status and causes of the excess inventories.

• Marketing—The burden of disposing of excess inventory usually falls to sales and marketing. This is not a welcome task and often has a lower priority than new product or key account programs; however, it must be done. Marketing should be among the most enthusiastic supporters of programs to prevent excess inventory. They can help by working more closely with customers to obtain better forecasts of customer demand; communicate with engineering and production about introductions of new products and phaseouts of discontinued products; participate in the reduction of production and delivery lead times to reduce the need for finished goods inventories; and become a closely integrated link in the company's planning and control system.

• Production—Several current movements in production and inventory management include a focus on reducing the level of inventories. Just-in-Time (JIT) includes a major emphasis on reducing the causes of inventory to reduce the absolute level of inventory. Materials requirements planning (MRP), when properly applied, will reduce excess and slow-moving inventory. Total quality management (TQM) attempts, among other things, to reduce the level of defects. Lower defects result in less uncertainty and fewer overruns on production orders. These programs help to reduce the cycle time from customer order to delivery and to improve on-time deliveries.

Changes in Accounting Practices

Accounting can help to identify, reduce and prevent excess inventory; however, they must change some of their practices, particularly about inventory valuation—changes necessary to make accounting information more useful to production/operations managers. These changes include how to value inventory, how to revalue inventory over time, how to reduce buildup of excess inventory through proper financial performance measures, and how income and cash flow must both be considered in planning inventory.

Initial valuation—The initial valuation of inventory should be a discriminating process to separate the planned and readily resalable product in inventory from the unplanned product with uncertain resalability. This process also should be dynamic, in that the status of certain products will evolve as they move through the product life cycle. To show the extremes of this method, a regularly sold, standard product could be valued with full absorption costs, as done currently; at the other extreme, inventory of nonstandard product generated as the result of a production overrun, could be valued at the scrap value of the material.

A factor to be considered in the initial valuation is the probability that the unit will be sold. In the standard unit described above, the assumption is that the probability of sale is near 100 percent and the unit can be assigned full cost value. In the overrun unit, the probability of sale as a completed unit is near zero, and the unit value is only the revenue generated when sold as scrap. The values for these extreme groups of products are logical; however, how about units of inventory that fall between the end groups? How does a company value them?

When the probability of sale is less than 100 percent, one approach is to value the units at some cost less than full absorption cost, such as the direct cost or the purchased material cost. This is a way of reducing the average cost of the units in inventory and allowing some costs to flow through as period expenses during the production period. However, it is an expedient method of devaluing, and does not address the logic of the situation, namely, what is the probability of sale?

Another approach is to value the units at full absorption cost and then group them in a category of "25 percent probability of sale," "50 percent probability of sale," etc. This forces an evaluation of the potential salability of the product, but it requires extensive additional attention and record keeping; however, it reflects the reality of the situation. In addition, it offers a way to assign responsibility to the source of the excess inventory, thereby suggesting a way to prevent reoccurrences.

Revaluation of inventory—The total inventory should be classified by major product lines, and by method of initial valuation. It should be reviewed regularly (higher usage, or "A" items more frequently) to decide the need for revaluation. As with the initial valuation, certain guidelines could be developed. Some parameters to be considered include the age of the inventory, its physical condition and shelf life, the degree of obsolescence, and the number of sales days on hand. These adjustments could be handled in an "Allowance for Inventory Revaluation," in much the same way as an "Allowance for Uncollectible Accounts Receivable."

While this method requires judgment, this judgment can be systematically applied, and the process will identify major areas of concern or potential liability to the company. Adjustments in inventory value are not unheard of.

Retail stores do it through the markdown procedure. This reduces the income when product is sold, and cost is matched with the sale. Wholesale companies, because of very narrow gross profit margins, sometimes revalue inventories higher when notified of price increases by suppliers. This has the effect of increasing income at the time of purchase, not at the time of sale, presumably because the inventory has increased in value. These adjustments make sense and are convenient; something similar should be done for manufacturing inventories, though it is less convenient and more difficult to determine the true value.

Clearly, the processes described above for valuation and revaluation of units of inventory would be time-consuming and an added expense; as a result, the emphasis should be on prevention of excess inventory, not accounting for it, or disposing of it. As with many problems, the best answer is avoidance, not correction.

Integration of Organization Functions

Identification, disposal and prevention of excess inventories requires a coordinated effort by all functions of a business, particularly marketing, operations and accounting. This coordinated effort starts with the strategic planning process and carries through to the day-to-day operations.

If all parties concerned were more aware of the effect of inventory changes on both income and cash flow, better decisions could be made about the best levels of inventory and the most desirable product mix. This requires better communications among the operating groups and accounting during the business planning process and recognition of the responsibilities of the marketing and production groups in the cash management program.

Inventory is not an asset to a company if it is excess inventory. The sooner production/operations management and accounting recognize this and adjust their performance measures and operating practices, the sooner companies will be motivated to identify and reduce, or better still, to prevent excess inventory.

References

1. Beddingfield, Thomas W., "Reducing Inventory Enhances Competitiveness," *APICS— The Performance Advantage*, September, 1992, pp. 28-31.
2. Dixon, J. Robb, Alfred J. Nanni and Thomas E. Vollman, *The New Performance Challenge, Measuring Operations for World-Class Competition,* Dow Jones-Irwin, Homewood, Illinois, 1990.
3. Farmer, James R., "Re-engineering, Achieving Productivity Success, *APICS —The Performance Advantage,* March, 1993, pp. 38-42.
4. Fry, Timothy D., "Manufacturing Performance and Cost Accounting," *Production and Inventory Management Journal,* Vol. 33, No. 3, pp. 30-35.
5. Gaither, Norman, *Production and Operations Management* (Fourth Edition), The Dryden Press, Chicago, 1990.
6. Jenkins, Carolyn, "Accurate Forecasting Reduces Inventory," *APICS—The Performance Advantage,* September, 1992, pp. 37-39.
7. Lee, Hau L. and Corey Billington, "Managing Supply Chain Inventory: Pitfalls and Opportunities," *Sloan Management Review*, Spring, 1992, pp. 65-73.
8. Rosenfield, Donald B., "Disposal of Excess Inventory," *Operations Research*, Vol. 37, No. 3, May-June, 1993, pp. 404-409.
9. Schaeffer, Randall, "A New View of Inventory Management," *APICS—The Performance Advantage,* January, 1993, pp. 21-24.
10. Sharma, Ken, "Adding 'Intelligence' to MRP Systems," *APICS—The Performance Advantage,* March, 1993, pp. 53-58.
11. Umble, M. Michael and M. L. Srikanth, *Synchronous Manufacturing,* SouthWestern Publishing Co., Cincinnati, 1990, p. 29.
12. Vollman, Thomas E., William L. Berry and D. Clay Whybark, *Integrated Production and Inventory Management*, Business One Irwin, Homewood, Illinois, 1993.
13. White, R. Douglas, "Streamline Inventory to Better Serve Customers," *The Journal of Business Strategy,* March/April, 1989, pp. 43-45.

Reprinted from *Production and Inventory Management*, Fourth Quarter, 1985.

The Impact of Reduced Setup Time

Yale P. Esrock

The APICS zero inventory crusade is sparking much interest in Japanese manufacturing techniques. When considering these techniques, however, universally applicable concepts must be distinguished from cultural trappings which are not readily transferable to the U.S. environment. One concept fundamental to the pursuit of stockless production in Japan and readily adopted in the United States is that machine setup times should be reduced to a minimum. The goal in Japan is known as SMED—single minute exchange of dies—which implies that setups should be performed in less than ten minutes. That this can be accomplished, even with 800-ton presses, is impressively demonstrated at some Japanese companies.

Projects to reduce setup times are not difficult to organize. Thorough analysis of the setup process and a large dose of ingenuity can often produce marked results without the necessity for large capital outlays. The big question is, why do it? Many companies may not be interested in, or may not be good candidates for, stockless production systems. So why spend the effort to reduce setup times? The fact is that setup time has a pervasive influence on manufacturing operations. Viewing setup time as a variable that can be changed and improved opens the door to a whole range of benefits, some of which will be explored below.

The following notation will be referenced in the discussions: A is the annual usage (units), S is the cost per setup, ST is the time per setup, SW is the setup wage rate (dollars per hour), C is the cost per part, i is the carrying cost (percent of unit cost), EOQ is the economic order quantity, RT is the run time per piece, LT is the lead time. Although many of the following examples use the EOQ concept to help quantify results, achieving the types of benefits described does not necessarily require its use.

Cost per Setup

The most obvious effect of reduced setup time is reduced cost per setup. Since cost per setup is the product of time per setup and the setup wage rate [Equation (1)], any reduction in setup time translates into a directly proportional reduction in cost per setup:

$$S = (ST)(SW). \qquad (1)$$

Lot Size

The well-known formula for computing economic order quantity is

$$EOQ = \sqrt{\frac{2AS}{iC}} = \sqrt{\frac{2A(ST)(SW)}{iC}} \qquad (2)$$

This relationship shows that a reduction in setup time would result in a lower EOQ. Specifically, if setup time were reduced by $K\%$, EOQ would be reduced by $100(1 - \sqrt{1 - 0.01K})\%$. For example, a 75% reduction in setup time results in an EOQ reduction of $100\ (1 - \sqrt{1 - 0.75}) = 50\%$. As a further example, if an operation had a one-hour setup and a resultant lot size of 1000 parts, reducing setup time to one minute would reduce the lot to 129 parts. Such substantial lot size reductions increase flexibility of operations, reduce space requirements, and allow earlier detection of quality problems.

Total Annual Setup Cost

While the effect of reduced setup time on cost per setup is straightforward, the effect on total annual setup cost is less obvious. Total annual setup cost (TASC) is the product of the number of setups per year and the cost per setup:

$$TASC = \frac{A(ST)(SW)}{EOQ} \qquad (3)$$

Although reducing setup time reduces the EOQ, more setups per year are required to achieve the same volume of production. The question to be answered is: do more setups at less cost per setup increase or decrease total cost?

Substituting the EOQ formula into the expression for total annual setup cost results in an expression that clearly shows the answer:

$$TASC = \sqrt{\frac{AiC(ST)(SW)}{2}} \qquad (4)$$

We see from this expression that reducing setup time also reduces total setup cost. In fact, the relationship is the same as was illustrated for the EOQ; namely, a 75% reduction in setup time reduces total annual setup cost by 50% and, depending on the method of accounting, results in lower factory overhead.

Cost of Lot Size Inventory

Lot size inventory is the stock of finished parts carried in storage as a result of producing a standard lot size (exclusive of safety stock). Assuming continuous demand and instantaneous replenishment, lot size inventory fluctuates over the replenishment cycle between a maximum value equal to the EOQ and a minimum of zero. On the average, the number of units in the lot size inventory is approximated by one-half of the EOQ, and the cost of carrying (CC) this inventory is calculated as shown below:

$$CC = \frac{iC(EOQ)}{2} = \sqrt{\frac{AiC(ST)(SW)}{2}} \qquad (5)$$

Productive Capacity

A machine, work center, or plant has a limited amount of available capacity. Of this capacity, a portion is required for setup, leaving the remainder available for actual production.

The total annual setup time (TAST) required to produce an item is derived by dividing the total annual setup cost developed earlier [Equation (4)] by the setup wage rate, as shown below:

$$TAST = \frac{TASC}{\text{Setup Wage Rate}} = \sqrt{\frac{AiC(ST)}{2(SW)}}. \qquad (6)$$

This expression shows that reducing setup time reduces total annual setup requirements. As a result, productive capacity increases and, if the work center is a bottleneck where demand exceeds capacity, profitability is improved due to higher throughput.

Observe that reduced setup simultaneously increases productive capacity and reduces inventory investment. Inventory investment can also be reduced by inflating the inventory carrying cost parameter i to force lower lot sizes; however, as Equation (6) shows, this approach has the undesirable side effect of increasing setup requirements and, thus, decreases productive capacity.

Run Time

Run time is the length of time parts spend on a machine. When processing batches or lots of parts, total run time is equal to the number of parts in the lot multiplied by the standard run time per part:

$$\text{Total Run Time} = (EOQ)(RT). \qquad (7)$$

Because reduced setup reduces the lot size, run time per lot is correspondingly reduced.

Queue Time

Queue time is the length of time a batch of parts waits for a machine to free up so that setup can begin. Total queue time for a batch is the sum of the setup and run times for those batches ahead of it at the work center. By reducing both setup and run time for those batches, reduced setup time decreases the average unproductive time that parts wait in queues. This is significant because studies show that, in many plants queue time accounts for 75-95% of total lead time.

Although queue time reduction cannot be computed exactly, the magnitude of the reduction can be estimated. First, assume the average number of jobs in queue at a work center is constant. Next, determine the ratio of average run times to average setup times for these jobs. Suppose this ratio is Q:1. The reduction in average queue time can be approximated as a weighted average of the reduction in setup and run times for the jobs in queue. If reduction in setup is denoted as RS and reduction in run time is denoted as RR, we have:

$$\text{Queue Reduction} = \frac{RS + Q(RR)}{1 + Q}. \qquad (8)$$

For example, a 75% reduction in setup time reduces job run time by 50% (due to smaller lot size). If the average job run time is four times the setup time, approximate reduction in queue time is $(0.75 + 4 \times 0.5)/(4 + 1) = 0.55$, or 55%.

(Note that this analysis has assumed that all jobs require a new setup. It can be adjusted accordingly if shared setups are prevalent.)

Wait and Move Time

Wait time is the length of time parts wait to be moved to the next work center; move time is the actual transit time. Although reduced setup time may have no significant effect on wait and move times, in some instances it can. For example, suppose production lots are of such size that it takes a fork lift two trips to move the lot to the next work center. If reduced setup allows the lot size to be cut in half only one trip will be required, thus reducing both move and wait.

Lead Time

Lead time is the total time required to complete a batch of parts, and is composed of the previously described components of setup time, run time, wait time, move time, and queue time. Since reduced setup time can affect all of these components, the impact on lead time can be substantial. With shorter lead times the plant is more flexible, can react more quickly to changes, and can be more responsive to customers.

To approximate the overall effect of reduced setup on lead time, assume move and wait times are negligible and the ratio of run time to setup time is the same used for the queue reduction calculation. Under these assumptions, the percentage reduction in total lead time equals the percentage reduction in queue time. This fact is illustrated by the example below.

Assume Lead Time = Setup + Run + Queue
Run = 4(Setup)
Setup Reduction = 75%

Element	*Before setup reduction*	*Percentage improvement*	*After setup reduction*
Setup	10	75%	2.5
Run	40	50%	20.0
Queue	100	55%	45.0
Total Lead Time	150	?	67.5

Percentage improvement in total lead time = (150 − 67.5)/150 = 55%.

Work-in-Process

The average level of work-in-process (AWIP) is directly related to lead time (in days) as follows:

$$AWIP = \frac{A(LT)}{365}. \qquad (9)$$

By reducing lead time, reduced setup results in a correspondingly lower level of work-in-process.

Safety Stock

Safety stock is inventory carried as protection against stockouts. For independent demand items which have forecasted requirements, safety stock acts as insurance against demand exceeding forecast. Because of this link, safety stock levels should be proportional to historical forecast error. That is, if forecasts are accurate, little safety stock is required; if forecast error tends to be large, higher safety stock levels are needed.

What has this to do with setup time? Forecast accuracy is measured as an average over an item's lead time and is inherently greater over shorter periods. By shortening lead time, reduced setup time improves forecast accuracy and thus lowers the requirement for safety stock.

The ultimate effect on safety stock, however occurs in one of two ways. If a manufactured component is controlled by a reorder point inventory system, the component's safety stock is influenced as described above. If the component is controlled as a dependent demand item in a material requirements planning system, the primary influence is on the safety stock of the end item in which the component is used. This occurs, however, only if the component is on the end item's critical path for lead time. In this case, reducing the component's lead time also reduces the end item's lead time, and thus its required safety stock.

Productivity

Productivity is a measure of how effectively resources are used. Although there are many measures of productivity, all compare output produced to input consumed. If the total time required to set up and run a batch of parts is B times the setup time, reducing setup time by K% increases productivity (measured by parts produced per hour) as shown in Equation (10):

Percentage increase in pieces produced per hour

$$= \frac{100(1 - \sqrt{1 - 0.01K})}{B - 1 + \sqrt{1 - 0.01K}}. \qquad (10)$$

For example, if it takes half an hour to set up and a total of 2.5 hours (including setup) to process the batch, then $B = 5$. In this case, a 75% reduction in setup time improves productivity by 100 × $(1 - \sqrt{1 - 0.75})/(5 - 1 + \sqrt{1 - 0.75})$ = 11%. The following illustration will help to better understand this effect:

Element	*Before setup reduction*	*Percentage change*	*After setup reduction*
Setup (hours)	0.5	−75%	0.125
Lot size	1000	−50%	500
Run time (min/piece)	0.12	0	0.12
Total run time (hr)	2	−50%	1
Total setup and run	2.5		1.125
Pieces per hour	400	+11%	444

Profitability

Because of the many factors that affect profitability, the bottom line impact of reducing setup times is difficult to quantify. Nevertheless, the many factors already discussed affect profitability in several ways:

- The cost of financing and carrying inventory is lower due to smaller lot sizes, improved
- Factory overhead is lower and gross margin is higher due to reduced annual setup costs and reduced space requirements.
- Sales potential is higher due to increased throughput and enhanced ability to respond quickly to customer demand.

Summary

Setup time affects many areas of manufacturing. By instituting a program aimed at substantially reducing setup times, some or all of the following benefits can accrue:

- Reduced cost per setup
- Reduced annual setup costs
- Smaller lot sizes
- Lower finished parts inventory
- Lower work-in-process inventory
- Lower safety stock levels
- Reduced space requirements
- Shorter run times
- Shorter queue times
- Shorter lead times
- Greater productive capacity
- Higher throughput
- Greater plant flexibility
- Improved forecast accuracy
- Lower factory overhead
- Increased productivity
- Increased profitability

Although each of these results is well known the full impact of reduced setup times can be appreciated only by viewing them collectively. Achievement of these benefits can more than justify the cost of a setup time reduction program and enhance the company's competitive position.

About the author

Yale P. Esrock, CPIM, is a manager in the Management Consulting Services Division of Coopers & Lybrand and is head of the manufacturing industry consulting practice in the St. Louis office. Prior to joining Coopers & Lybrand, he was a senior manufacturing consultant with McDonnell Douglas Automation Company (McAuto) and served as assistant to the president and project leader for manufacturing systems at James David Incorporated in St. Louis. He received a BS in industrial engineering from Purdue University and an MS in industrial administration from Carnegie-Mellon University.

Reprinted from *Production and Inventory Management Journal*, Vol. 25, No.3, 1984.

Lead Times Revisited

Ed Heard and George Plossl

In the never ending war against poor customer service, manufacturing inefficiency and high work-in-process, several battle cries reverberate across the sites of numerous successful and some not so successful engagements.

Lock your storeroom; clean up your data base; increase your transaction reporting accuracy!

Get realism in your master schedule!

Plan your priorities and keep them current with MRP!

Control your priorities with better dispatching; don't just expedite, de-expedite too!

Identify your effective capacities; find out how much you need!

Control your input and output; starve your gateways!

Shorten your lead times; reduce your work-in-process!

Don't commit your resources until the last possible moment!

So, management at your plant heard and heeded. MRP, CRP, I/0, a realistic master schedule, and an effective dispatching system—you have them all. In fact, your plant has made it all the way to Class A MRP user status. Customer service is up significantly, labor and materials cost as a percentage of sales is better than ever, and work-in-process is down. But, after careful scrutiny, it appears that inventory is only turning four times a year. To make matters worse, it was turning, as the controller enjoys pointing out, 3.8 times before all this started. How can this happen?

The Obvious Answer—Long Lead Times

Any time inventory turns are low, average throughput time is high. This is one of the basic truths of production and inventory control.

$$\text{Number of Inventory Turns} = \frac{\text{Cost of Goods Sold}}{\text{Average Inventory at Cost}}$$

and

$$\text{Average Throughput Time} = 1 \div \text{Number of Inventory Turns}$$

But just what is *average throughput time? It is the average length of time it takes a dollar of materials, labor, or labor-related costs to flow through a plant.* The process is initiated when raw materials are received. Until raw materials are released, no labor or labor-related costs are incurred. But, once manufacturing begins, those same materials acquire more and more value as labor and burden are added. Ultimately, completed items go into finished goods inventory and from there, are shipped. Clearly, reductions in throughput time will lead to equivalent increases in inventory turns.

The process of inventory value (cost) accumulation is illustrated in simplistic fashion in Figure 1.

The slope of the line represents an approximation of the rate at which labor cost is added to materials on the floor. The two steps in the line should be interpreted as the addition of manufacturing burden to the cost basis of the materials at intermittent points in time. (This is not necessarily the convention that is or should be followed by all inventory accounting systems; it is merely representative.) The level line segments indicate that materials do not change value while in raw material or finished good inventories.

Manufacturing Cycle Time

It is apparent from Figure 1 that throughput time consists of raw materials inventory turnover time, manufacturing cycle time, and finished goods inventory turnover time. What is not obvious from Figure 1 is that still another inventory turnover time is a major part of manufacturing cycle time. In a fabrication-subassembly-final assembly plant, materials may move into and out of stores several times between initial release to the floor and transfer to finished goods. Figure 2 portrays cost (value) accumulation for a manufacturing installation where labor and burden are applied simultaneously and where materials may move into and out of stores multiple times.

The time between order completion for a subordinate item and its consumption in an order for one of its parents is stores turnover time (zero for parts produced using lot-for-lot order policy and consumed directly on the floor in the phantom bill sense). Manufacturing cycle time is defined as the sum of the critical path activities required

FIGURE 1

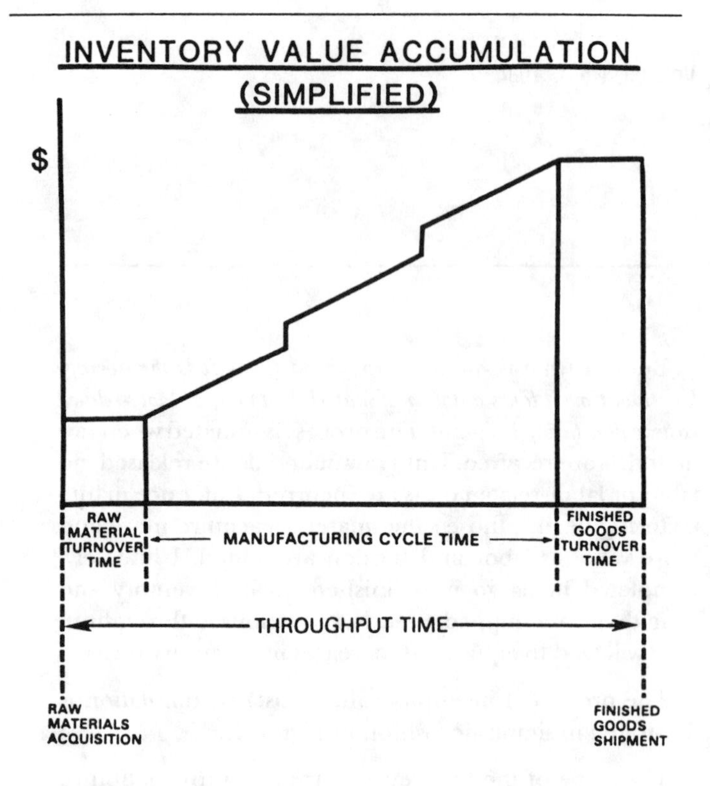

Figure 1

FIGURE 2

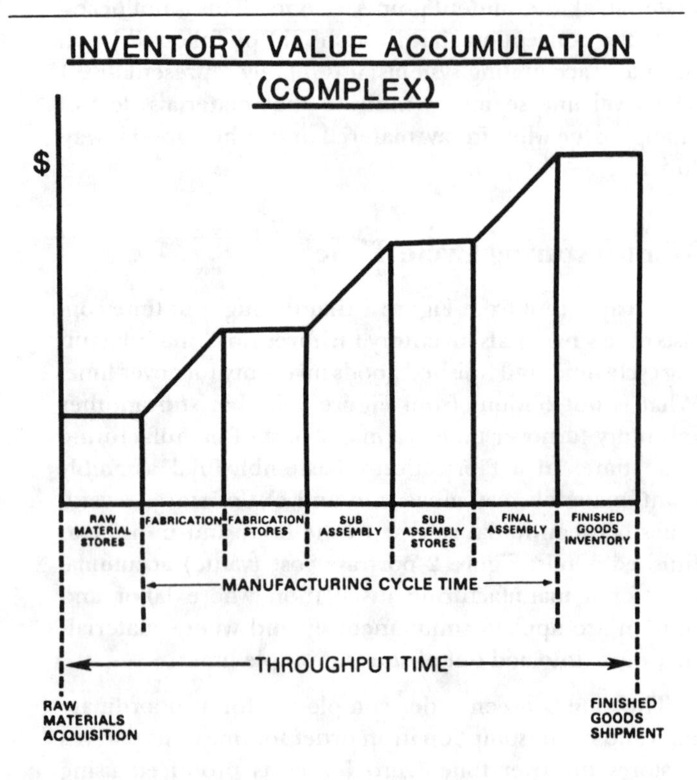

Figure 2

FIGURE 3

PLANNED LEAD TIME COMPONENTS

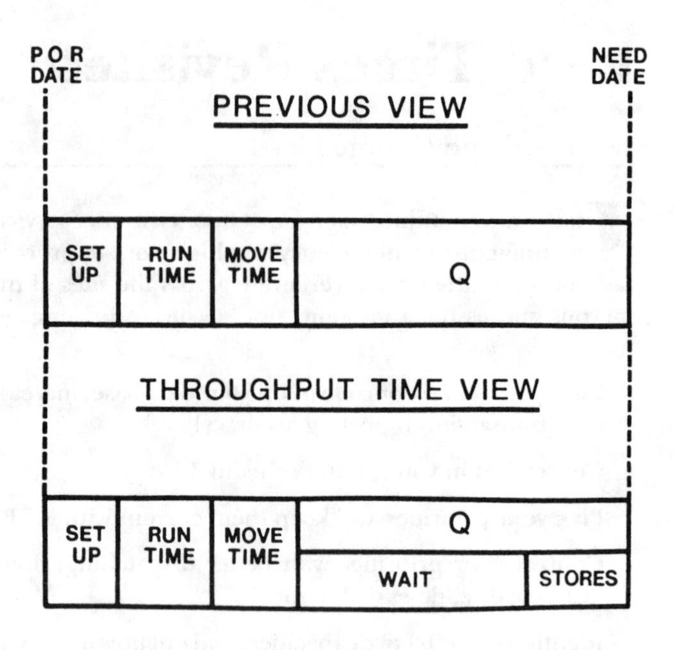

Figure 3

to produce a product. Consequently, when subordinate parts must be booked back into stores before they can be used for parent production, stores turnover time is part of manufacturing cycle time as shown in Figure 2.

Importance of Stores Turnover Time

As indicated in Figure 3, past practice has been to describe *order lead time* as consisting of setup time, run time, move time, and queue time. As a definition of *the time a work order spends on the shop floor,* this is a correct statement. But, as a specification for order planned lead times, it is inadequate. It ignores the time between completion of the last part on a subordinate item work order and the actual release of those parts for a parent level work order. It ignores the storeroom receiving, and possibly counting, activity, the physical placement in storage of the items, the transaction time to update records, and the actual time on the shelf until release for the next higher level work order. A purist reaction at this point might well be so what—that's the kind of lead time we are trying to avoid. And that is a correct reaction, up to a point. *Even though we do want to avoid stores turnover time, pretending it doesn't exist won't eliminate it; understanding it and attacking it with the right tools can.*

Fortunately, the significance of stores turnover time has been implicitly recognized in previous discussions of order planned lead times. The stacked order planned lead time

FIGURE 4

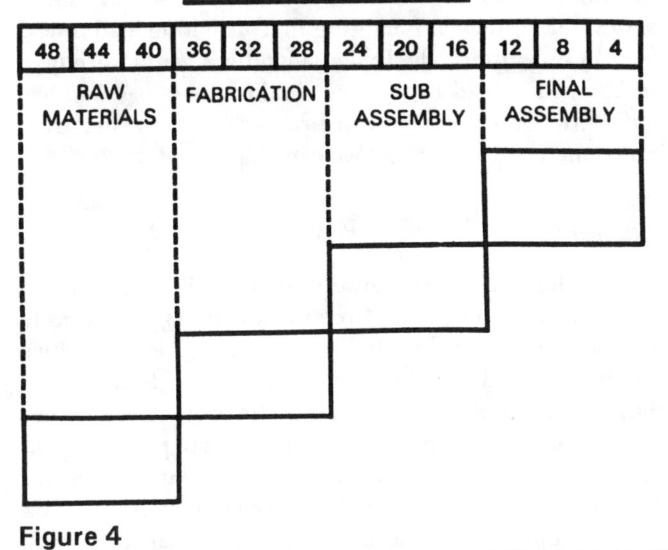

Figure 4

FIGURE 5

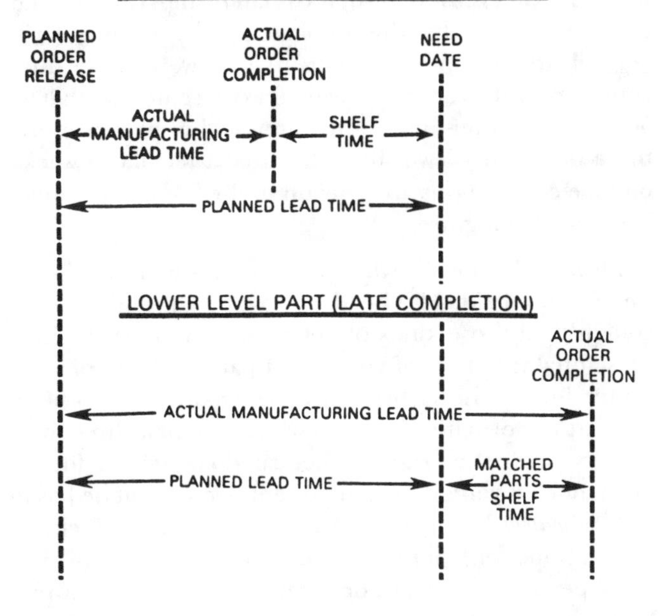

Figure 5

relationships in Figure 4 help to illustrate this point. It is clear from this illustration that planned lead time must extend all the way from planned order release date at one level to planned order release (need) data at the next higher level. Since an item not directly consumed on the floor in the phantom bill sense becomes part of stores until the planned order release calling for it becomes a scheduled receipt, order planned lead times clearly must accommodate stores turnover time.

Although much has been written about lead time management, most previous authors have concentrated on queue management. This concentration has been justified on the basis that queue time typically accounts for 90-95 percent of work order lead times. We have no quarrel with that claim. We do contend, however, that queue times account for substantially less than 90-95 percent of manufacturing cycle time. The remainder of manufacturing cycle time is, in fact, stores turnover time. And in complex manufacturing systems, stores turnover time can be a highly significant factor (See Figure 2). But do long stores turnover times explain our failure to meet inventory goals?

The Real Answer—Highly Variable Lead Times

The importance of lead time length is evident. The significance of variability in lead times is not as evident. Manufacturing control systems are notoriously one-sided with respect to completion date and quantity performance. Rarely are manufacturing or production control people yelled at for finishing too many parts too early. Performance measurement systems typically measure percentage of deliveries late, percentage of work orders late, etc. The percentage of parts and work orders finished early is usually ignored. Nobody is penalized for early performance which strongly indicates that the problems caused by early completion of individual work orders are neither appreciated nor understood. And yet, *early completions go straight into inventory and sit there until they are needed,* thus increasing stores turnover time significantly.

Likewise, materials and *capacity devoted to completing unneeded work orders early can't be used to complete needed work orders on time.* Work orders that are needed get further behind until someone notices them. Then we expedite like mad to get them back on schedule. But, by that time, the other parts that are supposed to make up the matched sets are already in stores on the shelf. They can't be released because of missing parts—the late work order. So early completion of work hits twice (see Figure 5). First, the order that is completed early sits on the shelf an unnecessarily long time. And second, other parts sit on the shelf awaiting completion of the parts delayed by the original

TABLE 1

INVENTORY TURNS A THROUGHPUT TIME

INVENTORY VALUE	PERCENTAGE	SALES REVENUE	PERCENTAGE
8,000,000	.80	8,000,000	.20
2,000,000	.20	32,000,000	.80
10,000,000	1.00	40,000,000	1.00

TURNS	WEIGHTED TURNS	TURN DAYS	WEIGHTED TURN DAYS
1	.8	360	72
16	3.2	22.5	18
AVERAGE TURNS	4.0	AVERAGE TURN DAYS (THROUGHPUT TIME)	90

Table 1

misguided early completion. The net result is unnecessarily long stores turnover, and thus, throughput time.

Example One

A little lead time variability goes a long way. We are reminded of a recent case in which a materials manager assured us that his manufacturing cycle time to respond to a customer from order entry to shipment was down to 4-5 weeks. He cited that kind of performance on 80 percent of his customer orders. Interestingly enough, inventory in this plant was turning 2.8 times per year which in turn implies that true average throughput time was around 18 weeks. Ineffective capacity utilization and poor priority control were the culprits. High lead time variability was the symptom. Parts made early were put on the shelf to sit and sit and sit! At the same time, other parts couldn't be released because of missing matched set components.

Not too long ago, this type of situation was all too common. In fact it is institutionalized in the production and inventory control literature as the 80/20 rule. That is, it is generally accepted that 20 percent of an inventory accounts for 80 percent of annual sales. In fact, as the concept was originally intended, 20 percent referred to part numbers. But to dramatize the situation, we're going to apply the 20 percent to inventory value, not part numbers—also a fairly common practice. (See Table 1.) Notice that 20 percent of the inventory is turning over very rapidly to generate 80 percent of the sales. But the other 80 percent of inventory, which is barely turning at all, is destroying inventory turns. The plant may be providing excellent customer service and getting good manufacturing efficiency but its inventory performance leaves a lot to be desired. And what is causing that? Is it long lead times? Yes, but only indirectly. In actuality it is a whole variety of problems that lead to the real villain here—*high lead time variability.* Some parts get finished early, others late, when in fact matched sets are all we can ship!

Example Two

Consider four work centers involved in producing a single product. The first three work centers produce entirely different parts but their basic function is to produce matched sets of parts for assembly in the fourth work center. Management specifies that the fourth work center should finish 90 percent of its work orders in plus or minus three days. This goal is translated into tolerance limits for the queues at the three feeder work centers. After a few weeks of operation it becomes apparent that the fourth work center is not meeting its goal. In fact, on-time completions within plus or minus three days are in the 60 percent range. After rethinking the relationships, someone suggests that the feeder queue tolerances are too loose. New queue tolerances of plus or minus one day are set. After another few weeks, it becomes apparent that on-time completions at the fourth work center have gotten worse. Further rethinking of the relationships causes someone to recognize that the problem is really one of priority control. In fact, our hero says that all we have to do is control priorities at the individual work centers so that we get 90 percent on-time completions within plus or minus three days and all will be well. After a few more weeks, on-time completions are only up to the 70s and our hero has fallen from grace.

Meanwhile the fourth work center supervisor keeps smiling and shaking his head. He says he knew all along he couldn't get those kinds of deliveries without stockpiling substantial numbers of completed parts in front of work center four. Is he right or wrong? That depends—if 90 percent performance is the best that the first three work centers can do, he's right. If they can do better, he doesn't need much inventory of component parts. What he has to have is *matched sets of parts.* And the best on-time delivery he can hope for from the three work centers is a .9 .9 .9 or 72 percent if they are only capable of 90 percent performance.

Why did performance degenerate when queue tolerances were tightened? Planners had to violate scheduled release dates by wider margins—some sooner and some later—to maintain near constant queues. And an inadequate priority control system was not selecting the right jobs for processing. The root problem was excessive lead time variability due to large lot sizes, long set-up times, etc. Tighter queue tolerances amplified the problem to the point where even the best priority control system simply couldn't overcome it.

Sources of Lead Time Variability

The bottom line is:

- Throughput control is a capacity management problem.
- Capacity requirements planning is a capacity management technique.
- Queue control is an average lead time management problem.
- Input/output control is an average lead time management technique.
- Managing actual lead times involves controlling average lead time and lead time variability.
- There are no CRP or I/O solutions to lead time variability.

A major source of lead time variability is ineffective manufacturing engineering practices. Manufacturing engineering creates high lead time variability through ineffective execution of its responsibilities for plant layout, processing methods selection, and setup/tool/fixture/jig design. How so? Poor practice in these areas leads to long manufacturing cycle times, and, while average lead time length and lead time variability are different concepts, the length of planned lead times limits the range of actual lead times that can occur. Patterns like these are common and normal:

Planned Lead Time	Lead Time Range	
5	5	4
10	10	9
20	20	19

Plant Layout

Just how do manufacturing engineering practices influence planned lead times? Manufacturing engineering is responsible for managing flow patterns within the plant. In carrying out this responsibility, work center layouts are supposedly designed, monitored, and revised to accommodate changes in product mix associated with the various product life cycles. Historically, manufacturing engineering has interpreted this responsibility as an assignment to minimize physical materials handling costs. In general, this results in layouts with minimum length flows in continuous processes, but for batch/intermittent processes, manufacturing engineering appears to have abdicated its responsibility. Machines are grouped by function and, as time passes, new machines replace the old without the kind of flow analysis necessary to minimize flow distances. In the past the number of possibilities in batch/intermittent processing was so great and computing power so limited that a purely intuitive approach was justified. With today's computing power and massive data bases, this is no longer the case. *Detailed flow/routing analyses can lead to shorter flows, less movement, shorter lead times, and lower work-in-process.*

Manufacturing engineering's responsibility for processing methods involves determination of how the product is to be built. In a functional layout, manufacturing process methods can be too fragmented. That is, material may move to a work center for a single operation, back to stores or to a distant work center for another operation, etc. All this movement takes time, adds queues and creates control problems. Lead times tend to be proportional to the numbers of separate operations and locations on a part's routing. When combined with layout problems, highly fragmented routings create unnecessarily long lead times and high lead time variability. Group Process Technology recognizes both the layout and fragmented process problems and addresses them directly. It is a sad commentary that although GT made its debut in US manufacturing 15 years or so ago, it has gained very little acceptance and use. By contrast, *GT is an integral part of Japanese synchronized flow manufacturing systems.*

Setups and Lot Sizing

A third way that manufacturing engineering contributes to long and highly variable lead times involves setup design. Large manufacturing run quantities are seen as spreading setup costs better and keeping unit processing costs down. Because "engineering" quick setups has little potential for reducing unit costs but appears to lead instead to increased capital investment in tooling, it is usually ignored. However, long setup times and large run quantities lengthen work order lead times and stores turnover times. Lead time variability also increases because of the impact of large batches on waiting times. Work tends to arrive at work centers in large clumps at infrequent intervals as opposed to a semi-continuous flow of small batches. *The relationships between long setups and excessive lead time, high work-in-process, etc. have not been well understood by manufacturing engineering in the past.* The Japanese are again leading the way in this area.

The net result of the engineering practices described previously is unnecessarily large variations in input to individual work centers and to stores. Work center queues and work-in-process stores have to be maintained at high levels to accommodate high input variability Even though queues can be controlled to the lower limit required by actual input variability, that lower limit may well be much larger than needed. As a consequence, planned and actual lead times have very real and large lower limits. And *actual lead time variability increases with the length of planned lead time.*

Ineffective Capacity Utilization/Priority Control

Lead time variability is further amplified by ineffective capacity utilization and priority control practices. Because long setups require so much machine downtime, families of part numbers are run back-to-back when they share identical or similar setups. In a few companies, these joint setups are planned in the ordering system—easy for gateway operation but difficult for secondary work centers. If equal runout time order quantities are used with joint setups, there is no negative effect on lead time variability. But in most cases, joint setups are used by machine operators and foremen to improve their performance against budgeted standards. Unfortunately, the impact of joint setups that are not based on equal runout time order quantities on lead time variability is not widely appreciated. When two part numbers are run sequentially using the same setup, they are usually being run because one of the part numbers is needed now. The other one will be needed at some point in the future—maybe a few days or perhaps weeks. The completed quantities of these parts represent items going into inventory prior to their need dates with potentially disastrous consequences for throughput times.

Poor order releasing practices further contribute to high lead time variability. It is common practice to level input to gateway work centers. It is not common practice to look at the implications of the work about to be released for downstream work centers. This is surprising in light of the ratio loading techniques that have been around for some time. Although ratio loading techniques don't guarantee level loads at downstream critical work centers, they represent the best available tool to minimize the peaks and valleys in actual load arrivals at those work centers.

Support Functions and Lead Time Variability

Lead time variability is also exaggerated by lack of attention to two other areas. If several work orders with identical due dates need the same tool at the same time, something has to give. Only one work order can be processed at a time. Meanwhile, the other work orders wait, thus further increasing lead time variability. Tool capacity planning and priority scheduling is the obvious answer.

The same comments are applicable to inspection and maintenance capacity planning and scheduling. One inspector or one maintenance man can be no more than one place at a time. Consequently, capacity requirements for these activities must be determined, the capacity made available, and priority decisions arrived at in a coherent fashion. Lead time variability increases in almost direct proportion to the extent these things are not done.

Finally, priority control requires that the decision maker be aware of all relevant shop floor information. This, in turn, implies timely, accurate shop floor reporting. Machines down, tools missing, tools broken, operators absent, inspector absent, parts missing, etc., are all relevant to priority validity. Anything that interferes with the timely flow of accurate information from the floor to the dispatcher causes him to base priorities on incorrect and out-of-date information, i.e., fallacious assumptions. Lead time variability decreases in direct proportion to the timeliness and accuracy of shop floor reporting, i.e., priority validity.

Management Reaction to Existing Conditions

To many managers, the details described previously are overwhelmingly complex. After attempting to understand the relationships between the variables in manufacturing, many surrender to this complexity. Many conclude that the answer lies in better priority control. This group has funded much of the development of finite load scheduling systems. Their order releasing philosophy is that if they get enough work on the floor and materials in stores, they can always make anything we need. Sometimes this results in high customer service. But, more often, the congestion takes its toll on manufacturing efficiency. In any event, we are glad we don't have to pay interest on these managers' WIP and stores.

Other managers conclude that the only route to salvation is better planning. In fact, they believe that if they plan far enough ahead, anything is possible. They plan, replan and plan some more. But they are still mystified when customer service is low and work-in-process is high.

What do these groups have in common? Two things. Eventually they both develop a lack of confidence in the ability of their plants to execute realistic plans. Secondly, they both tend to rely on long planned lead times to overcome this deficiency. As has been seen previously, long lead times result in invalid priorities which result in highly variable actual lead times and inventory shelf turns. In turn, these factors require high inventory investment.

FIGURE 6

THROUGHPUT TIME CONTROL

		MONTHS			
		1	2	3	4
*	PLANNED SHIPMENTS	2,600	2,800	2,700	2,750
	ACTUAL SHIPMENTS	2,500	2,900	2,750	2,650
	DEVIATION	-100	+100	+50	-100
	CUMULATIVE DEVIATION	-100	0	+50	-50
*	PLANNED INVENTORY	8,000	8,000	8,000	8,000
	ACTUAL INVENTORY	8,250	8,500	8,000	7,750
	DEVIATION	+250	+500	0	-250
**	PLANNED INVENTORY TURNS	3.9	4.2	4.1	4.1
	ACTUAL INVENTORY TURNS	3.6	4.1	4.1	4.1
	DEVIATION	-.3	-.1	0	0
***	PLANNED THROUGHPUT TIME	92	86	88	88
	ACTUAL THROUGHPUT TIME	100	88	88	88
	DEVIATION	+8	+2	0	0

* ALL NUMBERS IN THOUSANDS OF DOLLARS
** ANNUALLY
*** ALL NUMBERS IN DAYS

Figure 6

Getting Throughput Time Under Control

What can we do about long average throughput time? Obviously there are some answers in the manufacturing engineering area but most of them are long term. Likewise, there are some other answers in the capacity utilization/priority control areas that can only be realized after dedicated effort for a substantial period of time. In the short run, what is needed is a way to get average throughput time under control and to benchmark performance so that we can measure the effectiveness of continuing effort in this direction.

The example in Figure 6 represents one way of doing this. A close look at the example reveals that it is simply a different way of portraying inventory data. The first section of the table portrays planned versus actual shipments as measured by cost of goods sold during each period. The second section describes total wall-to-wall inventory value for each period. The third section illustrates the annualized inventory turns indicated by the two previous sections. Shipments are multiplied by 12 and divided by the inventory value to develop inventory turn figures. Finally, in the last section, average throughput time was computed by dividing 360 days by the number of inventory turns.

The rationale for this approach is that it focuses attention on the right variable—time. The numbers in the top three sections of Figure 6 are in dollars. Since inventory and COGS are usually adjusted monthly as opposed to weekly, it is likely that the period of control would also be months. In the event that the accounting system is capable of generating weekly updates, tighter control would be possible.

Conclusions

Average throughput time represents the aggregate consequences of management practices in all areas of the business. It is this time that must be reduced. Until it is, any claimed improvements in inventory performance are just that—claims, not facts. The first step toward reducing average throughput time is to identify all the pieces and understand their relationships-queue times and inventory turnover times. The second step toward reducing average throughput time is bringing the individual elements—queues and stores—under control. After that, further reductions can only be achieved by waging war against the real enemies—variability of demand, supply, lead times, materials flows, etc. Variability can't be eliminated by production and inventory control personnel operating autonomously. It can be substantially reduced by a dedicated, coordinated campaign involving marketing, design engineering, manufacturing engineering, purchasing, manufacturing, materials control, production control, plant engineering, quality control, and shipping and receiving. Reductions in planned lead times can improve actual lead time and inventory performance to a point. Beyond that point, further reductions in planned lead times must be accompanied by simultaneous reductions in lead time variability if significant gains are to be realized.

About the authors

ED HEARD, CPIM, is a principal in Plossl & Heard and in Ed Heard and Associates, management services companies engaged in manufacturing control systems education, counseling, use, and development. Mr. Heard is a frequent speaker at professional society meetings, conferences, and seminars. His background includes a combination of hands-on practical experience and academic know-how. He has been consulting, publishing, and teaching for a dozen years and currently serves on the faculty of the University of South Carolina College of Business. Mr. Heard has published in production and inventory management, accounting and data processing trade and academic journals. He is certified at the fellow level by APICS and is active in both APICS and AIIE. He earned MBA and DBA degrees in Production Management at Indiana University and a BBA degree in Management from Georgia Southern College.

GEORGE PLOSSL, CPIM, is President of both G. W. Plossl Co., Inc. and George Plossl Educational Services, Inc., Atlanta-based management education and counseling firms with clients throughout the U.S. and in Europe and Africa. He has authored numerous articles and several books on production and inventory management including INVENTORY CONTROL: Principles and Techniques (co-authored with O. W. Wight). Mr. Plossl has been active in professional organizations, holding offices and directorships in APICS, AIIE and other technical societies. Earlier in his career, he served as plant manager for the Stanley Strapping Systems Division of the Stanley Works and as materials manager of the Stanley Tools Division. He received AB, BS and MS degrees in Mechanical Engineering from Columbia University.

 © APICS

Reprinted from *Journal of Cost Management*, Incremental, Separable, Sunk, and Common Costs in Activity-Based Costing, by Maurice L. Hirsch, Jr. and Michael C. Nibbelin, Spring 1992, pp. 39-47. Copyright ©, Warren Gorham Lamont. All rights reserved. Used by permission.

Cost Management Concepts and Principles: Incremental, Separable, Sunk, and Common Costs in Activity-Based Costing[1]

Maurice L. Hirsch, Jr. and Michael C. Nibbelin

Activity-based cost (ABC) systems—which assign costs based on activities or transactions—can lead to better decision making: They trace indirect costs more accurately and also direct managers' attention toward the *causes* of costs. Nonetheless, problems with product costs can occur even within ABC systems. Specifically, managers must address certain basic issues that arise in both ABC cost systems and traditional, volume-based cost systems, including: (1) the handling of incremental, separable, and sunk costs; and (2) the treatment of common costs. Managers must always consider which costs to include and which to exclude for different types of decisions.

Assigning costs based on activities or transactions undoubtedly alleviates some major problems associated with product costs. For example, replacing an allocation based on labor hours with assignment of costs based on relevant activity drivers can undoubtedly lead to more accurate product costs and to better measures of performance, especially in settings where labor hours have become insignificant in terms of total product costs.

While the basic ideas underlying activity-based cost (ABC) systems are sound, several problem areas have not yet been fully addressed. These problem areas should be studied so that managers do not rush to adopt an ABC system only to learn later that their new cost system incorporates some of the same flaws that traditional, volume-based cost systems have.

Tracing vs. allocation

Throughout this article, it is important to distinguish between costs that are *traced* and costs that are *allocated*. Costs are *traced* to a product or cost object when a causal relationship exists between the incurrence of the cost and the object. On the other hand, costs are *allocated* to products or cost objects when no such causal relationship exists, such as when common costs are assigned using some reasonable basis. (The term *assignment* is used in this article as a neutral term; it implies neither causality nor the lack of it.)

Cost allocations are *arbitrary*, because they are based on fairness or reasonableness, rather than on a strictly causal relationship.[2] The term *allocation* is used in this article only when there is no causal relationship. A failure to recognize the difference between tracing and an allocation of costs may leave companies with the false impression that their costs are more accurate than they actually are. To the extent that costs are traced to products, the costs are more accurate. *Allocations* of costs from activity centers to products, however, do not lead to more accurate costs.

Companies need to understand that ABC systems are themselves subject to many of the same pitfalls and problems that traditional cost systems have. Specifically, this article addresses two basic problem areas:

1. Handling incremental, separable, and sunk costs; and
2. Dealing with the general problem of common costs.

Overview of activity-based costing

ABC systems are founded on the notion that costs often cannot be accurately traced using a single activity driver or even several activity drivers if all of them are based on volume (e.g., machine hours, direct labor hours, or units). The general idea of ABC systems is to trace as many costs as possible by relying on relationships between the consumption of resources and the causes for this consumption.

This is not a new idea in management accounting; many aspects of ABC systems have been accepted in management accounting for decades. For example, management accountants have long used regression analysis to determine whether causal relationships exist; they have also employed the reciprocal method for assigning variable interdependent service department costs. Until recently, management accountants have relied on direct labor hours as an accurate, causal activity driver. With changes

Exhibit 1. *HCA Company Unit Costs*

Per Unit		Product 1		Product 2
Direct Materials		$ 5.00		$ 6.00
Direct Labor				
Hours	0.3		0.5	
Rate per hour	$15.00			
Cost per unit		4.50		7.50
Variable Overhead				
Rate per hour	$9.00			
Cost per unit		2.70		4.50
Fixed Overhead				
Rate per hour	$5.70			
Cost per unit		1.71		2.85
		$13.91		$20.85

Note: Overhead is applied based on direct labor hours (DLH).

Annual fixed overhead	$570.000
Divided by annual direct labor hours	100.000
Fixed overhead per direct labor hour	$5.70

Exhibit 1 *HCA Company Unit Costs*

over the past few decades in the internal manufacturing environment and in the external competitive environment, however, the use of only one (or, at most, several) volume-based drivers has become inappropriate.

Inappropriate use of volume based drivers. Most companies whose product costs are suspect have relied on direct labor hours as the sole basis for assigning indirect costs, even if there is little or no relationship between direct labor hours and the consumption of most factory overhead.[3] Undoubtedly, direct labor was once the driving force in many companies for the incurrence of indirect costs; direct labor therefore became the focus of managerial attention. Problems arise, however, when direct labor hours continue to be used as the assignment base when direct labor costs constitute only a small percentage of total costs.

Activities other than direct labor can cause costs—especially support department costs.[4] For example, it takes more resources to keep track of 50 orders of 1,000 units each than one order of 50,000 each. Under ABC systems, the focus changes from *assigning* costs to determining *why resources are in place.* ABC systems help managers determine what drives costs; it also focuses on tracing costs to (for example) units of particular products, product lines, or processes. Tracing costs is made possible through interviews, the use of common sense, and application of statistical methods (e.g., linear regression). Thus, rather than dealing with support department costs by deciding whether square feet or number of employees is a "good" way to assign costs to operating departments, managers should instead ask "why do the supporting resources exist?" Costs are assigned based on the answer to this question. ABC directs management's attention toward *reducing* support department costs rather than simply deciding on a fair way to allocate them.

Activity cost assignments

To illustrate the two problem areas identified, assume the following example involving HCA Company, a hypothetical company with two products. All of HCA's overhead is applied using direct labor hours. Exhibit 1 shows the unit costs generated by HCA's conventional, direct labor-based cost system. While variable overhead might change in relation to direct labor hours, there is no evidence that fixed overhead is in any way affected by direct labor hours or by any other volume-based measure. Indeed, basic cost-volume-profit notions indicate that fixed overhead is not a function of any volume-related activity, but is instead simply a function of time and relevant range (capacity).

First- and second stage assignments. ABC systems involve a two-stage process. First, costs are assigned to an activity. In the second stage, they are assigned to cost objects. The HCA example used in this article examines the second stage of the process. In this case, the cost objects are products. Assume that HCA's managers become concerned that using direct labor hours is not a reasonable way to apply fixed manufacturing overhead, so they conduct a study to see if costs that were formerly classified as common are actually separable by product. Exhibit 2 shows the result of that study.

One of the arguments in favor of ABC systems is that they are more accurate.[5] Exhibit 3 compares the product costs generated by HCA's traditional cost system with the costs generated by a new ABC system in which costs are first traced to products, then common fixed overhead continues to be allocated using direct labor hours. (Note that there might be a rationale for continuing to use direct labor hours even under ABC, because the single largest overhead item is variable overhead of $900,000—i.e., 100,000 hours at $9 per hour. Since variable overhead is the largest overhead item and since it is associated with direct labor hours, managers might well choose to assign common fixed overhead based on direct labor hours, especially if doing so meets the general criteria of being reasonable and fair.)

As Exhibit 3 shows, substantial changes occur in the costs for Product 1, though the change for Product 2 is relatively small. Since separable costs are traced to each product, the ABC costs are more *accurate* with respect to these costs.

Exhibit 2. HCA Company
Schedule of Overhead

	Total	Product 1	Product 2	Common
Fixed Manufacturing Overhead				
Supervision	$100.000	$ 25.000	$ 25.000	$ 50.000
Building costs	150.000			150.000
Depreciation	100.000	30.000	20.000	50.000
Engineering	80.000	60.000	20.000	
Maintenance	80.000	12.245	47.755	20.000
Material handling	60.000	24.000	36.000	
Annual fixed overhead	$570.000	$151.245	$148.755	$270.000

Note:			
Annual production (units)		10.000	194.000
Units per batch		1.000	5.000
Number of setups		10	39
Total setups	49		
Annual setup costs	$60.000 (traceable to the setup function)		
Cost per setup	$1.224.50		

Exhibit 2 *HCA Company Schedule of Overhead*

Exhibit 3. HCA Company
Comparison of Costing Methods

	Product 1	Product 2	
Production	10,000	194,000	
Variable cost/unit	× $12.20	× $18.00	
Total variable cost	$122.000	$3.492.000	
Direct overhead			
Supervision	25.000	25.000	
Engineering	60.000	20.000	
Material handling	24.000	36.000	
Depreciation	30.000	20.000	
Setup costs	12.245	47.755	
Common overhead	8.100	261.900	$570.000
Total	$281.345	$3.902.655	$4.184.000
Direct labor hour-based total	$139.100	$4.044.900	$4.184.000
Dollar change—Total	$142.245	$(142.245)	
Cost per unit	$28.13	$20.12	
Direct labor hour-based cost per unit	$13.91	$20.85	
Percent change	102.26%	-3.52%	
Dollar change—per unit	$14.22	$(0.73)	

Note: Traceable costs are assigned per information in Exhibit 2.
Common overhead is applied based on DLH:
$270.000 from Exhibit 2
÷ 100.000 annual direct labor hours
$2.70 per direct labor hour

Exhibit 3 *HCA Company Comparison of Costing Methods*

Effect on managerial decision making

For purposes of management decision making, the change in the computed cost of Product 1 might change a manager's pricing decisions and evaluations about the product's profitability. While the ABC costs for Product 2 are also more accurate, there is no substantial change in the product's total cost per unit. Thus, although the new ABC system's costs are more accurate, they do not provide strikingly different information about Product 2. The main reason for the dramatic change in the costs for Product 1 is that Product 1 is a low-volume product compared with Product 2. (Note, however, that the fact that one product's cost changes while the other remains about the same is a function of the illustration and not ABC in general.)

Incremental, separable, and sunk costs

The HCA Company example focuses on product costs based on full-absorption costing, as required for financial reporting purposes. These costs are used as follows:

As a basis for pricing;

As part of the calculation of return on investment (ROI); and

As a basis for assessing segment profitability.

Different costs for different purposes. Management accounting has long advocated different costs for different purposes. Changes in the internal and external environments have brought about an increasing awareness of the need to separate product costs for financial accounting purposes from the cost of products for purposes of managerial decision making and the cost for purposes of operational control.

In the case of the cost of products for managerial decision making, the financial accounting distinction between product and period costs is eliminated. Managers are interested in separable costs. Whether they are manufacturing costs or (to give one example) sales costs. In a decision about whether to reprice or drop a product, all costs that are traceable to that product are relevant. Two questions that need to be asked are:

1. What costs would be eliminated if the product were discontinued?

2. What costs are appropriate to use when trying to determine the price of products?

Should these two questions be answered using the same product cost?

Some costs are not really incremental

ABC systems are now focusing managers' attention on what *causes* resources to be consumed; thus, ABC systems have expanded the idea of incremental costs. Previously, managers have usually thought of incremental costs in terms (for example) of the additional material required to make an extra 100 units or of the need to hire a new product manager if a new line is produced. Now managers attention is also being directed toward the costs of complexity. It is important to recognize, however, that some of the costs assigned to products under ABC are *not* incremental. They should therefore be ignored when making decisions for which only incremental costs are relevant.

Suppose, for example, that a company has several products. The industrial engineering department manager is asked to find out how engineering resources are used. Suppose that one engineer spends about half his time on one product (Product A) and the other half on tasks that benefit several products (i.e., common costs). An ABC system might assign one-half of that engineer's time to Product A. However, if the company decided to drop Product A, that cost would not disappear. In other words, the cost is traceable, but not avoidable. While one might argue that the half-person capacity freed by dropping Product A would be available for a new product or for some other activity, the cost assigned to Product A is not really incremental, even though the cost may be traced to Product A under an ABC system. (Such a cost would be incremental if, for example, the use of that half-time position would allow the company to avoid hiring another person for needed activities.)

This is an example where managers must be as wary of costs generated by an ABC system as they would be of costs reported by a traditional, volume-based cost system. Managers cannot simply trade the old paradigm for a new one. Costs of products that are not really incremental should be clearly identified in any cost system.

Some traceable costs are sunk

Depreciation is a sunk cost. It represents neither replacement cost nor resale value, since it is based on the original cost of an asset. As many writers point out, today's investment in computer-integrated manufacturing (CIM) equipment is quite large, and can only be justified over a lengthy period of time.[6] Such equipment yields large annual depreciation charges. While single-purpose or dedicated machinery costs may be directly traceable to a group of components or products, the depreciation assigned to a product does not seem useful for most managerial decisions.

Consider the HCA example again. As Exhibit 2 shows, certain pieces of machinery are evidently associated with each of the two products, while other equipment is common to the overall operation. Managers using an ABC system (even if they are looking at the cost of products for managerial decision making) might believe that all assigned costs are relevant.[7]

If a product that uses single-purpose machinery were discontinued, the machinery would be sold. The accounting system would consequently show a reduction in annual depreciation, but that reduction is not indicative of a real savings. The economic event of note in the disposition of dedicated assets is a single period cash inflow (assuming that the equipment has a salvage value). That cash inflow is relevant to the decision; annual depreciation expense by itself—even depreciation for separable equipment—is not. The lost tax shield from depreciation on the equipment would also have cash flow effects in subsequent periods, but this is not reflected in the allocated cost. Managers must therefore recognize that a portion of product costs are sunk costs. These sunk costs must be eliminated and converted to cash flows when evaluating a product line.

Short-term vs. long-term decision

Some managers distinguish between short-term and long-term decisions when deciding whether to include depreciation as a "relevant" cost. Managers at one company, for example, concluded that depreciation should not be included in assessing product profitability or in making pricing decisions in the short run when the plant operates at below capacity. At this company, depreciation was classified as a common cost; that is, it was not allocated to products (or product groups) for purposes of managerial decision making or for operational control. For long-term decisions regarding capacity (the process), however, depreciation was included.

The team that implemented an ABC system at this company thought that depreciation reflected some capacity cost and would be useful in looking at ROI. Since the equipment had been bought several years before, however, both technology and the cost of productive capacity had changed since the equipment was purchased. Whcn this was pointed out, the managers agreed that the depreciation costs were sunk and did not represent an opportunity cost associated with even long-term capacity decisions.

Assigning the cost of a cow. Another example of the confusion over how to handle sunk costs in ABC comes from academia. In one recent article,[8] the authors sought to determine an appropriate ABC model to help ranchers make better decisions about keeping or selling calves. They took the historical cost of the mother cow and allocated it to each calf, using a potential number of offspring as a denominator. Annual feed costs for the cow were also assigned to the calf. Unfortunately, both these costs are sunk, and thus are irrelevant to the decision of whether to keep a calf or to sell it.

As these examples show, real confusion exists among both managers and academics about how to deal with sunk costs, whether they are traceable or not. Whcn dealing with a decision that should rely on incremental costs, the inclusion of separable sunk costs seems inappropriate.

Allocating common costs

This section considers the problems that exist in allocating common costs—a problem that exists regardless of the cost system whenever all manufacturing costs are assigned to products. While nothing in ABC systems inherently requires assignment of nontraceable costs, managers often want full-absorption costs.

Allocation of common support department costs. As Exhibit 2 shows, some of the fixed overhead costs for HCA are clearly associated with each of the two products and can therefore be traced to the products. Supervision costs, for example, include traceable costs of a manager of each product at $25,000 per product plus common supervision costs of $50,000 for a plant manager. Therefore, we can assume that if one of the products were discontinued, the costs associated with its manager would cease within some reasonable period of time.

In this example, assume that the $60,000 in setup costs consists of the salaries and benefits of employees who perform setups. The level of costs is based on the current capacity of the plant. Therefore, unless the basic structure of the plant were to change, these costs are fixed. (In other words, this level of costs is the minimum amount of resources that HCA needs for the setup function.) Thus, while these costs are attributable to setups, they are common to the two products. Any assignment of these costs involves an allocation, which means that a cost per setup or some other method of allocation must be determined.

If HCA had previously used direct labor hours to assign all support costs, the change to a cost per setup would lead to a fairer allocation, because higher costs would be assigned to products that required more setups. While this seems more reasonable than using direct labor hours as an allocation base (since, direct labor is unrelated to the setup function), note that when setup costs are allocated in this manner, the assumption is that all setups take the same time to complete, which might or might not be the case. Even if setups took a different amount of time and, consequently, setup time were used as the driver, the same problem previously discussed arises, because a cost that is not incremental (i.e., avoidable) is assigned as if it were.

Supervisory costs. Supervisory costs provide another insight into allocations under ABC. As before, assume that there is one supervisor in the HCA example for each product and that the remaining supervision costs represent common costs of a general supervisor. Thus, 50 percent of the costs of supervision can be directly traced to the products, while the remaining 50 percent is common to the two products. The question persists of what to do with this 50 percent that is a common cost. Some companies argue that these costs should be divided based on the ratio of separable costs.[9] The rationale is that since traceable costs are evenly divided between the two products, the common costs for that area should be divided evenly as well. Again, although this may be fair, it is not more accurate.

Exhibit 4. *HCA Company*
Overhead Application

	Product 1	Product 2	
A. Direct Labor Hour Base			
Variable overhead	$2.70	$4.50	
Fixed overhead	1.71	2.85	
Total	$4.41	$7.35	
B. Activity Base—Option 1			
Variable overhead	$ 2.70	$4.50	
Fixed overhead—traceable	13.90	0.52	
Setup cost	1.22	0.25	
Common fixed overhead	0.81	1.35	
Total	$18.63	$6.62	
Dollar difference	$14.22	$(0.73)	
Percent difference	323%	-10%	
C. Activity Base—Option 2			
Variable overhead	$ 2.70	$4.50	
Fixed overhead—Traceable	13.90	0.52	
Setup cost	1.22	0.25	
Common fixed overhead	13.61	0.69	
Total	$31.44	$5.96	
Dollar difference	$27.03	$(1.39)	
Percent difference	613%	-19%	
Common fixed overhead			$270,000
Activity-based overhead	$151,245	$148,755	$300,000
Percent	50.41%	49.59%	100.00%

Exhibit 4

In the case of the supervision example, the reported costs of the ABC system would be more accurate insofar as the separable costs were concerned, but they would not be more accurate regarding the division of common costs. Management can subjectively assess whether they are "better" because they are more reasonable, but managers should exercise caution when using these cost figures for managerial decision making. The costs should be clearly identified as allocations so that managers will not think that the costs were all traced.

Allocation of general common costs

As much as management accounting texts and literature argue that managers should not use full-absorption manufacturing costs as the basis for decisions, evidence shows that they do.[10] ROI (using full-absorption cost of goods sold in determining income) is still the most important basis for evaluating performance of segments,[11] even in the face of calls for new measures. Until managerial practice changes, therefore, it is important to discuss the effect of allocations of common cost under ABC.

Common costs other than support departments. As long as managers want fully absorbed costs, it is important for them to decide what to do with common costs. Assume that costs can be traced to some level: the company, a segment, a plant, a process, a product (or product line), a batch, or a unit. In some companies, costs that are traceable only to the process or above are quite large. They include items such as occupancy costs and general plant management. In the HCA example, $270,000 of the total of $570,000 in fixed manufacturing costs are common. (It might be argued that the proportion of common fixed costs is high in this example, but the point is relevant whenever common costs are significant. Moreover, even when the proportion of common costs was increased or reduced in this example compared with total overhead costs, no different conclusions were reached.)

Note that the HCA example carefully distinguishes between traceable costs and common costs and that it does not allocate common costs. If, for example, common supervisory costs were assigned based on the proportion of traceable supervisory costs, the pool of costs classified as "common" would be reduced. In some companies, if many such assignment were made, the amount of common costs left over might be fairly small.

Comparison of ways for dealing with common overhead. Exhibit 4 shows a comparison of different ways for dealing with common overhead. In Part A, overhead is applied using a single base—direct labor hours. In Part B, variable overhead is applied using direct labor hours (the causal variable), traceable fixed costs are assigned to products based on the analysis in Exhibit 2, setup costs are allocated based on the cost per setup in Exhibit 2, and common fixed overhead is allocated based on direct labor hours. (Thus, the results in Part B are the same as those found in Exhibit

3. The comparison of the costs shown in Part B to those shown in Part A is similar to the comparison shown in Exhibit 3. The percentages are different, since Exhibit 4 deals only with overhead costs, while Exhibit 3 includes all product costs.)

Other options exist for allocating common fixed overhead. One is to allocate based on the *proportion* of traceable costs, as shown in Part C of Exhibit 4. Variable overhead, traceable fixed overhead, and setup costs are assigned exactly as in Part B. The only change is in common fixed overhead. Since, in the example, costs generated by the ABC system are more accurate and more reasonable than would be the case if only a single activity driver were used, the choice of how to allocate common overhead leads to options such as those shown in Parts B and C of Exhibit 4. In this case, the difference is quite startling, as shown below:

	Per Unit Costs	
	Product 1	Product 2
Allocate common costs based on direct labor hours	$ 0.81	$ 1.35
Allocate common costs based on traceable costs	$13.61	$ 0.69

How managers will use cost information

As with the other issues illustrated above, the real question is how managers will use information generated by a cost system. Neither way of allocating common fixed overhead in this case is more accurate than the other. Given the basic premise that ABC provides more accurate product costs than allocations based on direct labor, the danger lies in managers' extending this perception to the fully allocated absorption costs of products.

Ideally, fully absorbed costs would not be used in decisions regarding, for example, whether a product is profitable. However, if managers insist on allocating common costs to units of product, then any list of product costs should distinguish between traceable and allocated costs.

In summary, costs of products for managerial decision making should show costs that are relevant for the decision at hand. If separable sunk costs are included, they should be identified as such. If costs are traceable but not really incremental, or if common support department or common general overhead costs are included, these too should be clearly labeled. Managers must have information that distinguishes between costs that can be fairly accurately traced as opposed to costs that are allocated.

Conclusion

The current interest in manufacturing accounting and the need for different costs for different needs is to be lauded, because the manufacturing environment has changed dramatically. U.S. companies face much stiffer competition from abroad and rapidly changing technology at home. ABC directs a manager's attention to the consumption of resources, and may thus help managers focus on ways to lower support department costs. ABC also ensures that product costs are more accurate and perhaps more reasonable.

Still, managers must be careful about how they use costs generated by ABC systems. While managers might believe that the "fix" they need in their accounting systems is to apply overhead based on activities, some of the problems associated with traditional cost systems persist even in ABC systems. Managers therefore risk adopting a new paradigm that includes many of the same problems that their traditional cost systems had. The new focus on causality should allow managers to create management accounting systems that remain flexible as competitive environments change.

Finally, managers must recognize when an ABC system—or any cost system—is being used to achieve behavioral results. For example, Tektronix, Inc. uses an ABC system that applies material-related costs based on the number of components that must be bought or made.[12] The objective was to reduce inventory and support-department costs related to inventory management. The reported results seemed promising, for the number of items in inventory dropped dramatically. However, cost systems with built-in incentives of this type can lead to dysfunctional behavior: Ultimately, a company's products could become less competitive if the system placed an unreasonably high price on using unique parts.

In many ways, ABC systems make use of basic axioms of management accounting: trace costs to products as accurately as possible, use different costs for different purposes, and focus attention on causes instead of symptoms. If ABC systems help managers regain these basic ideas, they are good and worthwhile. However, practitioners and academics must recognize that ABC systems have many of the same problems that traditional cost systems have; the basic problem areas do not go away.

Specifically, managers must differentiate the truly more accurate costs from those that are not. This can be done by determining whether costs are really incremental, determining which costs are sunk costs, and specifying which costs are allocated. Finally, managers cannot ignore the continuing problem of how to allocate common costs given the insistence of other managers on using fully absorbed costs.

Notes

1. The authors thank Thomas King, Joseph Louderback, and Linda Lovata for their helpful comments.

2. This definition is based on the works of Arthur Thomas. For example, see *The Allocation Problem in Financial Accounting Theory, Studies in Accounting Research, No 3* (Sarasota, Fla.: American Accounting Association 1969).

3. See, for example, James A. Hendricks, "Applying Cost Accounting to Factory Automation," *Management Accounting* 24-30 (Dec 1988).

4. See, for example, Michael O'Guin. "Focus the Factory with Activity-Based Costing," *Management Accounting* 36-41 (Feb 1990).

5. See, for example, Robin Cooper, "The Two-Stage Procedure in Cost Accounting: Part One," *Journal of Cost Management* 43-51 (Summer 1987).

6. See, for example, Robert E. Bennett, et al., *Cost Accounting for Factory Automation* 67-68 (Montvale, N. J.: National Association of Accountants 1987).

7. See, for example, Peter R. Santori, "Measuring Profitability in Today's Manufacturing Environment," *Journal of Cost Management* 19 (Fall 1987).

8. Cheryl L. Fulkerson & Amy H. Lau, "Application of the Activity-Based Costing Approach to an Agricultural Sector," *Proceedings—1990 Annual Meeting Decision Sciences Institute,* Vol. 1, 80-82 (San Diego Nov 19—21, 1990).

9. See, for example, "Schrader Bellows," *Harvard Business School Case Series* 186-272.

10. See, for example, Michael Cornich, et al., "How Do Companies Analyze Overhead Costs?" *Management Accounting* 41-43 (June 1988).

11. See Howell, et al., *Management Accounting in the New Manufacturing Environment* 52 (Montvale, N. J.: National Association of Accountants 1987).

12. John W. Jonez & Michael A. Wright, "Material Burdening: Management Accounting Can Support Competitive Strategy," *Management Accounting* 27-31 (Aug. 1987).

About the authors

Maurice L. Hirsch, Jr. is professor of accounting at Southern Illinois University at Edwardsville.

Michael C. Nibbelin is assistant professor of accounting at Eastern Illinois University, in Charleston, Illinois.

Reprinted from *P&IM Review,* January 1990.

The Manager's View of WIP

William E. Maginn

While an essential aspect of the manager's job is walking around the shop floor locating and solving problems, the fact remains that management reports are an important and necessary means of monitoring the production process. From a Production Control standpoint, the Work-in-Process (WIP) group of reports represent a crucial window to the shop floor.

A common analogy used when talking about WIP is the bathtub analogy. The incoming water from the spigot represents the inputs to the system, the water exiting through the drain represents the outputs, and the resulting level of water in the bathtub is the WIP level. The level of water in the bathtub is an indication of the difference between the input and output levels of the system. For example, if the incoming water is increased while the rate of drainage is unchanged, the water level will increase, but if the incoming level stays constant and the drain is opened up a bit, the water level will drop. Of course, if the relationship between the input and the output remains the same, the water level will also remain constant.

The three key measurements of the WIP system are: WIP levels (the water level), output (the water released from the bathtub), and WIP turns (the number of times the water is cycled through the system over some period of time). These three measurements can be used by managers to determine what is happening on the shop floor, and to make decisions based on this information.

WIP Level

A simple, easy to understand report of the total units or dollars in process on the shop floor should be one of the main reports maintained and reviewed by the Production Control Manager. If the production process involves the manufacturing of many different units, in job shop or batch fashion, the report is most easily understood in dollars. For assembly line or process production environments, the report is usually in the form of units of production. For purposes of consistency, the WIP level and other measurements presented here will be in the form of dollars.

Most computerized systems have a means of collecting and reporting WIP levels, and these can be separated by division, department, product line, etc. This report can allow managers to see just how much of a company's assets in the form of inventory are tied up on the shop floor, and can be used as a measurement of savings as lead times are reduced. For example, if lead times are currently at 10 days and the average WIP level is $1,000,000, the firm is paying approximately $120,000 annually in carrying costs (at 12 percent interest rate). By reducing lead times by two days, the WIP level will drop to $800,000 and carrying charges will therefore drop to $96,000 annually, saving the company $24,000 a year. This sort of analysis has proven useful in convincing senior management that reducing lead times should be an objective of the firm.

WIP levels can also serve as a control statistic to alert management to problems developing on the shop floor. Following the premises of Statistical Process Control, if the WIP level rises or falls outside of a certain statistically determined acceptable range, managers are alerted to the fact that a problem has possibly developed and should be investigated. Parts shortages, machine breakdown, and insufficient capacity can all result in an increase in WIP levels.

Output

Output, the water drained out of the bathtub, can be a difficult measurement in some situations, especially in subassembly departments who "sell" multiple products to other divisions or departments within the same company. However, the number can be arrived at through a simple algebraic equation. The variables used in this equation are the input to the system (water released through the spigot), the beginning WIP level (water level at the beginning of the period), and the ending WIP level (water level at the end of the period). The algebraic equation is: $E = B + I - O$. where

E = Ending WIP level

B = Beginning WIP level

I = Inputs to the system

O = Outputs from the system

The beginning and ending WIP levels should be readily available, as mentioned above, leaving the input levels to be determined in order to arrive at the output for the period. Material inputs are stockroom disbursements; labor inputs are standard hours earned or actual reported hours (depending on which form of hours are being measured in the WIP level, apples need to be compared with apples). Once this number is determined, the formula needs to be manipulated to: O = B + I - E.

The numbers can now be plugged into the formula and output can be determined. Suppose that the beginning WIP level was $1,100,000, the ending inventory level was $1,000,000, and the inputs in material and labor were $1,400,000. The solution to the equation would then be:

O = $1,100,000 + $1,400,000 – $1,000,000

O = $1,500,000

This figure of gross output can then be used to determine output per payroll hour, output per day, or any other form of output.

WIP Turns

WIP turns is a good measure of asset utilization overtime, as it relates WIP levels to outputs of the system. To determine the WIP turns, the period output must be determined, then annualized to simulate a full year's worth of output. This annual output is then divided by the period's average WIP level to determine the WIP turns. This measurement does not penalize higher WIP levels if higher output levels are being achieved, and doesn't reward lower WIP levels if lower outputs are being realized.

The equations used to determine WIP turns are: T = A/W

where

A = P • N

W = (B + E) /2

T = WIP turns

A = Annual output

P = Period output

N = Number of periods in a year

W = Average WIP level

B = Beginning WIP level

E = Ending WIP level

Suppose that the output for a period (one month was $1,500,000, the beginning WIP level for the period was $1,100,000, and the ending WIP level was $1,000,000. The solution to the equation for annual turns would then be:

A = $1,500,000 12

A = $18,000,000

W = ($1,100,000 + $1,000,000) / 2

W = $1,050,000

T = $18,000,000 / $1,050,000

T = 17.14

The WIP inventory will turn over 17 times per year, or once every 15 working days (260/17.14).

Again, the WIP turns measurement allows managers to compare WIP levels over time as they relate to output levels. This measurement should be more stable than the overall WIP levels, which change according to output.

Conclusion

The analogy of the bathtub has been used to picture the production process, with the water from the spigot representing inputs, the level of water the WIP level, and the water released from the drain the output. This simple analogy shows that relationship between inputs, outputs, and levels of any production system.

I have shown three simple measurements for monitoring asset utilization on the shop floor. Since the dollars represented in Work-in-Process could just as easily be spent on other productive assets, it is important for managers to monitor the level of WIP, the output from the system, and the WIP turns as the relationship between the two. These reports are a mathematical representation of what is happening on the shop floor and should be a key aid in the management decision making process.

Reprinted from APICS 1987 *Conference Proceedings.*

Lot Traceability Isn't Just for Regulated Industries

Jeffrey W. Moran

Introduction

FDA-regulated industries have been required for many years to control inventory by lot number to comply with quality standards and to help with product recalls. The lot number has served as a control point to identify a quantity of material supplied from a particular vendor, produced on the same piece of equipment, or found to have unique quality characteristics related to potency or color. Many non-regulated industries are now beginning to realize the benefits of lot traceability and control to improve quality, achieve better inventory accuracy, and to support serial numbering.

This presentation illustrates applications for on-line lot traceability systems that can be used by hardgoods manufacturers. First, the basic concepts of lot traceability are covered—tracing vs. control, lot creation, lot number assignment, and control of (QC) statuses. Then, new applications are described. For instance, lot number control can be used to improve product quality and isolate sources of defects that may be caused by faulty setup, tooling, handling, or testing. Cycle counting of lots can help push inventory accuracy levels to near 99%. Also, lot numbers can help to ensure that different component revision levels for a product are not shipped to the same customer.

The lot number can, in many cases, be more valuable than reason codes or text narrative in providing an audit trail of what happened to material. Lot numbers can be assigned to identify not only when and where material was produced, but also who made it, who tested it, how it was produced, and how it was transported.

Why Companies Maintain Lot Data

Lot traceability systems have been traditionally used by FDA-regulated manufacturers of foods, drugs, cosmetics. animal products, medical devices (tongue depressors, pacemakers), and electronic products that emit radiation, as well as by manufacturers of paper, plastic, and rubber products that come into contact with food and that must be certified as "food-grade." They have also been used by manufacturers of wine and spirits to satisfy Bureau of Alcohol, Tobacco and Firearms and state production reporting requirements. In addition, the Department of Defense has required many aerospace and defense contractors to track lots in case of product recalls.

These companies have used lot traceability systems to help them in the following areas:

Conformance Reporting—to show that products and practices comply with FDA regulations and Good Manufacturing Practices related to sanitation and inspection.

Product Recalls—to allow forward and backward traceability of lots through the manufacturing process, from vendor to customer and vice-versa, so that defective lots can be quickly recalled from market.

Quality Control—to support the manufacture of quality products through the use of tools provided by lot traceability systems such as retest and expiration reporting, last of lot notification, and lot receipt flags.

Retrievability of Data—to store and provide on-line access to tremendous amounts of data, eliminating manual 3-ring binder practices.

A distinction is often made between "lot tracing"—tracing lots forward and backward through a process, and "lot control"—controlling inventories by lot number without necessarily requiring tracing capabilities. This distinction can be supported through company policies and procedures as well as system parameters for handling traced vs. controlled items.

Creating Lots

A lot can be defined as a quantity of material with similar characteristics, such as:

- supplied by the same vendor (or plant or warehouse)
- produced on the same day (or hour or week)
- produced on the same piece of equipment (or mill or extruder)
- found by inspection to have the same potency, purity, color, cure rate, tensile strength, etc.

In making the decision to go with lot control, we are saying it is not sufficient to merely issue component items from stocking locations to work-in-process, and then receive finished items into inventory, and still expect to control our process as we have typically done in hardgoods manufacturing. By virtue of some characteristic of the material itself (it has a shelf life, it is hazardous, it becomes defective) we must break down its item number identity into smaller elements called "lots," and then be sensitive to the fact that individually these lots may expire, may be consumed, and may or may not be usable with certain other lots.

Associated with each lot is a quantity balance, a QC status, and a create and expiration date. This data is normally stored in a lot master or lot-item file.

The appropriate time to assign a new lot number is when purchased material is received from a vendor, or newly produced intermediates or finished goods are received out of work-in-process. However, the task of manually assigning lot numbers to tens of thousands of new lots each year can be burdensome. Fortunately, lot traceability systems can assign lot numbers automatically when material is received to a purchase order or a manufacturing order.

In the case of a purchase order, a lot number identical to the purchase order number can be created to allow traceability back to the original order the material came in on. The vendor's own lot number can also be tagged to the receipt for reference purposes. The user can then designate an internal lot number (or the system can assign one) to be used from this point forward.

As internal component lots are issued to manufacturing orders, parent lots are created which can then be received against at order close. A lot number identical to the manufacturing order number can be assigned by the system; this lot can in turn be issued to produce higher level lots, until the finished product is created.

Eventually, finished product lots are issued to customers. The system can create a customer order lot with a lot number identical to the customer order number.

This process of issuing and receiving material to orders can behind the scenes create all the lot relationships necessary to trace which component lots have gone to a specific customer, or which customers have received a specific component lot. Since all necessary lot numbers can be assigned automatically, creation of the lot traceability data base is for the most part transparent to the user. Very little additional clerical overhead is needed to support a lot traceability system.

In general, lots are created in the following ways:

- upon RECEIPT to a purchase order
- upon ISSUING component lots to a manufacturing order
- upon ISSUING finished goods lots to a customer order
- when splitting a lot—perhaps to segregate the defective portion of a lot for reworking
- when creating a lot manually—for instance, to identify material that is to be destroyed.

The standard types of lots normally identified in a lot traceability system are as follows:

Purchase Order Lot—Created when material is received from a vendor. Lot number = purchase order number. Lets you trace back to original purchase order. This is a "paper lot" its quantity = 0.

Vendor Lot—The vendor's own internal lot number. This is a "paper lot;" with quantity = 0, and lot number manually entered.

Receiving Lot—The user's in-house lot number that will proceed through the process. This is created by the receipt, with a lot number automatically assigned based on a user format. This is a "physical lot," with quantity not equal to 0.

Manufacturing Order Lot—Created when component material is issued to a manufacturing order, with lot number = manufacturing order number. Initially, quantity = 0. This lot eventually gets populated as receipts occur.

Customer Order Lot—Created when finished product is issued to a customer order. Lot number = customer order number. Allows you to trace material to the ultimate consumer.

Internal Lot—A new lot created by splitting a portion of an existing lot for rework, inspection, or nonstandard handling. Results from a lot splitting or transfer transaction. Lot number is manually assigned.

Destruction Lot—Manually created to record the destruction of material. Used when the desired audit trail calls for transferring defective material to a new lot. Lot number is manually assigned.

Figure 1 shows the creation of the various types of lots via issue and receipt transactions during production of a multilevel product.

Control Of QC Status

Lot traceability systems have commonly been implemented and administered by a company's Quality Control organization. Of key importance to maintaining integrity of the lot relationship data is that Quality Control be able to assign quality control statuses to individual lots or material within a lot. This function is performed on a security

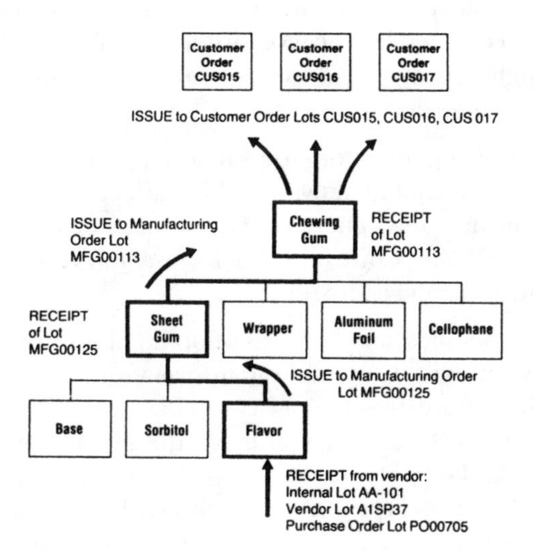

Figure 1 *Creation of Lot Relationships*

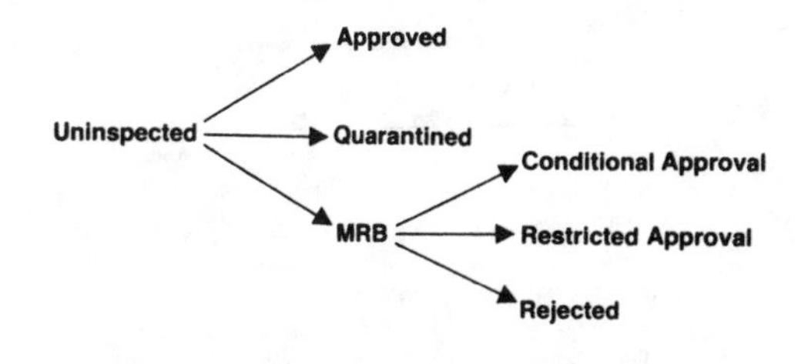

Figure 2 *Typical Sequence of QC Statuses*

controlled screen to which only Quality Control has access. As changes are made to the status of a lot, the inspector can enter reason codes or text to describe the reasons for the status change to create a complete audit trail.

QC status should include:

Uninspected—The lot has been processed or received, but not inspected yet. Quality is unknown. This is often the default status for newly created batches.

Approved—The lot has been inspected and approved. Quality is confirmed.

Conditional Approval—The lot has been inspected with conditional approval. Its quality cannot be fully determined until the parent material it is used in is completed and inspected

Restricted Approval—The lot has been inspected and approved for restricted use in some but not all parent items.

Material Review Board—The lot failed initial inspection and is awaiting final disposition. This material is not available for MRP projected inventory calculations.

Rejected—The lot has been rejected and will be reworked, scrapped, or returned to the vendor. This material is not available for MRP projected inventory calculations.

Quarantined—The lot has been received but must be isolated for a period of time. The material must be set aside for a time before its quality can be determined (e.g., to see if bacteria develop).

A typical sequence in which Quality Control might assign QC statuses to lots is shown in Figure 2. Newly purchased or manufactured material is inspected and is either Approved, Quarantined, or sent to the Material Review Board if defective. From there, it can be dispositioned as Conditional, Restricted, Rejected, or Approved.

Inquiry and Archiving

To be able to trace defective lots, isolate questionable material, and perform product recalls, Quality Control personnel require a lot traceability system to produce reports that:

- display multilevel lot source (explosion) and lot where-used (implosion) relationships
- show all issues of traced material with exception conditions
- display order history when an order closes
- show all inventory transactions and QC status changes affecting traced items

The multilevel lot source and lot where-used displays are typically available as on-line inquiries. These can include the Single Level or Indented Lot Source, Single Level or Indented Where-Used, and the Next Level-End Level Where-Used, which can be especially useful during prod-

INDENTED LOT WHERE USED INQUIRY 12/01/87

COMPONENT ITEM	UM	COMPONENT LOT	TYPE	VENDOR
FLAVOR	KG	A1FL37	VEN	A1 FLAVORS

..+....	PARENT ITEM	UM	PARENT LOT	TYPE	RELATIONSHIP QTY
1	FLAVOR	KG	AA-101	INT	3000
2	SHEET GUM	LB	MFG00125	MFG	80.5
3	CHEWING GUM	CS	MFG00113	MFG	600
4	CHEWING GUM	CS	CUS015	CUS	120
4	CHEWING GUM	CS	CUS016	CUS	180
4	CHEWING GUM	CS	CUS017	CUS	60

Figure 3 *Intended Lot Where-Used Inquiry*

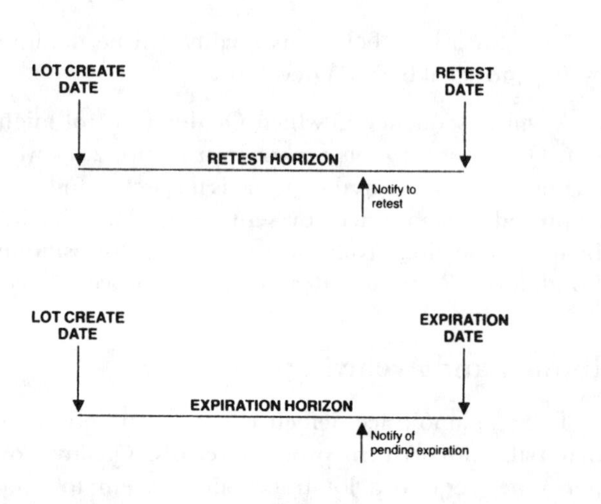

Figure 4 *Retest and Expiration Dates*

uct recalls. A sample Indented Lot Where-Used Inquiry is shown in Figure 3.

Hard copy reports listing issues of traced material with exception conditions are valuable to Quality Control personnel because they make all nonstandard activities which may affect the quality of traced material highly visible. Issue exception conditions include overissues, late or early issues, issues that result in the mixing of lots on an order, and issues of conditional or restricted material.

Order history reports are useful for reconciling accepted and rejected balances on orders as well as providing a thorough history of all issues and receipts of traced material to an order.

Reports listing inventory transactions are useful in providing an audit trail of activities which affect the status or use of individual lots. These would normally be requested only when Quality Control wants to research transaction history on a specific problem lot.

One of the necessary features of on-line lot traceability systems is the ability to archive old information onto history files so that future archaeologists can have ready access to historic data. FDA requirements for the maintenance of past data can be fully met using tape history files in place of 3-ring binders. Types of data that can be archived include lot master records, parent/component lot relationships, and lot transaction activity. Archiving of records typically takes place a certain number of days (user defined) after the last maintenance activity to a record.

Lot Control

Some companies never need to trace lots, but they do still need to control material by lot number. Lot traceability systems provide additional tools to monitor and achieve better control of inventory.

Retest and Expiration Reporting: When a new lot is created, the lot traceability system can add to the create date a user-defined retest or expiration horizon to establish future retest and expiration dates. The retest and expiration horizons are stored on the item master record. The system can then monitor their approach and notify the user when to retest or consume a particular lot. Figure 4 illustrates the calculation of retest and expiration dates from the create date.

Retest reporting applies to items whose quality may vary over time due to exposure to heat, sunlight or contamination but that don't ordinarily expire. If the user doesn't reinspect a particular lot by its scheduled retest date, the system should change its QC status to conditional.

Expiration reporting would be used for true shelf-life items that become unusable after a period of time because they spoil, cure, or lose their potency. If a lot is not consumed by its scheduled expiration date, the system should regard its QC status as rejected and unavailable for MRP projected inventory calculations.

Quantity Thresholds: If the user can define a minimum quantity threshold below which a lot or lot/location balance is considered empty, the lot traceability system can alert planners when a lot has been consumed. The quantity thresholds are typically stored on the item master record.

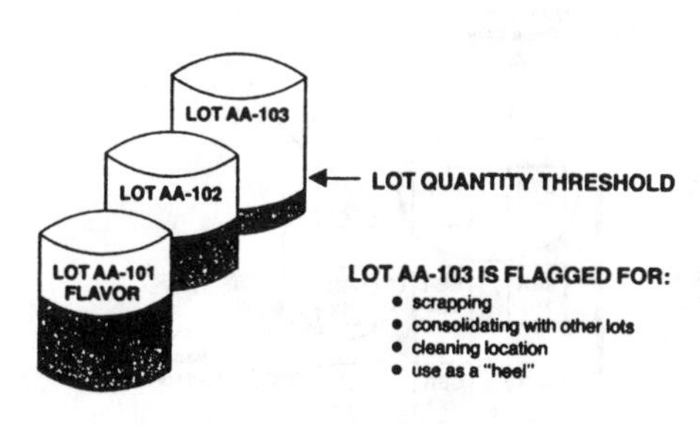

Figure 5 *Quality Threshold*

A daily report is generated listing lots that have reached or gone below their thresholds. This can serve as a trigger to empty out the location, to consolidate the material with other lots, or to use the remaining material as a "heel" to start a new process to produce more of itself. Figure 5 illustrates the use of the quantity threshold trigger.

Lot Receipt Flags: This feature allows the user to flag an incoming lot that may be defective and prevents receipt of the material or provides an on-line warning message. It can be used to prevent receipt of defective material in transit from a vendor, or to display special handling procedures for manufactured material.

Allocation by Lot Number: To support FIFO stock rotation of perishable items, the lot traceability system should allocate material to orders by lot number based on the receipt date of the material. Allocated lot quantities should also print out on a pick list to assist stores personnel in picking the correct lots.

New Applications for Nonregulated Industries

Lot traceability systems are being used today by manufacturers of disk drives, radios, medical equipment, automotive components, telecommunications equipment, and defense systems to improve product quality, achieve better levels of inventory accuracy, and to support serial number control. Many of these companies are taking the opportunity to install lot traceability systems as part of their MRPII implementations. They are not using lot traceability control on the majority of their items. In some cases, they are maintaining lots on as little as five percent of their total items. It is not unusual to see them "turn on" and "turn off" lot control on specific items many times over their life cycles as they feel the need to occasionally subject them to greater control.

Improving Product Quality: The use of lot traceability systems to improve product quality is increasing as companies expand their SPC programs to include measurement of quality by lots. They can obtain a better time-phased audit trail of events affecting quality and can better assess the impact certain variables have on ultimate product performance .

Traditionally, wherever a quality defect has shown up, the function of lot traceability has been to pinpoint which lot of material was the source of the defect, and then determine who else received it. Nonregulated companies can twist this logic to fit their own needs to trace:

- who made it
- who tested it
- what tools were used
- how it was set up
- how it was transported
- how it was stored

This simply requires a creative redefinition of what a lot is. Instead of using the lot to identify the customary vendor, time of day, equipment, or potency associated with the material, it can be used to identify:

- a group of material run on the same setup
- a group of material subjected to the same test procedure during a particular period
- a group of material tested by the same inspector
- a group of material going through the same handling or storage procedure
- a group of material made with the same tooling, die or press
- a group of material using reworked components

The idea here is to trace the effects on quality throughout the rest of the production process of a variable that could affect quality at some level. Material accumulated into "lots" as defined here would likely come from multiple manufacturing orders, rather than one order to one lot. Lot numbers would be assigned manually. Quality Control could then do statistical analysis on finished products to determine how the variables have affected quality, and quickly trace all lots involved in a defect. An example of

INDENTED LOT SOURCE INQUIRY 12/01/87

PARENT ITEM	UM	PARENT LOT	TYPE	CUSTOMER
O8-SR COMPUTER	EA	MFG-5101	MFG	

• • • + • • •	COMPONENT ITEM	EA	COMPONENT LOT	TYPE	RELATIONSHIP QTY
1	COMPUTER SUBASSY	EA	MFG15307	MFG	15
2	PC BOARD	EA	MARLA/8-14-87	INT	12
2	PC BOARD	EA	IRMA/7-30-87	INT	20

Figure 6 *Use of Lot Traceability to Determine Who Stuffed PC Boards*

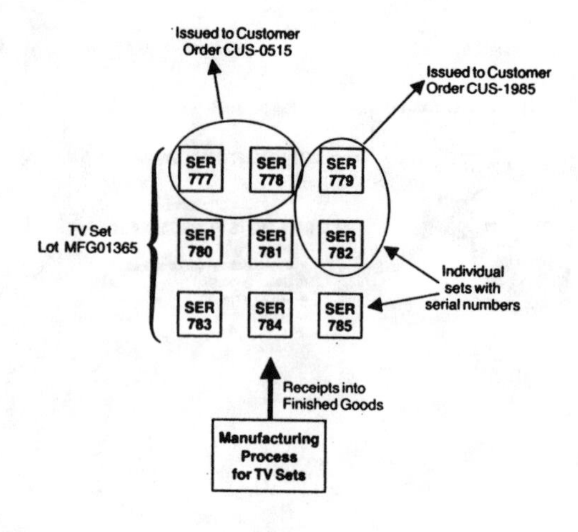

Figure 7 *Serial Numbering*

this is shown in Figure 6. An inspector has identified a defective product. An Indented Lot Source Inquiry is initiated to determine who stuffed the PC boards that went into the product. A hold order may be placed on other computers using PC boards stuffed by this worker.

As new variables are added or altered (new setup procedure, new vendor, etc.), the user can temporarily "turn on" traceability for all items concerned, wait to see if defects occur, then later "turn off" traceability.

Improving Inventory Balance Accuracy: By cycle counting individual lots of material, a greater degree of control can be obtained, boosting inventory accuracy to 99% or better. Some companies use quantity thresholds as a trigger to stockroom personnel to count material. They typically define lots in this case to represent an order's or a shift's worth of production to identify groups of material that move in and out of stock together.

Tracing Costs of Rework: Some nonregulated companies use lot traceability systems to trace defective component material back to the vendor so they can charge the costs of rework to that vendor.

Sorting Shipments to Customers: Lot traceability systems can be used to mix lots of material sent to customers to minimize the impact of a recall of one particular lot. Also, they can be used to ensure that products using subassemblies built at different revision levels aren't mixed, so the customer gets a homogeneous shipment.

Serial Numbering: In some companies, it is necessary to track material at an even greater level of detail—the serial number. A serial number is a unique identifier assigned to an individual physical component or finished good for warranty verification or liability reporting. The quantity of a serial number is assumed to be one. A finished lot can contain hundreds or thousands of parts stamped with serial numbers. Serial numbers can be assigned at the time finished product is produced and received, or when it is shipped to a customer. Serial numbering is not practical for manufacturers of drugs, food products, or chemicals because of the large volume of physical units (tablets, cans, jars) produced. It is commonly used by aerospace and defense, automotive, appliance, and electrical consumer products manufacturers.

Lot traceability systems handle the serial number as a special type of lot. To be practical, the system should allocate a range of serial numbers as finished product is received, and allow for the designation of serial numbers on issue transactions. The user can then retrieve information on which particular serial numbers have gone to a customer as well as which lots. Figure 7 illustrates the relationship between serial numbers, lots, and customer orders. We are primarily interested in verifying which serial numbered TV sets went to which customers.

Policy Decisions

Before a lot traceability system can be installed, the user must make a number of policy decisions related to how the system will function in the user's particular environment.

Policy decisions could include the following:

- Must individual lots be homogeneous with respect to QC status, or can a lot contain material with multiple QC statuses?
- Who will have security access to lot traceability screens, especially screens on which QC statuses are assigned?
- Which items will be traced vs. nontraced?
- How will lot numbers be assigned—manually or automatically?
- Will lot mixing—issuing multiple lots of a given component to the same order—be allowed?
- How will the scrapping of lots be reported—inventory adjustments, issues to a "destruction order," transfer to a Destruction lot?
- How long will lot data be retained on the on-line data base before being archived to history?

Conclusion

Lot traceability systems provide a versatile way to record and store a series of events and relationships. By creatively defining what the lot is, companies can isolate sources of quality problems, improve inventory accuracy, sort material for shipment to customers, and achieve on-line serial number control. New applications for lot traceability systems are just now coming to light.

About the author

Jeff Moran is currently Manager of Software Instruction for MSA Advanced Manufacturing, where he is responsible for training instructors, and scheduling and teaching AMAPS workshops. Prior to this he held materials, production control, and quality control positions in companies that manufacture custom molded rubber products, radios, and electrical transformers. He holds an MBA degree from the University of Minnesota, and is CPIM certified by APICS.

Reprinted from the 1991 APICS *Conference Proceedings.*

The Relationship between Manufacturing Lead Times and the Level of Work-in-Process Inventory in Complex Manufacturing Environments

Joseph Munn and Van D. Gray

Abstract

The purpose of this presentation is to examine the relationship between manufacturing lead times and levels of work-in-process inventories in complex manufacturing environments. Classical inventory theory indicates that as lead times increase, the level of work-in-process (WIP) is not affected. On an average basis, WIP remains relatively constant. This "understanding" rests on the assumption that plant utilization is less than 100%, and therefore all backlog situations are only temporary in nature. However, John J. Kanet reports that while most practitioners "know" that increases in lead time tend to increase Work-in-Process, the reasons for this are not obvious. The authors' experience, both in industrial environments and through classroom exercises, led to the notion that the WIP increases as manufacturing transfer batch size increases. The presentation will examine the effects on Work-in-Process, and output resulting from an increase in lead time.

A simulation model was constructed in an effort to examine the degree of fluctuation of WIP as manufacturing lead times are allowed to vary. The model depicts a manufacturing environment producing two separate products made with common components. In this environment, incoming materials arrive periodically and are processed in lots. Lot size is determined by lead time targets. The levels of WIP are observed as both lead times and lot sizes change. This paper discusses the relationship between lead times and WIP and describes the effects that varying lead times have on the level of WIP.

The Importance of Lead Times and Inventory

Classical inventory theory indicates that as lead times increase, the level of Work-in-Process is not affected. On an average basis, WIP remains relatively constant. This "understanding" rests on the assumption that plant utilization is less than 100%, and therefore all backlog situations are only temporary in nature. However, Kanet reports that most practitioners "know" that increases in lead time tend to increase Work-in-Process, but that the reasons for this are not obvious [Kanet]. The authors' experience, both in industrial environments and through classroom exercises, led to the notion that the WIP increases as manufacturing transfer batch size increases.

The relationship between batch sizes and Work-in-Process is obvious. As batch size increases, naturally there will be a larger quantity of products in the system, leading to increased levels of Work-in-Process. Likewise, an increase in manufacturing lead-time intuitively will lead to an increase in Work-in-Process inventory. As products are produced, parts enter the system in time frames sufficient to keep the production process loaded. The more time allotted, the more parts will enter the system, leading to increased levels of Work-in-Process. But what about the effect on output? Traditionally, longer lead times and larger batch sizes have been believed to be required in order to produce in sufficient quantities to meet specified demand. As batch sizes drop, lead-times drop, but output will also drop. Whether this is the case remains to be seen.

Simulation Model

To analyze the effects of batch size, manufacturing lead-time, output, and Work-in-Process, a "balanced" complex production line model was constructed. The model, depicted here in figure 1, is a three stage process in which parts arrive at intervals consistent with batch size objectives (periodic replenishment) and service times are identical.

The model depicts a typical assembly process of two products: Product A and Product B. Further, these two products share a component part illustrated in figure 1 as the convergence of points 14 and 15 at node 18. Stations identified as 1 through 8 represent raw material release points. Processing activities are identified as A0, Al, A2, A3,

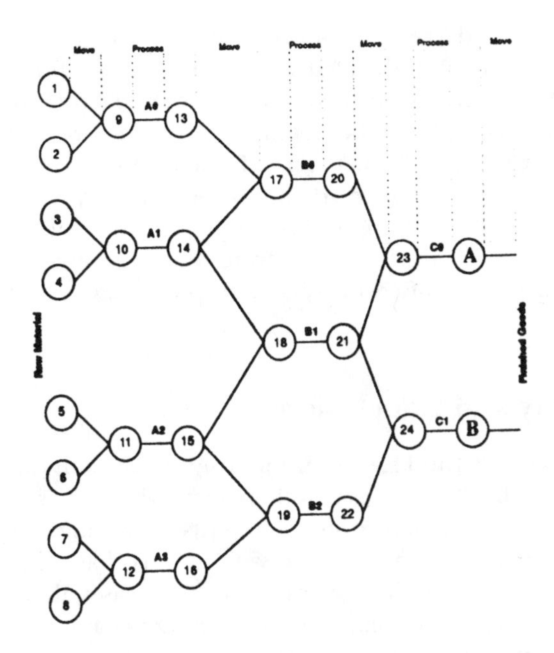

Figure 1

Batch Size	PRODUCT A Mfg. Lead-time	PRODUCT A Total Output	Total WIP	PRODUCT B Mfg. Lead-time	PRODUCT B Total Output
1					
Mean	326.60	1318.00	172.20	277.00	1335.20
Std. Dev	85.97	28.08	85.88	68.89	9.58
Range	188.00	70.00	228.00	175.00	20.00
5					
Mean	422.00	1329.00	456.00	437.33	1296.67
Std. Dev	82.21	8.54	163.45	51.48	23.63
Range	156.00	17.00	355.00	99.00	45.00
10					
Mean	843.60	1281.80	618.00	698.60	1266.00
Std. Dev	284.55	84.66	228.30	91.18	30.50
Range	744.00	162.00	520.00	217.00	80.00
20					
Mean	1012.00	1290.40	624.00	902.40	1285.80
Std. Dev	434.09	78.96	286.50	120.79	46.78
Range	1101.00	162.00	680.00	305.00	120.00
40					
Mean	1092.40	1287.80	1208.00	1216.80	1246.00
Std. Dev	168.32	51.81	388.23	410.66	74.70
Range	437.00	119.00	880.00	899.00	170.00

Table 1. Calculated means, standard deviations, and ranges of 25 simulation runs for a typical production environment with varying batch sizes. (Manufacturing lead-times are reported in hours, while output and WIP are reported in units. WIP is not product specific.)

Table 1

Variable	PRODUCT A F-test	PRODUCT A p	PRODUCT B F-test	PRODUCT B p
Mfg. LT	6.231	.002	12.452	.0001
Output	.287	.8828	2.913	.0475
WIP	11.228	.0001		

Table 2. Analysis of Variance of Batch Size and the effects on Manufacturing Lead-time, Output, and WIP. (WIP is not product specific.)

Table 2

B0, B1, B2, C0, and C1. Finished products are shown at the far right of figure 1 as node A and node B. Once raw materials enter the system, they are transferred to each process in batches of either one, five, ten, twenty, or forty units. Each move or transfer consumes an average of two minutes, while the average process time per part is ten minutes. In this system, then, the average minimum cycle time for a single product would be thirty-eight minutes. For the purposes of this paper, demand for Product A and B is considered to be equal, and no setup times or breakages at the various process steps are incurred. The single question of the effects that batch size has on the manufacturing lead-time, total output, and the associated levels of Work-in-Process is best illuminated within this "balanced, and perfectly maintained," environment.

Methodology

Simulations were conducted for batch sizes of one, five, ten, twenty, and forty units each for a duration of 13,520 hours. A series of five replications for each batch quantity brought the total number of simulation runs to twenty-five. The five observations for each batch condition were averaged to produce the values reported in table 1.

Results

Additionally, an analysis of variance was conducted to determine the significant differences, if any, that exist between the various batch size policies and the manufacturing lead-time, total system output and level of Work-in-Process inventory. Table 2 summarizes the results of the analysis of variance, indicating that there is a highly significant relationship between batch size and manufacturing lead-time for both Product A and B. There is also a strong relationship between the batch size and the level of WIP.

BATCH SIZE COMPARISON	PRODUCT A	PRODUCT B
1 vs. 5	——	*
1 vs. 10	*	*
1 vs. 20	*	*
1 vs. 40	*	*
5 vs. 10	——	——
5 vs. 20	*	*
5 vs. 40	*	*
10 vs. 20	——	——
10 vs. 40	——	*
20 vs. 40	——	*

Table 3. Group-wise Contrasts of Batch Size and the effects on Manufacturing Lead-time. (* denotes that the Fisher PLSD was significant at 95% level.)

Table 3

BATCH SIZE COMPARISON	PRODUCT A	PRODUCT B
1 vs. 5		
1 vs. 10		*
1 vs. 20		
1 vs. 40		*
5 vs. 10		
5 vs. 20		
5 vs. 40		
10 vs. 20		
10 vs. 40		
20 vs. 40		

Table 4. Group-wise Contrasts of Batch Size and the effects on Total Output. (* denotes that the Fisher PLSD was significant at 95% level.)

Table 4

BATCH SIZE COMPARISON	PRODUCT A & B
1 vs. 5	
1 vs. 10	*
1 vs. 20	*
1 vs. 40	*
5 vs. 10	
5 vs. 20	
5 vs. 40	*
10 vs. 20	
10 vs. 40	*
20 vs. 40	*

Table 5. Group-wise Contrasts of Batch Size and the effects on Work-in-Process Inventories. (* denotes that the Fisher PLSD was significant at 95% level.)

Table 5

Clearly, the results indicate that as batch size increases, the lead-time and level of Work-in-Process also increase. From the analysis, total output for the system does not seem to be highly dependent on batch size.

Tables 3, 4 and 5 report contrasts between varying batch size policy and the associated effects on manufacturing lead-time, system output, and system levels of Work-in-Process inventory. It can be noted that lead-time was not significantly different for batch sizes from one to five or for batches from five to ten. Work-in-Process inventory levels were not found to be significantly different for batches from one to five, five to ten, or from ten to twenty. No difference was identified for system output as batch sizes changed.

Summary and Conclusions

From tables 3,4 and 5, some interesting conclusions can be drawn. Table 3 indicates that there may exist a series of plateaus or logical improvement points regarding the firm's batch size policy. The message here is that while lead-time increases as the size of the batch increases, there exists some degree of tolerance to batch size changes. It appears that as batch sizes increase from one to five, a significant deterioration in the firm's manufacturing lead-time does not seem to occur; however, further increases in the batch size have a serious effect on the firm's lead-time. The same phenomenon is depicted as batch quantity moves from five units to ten units, and from ten units to twenty. Table 5 illustrates a similar pattern regarding increases in the level of Work-in-Process inventory as batch size increases. As one changes the batch policy, there appears to be some tolerance to the negative effects that change has on the WIP (and the associated investment in materials) and on manufacturing lead-time. This suggests that a batch size change from an ideal size of one to that of two or three may not yield significantly longer lead-times or greater levels of investment in inventory. Likewise, a batch size of six, seven, or eight may not be significantly different than a batch size of five. Perhaps this information will be useful in dispelling the notion that there is a single "best" batch size value. Rather, there are degrees of "best." If other competitors in the industry normally operate with large batch sizes, then to increase ones ability to quote shorter lead-times, and reduce the level of investment in inventory (and thus freeing cash for other activities while maintaining the same output), simply reduce batch size to the next lower level. A proposed rule-of-thumb suggested by this analysis would be to cut batch size in successive one-half increments, until performance measures indicate that lead-time and inventory improvements have been realized.

Table 4 suggests that while manufacturing lead-time and WIP are adversely affected as the batch size is increased, total output for the system does not seem to change. Stated simply, the firm tends to produce the same number of total units regardless of batch quantity. However, as the size of the batch increases, the firm's responsiveness diminishes. A large batch size inhibits the firm's ability to change. The large-batch firm produces as much as the small-batch firm; it just takes the large-batch firm longer.

The implications from this study are clear: as lot size increases beyond Just-in-Time or near Just-in-Time ideals, WIP and manufacturing lead-time soar. However, the authors would like to caution against generalizations to all cases based upon this narrowly defined exercise. Nevertheless, reducing the batch size appears to enable the firm to reap the benefits associated with reductions in manufacturing lead-time, and reduced levels of investment in Work-in-Process, while maintaining or gaining a slight increase in the level of goods produced by the system

References

[1] Kanet, J. J. "Toward Understanding Lead Times in MRP Systems," P&IM Review, 3rd qt., (1982), 1-14 .

[2] Orlicky, J. Material Requirements Planning, McGraw-Hill (New York, 1975).

[3] SLAM II version 4.03 by Pritsker and Associates, (West Lafayette, Indiana, 1983).

About the authors

VAN D. GRAY is assistant professor of management at the Hankamer School of Business where he teaches production/operations and inventory/resource management. Van earned a BS degree from Houston Baptist University, and both MBA and PhD degrees from the University of North Texas. He joined the faculty in 1986 after teaching for 7 years at the University of Missouri at Columbia.

He is a member of the American Production and Inventory Control Society, Decision Sciences Institute, and the Association of Computing Machinery. Recently, Van has been involved with the Avraham Y. Goldratt Institute, where he is assisting in the implementation of information systems in constraint theory environments.

JOSEPH R. MUNN is currently an assistant professor at Baylor University. He holds a Ph.D. from Texas A&M University and is recognized as a CPIM by APICS. His articles have appeared in Decision Sciences *and the* Journal of the Operational Research Society*, in addition to a number of conference proceedings. His research interests include the management of quality programs, Just-in-Time/TQC production systems, manufacturing maintenance systems, application of simulation modeling to productive systems, and distribution and logistics.*

He is a member of the American Production and Inventory Control Society, Decision Sciences Institute, the Institute of Management Sciences, and the Association of Computing Machinery.

Reprinted from the *1996 APICS International Conference Proceedings.*

Accounting and the Theory of Constraints

Charlene W. Spoede, Ph.D., CPA, CMA

Until recently, theory of constraints proponents have paid far more attention to criticizing cost accounting than to encouraging its adaptation to support TOC decisions. At best, practitioners were told to "forget costs" and concentrate on throughput. However, no firm can afford to ignore costs. And most of our performance measures reinforce the importance of costs. Fortunately, there is a way that cost accounting can be adapted to generate information that focuses on throughput as well as costs.

This paper will try to reconcile cost accounting and the Theory of Constraints. The first section will review a bit of the history of cost accounting, so that we know how we arrived where we are today and why our traditional cost systems no longer provide the information we need. To validate this section and to clarify your own cost accounting beliefs, you should take the Accounting True/False Test included in Appendix 1 to this paper.

The second section of this paper will discuss "throughput" accounting as it is being used today, and how it might be integrated with activity-based accounting. This section also reviews a model for presenting the income statement in a segmented format. Segments might be defined as products, business lines, geographic areas, customers, or any other cost object of interest.

The subject of the final section is using appropriate costs in decision making. Capacity availability and utilization are critical pieces of necessary decision information. This section includes suggestions for identifying relevant items and some simple examples of relevant items for some common decisions.

Traditional Cost Accounting

Assumptions upon Which Cost Accounting Was Built

Cost accounting was originally designed to give decision makers relevant information to make informed decisions on adding additional products, automating operations, making or buying component parts, increasing capacity and other decisions we still make today. The assumptions underlying the system as it was developed reflected the reality of that time period. The assumptions were that direct materials were a purely variable cost; direct labor, which was paid on a piecework basis, was a purely variable cost; and overhead existed primarily to support direct laborers and was a portion (less than 10%) of total product cost.

With these assumptions and some reordering of record keeping, F. Donaldson Brown, in the early part of this century, was able to develop a system for Du Pont and later General Motors that gave them a tremendous advantage over competitors.[1] Overhead was firmly established as a function of direct labor, and total production costs were carried down to the unit level. At some point, we became enamored of "cost per unit" and forgot the basic assumptions upon which it was built.

A basic truth about cost allocation is that the relative total of whatever base is used to allocate a total cost, over time, will decrease. All that is required for this "truth" to hold is that people are rational. That is, once people know that they will be "charged" for their use of the base, they will try to decrease their consumption of the base. Because the original base was direct labor, there was tremendous incentive for all parties (engineers, operating managers, etc.) to reduce the quantity of direct labor in all operations. Hence, automation almost was assured once the base was chosen.

Also, because overhead was spread over all users and no one decision-making manager was directly responsible for all overhead items, there was every incentive not to expend considerable effort to control or reduce overhead spending. Thus, we might logically have predicted the occurrence of the current situation of greatly decreased direct labor and tremendously increased overhead.

Violation of Basic Assumptions

Today, labor is not a significant part of total product cost (on average, about 10 percent and falling), and generally workers are paid by the hour or week, not by each piece produced. Overhead, rather than being a small portion of total product cost, now is a major cost item representing about 50-60 percent of total product cost. Two of the three major assumptions upon which our traditional cost systems were built currently are invalid, yet we remain in love with the unit product costs resulting from this flawed system.

To see how entrenched this system has become, answer the 15 true/false questions in Appendix 1 to this paper. While all of the questions have some truth in them, the general answer to each one is "false."

Current Accounting Axioms That Frequently are Violated

In a working paper case study (1995), Eric Noreen has summarized some basic cost axioms that seem entirely reasonable and acceptable:

1. The sum of product costs should equal total (manufacturing) costs. [The sum of the parts is equal to the whole.]
2. No cost should be assigned more than once. [There should be no double-counting of costs.]
3. Given a fixed production technology and the prices of inputs, the cost of a product is a constant. [There is a true and immutable cost for every product or service.]
4. If fabrication of a product consumes a costly resource and the amount that is consumed is known, then a portion of the cost of that resource should be assigned to the product. [All production costs should be assigned somewhere.]

While these four axioms seem entirely reasonable, they routinely are violated by all traditional cost systems. The first axiom justifies our concentration on total manufacturing, as opposed to total costs of getting product or service into customers' hands and fulfilling all warranties. The second axiom implies that once actual costs have been covered, we cease the allocation process. Of course, we do not discontinue allocations, we merely end the period in an "overapplied" status. The third axiom assures us that there is a true product cost and all we have to do is find it. Unfortunately, this "truth" is entirely governed by our assumptions, which we can change at will. Finally, the fourth axiom states that all production costs must be assigned, not that they must be assigned in a way that is defensible to all parties. There is no axiom relating to assignment/allocation of selling and administrative expenses because we generally have ignored these things when we design cost systems.

In spite of the fact that the foundations of our traditional cost systems have crumbled, our managers use the results of their systems as if they reflected reality. The real problem is not that the wrong overhead base was selected, or that we should have switched bases at some past point in time. The real problems are the assumptions that (1) there is a cause-effect relationship between the base and the cost to be allocated, and (2) that cost behavior can be ignored. The theory of constraints addresses these two issues.

Theory of Constraints Accounting

Throughput Accounting

The theory of constraints, as well as just-in-time and total quality management concepts, emphasizes the revenue or "throughput" side of the net income equation. Throughput is generally defined by the people who developed the theory of constraints as revenues minus the costs paid to people outside the firm such as vendors, subcontractors, etc. Because materials and subcontracting work are variable costs, it is a small step to enlarge the definition of throughput to revenues minus all variable costs. This definition also fits the broader philosophy that "cost" should include whatever it takes to deliver a product or service to a customer since it would include items such as sales commissions determined on a percentage of sales (or, more uncommonly, gross margin or contribution margin) basis.

Once we have modified the definition of throughput to revenues minus variable costs, the result, called contribution margin, is widely recognized by accountants and business school graduates. This contribution margin format forms the basis for direct or variable costing income statements, now referred to as "throughput accounting," as well as the basic structure for cost-volume profit (break-even) analysis.

Direct (Variable) Costing or Throughput Income Statements versus Traditional Income Statements

Throughput accounting, like direct or variable costing accounting, focuses on the behavior of costs. All costs must be divided into their fixed and variable components. However, this process need not be precise—if a cost is mostly variable or mostly fixed, it can be treated according to its more heavily weighted behavior.[2]

An example of a variable costing (throughput) income statement and a traditional (absorption costing) income statement is shown below for a company that has no beginning inventories of work-in-process or finished goods, produces 20,000 units, and sells 15,000 units for $20 each. There is no ending work-in-process inventory. Costs are shown in Figure 1.

The traditional (absorption costing) income statement shows $97,500 - $82,500 = $15,000 greater income than the variable costing (throughput) statement. This is because the traditional statement has deferred to another period a portion of the fixed manufacturing overhead costs assigned to the units produced but not sold. The variable costing statement has expensed all fixed manufacturing overhead costs in the current period.

When inventories are increasing, the traditional income statement always will show greater income.[3] Since the example company increased its inventory by 5,000 units, the traditional income will be 5,000 units x $3 fixed manufacturing overhead cost per unit = $15,000 greater than the variable costing statement. If inventories decrease, the opposite effect occurs: variable costing operating income is higher than traditional operating income.

Note that total selling and administrative expenses, while shown on different parts of the two statements, are identical in total amount. Also, note that variable selling and administrative expenses vary with sales, not production.

Cost Item	Details	Total	Per Unit
Direct materials	40,000 units @ $2	$ 80,000	$4.00
Direct labor	2,500 hours @ $8	20,000	1.00
Variable manufacturing overhead	4,000 mach. hrs. @ $10	40,000	2.00
Fixed manufacturing overhead	4,000 mach. hrs. @ $15	60,000	3.00
Variable selling and administrative		22,500	1.50
Fixed selling and administrative		30,000	2.00
Total costs incurred		$250,000	

Variable Costing (Throughput) Inc. Stmt.

Revenues (15,000 units)		$300,000
Variable costs		
Direct materials	$60,000	
Direct labor	15,000	
Variable mfg. OH	30,000	
Var. sell. & ad.	22,500	
Total variable costs		127,500
Contribution margin		$172,500
Fixed costs		
Manufacturing	$60,000	
Sell. and admin.	30,000	
Total fixed costs		90,000
Net operating income		$ 82,500

Traditional (Absorption Costing) Inc. Stmt.

Revenues (15,000 units)		$300,000
Cost of goods sold		
Beg. Fin. Goods	0	
Cost of goods manufactured	$200,000	
Less end. Fin. Gds.	50,000	
Cost of goods sold		150,000
Gross profit (margin)		$150,000
Sell. and admin. expenses		
Variable	$ 22,500	
Fixed	30,000	
Total sell. and ad. exp.		52,500
Net operating income		$ 97,500

Figure 1. *Costs*

Killen Company

	Product 1	Product 2	Product 3
Revenue	$150	$120	$ 90
Variable costs	60	40	45
Contribution margin	$ 90	$ 80	$ 45
Constraint time	20 min.	20 min.	5 min.
CM per constraint time	$4.50/min.	$4/min.	$9/min.

Figure 2. *Killen Company*

Importance of Capacity Information

Throughput accounting requires information on capacity availability and capacity utilization as well as contribution margin, to make appropriate decisions. Assume the Killen Company has an internal physical production constraint and three products with contribution margins of $90 for Product 1, $80 for Product 2, and $45 for Product 3. Products 1 and 2 require 20 minutes of time on the constraint to produce each finished unit; Product 3 requires 5 minutes. Even though it has the lowest contribution margin, the firm's best product in this situation is Product 3. Product 3 is the "best" product, because its contribution margin per constraining factor is $9 per minute, versus $4.50 for Product 1 and $4 for Product 2 (See Figure 2).

Therefore, Killen Company should concentrate on producing and selling Product 3 until it exhausts its demand in the marketplace. Then it should concentrate on Product 1 until its demand has been entirely filled. Finally, any remaining processing time should be devoted to Product 2.

Notice that total processing time on all resources is not a required piece of information once a constraint has been identified.[4] While individual resource processing times might be used by an activity-based accounting system to assign costs to products, these costs usually are not relevant for decisions. (The last section of this paper will discuss relevant items.)

Selecting the appropriate product mix, using the concept of contribution margin per constraining factor, is a central piece of the logistics portion of TOC. However, the idea of contribution margin per constraining factor has appeared in management accounting textbooks (usually in an abbreviated treatment) for over two decades.

Segment Margin Income Statements

The two income statements shown above are aggregated for the entire firm. If detailed information on product lines, areas, or customers is desired, the fixed costs can be treated in a better way. Rather than grouping all fixed costs together, they can be separated into traceable fixed costs that can rationally be linked to the cost object of interest—and therefore easily assigned—and common fixed costs that only can be assigned on some arbitrary basis and are best kept together and not assigned or allocated.

For example, a traceable fixed cost is a cost for an item either used exclusively by the cost object (such as an inspection device used for only one product) or is a joint cost, where several cost objects have pooled their resources to provide more efficient, effective service (such as a centralized purchasing department or a centralized graphics lab). The definition of the cost object, what fixed costs are "traceable," and what fixed costs are "common" to all units must be decided by each company. A tracking system such as activity-based costing would provide the information for determining traceable fixed costs. This process can result in segment margins statements such as the following one for the Killen Company in Figure 3.

Killen Company

	Product 1	Product 2	Product 3	Total
Revenues	$13,500	$1,200	$7,200	$21,900
Variable costs	5,400	400	3,600	9,400
Contribution margin	$ 8,100	$ 800	$3,600	$12,500
Traceable fixed costs:	2,600	500	1,900	5,000
Segment margin	$ 5,500	$ 300	$1,700	$7,500
Common fixed costs				7,000
Operating income				$ 500

Figure 3. *Segment margins statements*

The advantage of showing traceable fixed costs is that it clarifies how past decisions have impacted current profitability. Thus, to the extent possible, managers are encouraged to control[5] traceable fixed costs and find ways they can be used more effectively.

While the segment margin describes each product's contribution to cover common fixed costs and operating income, it does not in any way define the "best" product. This is because most of the traceable fixed costs may be sunk, meaning that even if the product goes away, the cost will not. Therefore, this statement format can be used only to compare actual results with expectations for the period and to make product (segment) managers aware of the fixed costs for which they are responsible.

The use of costs in decision making requires that we first identify which costs are relevant to a particular decision. The final section of this paper addresses relevant items.

Using Costs in Decision Making

The Danger of Arbitrary Allocations

There is a fundamental truth about cost accounting. The moment the company begins arbitrarily assigning costs to areas or segments, it causes people to begin to focus on the wrong thing(s) for decision-making purposes. As we saw in the Killen Company example, even nonarbitrary assignments of fixed costs can cause us to come to erroneous conclusions.[6] The key to making good decisions is the ability to recognize what is relevant to a particular decision.

Items That Are Relevant for Decisions

A relevant item is easy to define, but hard to practice. A relevant item (revenue or cost) is one that will occur in the future and will be different for the alternatives under consideration. Relevant items are those things that make a difference in a decision. For example, if revenues will be the same no matter which equipment is purchased, revenues are irrelevant to the equipment purchase decision. Likewise, expenditures that occurred in the past are sunk costs, and book values are irrelevant. However, if a previously purchased item has a current market value, that amount is relevant to a replacement decision.

In throughput accounting, most decisions can be made by checking the impact on three critical measures: throughput, inventory, and operating expense. The idea is to increase throughput, decrease inventory (to shorten manufacturing lead time and increase future sales), and decrease operating expense. Of course, all three desirable movements do not have to happen for each decision. In fact, inventory or operating expense may increase if they are more than offset by an increase in throughput.

In the Killen Company example in the previous section, individual resource capacity availability and utilization were necessary in order to know if an internal constraint existed. Assume that Killen Company has determined that the market will buy a maximum of 90 units of Product 1, 50 units of Product 2, and 80 units of Product 3. A complete schematic of the Killen Company's production process, showing flows, times, capacities, costs, sales prices, and market demand, is included in Appendix 2 to this paper.

The Killen Company accumulated the data in Figure 4 to identify a constraint. Even if Resource A had been loaded more than 100%, but less than 133%, resource B would still be the most binding constraint. Therefore, the theory of constraints suggests a type of step-wise optimization algorithm. Companies can focus on the "worst" constraint until it no longer is a problem, then go to next constraint.

Most companies, however, would identify an internal constraint using logic and intuition (cause-and-effect analysis from the theory of constraints thought process), not analytic data. The primary reasons why analytic data cannot be used to identify a constraint are that our data are notoriously corrupt, and our processes are so complex and changing that by the time we establish a computer program to precisely calculate resource loads, the entire environment

Killen Company

	Units Demanded	Time required on each resource for each unit produced[7] A	B	C	D	Total
Product 1	90	10	20	5	10	45
Product 2	50	5	20	5	5	35
Product 3	80	15	5	10	10	40

Total Time Required on Resources (in minutes):

	A	B	C	D
Product 1	900	1,800	450	900
Product 2	250	1,000	250	250
Product 3	1,200	400	800	800
Tot. Min. Needed	2,350	3,200	1,500	1,950
Total Min. Avail. (Capacity)	2,400	2,400	2,400	2,400
Resource Load	98%	133%	63%	81%

Figure 4. ***Killen Company***

is likely to have changed. It is possible, however, for a company to decide what markets they will serve or what products they will produce, and not be subject to the whims of every customer that comes to the door.

Once a constraint is identified, the time required on the constraint (not the time required on all resources) is needed in order to compute the contribution margin per constraining factor. Using this information for the Killen Company, Product 3 was determined to be the best product, Product 1 next best, and Product 2 the third best product.

Therefore, relevant information for the Killen Company product-mix decision is (1) contribution margin per constraining factor (resource B), and (2) market demand. Given the current resource base, the product mix of 80 units of Product 3, 90 units of Product 1, and 10 units of Product 2 permits Killen to earn the highest weekly operating income possible. This plan also determines exactly how much inventory is required (sufficient to only cover items produced). Excess inventory in the system almost surely will guarantee that the preferred mix will not be produced because of worker confusion regarding what they should work on next when they have too many choices.

In a make-or-buy decision, the relevant cost to make a component are the costs that go away if we buy. Generally, these costs include direct materials and little else. However, if the component we are considering outsourcing requires time on an internal constraint, the additional contribution margin the company could generate if additional time on the constraint were available is an opportunity cost of continuing to make the component (or, alternatively, an "opportunity revenue" of purchasing, which reduces total purchase cost).

Looking for opportunity costs and opportunity revenues can be accomplished by maintaining a logical cause-effect-cause orientation to potential changes. This process does not require a genius, it merely takes someone familiar with the operation who is willing to spend some time thinking about the implications of changes. Theory of constraints training provides this ability.

Accountants generally are not good at identifying opportunity costs and revenues because they are too removed from actual operations. Managers close to the process must communicate these opportunities to accountants if accountants prepare decision analyses. Alternatively, operating managers must learn how to structure a decision analysis.

Other short-term decisions such as deciding to sell as-is or process further, setting priorities for quality improvement projects, and scrapping or reworking defective units, follow the same general pattern. Prioritizing quality improvements is particularly difficult because we are in the habit of looking at quantities of defects, rather than the "cost" of defects. The total cost of defects, of course, includes time lost on a constraint (that is lost forever) and not total time on all resources because most resources have excess capacity and are idle a good part of each day.

The only relevant costs (or revenues) are those that will be different for the various alternatives being considered and that are future costs. Also, opportunity costs (or opportunity revenues) are relevant pieces of information that must be included in the analysis.

Long-Term Decisions

In addition to short-term decisions, long-term capital budgeting decisions also must include relevant costs and revenues. To appropriately do this, the impact on the entire system must be considered, not merely what an individual resource might accomplish if it were independent of all other resources. Most resources are part of a chain of dependent operations. Unless the entire chain is strengthened, any improvement or additional investment is wasted.

Our present capital budgeting techniques, such as net present value and internal rate of return, work well when all relevant items are included in the analysis. However, the procedure is difficult for some employees to understand.

TOC people recently have developed a new long-term decision technique called Flush that calculates the point not only when all cash will be returned (as payback models do), but also when all the days of cash investment have been matched by an equal number of days of cash inflows. This is an intriguing technique, but, because of space limitations, it will not be pursued in this paper.[8]

Conclusion

One thing that activity-based cost accounting and activity-based management ideas have done for the accounting profession is to make clear to accountants and nonaccountants that cost accounting systems not only must be changed, they can be changed. A "standard" financial reporting system will not provide the information managers require.

The solution is not as easy as adding nonfinancial measures to our reports. Developing and implementing management reporting systems that help our managers, rather than put them on the defensive each month or each quarter, certainly is within our capabilities.

To do this, however, we must be willing to question all the assumptions that underlie our reports. We also must be much more system oriented and less "locally" oriented.

Consider the Following Question

Rather than focusing our attention on a more detailed reallocation of costs, would we be better off concentrating on the efficient use of our current resources?

Appendix 1

Accounting True/False Test

1. You need to know the fully absorbed unit cost of your product before you can prepare a bid or decide whether to accept a price offered by the customer.
2. A company can measure its company-wide efficiency by measuring the efficiency of each individual worker and/or machine.
3. Worker processing time on a component must be tracked 100% of the time to have accurate measures for standards, for cost allocations, and for efficiency calculations.
4. The only negative effect of carrying excessive work in process inventory is that it ties up working capital.
5. If each area of the company does its best, the entire company will do its best.
6. Measuring an employee's achievement of actual amounts to budgeted amounts is a good way to evaluate performance.
7. Detailed direct labor reporting enables a company to accurately summarize the total direct labor costs of each job.
8. The largest opportunities for improvement for a manufacturing firm are on the plant floor.
9. Just-in-Time and Total Quality Management and Theory of Constraints concepts are applicable only to physical product flows.
10. Direct materials and direct labor are variable costs.
11. A company can earn satisfactory profits if it makes sure that each price proposal that it offers customers covers fully absorbed unit cost plus an adequate margin.
12. The only legitimate concern about capacity is that, on average, it be almost completely (fully) utilized.
13. There is a true and immutable cost for every product or service.
14. Service organizations do not have work in process.
15. Service organizations generally do not need to be concerned about logistics and scheduling.

Notes

1. See F. Donaldson Brown, *Some Reminiscences of an Industrialist*, (Easton, PA: Hive Publishing, 1977, reprint of 1958 ed.). Also see an evaluation of Brown in Peter F. Drucker, *Adventures of a Bystander,* (New York: Harper & Row, 1978), 263-266.
2. There are fairly simple ways to do this ranging from "best guess" to regression analysis.
3. This frequently serves as an incentive for many managers to increase inventories at the end of a period, despite ongoing inventory reduction programs.
4. Be aware that an organization's real constraint is not likely to be in production but rather in order entry, engineering, sales procurement, or some other area.
5. In today's environment, "control" means reduce.
6. Product 1 is not the "best" product even though it has

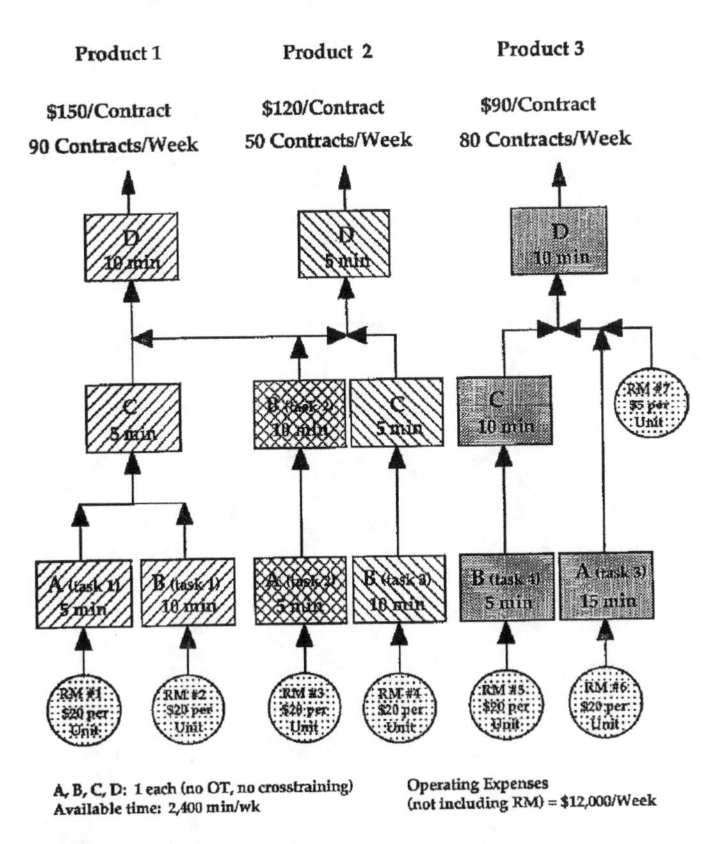

Appendix 2. *Killen Company*

the largest segment margin. With the company's current resource base, Product 3 is the "best" product.

7. See the times required for each operation in Appendix 2.
8. The A.Y. Goldratt Institute's Project Management course includes a detailed explanation of *Flush.*

About the Author

Charlene W. Spoede, Ph.D., CPA, CMA, is Professor, Accounting Department of Baylor University in Waco, Texas. She holds the Emerson O. Henke Chair in Accounting and is Director of the Center for Manufacturing Excellence at Baylor. She is also the owner of Spoede Consulting. Ms. Spoede is a member of the American Institute of Certified Public Accountants, the Financial Executives Institute, the American Accounting Association, and the Institute of Management Accountants.

Ms. Spoede has authored numerous books and articles, including Fundamental Financial and Managerial Accounting, *coauthored with Kermit Larson and Paul Miller, and* Cost Accounting: Managerial Use of Accounting Data, *coauthored with Emerson Henke.*

Reprinted from the *Production and Inventory Management Journal*, First Quarter, 1995.

A Structure for Lot-Tracing Design

Daniel C. Steele, CFPIM

Lot tracing is a requirement for an increasing number of companies. Product liability risks and government regulation mean companies must do more than produce good items. They must identify source material and processes; and if an item is defective, they must find the other items related to suspect sources. Even routinely, customers demand that firms track or certify compliance with quality specifications.

Exactly what are the activities included in lot tracing? When an original equipment manufacturer (OEM) of automotive parts received a lot-tracing requirement from a major customer, the staff found little help in answering that question. One could install a fully integrated manufacturing control system that included predefined lot control, but to do so was expensive and unattractive. The alternative was to change current procedures and systems to gain the traceability. However, little guidance for identifying the key elements of traceability was available in published work.

The purpose of this article is to define the basic elements of lot tracing in repetitive, discrete item manufacturing. The elements of lot tracing proposed in this article were benchmarked against a well-run lot tracing system and found to effectively identify required design decisions. When used to evaluate the system in the OEM facility, the proposed elements provided a useful road map and helped identify shortcomings in one important element. The evaluation of that element, physical lot integrity, and its effect on tracing resolution is demonstrated. Overall, these elements of lot tracing are proposed as a useful starting framework when beginning to evaluate or design lot-tracing functions.

Lot Tracing

Lot traceability is defined by APICS as "the ability to identify the lot or batch numbers of consumption and/or composition for manufactured, purchased, or shipped items [1]." With lot tracing, one identifies suspect items once faulty component material or processes are uncovered. Eads [3] likened lot traceability to a bill of material explosion or implosion (where-used) process. The traceability process explodes from end use to an earlier state and then implodes from an earlier state to all end uses.

As a result of data collected within a lot-tracing system, a number of questions can be answered:

- Which processes or component material were used to make this item? Which resulted in this item being the way it is?
- What were the characteristics of the processes or component material used? What process records, component material sources, letters of analysis, or certificates show the level of compliance to specifications?
- If processes or component material are suspect, what other items may be defective as well? Which items may need inspection or repair?

Others have defined the data used in lot tracing in some detail. Petroff and Hill [4] largely identified the data content and transactions required of a lot-tracing system. For example, they pointed out that the characteristics of an item determine to what detail it is traced. They highlighted the importance of quality information, the types of orders that could be tracked, and the transactions that might be required. Using the types of features that might be found in a computerized tracing system, they showed how the system could be used to gain needed information.

Still, if a computerized system has not defined the lot-tracing system, there is little information on how to organize the actual lot-tracing functions. Lots being traced are not necessarily job orders or containers, particularly in a repetitive environment. And if tracing requirements are not standard, one needs an overall structure that defines the needed functions, regardless of how they are to be implemented.

Elements of Lot-Tracing Design

Four elements define the design of a lot-tracing system: physical lot integrity, data collection, lot-process linking, and reporting. Together, these elements define the full scope of lot traceability. Individually, each element identifies a set of decisions that ultimately create the total system.

Physical Lot Integrity

A lot is a physical grouping of material that is controlled as a unit. A lot is uniquely identified and serves a truer understanding of the costs of services rendered. Tracking the lots, the component material used in them, their transformation to or inclusion in other lots, and, finally, their use as a shipped item is the primary function of traceability. How lots are defined and controlled is an essential design question.

One important aspect of lot definition is resolution. How large the lot is and how well lot integrity or separateness is maintained determines the resolution or precision of the traceability system. Resolution means how narrowly one can identify the grouping of material, components, or other items associated with a lot being traced. For example, a large lot size provides less precision since a single item can only be identified as one of a large batch. Resolution thus determines the exposure to contamination. When exploding from a defective item, a wider resolution means more component material and processes are exposed as possible sources. Also, when a defective component material or process is identified, a wider resolution means more items are exposed as possibly defective.

The size of the lot does not fully define resolution, however. Any loss in integrity of the defined lot widens resolution beyond the lot size. For example, if one lot is mixed with the adjacent one in any way, then both must be included as potentially defective. Loss in lot integrity can take place three ways:

Lot mismatching—where a lot is transformed into a new lot, but the new lot does not exactly match the source lot. As a result, the new lot contains some of two or more source lots (or a source lot was used in two or more final lots). If the new lot quantity does not match the source lot quantity, then mismatching must result.

Lot-end mixing—if lots are processed in continuous or repetitive batches, failure to maintain clear separation between adjacent lots of the same part will result in mixing at the end of one lot and the beginning of the other lot.

Lot-sequence mixing—if control or record keeping depends on a first-in, first-out (FIFO) process, then failure to honor FIFO will result in mixing. A special case of this is rework when not accomplished as part of the original lot or redefined as a new, separate lot. Rework saved for later is out of sequence. If delayed, then mixed with a following lot, integrity is lost and resolution widened.

Regardless of how data collection is accomplished, physical lot control and its level of integrity determine the minimum resolution the system will have. Of course, the nature of the process constrains alternatives in this design element. To move away from existing physical flow can be difficult and expensive. For continuous or repetitive processes in particular, this can be a major issue.

Data Collection

Two types of data are collected—lot-tracing data and process data. Lot-tracing data record the occurrence of movement into processing or storage and the merging or transformation of one lot into another lot. An inventory control system might contain such information. Process data record important production process information, such as statistical process control or quality assurance information.

For lot tracing, Petroff and Hill [4] and Eads [3] provide excellent detail on data requirements. Software designs also structure such data. For process data, the design will usually depend on its original purpose. A statistical process control system, for example, may be manual or electronic, local or networked, and primarily provides for the process control. Regardless of how the data is collected, the lot record and the process data must then be linked.

Lot-Process Linking

Lot-process linking is the cross-referencing of process or component material data to physical lots. In particular, it is the method by which process data is identified with a corresponding production lot. The most straightforward way to link this data is by a lot identification number. That means simply recording both physical lot tracing and process data by the same physical lot identification number. If the information is readily obtained and recorded, the linking is tight and accurate.

Likewise, raw material usage can be clearly recorded by lot number or, in some cases, even marked directly on the part or item. Either provides concise cross-referencing.

A third method not frequently discussed is to link by time and date. Both lot and process data are recorded by the time of processing. Then lot and process data can be collected independently and linked later only when needed. The major advantage is that it does not require existing systems to be tied together. When the time of lot processing is known, it is relatively simple to acquire the process data corresponding to the same period. For example, linking a particular lot to the corresponding process data from an SPC system may occur by simply knowing lot 15 was processed from 2 to 4 p.m. on January 5. Process records for that period can then be retrieved as required. The major disadvantage of time-date linking is that retrieval of that data can be cumbersome and time-consuming. Thus the required frequency and speed of reporting must be considered. Also, any loss of lot integrity (mixing) reduces its effectiveness.

Reporting

Reporting is the retrieval of data from the system. Reporting includes the explosion process of using the lot-tracing data to find source lots or component material associated with an item lot at question. When the source lot or lots are identified, it can also include finding the process data corresponding to the source lot. Reporting also includes the implosion process of identifying potentially contaminated item lots associated with a suspect process or component material.

The design of the reporting function is determined by how data is stored, the frequency access is required, the retrieval time permitted, and storage space limitations. If all data is recorded in a computerized system, data may be fully accessible under almost any condition. If the data is accessed infrequently and long access time is permitted, automated retrieval may not be necessary. Simple manual filing of key data, if well organized, may be sufficient. However, the possibility of considerable clerical effort and an increased risk of error do exist. Cross-linking by time/date might suggest manual retrieval. In any case, storage space for several years of data, electronic or physical, must be planned.

A Benchmark

Evaluation of lot tracing within the automotive OEM firm mentioned earlier took place using the preceding design elements. Two steps were taken. First, a benchmark for each element was taken at a firm known for excellent lot traceability. Second, current procedures at the OEM facility were individually audited for each element.

Four companies were evaluated to determine a good benchmark for lot traceability. The company selected as the benchmark was one where repetitive processing similar to the OEM manufacturer occurred, but also where customer and regulatory demands required a well-designed and complete system. A comparison with the company provided not only a benchmark of performance, but a test of the completeness of the design elements identified.

Table 1 compares the OEM company to the benchmark firm. The elements served as an effective structure for evaluation. No capability was found not included in a design element. However, between the companies, the degree of coverage was quite different.

The importance of traceability was considerably higher at the benchmark firm. Lot control was perfectly maintained, lot data was collected by an automated bar-coding tracking system, process data was collected by an indepen-

Table 1. *Benchmark Comparison*

Dimension	***Current Status***	***Benchmark Company***
Traceability Importance	Increasing	Critical
Nature of the product	Stable, but important	Hazardous
Traceability requirements	Moderate—customer driven	Stringent—regulated
Lot Integrity	Not fully maintained	Fully controlled
Lot mismatching	Frequent mismatched transitions	Fully matched transitions
Lot-end mixing	Mixing on transfer lines	Run breaks prevent mixing
Lot-sequence mixing	Mostly FIFO except rework (delayed to shift end) and assembly lot usage	Strictly FIFO; rework retained inoriginal lot or returned to raw material
Data Collection		
Sources available	Inventory; SPC; container and operation logs	Inventory; production activity; SPC and other special process control
Lot movement and transition	Container log	Bar-coded travellers
Process/Quality	Process logs; stand-alone SPC	Integrated process control
Lot-Process Linking	Lot and process data record by time-date	Process data recorded by container lot number
Reporting Capability		
Importance	Not very	Very
Frequency of reporting	Very infrequent	Very infrequent
Speed of retrieval	One day acceptable	Real time required

dent quality assurance system, and lot-process data was directly linked by lot number. Reporting, which was required infrequently but quickly, was immediately accessible on-line through an interconnected tracking and quality control system.

Audit of the OEM Firm

It was immediately recognized at the OEM firm that neither the importance of traceability nor any obvious need for an integrated computer system demanded total redesign of current procedures and systems. Rather, current systems were compared to each element to determine effectiveness. Any changes were likely to be justified on an incremental basis as experience and insight were gained. While the following is only an illustration, it reflects actual conditions found in the OEM plant. By far the biggest surprise was how poor resolution was with the degree of lot control employed.

Lot Integrity

Physical lot integrity was found to be far worse than suspected. The same product was often run for multiple shifts. Each shift represented about three containers released into fabrication, and each container defined a lot. With a process that was repetitive and often used automated transfer equipment, lot integrity was compromised far more often than was initially apparent. Relatively small losses in lot integrity cascaded into major losses in resolution.

Figure 1 describes the process and the containers used to identify lots. The fabrication process used automated transfer equipment and was fed from tubs containing 2,800 component units. Material flowed continuously through the process. When work was rejected, it was reworked at shift end and included with the final shift lot. At the end of the fabrication line, component units were packed onto pallets of 1,500 units and used in the assembly process.

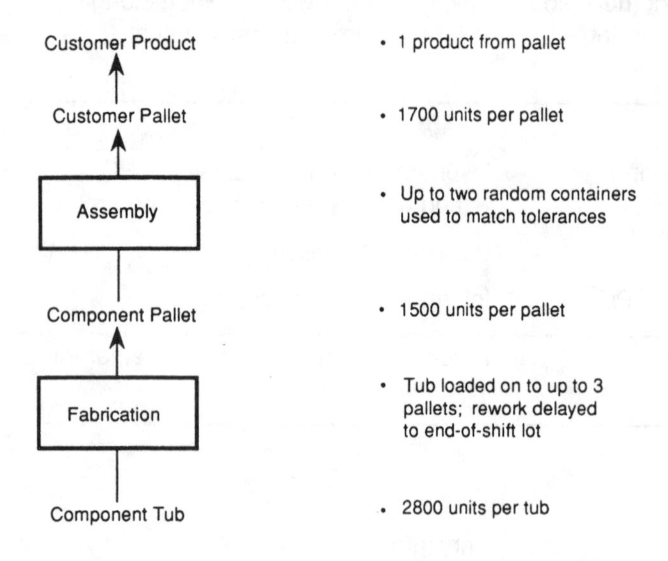

Figure 1 *Process and container flow*

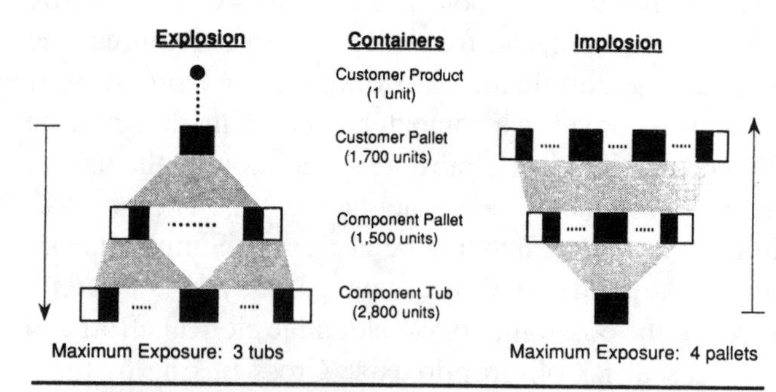

Figure 2 *Assembly and fabrication lot mismatching*

In assembly, a maximum of two pallets of 1,500 units were used to feed the line. Individual components were selected to provide offsetting tolerance, thus providing tight overall specification control. However, FIFO of the incoming pallets could not be maintained since tolerance demands changed. Finished products were packed onto customer pallets of 1,700 units.

Several lot-integrity losses are caused by this process, each reducing resolution. Overall, they become quite complex. To illustrate most clearly, lot mismatching is depicted as the base case. Then the effects of adding each of three other effects (lot-end mixing, rework-sequence mixing, and assembly-sequence mixing) to the base case will be shown individually and in turn. Finally, all will be combined to show the total effect.

Lot mismatching, the base case, and its effect on resolution is shown in **Figure 2.** It occurs because input and output lots did not match as they were transformed in the repetitive process. Exploding from a single defective product to the customer pallet was a direct identification fully recorded and is not considered further. However, exploding from the customer pallet through assembly to the component pallets means two supplying pallets were always involved (one 1,500-unit component pallet was not enough to fill a 1,700-unit customer pallet). A defective product could come from either component pallet. Further, exploding from the component pallet through fabrication to the component tubs shows that as many as three supplying tubs were involved. Since input to output containers did not match in quantity or timing, a component pallet usually contained input from the end of one component tub, one whole tub, and the beginning of a third. With component tubs in production sequence, two component pallets explode into three component tubs. That is, for one defective prod-

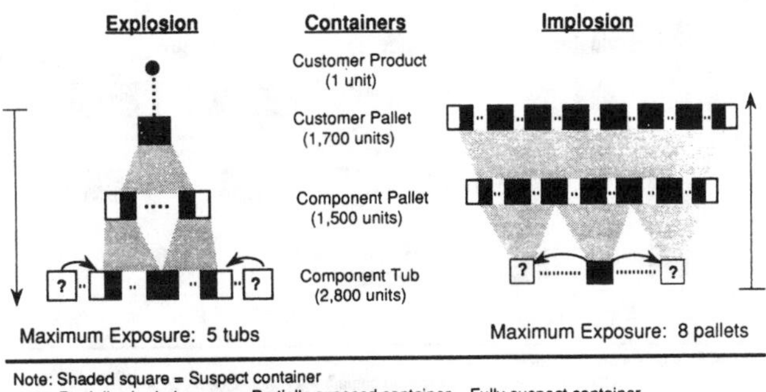

Figure 3 *Lot mismatching with fabrication lot-end mixing*

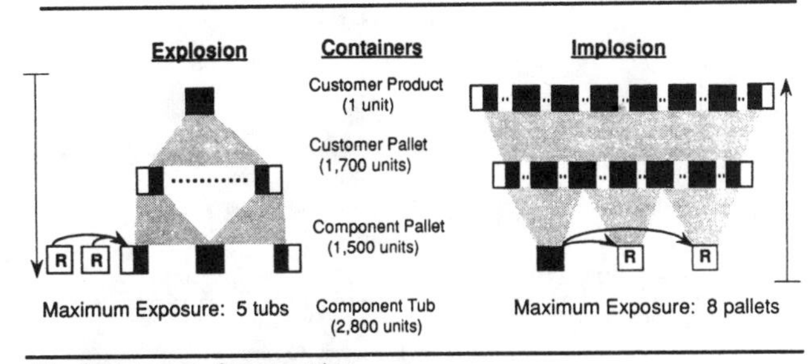

Figure 4 *Lot mismatching with fabrication sequence mixing (rework delayed until end of shift)*

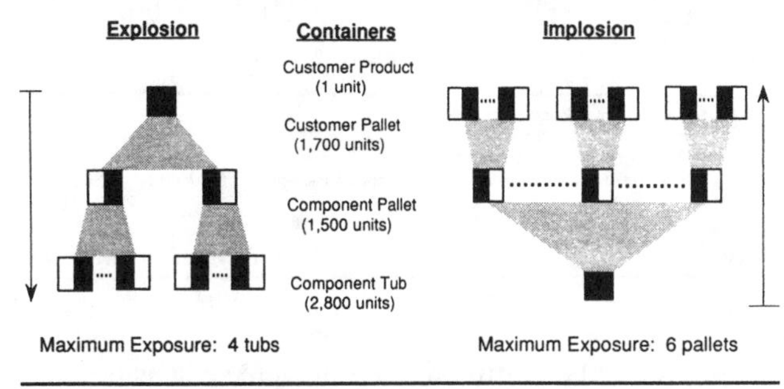

Figure 5 *Lot mismatching with assembly sequence mixing*

uct, it usually was not possible to identify the source with certainty to less than three-tubs resolution at the fabrication process.

Likewise, the implosion process displayed a similar loss in resolution. Having identified one suspect tub from process data, the suspect component material could be in as many as four customer pallets. And this was only from lot mismatching.

Lot-end mixing, when added to the base lot mismatching, is shown in **Figure 3.** Since no separation of components was maintained on the fabrication transfer line, from 1% to 5% of the components were mixed between adjacent lots by fabrication line end. Therefore, in exploding from a defective product, one must include the adjacent component tubs as potential sources of defective component material. Comparing to the base case (Figure 2), exposure was increased from three to five tubs (Figure 3). Likewise, the implosion exposure was increased, doubling from four to eight tubs.

Rework-sequence mixing was yet another loss in resolution at fabrication. **Figure 4** depicts the loss from this effect when combined with only the original base lot mismatching. Since rework was delayed until shift end, FIFO sequence was not maintained. The earliest rejects in a shift might be delayed and included in the third and last container of the shift. Similar to the previous example, Figure 4 shows the rework-sequence mixing increasing explosion exposure from the base of three (Figure 2) to five tubs and implosion exposure from four to eight tubs.

Assembly-sequence mixing effects (with only the base case lot mismatching) are shown in **Figure 5**. Since FIFO was ignored in assembly in order to match tolerances, each of the two input component pallets used were not necessarily adjacent to each other in fabrication sequence. A defective unit could have come from either independently produced component pallet. Without the sequence overlapping, explosion exposure was increased from the three tubs of the base case (Figure 2) to four tubs (Figure 5). The two-product pallets associated with each component pallet were always identified, but they were independently determined for each component pallet depending on tolerance needs. Thus, implosion exposure was increased from four to six tubs.

When all the losses in physical lot integrity are combined, the results are seen in **Figure 6.** A single defective product could be isolated to about 12 tubs at fabrication with certainty. This means an investigation into a single defective unit could involve the processing associated with all 12 tubs at fabrication. Likewise, a process error resulting in a single defective fabrication tub could be isolated to only about 22 customer pallets. Thus, at 1,700 units per pallet, 37,400 units would be suspect.

Clearly, physical lot integrity is a major issue when lot tracing in a repetitive environment. No matter how well data is collected, linked, or reported, resolution can be no better than physical lot integrity permits.

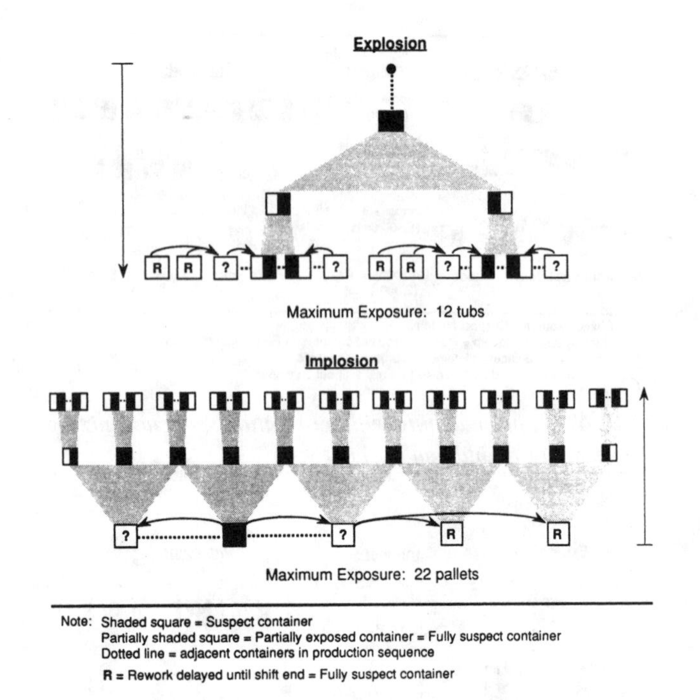

Figure 6 *Lot mismatching with all sources of mixing combined*

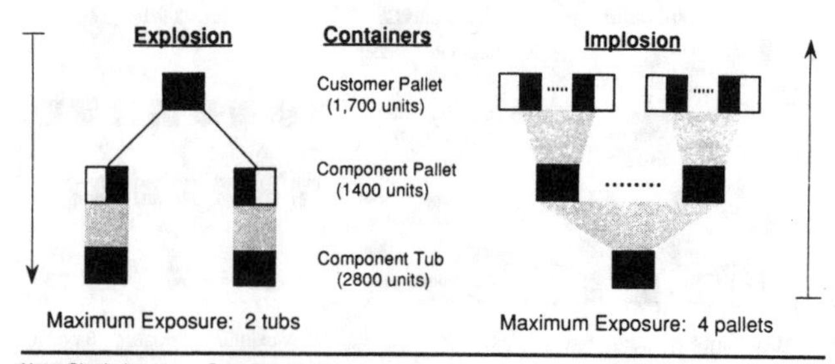

Figure 7 *Fabrication lot matching with no mixing*

Improvements within fabrication were seen as possible. Reducing the component pallet quantity to 1,400 units could permit lot matching. Then one component tub filled exactly two component pallets. Also, creating a separation between lots would eliminate end mixing and doing rework without delay could stop rework-sequence mixing. The separation between lots would produce idle time on the transfer lines, reducing capacity and efficiency. Also, providing capacity to accomplish rework immediately (to rejoin the original lot) meant extra resources. So with some expense, both were possible. However, elimination of the tolerance-matching assembly process would be extremely expensive. Still, resolution could be greatly improved from the fabrication changes alone.

Figure 7 shows resolution if only fabrication lot mismatching, end mixing, and rework-sequence mixing were eliminated. Assembly lot mismatching and sequence mixing were retained. The resulting explosion resolution is only two tubs and an implosion resolution is only four customer pallets. Compared to the previous condition in Figure 6 (12 and 22 containers), the potential for improvement was dramatic.

Data Collection

The collection of lot movement data was accomplished through paper records accompanying each lot, and only minor omissions and errors were found. All lot identities were maintained during processing and could be identified with transformation to new receiving lots. Raw material vendor and lot information were marked on each unit at the gateway process and was complete.

Necessary process data was contained within the local electronic statistical process control (SPC) system and other process logs. Information was adequate to identify process characteristics. No major changes were seen as necessary.

Lot-Process Linking

The lot and process data were linked by recording date and time. Container arrival and completion times were logged for each lot. Process SPC data were also recorded with time information. While linking process data directly via lot number would assist reporting, a costly reporting system would be required. Therefore, no major changes seemed appropriate. All linking could be accomplished through finding the time of lot processing, then finding the process SPC data associated with that time.

Reporting

Retrieval of data was possible, but untested. Since retrieval was permitted for a full day, it was deemed necessary only to ensure that the long-term storage of the records was well organized by date-time for both lot moves and processing information. Access could be time-consuming in terms of clerical labor-hours, but requests were expected very infrequently. No changes were seen as required to meet traceability needs.

Conclusion

In this article, four elements of lot tracing were proposed for repetitive, discrete item manufacturing. Physical lot integrity, data collection, lot-process linking, and reporting were defined and the function of each explained.

As a structure, these design elements were demonstrated as providing a starting point for designing or evaluating lot

 © APICS

tracing, particularly when combined with other literature on data requirements. If a computerized system is being upgraded or purchased, the system itself may offer a structure for the data-related elements such as data collection, lot-process linking, and reporting. But even with such a system, the element of physical lot control must be carefully evaluated, particularly in the repetitive environment. Overall, these elements provide insight into key functions required of any lot-tracing activity.

Acknowledgment

The contribution of Christopher R. Forsythe, D. Bret Gaskins, Steven Groth, Jennifer A. Servatius, and Agnes Szollosy is expressly acknowledged. These individuals participated in the study reported here and provided valuable contributions and insights.

References

1. *APICS Dictionary.* 7th ed. Falls Church, VA: American Production and Inventory Control Society, 1992: 27.
2. Connor, S.J. "Lot Number Control: Tracking and Tracing." *Readings in Production and Inventory Control and Planning*. APICS 27th Annual International Conference (1984): 62-64.
3. Eads, G., and H. Undhein. "Inventory Control with Lot Traceability and Quality Assurance." *Readings in Production and Inventory Control and Planning.* APICS 27th Annual International Conference (1984): 57-61.
4. Petroff, J.N., and A.V. Hill. "A Framework for the Design of Lot-Tracing Systems for the 1990s." *Production and Inventory Management Journal* 32, no. 2 (1991): 55-60.

About the Author

Daniel C. Steele, CFPIM, is an assistant professor in the College of Business Administration, University of South Carolina. Coming from an industrial background, Professor Steele holds a Ph.D. in operations management from the University of Iowa. He also has a BS in electrical engineering and an MS in industrial management from Purdue University. His most recent industrial responsibilities were as director of materials management and plant superintendent. His interests include manufacturing strategy, world-class manufacturing, cellular manufacturing, and manufacturing planning and control systems. Dr. Steele, who has prior articles in this journal, serves as vice-president for the Mid-Carolina chapter of APICS.

Reprinted from *Journal of Cost Management,* Winter 1992, pp. 54-60. Copyright ©, Warren Gorham Lamont. All rights reserved. Used by permission.

Cost Management Concepts and Principles: What an Activity-Based Cost Model Looks Like[1]

Peter B. B. Turney

The modern activity-based costing model has two dimensions: a costing dimension and a process dimension. The *cost* dimension contains cost information about resources, activities, and cost objects. It supports economic evaluations of the strategy and operations of an organization. The *process* dimension contains performance information about the work done in the organization. This information supports judgments about why work is done and how well it is performed. The process dimension brings the world of operations directly into the heart of the cost system. This article explains this new, more comprehensive view of activity-based costing and activity-based management.

A new definition of activity-based costing (ABC) was published in the last issue of the *Journal of Cost Management.* The definition reads as follows:

Activity-based costing—A methodology that measures the cost and performance of activities, resources, and cost objects. Resources are assigned to activities, then activities are assigned to cost objects based on their use. Activity-based costing recognizes the causal relationship of cost drivers to activities.[2]

In contrast to earlier definitions of ABC, which focused only on product costing,[3] this definition includes a wide range of cost and performance information. This expanded definition was selected for the glossary because it was believed to be descriptive of the practice of ABC in the early 1990s, and because an ABC model based on this definition is a powerful tool for improvement.[4]

Two-dimensional ABC

An ABC model based on this definition has two main views. The first is the *cost assignment view,* which is the vertical part of the model shown in Exhibit 1.[5] It reflects the need that organizations have to assign costs to activities and cost objects (including customers as well as products) to analyze critical decisions. These decisions have to do with issues such as the following:

Pricing,

Product mix,

Sourcing,

Product design, and

Setting priorities for improvement efforts.

The second part of the ABC model is the *process view,* which is the horizontal part of the model shown in Exhibit 1. The process view reflects the need that organizations have for a new category of information—information about what causes work, and how well that work is done. Organizations use this type of information to help improve performance and to increase the value received by customers.

The ABC Cost Assignment View

The cost assignment view identifies the significant activities of an organization and attaches costs to them. It also assigns costs to cost objects that use the activities.

Knowing the cost of activities makes it easier to understand why resources are used. Moreover, the information provided makes it much easier to address such questions as:

Which activities require the most resources?

What types of resources are required by these activities? and

Where are the opportunities for cost reduction ?

Cost objects. Cost objects take ABC far beyond product costing. For example, some ABC systems include the customer as a cost object. This makes sense, because customers often vary in their needs for support. Also, customer-support activities are costly in many companies. The use of customers as a cost object takes costing into new areas of an organization. Customer-support activities, for example, invariably take place outside the manufacturing plant—in marketing, order entry, and customer service.

Exhibit 1. Activity-Based Management
(Cost Assignment and Process Views)

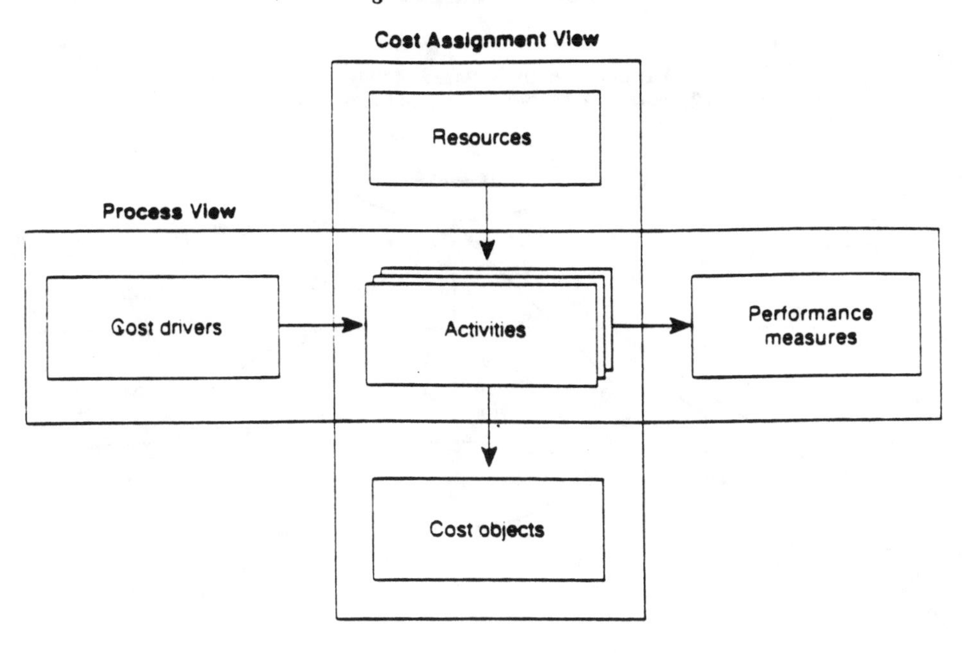

Exhibit 1

Building Blocks of the Cost Assignment View

The cost assignment view is constructed from several building blocks. The three main blocks are:

1. Resources,
2. Activities, and
3. Cost objects.

Resources are connected to activities via *resource drivers*, and activity to cost object via *activity drivers*. Activity centers, cost elements, and cost pools also help describe the motel (see Exhibit 2).

Resources are economic elements directed toward the performance of activities. They are the sources of cost. Resources in a manufacturing company include direct labor and direct material, production support (such as the salary cost of material procurement staff), indirect costs of production (such as the cost of power for heating the plant), and costs outside production (such as advertising). Examples of resources found in both manufacturing and service companies include the salaries of professionals and office support staff, office space, and costs of information systems.

Resources flow to *activities*, which are processes or procedures that cause work. In a customer service department, for example, activities can include processing orders, solving customer difficulties with products, processing returned products, and testing returned products (see Exhibit 3).

Typically, related activities are enclosed in an *activity center*. An activity center is a cluster of activities, which are usually clustered by function or process. In Exhibit 3, for example, the activity center contains all customer service activities.

Various factors, referred to as *resource drivers*, are used to assign cost to activities. These factors are chosen to approximate the use of resources by the activities. In Exhibit 3, customer service cost is traced to three activities. (It is assumed that the cost of resources used in the customer service department has already been determined.) The percentages shown (60 percent, 20 percent, and 20 percent) are based on estimates of the effort expended on each activity. This would be the case, for example, in a ten-person department, if six employees work full-time at solving customer problems, while the other four split their time between processing and testing returns.

Each type of resource traced to an activity (e. g., the salary cost of processing returns) becomes a *cost element* in an *activity cost pool*. The activity cost pool is the total cost associated with an activity.

Each activity cost pool is traced to cost objects via an *activity driver*. The activity driver is a measure of the use of

Exhibit 2. ***Activity-Based Management (Resources, Activity Centers, and Cost Objects)***

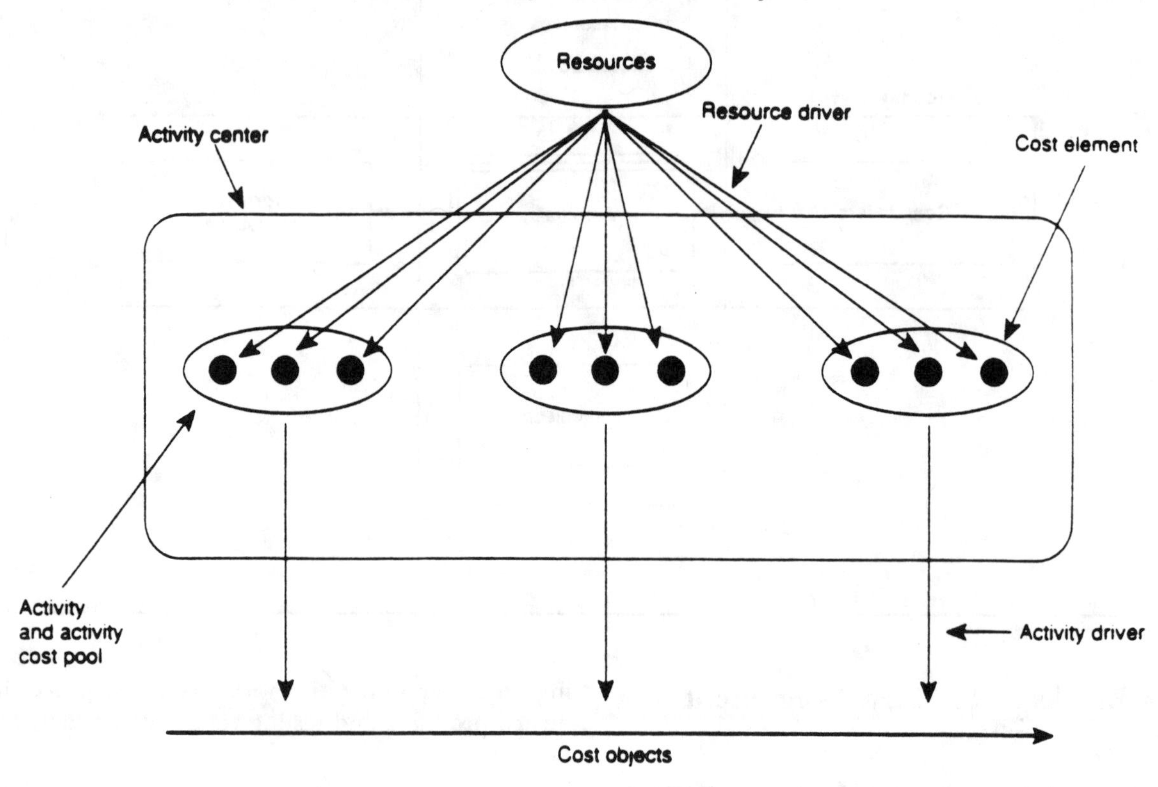

Exhibit 2

the activity by the cost objects. It is used to assign resources from the activities to the cost objects.

To relate this back to Exhibit 3, each activity has a unique activity driver to trace its cost to the products. "Solving product problems," for example, is traced to products based on the number of telephone calls. This is reasonable because the product that creates the most problems for customers is likely to generate the most phone calls.

The *cost object* is the final point to which cost is traced. A cost object is the reason why work is performed in the company. It may be a product or a customer. Engineering, producing, marketing, selling, and distributing a product require a number of activities. Supporting a customer is also comprised of a number of activities. The cost traced to each product or customer reflects the cost of the activities used by that cost object. This vertical flow of information in ABC defines the economics of the company and the organization of work within it. It also provides the basic building blocks for creating accurate and useful cost information about the strategy and operations of the company.

Process View of ABC

The horizontal part of the ABC model contains the process view (see Exhibit 1). It provides information about the work done in an activity and the relationship of this work to other activities.

To expand on this, a *process* is a series of activities that are linked to perform a specific goal. Each activity is a customer of another activity and, in turn, has its own customers. In short, activities are all part of a "customer chain," with all activities working together to provide value to the outside customer.[6]

 © APICS

Exhibit 3. *Activities in a Customer Service Department*

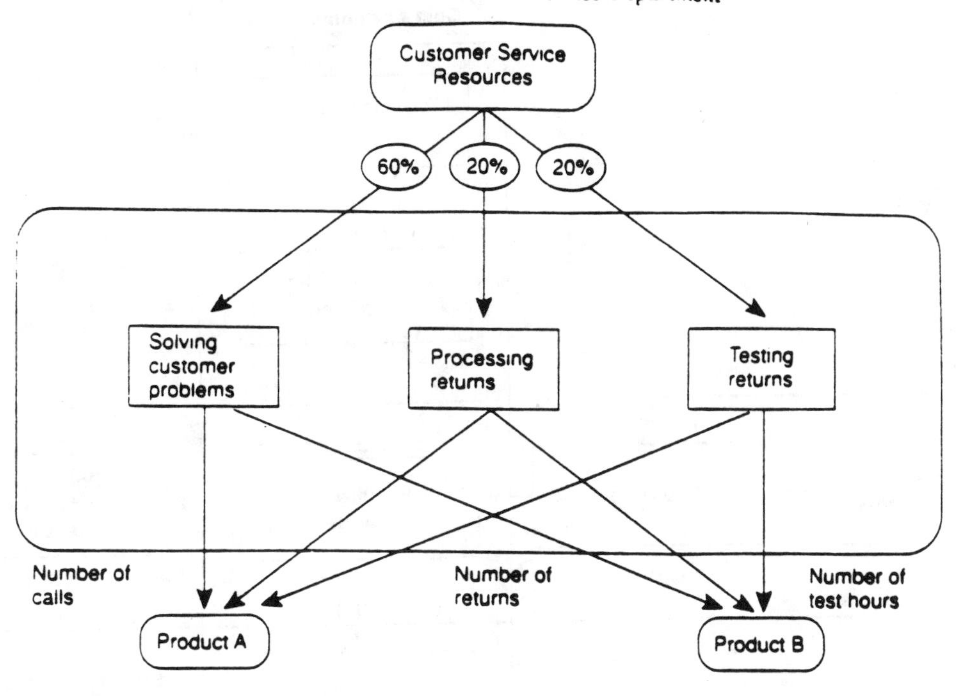

Exhibit 3

At a value manufacturer, for example, metal is melted in the foundry and then forwarded to molding. Molding pours the molten metal into molds, allows them to cool, and passes them on to an activity that breaks and removes the mold to reveal the parts inside. All these activities—and many more—work together to provide finished valves to the company's customers.

On a more detailed level, the process view of ABC includes information about cost drivers and performance measures for each activity or process in the customer chain. These cost drivers and performance measures are primarily nonfinancial. They are useful in helping to interpret the performance of activities and processes.

Cost drivers. Cost drivers are factors that determine the work load and effort required to perform an activity. They include factors relating to the performance of prior activities in the chain, as well as factors internal to the activity.

Cost drivers tell you *why* an activity (or chain of activities) is performed. Specifically, activities are performed in response to prior events. Scheduling a batch of parts, for example, is a response to a customer order or the scrapping of inventory—the why. In turn, scheduling the parts requires setting up equipment—the effort. Cost drivers also tell *how much effort* must be expended to carry out the work. A defect in the part or data received from a prior activity, for example, can increase the effort required. A requisition containing the wrong part number requires correction prior to completing a purchase order. An engineering drawing that fails to reflect the current process causes additional effort during machine setup.

Cost drivers are useful because they reveal opportunities for improvement. A reduction in the defect rate for incoming requisitions, for example, allows wasted effort and resources to be eliminated in the purchasing activity.

Performance measures. Performance measures describe the work done and the results achieved in an activity. They tell *how well* an activity is performed. They communicate how an activity is meeting the needs of internal or external customers. They include measurements of:

The efficiency of an activity,

The time required to complete an activity, and

The quality of work done.

Exhibit 4 *Illustration of Two-Dimensional ABC*

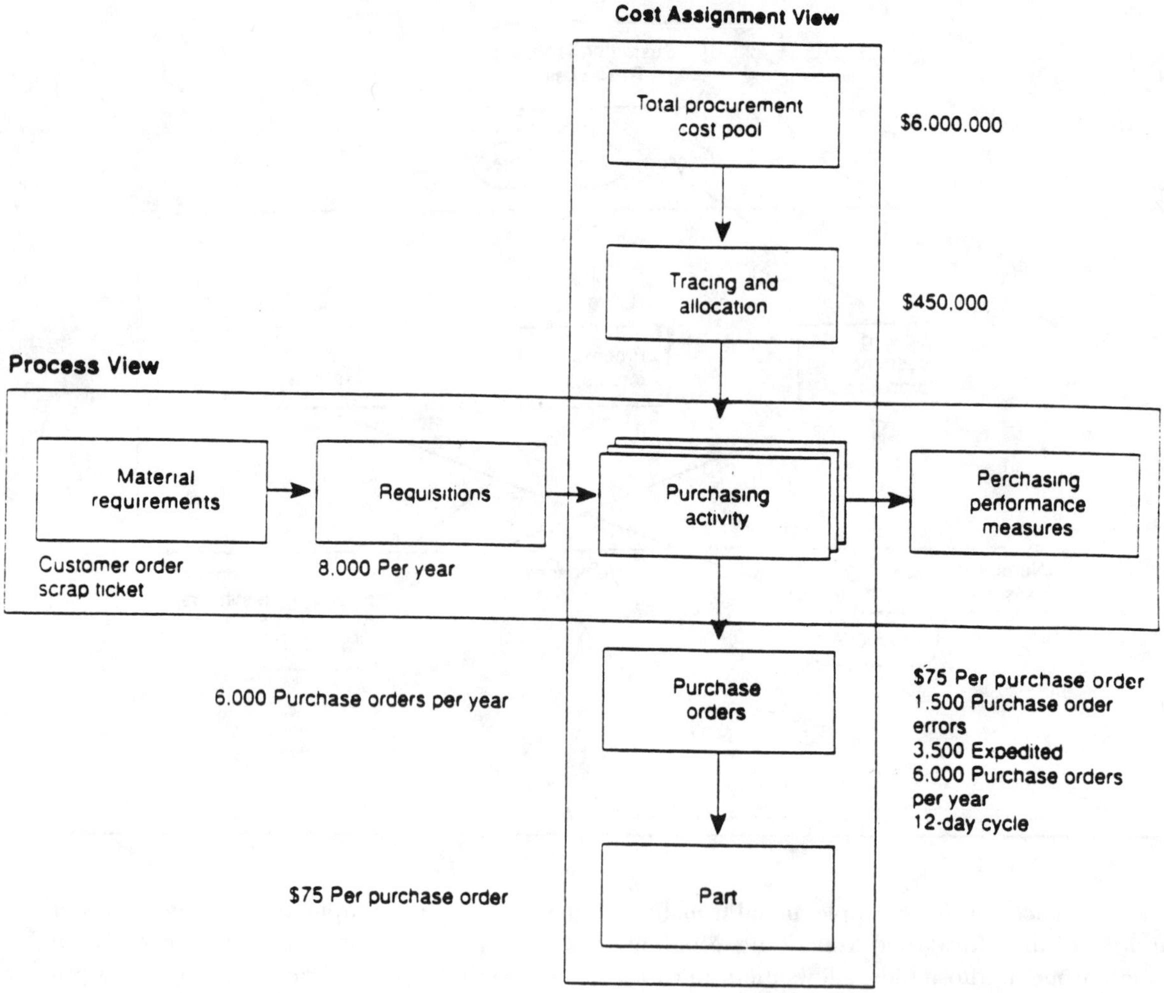

Exhibit 4

The *efficiency* aspect is judged by first determining the activity's output volume. This is then compared to the resources needed to sustain that activity and its output level. For example, the number of molds processed in a month is computed for a molding activity. This measure of output is then divided into the resources required by that activity during the month. The result is a cost per mold, say $20, which may be compared with internal or external standards of efficiency.

Still another dimension of performance is the *time* required to complete an activity. Measures of elapsed time are indirect measures of cost, quality, and customer service. The longer it takes to perform an activity, the greater the resources required. These additional resources include the salaries of staff required to do the work and the cost of equipment used to carry out the work. Also, the longer it takes, the more likely it is that work will have to be redone to correct mistakes or defects. Conversely, the shorter the elapsed time, the quicker the activity response will be to changes in customer demand.

A third aspect of performance is *quality*. For example, what percent of the molded parts need to be reworked, and what percent are scrapped? The higher this percent is, the lower the quality of the activity, the higher its overall cost, and the greater the detrimental influence will be on the next activity in the process. The value received by the customer may eventually be diminished as well.

Performance measures focus attention on the important aspects of activity performance and stimulate efforts to improve.

Operational intelligence. To recap, the ABC process view provides *operational intelligence* about the work going on in a company. This includes information about the external factors determining how often the activity is performed, and the effort required to carry it out. Operational intelligence also includes information about the performance of an activity, such as its efficiency, the time it takes to perform the activity, and the quality with which it is carried out.

An Illustration of Two-dimensional ABC

Exhibit 4 illustrates how two-dimensional ABC works. The total resource pool of $6 million is the total budget for the procurement department. $450,000 of this cost is traced directly to the purchasing activity. (The resource drivers include estimates of effort expended on the activity and a specific measurement of the use of supplies.) The cost of the purchasing activity is traced to part numbers via the number of purchase orders per part number (the activity driver).

The number of purchase orders measures the output of the activity (the number of times the activity was performed). Other performance measures include the number of errors made, the number expedited, and the elapsed time required to complete a purchase order. A volume of 6,000 purchase orders and an activity cost of $450,000 yields a cost per purchase order of $75.

In this example, the activity driver and the performance measure of output are one and the same. This matching of activity driver and performance measure is common in activity-based costing, though there are exceptions.

For example, if the number of purchase orders per part number is not captured by the company's information system, an alternative activity driver (such as the number of different parts) is required. Alternatively, if the effort required to complete a purchase order varies systematically from one type of part to another, a different activity driver (such as a direct measurement of the effort involved) may be necessary.

On the input side, the activity must cope with a volume of incoming requisitions of 8,000. A requisition is not a cost driver of the purchasing activity. Rather, it is the paperwork, or "trigger," that initiates the work.

The volume of requisitions is determined by two cost drivers—the number of customer orders and the number of scrap tickets. Customer orders and scrap tickets are factors that trigger preparation of a purchase requisition (and the need to complete a purchase order).

Exhibit 4 shows the demand for the purchasing activity coming from purchases of parts. The level of work, however, is determined by the cost drivers—demand for end products (number of customer orders) and the quality of the parts and their processing (the number of scrap tickets). An improvement in the quality of a machining activity, for example, reduces the number of scrap tickets and, in turn, reduces both the number of requisitions and the demand for purchasing replacement parts.

Performance is monitored by several measures. The cost per purchase order averages $75. The frequency of errors is one in four (1,500 out of 6,000 per year). Over half the purchase orders were expedited rather than completed in the normal processing cycle. It took an average of twelve days to complete the processing of a purchase order.

Conclusion

A modern ABC model has two dimensions. The cost dimension contains cost information about resources, activities, and cost objects. It supports economic evaluations of the strategy and operations of an organization.

The process dimension contains performance information about the work done in the organization. It supports judgments about why work is done and how well it is performed.

The process dimension brings the world of operations directly into the heart of the cost system. Cost and nonfinancial information join forces to provide a total view of the work done, thus facilitating management of activities and the improvement of performance.

Notes

1. Adapted from Peter B. B. Turney, *Common Cents: The ABC Performance Breakthrough* (Portland, Ore. Cost Technologies 1992).

2. Norm Raffish and Peter B. B. Turney, "Glossary of Activity-Based Management," *Journal of Cost Management* (Fall 1991): 53-63. This glossary was first published as *The CAM-I Glossary of Activity-Based Management*. ed. Norm Raffish and Peter B. B. Turney (Arlington, Texas: Texas Computer Aided Manufacturing-International, Inc., 1991).

3. See, e. g., Robin Cooper, "The Rise of Activity-Based Costing—Part One: What Is An Activity-Based Cost System?" *Journal of Cost Management* (Summer 1988) 45-54. This article contains a product costing definition of ABC, and describes a model that is consistent with this definition.

4. See Turney, *Common Cents: The ABC Performance Breakthrough*, Chaps. 7, 8, 9, for examples of successful applications of activity-based costing.

5. Exhibits 1 and 4 were adapted from figures included in *The CAM-I Glossary of Activity-Based Management*, eds. Raffish and Turney, which is the basis for the article, "Glossary of Activity-Based Management," Norm Raffish and Peter B. B. Turney eds., *Journal of Cost Management* (Fall 1991) 54-63.

6. Richard J. Schonberger, *Building a Chain of Customers Linking Business Functions to Create the World Class Company (New York, Free Press, 1990).*

About the author

Peter B.B. Turney is chief executive officer of Cost Technology, in Portland Oregon.

Reprinted from the 1991 APICS *Conference Proceedings.*

Throughput World or Cost World—What's the Difference?

Robert B. Vollum

The worldwide struggle to service the expanding demand for manufactured products has forced many contentious issues to light. One of the most volatile, and impactive, concerns the philosophy used to drive and evaluate our actions.

If it is true that performance follows measurement, then we are surely at a crossroads. The foundation upon which decision, measurement, and control have been based is under severe pressure to change.

This paper contrasts the new "Throughput World" processes of constraint management, synchronization, and money flow to the time honored "Cost World" procedures of efficiency, allocation, and costing.

The Throughput World and Cost World perspectives are in direct philosophical and procedural conflict with each other. At stake is how a company positions itself strategically, how it approaches its markets, how it values its products, how it plans and controls its manufacturing, and how it measures its performance.

Paradigm Shift

Since early in the twentieth century, the principles of cost accounting have dominated the way manufacturing companies have made decisions and measured results. We have practiced the cost procedures for so long that we have assumed them to be valid and sacrosanct.

Who would challenge logic that strives for maximum efficiency everywhere? Who would argue against minimizing cost at each step along the way? Who would question the assumption that each local improvement improves the overall process? And who could not value a system that purports to measure and report, in detail, performance against a standard for each operation and each product? The assumption is clear. Operate at high efficiency and low cost and you will maximize profit.

New management philosophies that focus on throughput rather than cost emerged during the 1980s. Total Quality Management (TQM), Just-in-Time (JIT), Theory of Constraints (TOC) and its logistical application, Synchronous Flow Management (SFM), all repudiate the Cost perspective.

The emphasis in each of these approaches is on doing those things that will put the company in the most favorable position to attract business. Each acknowledges the need to control operating expenses. However, expenditures are evaluated on their contribution to throughput enhancement, not cost recovery.

As viewed by TOC and SFM, most local efforts to optimize cost and efficiency are presumed to be inconsequential and often in conflict with the goal of the total company. The bottom line, not local performance, is the Judge of effectiveness.

Evolution Of Cost Accounting

The first applications of cost accounting reportedly surfaced in the early 1990s in DuPont and General Motors. However, the source of the invention is not clear. What is clear is the general business environment of the time. In 1900, the industrial revolution was in full swing, but Mechanization was not yet the rule. Most factories were labor intensive, often sweat shops. Workers were paid predominantly on a piece rate basis for acceptable work produced. Hourly wages were not yet an issue.

Material purchases were, by far, the largest expenditure of most companies, often representing seventy percent or more of the total operating outlay. Of the balance, direct labor often represented ten times as much as all other expenses combined. Material and labor typically represented ninety five percent or more of the expense associated with running a company. furthermore, material and labor expenses both varied totally and directly according to the quantity of product produced.

As products began to proliferate with increased consumer demand for variety and choice, the need to project the impact of new product introductions grew, also. The idea of allocating the small percentage of non-variable operating expenses to products based on the totally variable labor employed was a stroke of genius. It fit the times perfectly. The resultant approximations of "product cost" were easy to develop and were as accurate as needed. "Product margins" were a logical extension, as were the host of cost accounting procedures that followed.

By 1920, vertical integration and automation investments had altered the money flow profile of the typical manufacturing company. Material represented only fifty to sixty percent of total outlay. Labor represented a significantly smaller percentage of total cost than it had in 1900 and overhead had increased to be about equal to labor. Allocation had already ceased to be insignificant.

By 1940, labor reform had done away with sweat shops. Workers were paid on the basis of hours spent in the plant, not by the pieces produced of a product. Labor was no longer a totally variable expense, and overhead was consistently greater than labor. Two-tier allocations of overhead, first to work centers and then to products, became common practice. Efficiencies, budgets, and variances based on assumptions of product mix and factory performance took on added importance.

The technology explosion of the 1970s and 1980s has turned the 1990 manufacturing cost profile upside down from that of 1900. The percentage of material content today is typically about thirty five to forty percent of cost (half what it was in 1900). Labor has dropped from more than twenty five percent to between five and ten percent, sometimes as low as three or four. Overhead has grown from two or three percent of total cost to more than fifty percent.

In 1990 overhead is typically five to ten times greater than direct labor, and as automation increases the spread continues to grow. The effect now is that the impact of any movement, up or down and regardless of amount, in presumed labor content at any operation of a product is magnified several times by overhead allocation. This certainly does not reflect reality, and it is exactly the opposite of conditions in 1900.

The invention of cost accounting enabled industry to grow rapidly and profitably in the early decades of the century. The impact of investment decisions and product choices could be predicted with a level of accuracy not previously possible. Cost accounting was without a doubt one of the most powerful solutions ever introduced to industry.

Powerful solutions engender powerful reactions. Powerful reactions engender change. The more powerful the solution, the more pronounced the change. Eventually, powerful solutions tend to devour themselves through the changes they force. This has happened with cost accounting over the years. Unfortunately, the almost reverential respect we have given the procedures blinded us to the fact. We viewed the rules as though they represented "TRUTH" rather than a solution that was "valid" for the times it was designed to serve. As times changed, we strove to force the new conditions into the "rules."

The powerful solution that fit the times so effectively in 1900 is no longer valid in 1990. Conditions have changed.

a. Labor is no longer a major expense element, nor is it still totally variable. It is now only a small part of the total and is essentially fixed. We pay people for the time they are at work, not for the products they make. Labor no longer varies if we make one more or one less unit.

b. Overhead is no longer insignificant. Today, it is the dominant element of expense .

c. Most companies no longer make just a handful of products. The market has forced proliferation to the point where accurate allocation of expenses to specific products is impossible.

Emergence Of New Management Philosophies

Total Quality Management and Just-in-Time

Following World War II, a new perspective started to develop. Its impact was imperceptible at first. Even its originators did not understand until many years later that it represented a monumental shift in business thinking.

The movement was born essentially from the desperate need of devastated nations, principally Japan, to reconstruct their economies. Japan is a country with few natural resources and a burgeoning population. It must import resources for production, and it must export products to survive.

While the Western world, most notably the United States, was caught up in the business of mass production and "economies of scale," some progressive Japanese firms took a different approach. They concentrated on issues important to the consumer—things that would influence a customer to buy. From this beginning developed the philosophies known today as Total Quality Management (TQM) and Just-in-Time (JIT). JIT developed as an outgrowth of TQM.

In the 1950s and 1960s, the world laughed at what it viewed as "cheap junk" from Japan, but there was a market for inferior products if the price was right. We even accused the Japanese of selling below cost. We all know how the rest of the Japanese success story goes. What is not so widely understood, even by many experts, is the mechanism behind the success.

The steps taken to improve product quality, reduce setups, improve performance reliability, reduce lead times, improve delivery performance, reduce inventory, and speed up new product introduction cycles were not to reduce cost. Most of these issues are not even measured by financial reports. They are classified as non-tangible. In fact, the actions taken to get those kinds of improvements fly in the face of cost systems. They would generate negative variances. The better the company performed in each of those categories, the worse the variances would appear. Obviously, then, the reason for taking actions such as reducing batch sizes and increasing setups is not to get cost reduction. It is to put a company in position to sell more product by responding very quickly and very competitively to market needs. Over a period of many years, there was a paradigm shift from "cost world" to "Throughput world" thinking that is only now being recognized as such.

Taiichi Ohno, the late Executive Vice President of Production at Toyota and the inventor of Just-In-Time, claimed not to have understood why the system worked during the thirty or so years of its development. Ohno attributed much of the ultimate success to the ability, as he gained power in the company, to bar cost accounting and even the ideas of costing from the factories. He understood, intuitively, that efficiency measurements would stop progress and dictate counterproductive actions.

Today, there are scores of companies trying with great frustration and little success to put Total Quality Management and Just In Time programs in place while measuring performance with a cost system. The programs invariably fail because the measurement system eventually forces management to take protective action to mollify the measurements and get off the hot seat. We cannot evaluate actions designed to increase flow with measurements designed to reduce cost. A fundamental conflict exists. Is the goal to make money or save money?

Theory of Constraints and Synchronous Flow Management

The ideas of TOC and SFM emerged in the early 1970s from the fertile mind of Dr. Eliyahu M. Goldratt, an Israeli physicist. By 1980 Dr. Goldratt had incorporated his principles into a factory scheduling system, OPT, and had sold several copies of it to Fortune 20 companies. Over the next six years, from the experiences gained from those implementations and others, emerged a philosophy of management, a structured way of thinking, and processes for getting to the root of core problems and developing simple, practical solutions.

OPT is no longer marketed in North America, but the science of management that evolved from it is gaining worldwide notoriety and acceptance. Dr. Goldratt continues to expand the horizons through the work being done by the Goldratt Institute and its Associates and several major universities, worldwide.

Cost World Vs. Throughput World Comparatives

Many articles have been written, including several by this author, about the logistical issues of constraint management and factory synchronization. Very little exists about the financial and strategic decision making impact of this management philosophy. The balance of this article will expose some of the differences between throughput world thinking and cost world thinking. We will analyze several different strategic situations from both the cost and the throughput perspectives and will contrast the results. We will pay particular attention to the impact of constraints on the economics of the business.

Investment Justification

Case l. Let us assume that we are considering the replacement of a machine capable of producing 25 pieces per hour with one capable of 30 pieces per hour. The current machine is "up" 75% of the time. We anticipate the new machine to operate at 85% utilization. The plant operates 24 hours per day, 5 days per week. This equals 240 days per year considering a 2 week shutdown and 10 paid holidays. The operators for this equipment are paid $10.00 per hour. The burden rate is 500%. The total investment for the new machine would be $250,000.00. The permissible investment recovery period is two years.

Investment justification calculations are computed in a variety of ways, often depending on the creativity of the engineer involved. One common method is illustrated in figure 1.

This calculation indicates that the current machine is capable of producing 108,000 pieces per year at a cost of $3.2000 per piece. The new machine could produce 146,880 pieces per year at $2.3529 per piece, a saving of $0.8461 per piece. Considering only the differential in cost per piece for the quantity possible on the new machine, the calculations would indicate a savings of $248,550 over the two years. If that were not considered sufficient saving, additional justification could be found in the opportunity factor of the additional 38,880 pieces possible per year. The new machine would clearly pass the cost analysis test as a justifiable investment.

Constraint management requires a different sort of test. Its primary criterion for economic justification is anticipated impact on throughput and the bottom line. The first questions to be decided are whether the machines under consideration are constraints or non-constraints and what sort of flow relationships, if any, exist. See figure 2.

The plans are to replace the current Y machine, a non-constraint, which is capable of producing 108,000

Investment Justification

$250,000 New Machine Investment
Labor = $10.00 Per Hour
500% Burden Rate = $50.00 Per Hour

COST OF OPERATION

($10 Lab + $50 O/H) x 24hr/day x 240 days/yr = $345,600/yr
25 pc/hr x .75 Eff x 24 hr/day x 240 days/yr = 108,000 pc/yr
= $3.2000/pc
30 pc/hr x .85 Eff x 24 hr/day x 240 days/yr = 146,880 pc/yr
= $2.3529/pc

38,880 Additional pc/yr
$0.8461 Saving/pc
146,880 pc x .8461 = $124,275 Saving/yr

2 Year Saving = $248,550

Figure 1

Investment Justification

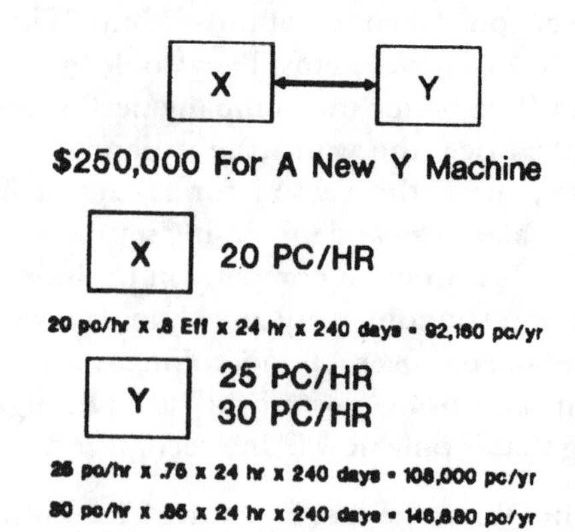

Figure 2

Investment Analysis

Work Week = 40 HRS = 2,400 Minutes
Labor = $10.00/HR = $0.16666/Minute
O/H = 500% = $50.00/HR = $0.83333/Minute
Market Potential Exceeds Plant Capacity

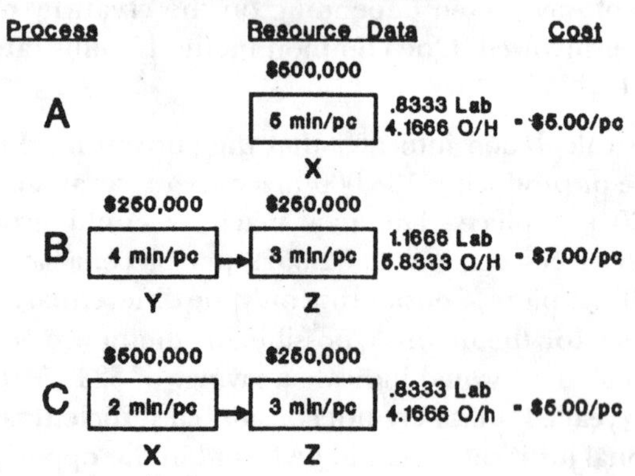

Figure 3

pieces per year with a more efficient new Y resource capable of 146,880 pieces per year. It so happens that the Y resource flows directly to or from, and is constrained by, an X machine that is capable of producing only 92,160 pieces per year. That limits the number of pieces that can be used from the Y resource to that number.

In this instance the throughput analysis would reject the proposal if the justification were strictly on the basis of economic value. The conclusion would be that the proposal was to replace one machine that already could produce more than could be used with one of even greater capacity. The result of such a purchase would be an expenditure of $250,000.00 with no pay back. The projected cost savings would have no significance.

Case 2. We must invest in equipment to produce a new part that has a market potential that exceeds our projected plant capacity. Labor for the new work center will be $10.00 per hour. The burden rate is 500%. The plant works a 40 hour or 2400 minute week. We are considering three process options. See Figure 3. Process A requires the purchase of a multi-task machine, X, that could perform the two operations required for each part in 5 minutes with one operator. The investment for this resource would be $500,000.00.

Process B requires the purchase of two single-task machines, Y and Z, for $250,000.00 each, a total of $500,000.00. Each resource would require its own dedicated operator. The total time per part split between the two resources would be 7 minutes.

Process C requires the purchase of multi-task machine X and single-task machine Z for a total of $750,000.00. Each machine would require a dedicated operator. The total time per part split between the two resources would be 5 minutes.

 © APICS

CONTRIBUTION FLOW ANALYSIS

FLOW PROCESS

	A	B	C
	(2,400 Minutes/Week)		
Pieces/Week Potential	5 Min/pc 480	4 Min/pc 600	3 Min/pc 800
S.P. $50/pc R.M. $25/pc			
Contr $25/pc	$12,000	$15,000	$20,000
Labor Incr		400	400
T Contr/Wk	$12,000	$14,600	$19,600

Figure 4

Product Costing

	A	B
Material	$1,000	$1,000
Labor-50Hrs@$20	$1,000	$1,000
300% Burden Rate	$3,000	$3,000
Total Cost	$5,000	$5,000
Selling Price	5,200	4,700
Net Profit (Loss)	$200	($300)

Figure 5

Based on the cost calculations, we would undoubtedly choose process A. It represents the lowest piece part cost, the least number of people, and the smallest capital investment.

A throughput analysis of the same opportunity would differ significantly. See figures 3 and 4.

The first step would be to identify the constraints in each process to determine what will limit throughput. Since market demand is greater than plant capacity, the constraint will be a physical resource within the plant. That means that the throughput potential of each process is limited by the capacity of the slowest resource. We see from figure 3 that process A can produce a part every 5 minutes. If the operations in process B are overlapped with a transfer batch of 1, the first part will take 7 minutes, but each succeeding one will take only 4 minutes. The same logic for process C indicates that each part will take 3 minutes to produce.

From figure 4. we see that at 5 minutes per part, process A can produce 480 parts per week. If each part sells for $50.00 and has a material content of $25.00, the throughput that it can contribute to the company is $12,000.00 per week. Throughput contribution is calculated as selling price less the raw material content of that sale. Processes B and C can produce 600 and 800 parts respectively, netting throughput contribution of $14,600.00 and $19,600.00 per week when the additional $400.00 per operator required for each of those processes is deducted.

It is clearly evident that process A, the one that would be the clear choice of a classical cost analysis, would produce the least money. Process B would generate $135,200 more throughput contribution per year at the same investment. Process C would generate $395,200 more per year for an additional $250,000 one-time investment.

Product Cost

Let us assume that a company makes two major products, "A" and "B." Let us assume also that its products are well respected and that it can sell as many of either, or both, of them as it chooses to make, at the established market price of $5,200.00 per "A" and $4,700.00 per "B."

The accountants at corporate headquarters have just completed a product cost analysis for the plant following a disappointing profit performance last quarter. These were the results. The material content of both products is $1,000.00 even though the material is different. Each product requires 50 hours of labor at a rate of $20.00 per hour. The burden rate is 300%. The figures show clearly that each product "A" produces a $200.00 profit and each "B" loses $300.00. See figure 5.

Based on this analysis, corporate staff made the decision for the plant to discontinue the production of product "B" and concentrate all the resources on Product "A." Unfortunately, the message came through garbled, and the plant manager understood the facts and the decision to be the opposite of that intended. One month later, having discon-

Product Costing vs Flow

	A	B
Material	$1,000	$1,000
Labor-50Hrs@$20	1,000	1,000
300% Burden Rate	3,000	3,000
Total Cost	$5,000	$5,000
Selling Price	5,200	4,700
Net Profit (Loss)	$200	($300)
1,000BN Hrs/Mo	1 Hr/Ea	
Units/Month	1,000	
Revenue/Mo	$5,200,000	
Less Material	-1,000,000	
Less Oper. Exp.	-4,000,000	
Net Profit	$200,000	

Figure 6

Product Costing vs Flow

	A	B
Material	$1,000	$1,000
Labor-50Hrs@$20	1,000	1,000
300% Burden Rate	3,000	3,000
Total Cost	$5,000	$5,000
Selling Price	5,200	4,700
Net Profit (Loss)	$200	($300)
1,000BN Hrs/Mo	1 Hr/Ea	.7 Hr/Ea
Units/Month	1,000	1,428
Revenue/Mo	$5,200,000	$6,711,600
Less Material	-1,000,000	-1,428,000
Less Oper. Exp.	-4,000,000	-4,000,000
Net Profit	$200,000	$1,283,600

Figure 7

tinued "A" and having made as many "B"s as possible, how deep is the hole?

Let us analyze the situation by first seeing what the results would have been if the plant had concentrated on "A"s, as intended. Before we start, though, let us introduce an element not considered by any cost system - constraints

Suppose there is a bottleneck in the plant that defines the limits of production and that there are 1,000 hours of its time available each month. And suppose further that 1 hour of the 50 total hours of labor required to make each "A" is done at that bottleneck. That means that 1,000 product "A"s could have been made during the month.

At $5,200.00 for each "A" sold, the plant could have generated sales revenue of $5,200,000.00. If we subtract out the $1,000,000.00 of material needed to make the product and net out the $4,000,000.00 that it takes to run the plant for a month, we find that the plant could have generated a $200,000.00 net profit, as expected, if it had concentrated only on "A"s. See Figure 6.

But the plant did not make "A"s. It made "B"s that show a loss of $300 each. Suppose that .7 hour is spent on the bottleneck for each "B" produced. That means that the 1,000 hours of bottleneck time available would have permitted production of 1,428 product "B"s in a month. At a $4,700 selling price, the plant could have generated $6,711,600.00 in revenue. Subtracting out the $1,428,000 of material content and accounting for the $4,000,000.00 of monthly operating expense we find the plant might have made an obscene profit of $1,283,600.00, not the expected loss of $428,400. See Figure 7.

Product Dynamics and Flow

The realities of product dynamics and flow are most often very different than cost analyses and projections believe them to be. The reliance most companies place on their cost systems to guide their strategic decisions is fraught with peril. The logic in those systems, given the conditions of today's manufacturing environment, is incapable of providing an accurate picture and often calculates the worst possible answer as its best advice.

Let us consider as a basis of discussion a company that manufactures only two products. The first product, "P," is assembled from three parts. One part that costs $5.00 per unit is used as purchased. The other two, part 1 and part 2, are fabricated in two-step operations. The material for part 1 costs $20.00 per unit as does the material for part 2. The processing for part 1 begins at resource A with a 15 minute operation then moves for a final 10 minute operation at resource C. Part 2 starts with a 15 minute operation at resource B and then moves to resource C for a final 5 minute operation. Parts 1, 2, and the purchased component are then made into a finished product "P" in a 10 minute assembly operation. The market will buy as many as 100 "P"s per week, no more, at $90.00 each. See figure 8.

Product "Q" is assembled from two parts: part 2 and part 3. Part 2 is the same one used in product "P," a common

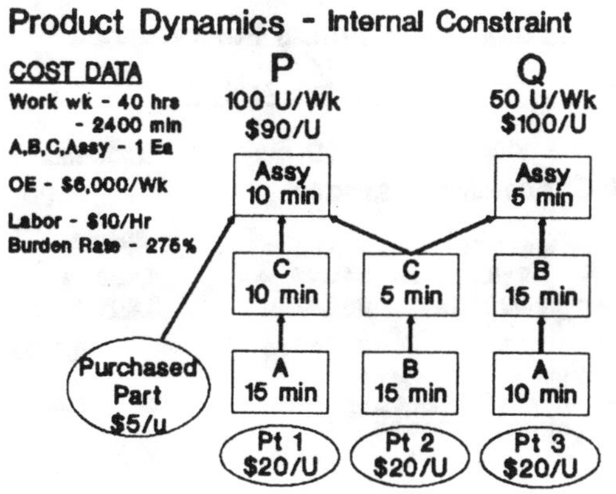

Product Dynamics - Internal Constraint

COST DATA
Work wk - 40 hrs
- 2400 min
A,B,C,Assy - 1 Ea
OE - $6,000/Wk
Labor - $10/Hr
Burden Rate - 275%

P
100 U/Wk
$90/U
Assy 10 min
C 10 min
A 15 min
Pt 1 $20/U
Purchased Part $5/u
C 5 min
B 15 min
Pt 2 $20/U

Q
50 U/Wk
$100/U
Assy 5 min
B 15 min
A 10 min
Pt 3 $20/U

Figure 8

P and Q Cost Analysis

		P		Q
Selling Price		90.00		100.00
Material	45.00		40.00	
Labor	9.167 (55 min)		8.333 (50 min)	
Burden 275%	25.209		22.916	
Cost of Sales		79.376		71.249
Gross Margin		10.624		28.751
		11.80%		28.75%

Figure 9

part. Part 3 starts with a $20.00 raw material and is processed first in a 15 minute operation at resource A and then at resource B for 15 minutes. Parts 2 and 3 are assembled in a 5 minute operation as a product "Q." The demand for product "Q" is for as many as 50 per week, no more, at $100.00 per unit.

The plant has one of each of the four resources, A, B, C and Assembly, each staffed with one dedicated employee. The plant works a one shift, 40 hour week (2,400 minutes). Each worker is paid $10.00 per hour and the burden rate is 275%. The total operating expense for the entire plant

Anticipated Performance

Cost System Analysis

	100P	50Q	Variance Analysis	
Sales	9,000.00	5,000.00		Plant OE
COS			Absorb	6,000.00
Mat'l	4,500.00	2,000.00		
Labor (55 min)	916.70	416.65 (50 min)	1,333.35	
Burden 275%	2,520.925	1,145.7875	3,666.7125	
Margin	1,062.375	1,437.5625		5,000.0625
Tot. Margin	2,499.9375			
Variance	(999.9375)			(999.9375)
Net Profit	1,500.00			

Figure 10

Capacity Analysis (Minutes)

	A	B	C	Assy
100 P	1,500	1,500	1,500	1,000
50 Q	500	1,500	250	250
	2,000	3,000	1,750	1,250
Available	2,400	2,400	2,400	2,400

↑ (B)

Figure 11

for one week is $6,000.00. Operating expense includes all labor and overhead but does not include the material cost for parts 1,2,3 and the purchased component.

The cost buildup shows product "P" has a material content of $45.00 and requires 55 minutes of labor to produce. The $10.00 per hour labor rate and 275% burden rate translate to $9.167 of labor and $25.209 of absorbed overhead. The total cost of sales is $79.376. The gross margin for product "P" is $10.624 or 11.80% of the selling price. See figure 9.

The corresponding calculation for product "Q" shows that it has a cost of sales of $71.751, a gross margin of $28.751 or 28.75% of the selling price. The analysis shows product "Q" to be almost three times as profitable as product "P."

Maximize P or Q?

	P		Q
Potential	100		50
Selling Price	90		100
Raw Material	45		40
T Contribution	45.00	⟷	60.00
Labor & Burden 275%	34.375	⟷	31.249

Which One?

	P	Q	
Demand	60	50	This
Time on Resource B	900	1,500	? or
Demand	100	30	That
Time on Resource B	1,500	900	

Figure 12

Maximize Q - Actual Performance

Cost System Analysis

	60P	50Q	Variance Analysis	
Sales	5,400.00	5,000.00		Plant OE
COS				6,000.00
Mat'l	2,700.00	2,000.00	Absorb	
Labor	(55 min) 550.02	416.65 (50 Min)	966.67	
Burden 275%	1,512.55	1,145.7875	2,658.3375	
Margin	637.43	1,437.5625		3,625.0075
Tot. Margin	2,074.9925			
Variance	(2,374.9925)			(2,374.9925)
Net Profit	(300.00)			

Figure 13

Maximize P - Actual Performance

Cost System Analysis

	100P	30Q	Variance Analysis	
Sales	9,000.00	3,000.00		Plant OE
COS				6,000.00
Mat'l	4,500.00	1,200.00	Absorb	
Labor	916.70 (55 Min)	249.99 (50 Min)	1,166.69	
Burden 275%	2,520.925	687.4725	3,208.3975	
Margin	1,062.375	862.5375		4,375.0875
Tot. Margin	1,924.9125			
Variance	(1624.9125)			(1,624.9125)
Net Profit	300.00			

Figure 14

Armed with these cost numbers and a sales projection of 100 product "P"s and 50 product "Q"s per week, the company would conclude that it could generate a total gross margin of $2,499.94 per week and would base its projections on that expectation. See figure 10.

Since 275% is the precise burden rate for this plant, there would be no assumed variances. In reality, there would be a $999.94 unfavorable variance. When this calculation is carried through, the maximum profit is seen to be $1,500.00 - $1,000.00 less than the assumption.

The burden rate has no actual impact on the $1,500.00 profit potential. That remains the same regardless of the value assigned. Product flow and expenses paid dictate what profit will actually be. What does vary as burden rates change is the profit assumption, from which decisions are made, and that assumption will be wrong no matter what rate is chosen.

A $1,500.00 per week profit assumes that all 100 "P"s and all 50 "Q"s can be produced. A review of the projected load in minutes imposed on each of the resources by those quantities shows that resource B does not have sufficient capacity.

A choice must be made. Either maximize "P" at the expense of "Q" or vice versa. Each element of the cost analysis in figure 12 shows in favor of product "Q." We should use as much of the time at resource B as is needed to make all the "Q"s we can and only then make as many "P"s as the remaining time permits. "Q" is clearly the superior choice.

There are 2,400 minutes per week available to resource B. Figure 8 shows that both part 2 and part 3 go across resource B for 15 minutes. 50 product "Q"s will require 1,500 minutes of B's time, leaving 900 minutes to make part 2 for product "P." In 900 minutes resource B can make enough part 2s for 60 product "P"s.

Using this preferred mix, the cost analysis would predict a $2,074.99 profit for the week. In fact, when the accounting books for the week were closed and variances were considered, the plant would show a $300.00 loss.

Since we are looking at an artificial environment that uses 100% of its resources for the products under consideration, variances can be shown exactly as they would be. In a real environment, there is no possible way to predict in advance where variances will occur, how large they will be, or whether they will be positive or negative. The results come as a surprise after the fact. That is why so much time must be devoted to reconciling variances to the budget.

If somehow the "wrong" choice were made and "P"s were maximized at the expense of "Q"s, we would still make $300.00. Only this time it would be profit, not loss. See figure 14. The difference is that the constraint, resource B, permits the production of twice as many "P"s as "Q"s in any given period of time.

The focusing procedures of the Theory of Constraints lead directly and immediately to the knowledge of how to set priorities on throughput opportunities. Expenditures are evaluated for their impact on throughput and the bottom line. There are no such things as budgets or variances.

In the example just completed, the choice of "P" in preference to "Q" can be arrived at very quickly and with great assurance. Each product "P" contributes $45.00 of throughput contribution ($90.00 sales less $45.00 material) and consumes 15 minutes of constraint time (resource B). Therefore, each minute of the constraint devoted to making "P"s returns $3.00.

The same calculation for product "Q" reveals that even though its throughput contribution is greater ($60.00), it returns only $2.00 per minute. It requires 30 minutes of constraint time, twice as much as "P."

As in the cost calculation, the choice is clear, but this time it is also correct. "P" is preferable to "Q", and the reason is intuitively understandable. The key to making the most money is in identifying and exploiting the constraint. That means learning how to maximize throughput contribution per unit of constraint consumed.

Summary

This paper has touched on a few areas of difference between cost world and throughput world thinking. Many equally important topics have not been broached. For example, how should labor be viewed? Is it possible to increase profit by adding significant time (cost) to the production of a product without reducing any other expenses? How do you know when to take business "at a price?" What can you do if your constraint is internal? - external? Every issue of strategic importance is viewed differently when the focus is on what should be done to increase throughput rather than what can be done to reduce cost.

Ironically, the companies that have adopted the throughput perspective are finding that they are not only reaping added value in the market. They are also getting the improvement in their operations that they had been chasing without success through cost.

The things that are critically important come to the fore quickly in the throughput world. All departments must pull together as though in a chain if the company is to improve. No part of the organization can stand off to the side. The fifth of the twenty-seven "Laws Of The Navy" that Plebes of my day at Annapolis had to commit indelibly to memory states:

"On the strength of one link in the cable,

Dependeth the might of the chain.

Who knows when thou mayest be tested?

So live that thou bearest the strain!"

Maximum performance can only be achieved when the weakest link is exercised to its limit, and true bottom line improvement can only happen when the weakest link is strengthened.

The cost procedures draw no distinction between links and assume that attention paid to any of them reap valuable benefits. The Throughput World continuously focuses on that one weakest link.

About the author

ROBERT B. VOLLUM has written, lectured, and consulted throughout the Western world for more than a decade. He has led the efforts since 1984 to mold the Goldratt "Theory Of Constraints" to industry applications and is the leading authority on Synchronous Flow Management as a manufacturing tool and a corporate strategy.

Bob is a graduate of the United States Naval Academy with advanced business studies at Union College and The College of William and Mary. He served his last several years in industry as Chief Operating Officer at divisions of two major corporations and as Chief Executive Officer of a company he founded. Prior duties were in manufacturing operations, materials management, sales, and marketing.

Bob is a certified Fellow of APICS and served as a Chapter president. He is a frequent contributor of technical articles and is in demand as a speaker. He is included in Who's Who in Finance and Industry *and* Who's Who in the World.

Reprinted from the 1991 APICS *Conference Proceedings.*

The Nemesis of Lead Time—Variability

Blair R. Williams

Objective

To understand the interrelationship of variability and capacity. To outline techniques for controlling variability and thereby increasing capacity.

How Much Capacity Is Available?

In a 1982 article Berry, Schmitt and Vollman referred to 62 sources and almost all of them dealt with estimating required capacity and not available capacity.

Conventional Approach

Capacity concepts are usually illustrated by Wight's funnel or trough, in which load is the volume of work in the system and capacity is the rate at which work is withdrawn from the system. Management has two controls over the amount of work in a system: input into the system and output from it. If output exceeds input the level of load will fall, while if input exceeds output the level of load will rise. Implicit in the model is that if input and output are equal, the level of load remains constant.

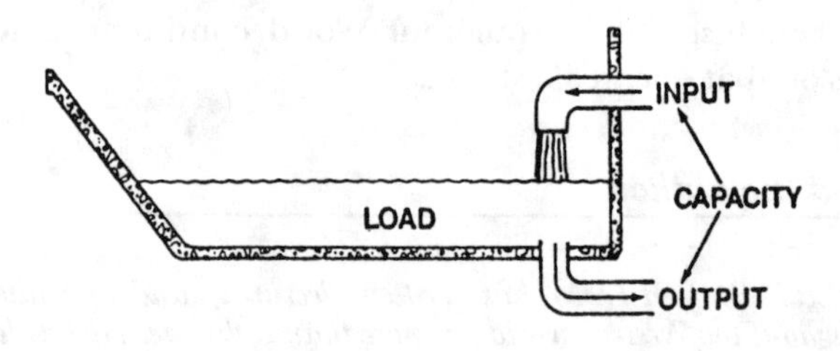

LOAD VS. CAPACITY

Why is that Model of Capacity Inadequate?

The trough model is valid only if the rate of input and output are constant. Since this is almost never the case, very few MRP II companies have an effective Capacity Requirements Planning module and factory operation is plagued with excess WIP, long lead times and on-time performance problems.

The reality of the workplace is that input and output rates are constantly varying and that this variability leads to changes in real time capacity. This is best illustrated by looking at a simple queueing example. If a customer arrives every 2 minutes and if he is served in a minute, there will not be a queue. Thirty customers will be serviced in an hour and the server will have 30 minutes of free time per hour. Now if two customers arrived together or if the server took more than two minutes, i.e. if there was arrival or service variability, then one of the customers would have to wait in queue, even though on an average there would be adequate capacity. As the inter service time approaches the inter arrival time, even small variations lead to formation of queues.

In a situation where arrivals and service times are random variables this can be graphically depicted as:

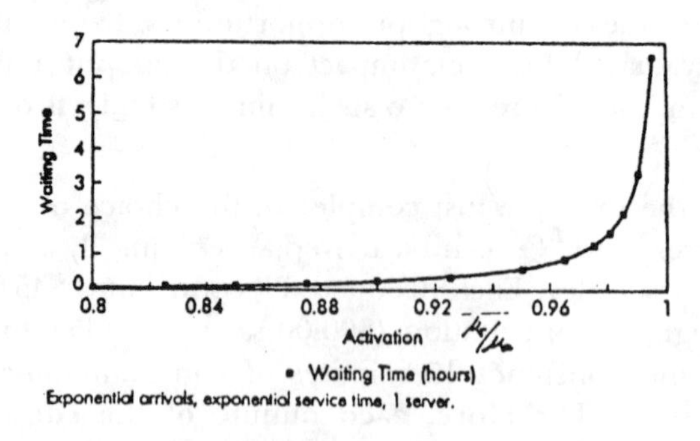

SERVICE TO ARRIVAL TIME AND QUEUES

A More Appropriate Model for Representing Capacity

We can thus see that it not just input and output that control the level of load, but also their variability. We can also see that a more accurate representation of capacity can be shown as under:

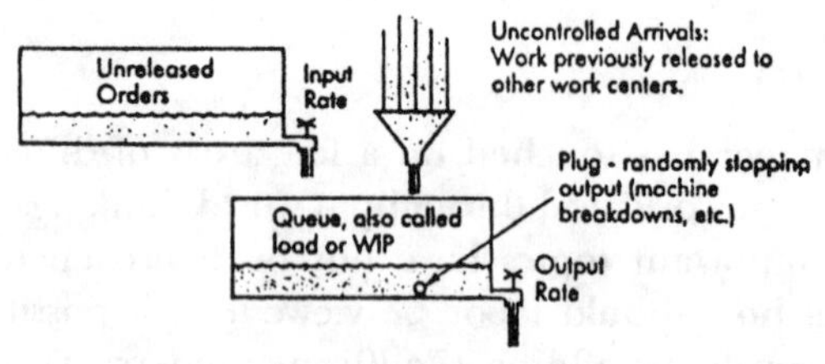

A MORE ACCURATE REPRESENTATION OF CAPACITY

 © APICS

A More Accurate Representation Of Capacity

Variability

An understanding of variability is essential if we are to understand available capacity. There are input or arrival variabilities due to release of new orders into the shop and arrival of orders from other in process work stations. Output or service variabilities are even more numerous as any variation in machine performance including downtime; in operator performance including absenteeism; or in the process including yield; all result in variation.

Variation is measured by a Coefficient of Variation, which is represented by:

Coefficient of

Variation = Variance/(Mean)^2

= (Standard Deviation)^2/(Mean)^2

The arrival variability and/or the service variability can easily be calculated by randomly recording the time of arrivals of various jobs at a work-center or their processing time, and applying the above formula. This is an essential first step to understanding how much of a resources' capacity can be used, and will eliminate our present approach of empirically attaching a 80% or some factor to the theoretical capacity.

Capacity vs. Throughput vs. Variability

One of the main reasons for increasing capacity utilization is to produce more required product by reducing its lead time or increasing its throughput.

Using a software packet a series of variability curves was generated for differing utilization (traffic intensity factors and the throughput was calculated. This is represented below:

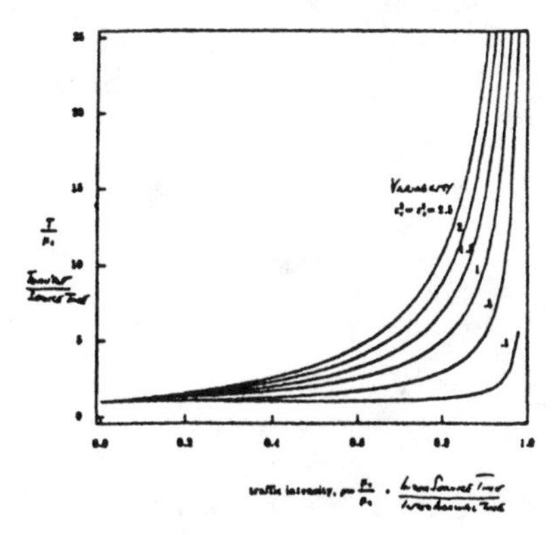

THE EFFECT OF VARIABILITY ON CAPACITY AND THROUGHPUT

Stated another way, for an constant lead time or throughput, increasing variability leads to reduction of capacity. What is particularly ironic is that generally when we have an increased variability and get behind schedule, we react by loading our facility even more and this creates more variability and longer delays. What is apparent is that when we have problems (variability), we should cut back on loading to meet the reduced capacity and thereby maintain the planned lead time according to which a customer order has been booked.

Variability and Inventory

We have seen that as variability increases, lead time increases and throughput decreases. The relationship of throughput and inventory was stated by Little's Law:

L (Queue) = R (rate) x W (Waiting Time)

(WIP) = Arrivals x Throughput

In other words for a constant loading WIP the inventory is directly proportional to the throughput which is itself a function of variability and capacity utilized.

Major Drivers of Variability and Suggested Controls

Facility Breakdown: This has a double effect. First we lose capacity in terms of actual time lost while the resource is down. Secondly we lose capacity as the variability of the process increases. Whenever possible we should schedule maintenance in small regular intervals of time as this way the variability is minimized. It is also essential that the machine is not allowed to be down for long periods of time as this increases variability.

Irregular Loading and/or Operator Tardiness: Surprisingly this is not as large a driver of variability as we would expect and while it should not be encouraged, it is not reason to get too worried.

LOT SIZE: This is the single most important driver of increased variability. Simulations reveal it to be about 100 times as detrimental as most other drivers. Perhaps the Japanese understood this intuitively when they focused on reducing lot sizes. Lot sizes are directly proportionate to run time. The factor preventing unlimited reduction of lot sizes is the set-up time. If lot sizes are reduced, there will come a point when no spent setting up the job. This can be seen in a graph which plots the lot size/set up time ratio against throughput for a family of utilization curves (Capacity curves).

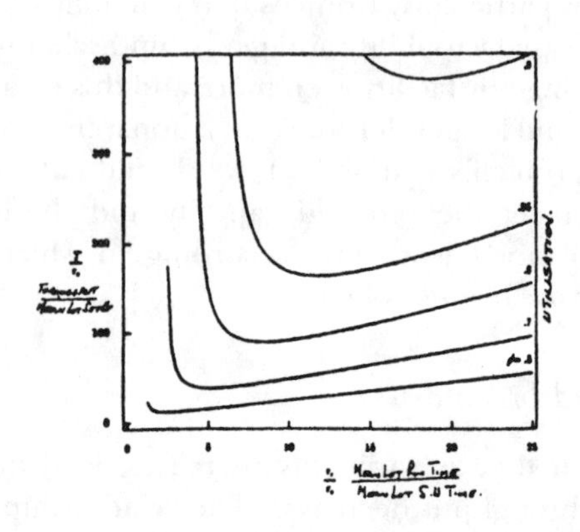

RELATIONSHIPS: RUN TIME VS. THROUGHPUT FOR VARYING UTILIZATIONS

Rule 2: As the Lot Size (run Time)/set-up Ratio Increases We Lose Either Capacity Or Throughput Or Both.

Understanding that lot size is proportional to variability, we see that this rule complements Rule 1. Thus we see the value of continuously reducing lot size up to the point when it is no longer efficient (i.e., the set up time is too high), after which we need to reduce the set up time and then continue to reduce the lot size. We are thus going down the same utilization curve and increasing throughput without loosing capacity.

High Variability Environment

There are product environments where either the process has unavoidable and unpredictable low yields or non repetitive, irregular demands and in these cases the above approach to increasing capacity has to be tempered by using some of the principles of Constraint Management. Constraints in the process have to be identified and an inventory buffer provided to maximize utilization of the constraint. This has to be considered as a "lesser of two evils approach," as reality has to be dealt with.

About the author

Blair is a Chartered Engineer (C. Eng.) from London and has an MBA from Loyola University. He worked for Pullman Incorporated out of Chicago and Indiana and held a variety of positions including Manufacturing Superintendent and Manager of Production Control. In 1982 he joined Worthington Pump in Harrison, N. J. as Materials Manager and in 1985 joined Lightolier as Director of Materials responsible for all the materials management functions of five factories. In 1988 he joined AT&T as a Technical Specialist responsible for Materials Management education in all AT&T factories, nationally and internationally. From September 1990 he has been the Materials Management and Engineering Manager at AT&T Submarine Cable Systems Division with responsibility for factories in Clark, N. J. and Reading, PA.

Currently Blair is an adjunct professor at Fairleigh Dickinson University teaching a graduate class in Strategic Materials Management. He has been an active member of APICS from 1981, having been recognized as a CPIM in 1982 and was a member of the Board of Directors of the Northern New Jersey Chapter. He has presented papers at numerous APICS user meetings, the most recent being the APICS Conference in 1990.

Reprinted from the *APICS 1990 Conference Proceedings.*

DRP: If We Knew Then What We Know Now

Clark Driscoll and Fred Tolbert, CPIM

Installing Distribution Resource Planning (DRP) software on your company's computer is a relatively easy task. Making the software work effectively for your organization is the hard part. Once the system is converted, the training classes completed and the consultants leave, what next? The objective of this paper is to present a case study of the lessons learned in facing the daily challenges of operating DRP in the 12 months following the system conversion. The focus of the paper is a series of issues which surfaced during the weeks and months following our DRP system conversion. Each topic includes how we chose to respond to the issue using sound DRP and inventory management principles. The list of issues includes:

- People Issues
- Item Analysis
- Sales Forecasting
- Disciplined DRP Procedures
- Performance Measures

The first 12 months following a DRP system conversion are full of roadblocks and challenges. Many of these were not anticipated prior to the system conversion. If we knew then what we know now, our road to Class A DRP status would be much smoother.

DRP Project Overview

Our company, Contel Material Management Company, is the procurement and distribution division of Contel Corporation. We purchase, warehouse, and distribute telecommunications products to the various operating divisions of Contel. We found ourselves having all of the typical inventory control problems. Customer service was down, inventory was up, and everyone blamed the system for our problems. We recognized the need to migrate from our existing reorder point system to a DRP system.

We chose an implementation approach which utilized personal computer based sales forecasting and DRP software. The PC software was integrated onto our existing mainframe system using file download and upload programs to transfer data between the mainframe and PC systems. We utilized the pilot project approach for installing the DRP system. This approach works by beginning DRP processing for one small product line, showing performance improvements and then phasing in the other product lines. Using the pilot project approach, we successfully implemented the PC based forecasting and DRP system over an eight month period.

If We Knew Then What We Know Now

Our project implementation approach included all of the textbook project management steps. We had a management steering committee, an implementation project team made up of system users, and a DRP education and training plan. We met the primary target completion dates and converted the system according to the work plan.

However, during the first 12 months of production DRP operations, our user community still did not completely trust the new system. Our resulting inventory management performance measures were mixed. We significantly improved our customer service, with our Line Fill Rate improving from 82% to 93%. At the same time, our total inventory gradually increased and our inventory turnover fell from 6.4 to 5.4 turns.

The following sections provide an analysis of the major issues which we have attempted to address during our first year of DRP operations. Each issue provides insights on the significant lessons we have learned while actually operating DRP in a production environment. Following each issue is a list of items that we would try differently if we had the past 12 months to do all over again.

If We Knew Then...—People Issues

Most of the efforts of our DRP Project Team and Steering Committee focused on the technical side of DRP operation. We read the books and listened to consultants talk about how people issues make or break an implementation. One book indicated that success was 80% people and 20% systems. We agreed, but went on without fully appreciating the importance of this principle and how the people and organizational decisions affect the outcome of the project.

Our company is organized under a product management concept where a Product Manager has "cradle to grave" responsibility for marketing, purchasing, and inventory control for specific product lines. A separate staff organization provides sales forecasting and DRP project management functions. This staff function provided the initial motivation for DRP implementation, and they remained the driving force behind the project. The company's DRP "Rambo" who served as the project team leader was from the staff organization. He did not have the related MBO's of decreased inventory and improved line fill rates that would hopefully result from the DRP project.

As you might imagine, this project organizational structure had built-in difficulty. The situation, which created an us-versus-them mentality, caused conflicts before and after the system was converted. Each camp found themselves thinking, "I have responsibility without the authority to act." The two groups lacked the necessary trust in each other for information to properly flow.

A second people-related issue which surfaced was the fear of job change and/or job loss. A theory among system users that the basic motivation for installing DRP was "getting rid of people." Questions surfaced like:

- Will I still have a job?
- Will my job be eliminated?
- Will my job change?
- Did anyone consider my unique needs?

Third, the manager ranks were given some, but not enough, consideration and response to their concerns about the system. As a result some of the managers became a part of the "underground resistance movement" to the DRP system. Here are a few of their typical concerns:

- I am not convinced DRP is better for me, so why should I support your system?
- Why were my concerns and unique needs not taken into account?
- This formal systems approach seems to require too much work, so where are the extra people?

The Product Managers' attitude influenced the behavior of their subordinates as well. We found that managers or supervisors in full support of the process will multiply the speed and effectiveness of the system's implementation.

...What We Know Now—People Issues

People are the key to success in any new system. If turf issues, control issues, and fear creep into the process, the project will suffer. If we could start over at Day 1 in our project, here are things we would do differently in the area of people issues.

- *Develop DRP "Rambos" in the Line Organization.* The inventory staff function members were convinced that DRP was the way to go. They tried to force-feed DRP concepts to the Product Managers and the Inventory Planners. A more effective way would be to develop DRP Rambos within the line organization actually responsible for inventory turns and customer service. Spend more time in DRP education and training activities. Visit other DRP installations and introduce Inventory Planners to others who have "been there." Building this positive momentum for change is critical to overcoming organizational roadblocks.
- *Address Job Security Issues.* Ensure that all personnel know the projected staffing plan and organization structure as soon as possible in the project. The nervousness and fear of the unknown about people's position, job title and compensation slows productivity and hinders the project implementation. These fears can be continuously alleviated by providing continuously project status and other relevant information.
- *Promote Line Manager Buy-in.* A successful DRP project has to have the support of the line managers responsible for the system users. There is no substitute for the motivation that a good leader provides in building and creating an environment for teamwork and personal growth. A good top management leader will help this process by focusing everyone's attention on company and department goals. This shifts the focus from the personal issues to working together on the business issues.

If We Knew Then...—Item Analysis

Item analysis is a review and validation of the key data elements and parameters input into the DRP system. DRP assumes that the data you are providing is correct. If it is not, you cannot expect to achieve planed results. Item analysis tasks deal with ensuring that the various item parameters are 100% accurate. The primary item analysis tasks to complete are:

- *Verify Standard Pack Size.* DRP recommends planned orders, expedites, and de-expedites in multiples of the item's standard pack size. Maintain the data base to ensure the standard pack size for each item is the correct order quantity.
- *Purge Invalid Open Purchase Orders and Sales Orders.* An invalid open purchase order or sales order quantity gives DRP an incorrect signal, and the system will give you a false action message. A periodic review of old sales orders and past due scheduled receipts helps to reduce excess inventories and potential customer backorders.
- *Items in Transition.* SKUs newly added to stock and items flagged to be deleted from the data base require a review and maintenance process to ensure the sales forecast, on-hand balance and on-order quantities are correct. These key processes, especially for items in a short product life cycle environment, ensure high service levels on new items and the prevention of obsolescence on old items.
- *Cost and Price.* Not only does your base business survive on these two data elements, but quality forecasting and DRP summary management reports must have 100% accurate cost and price data.

• *Inventory Deployment.* In a multi-warehouse environment all products are typically not stocked in all warehouses. How do you decide what to stock where? A criteria and policy must be established based upon balancing service, turn, and freight objectives. For example, should an item be stocked if there are six demands forecasted annually? Review inventory deployment strategies at least annually.

• *Inventory Balancing.* Once the deployment process is set, a periodic review of inventory transfers vs. buys decisions should take place. DRP provides a pegging report which can assist the Inventory Planner in weighing the cost/benefit of transferring excess product from one warehouse to another or buying more from the supplier.

• *Lead Times.* Variability of supplier lead times between quoted delivery intervals and actual lead times can disrupt the DRP planning process. Of all the item analysis elements noted above, accurate lead times can lead to immediate benefit. Supplier delivery performance is one of the single largest cost drivers to a distributor. Maintaining the data base with realistic lead times is mandatory to having valid DRP planning schedules.

At the beginning of our implementation item analysis was thoroughly executed. However, over time, lack of consistent, methodical approach to item analysis eroded the quality of our data base. The more attention we paid to the input data to DRP, the less override and change that was made to planned orders and expedite/de-expedite messages.

...What We Know Now—Item Analysis

Item analysis is important for beginning initial DRP operations for a product line. It is a more important ongoing activity essential for quality DRP processing. Here is a list of areas relating to item analysis that we would concentrate more on during the first year of DRP operations.

• *Educate users why item analysis is essential.* We need to better educate our users how DRP logic responds to incorrect data. The pilot implementation approach provides a good opportunity to use real life data to demonstrate how DRP responds if standard pack sizes, lead times, open purchase orders and the other item analysis components are not 100% accurate. We need to reinforce the concept that DRP assumes that the data you are providing it is accurate. Users need to fully understand the consequences of not maintaining a data base that is 100% accurate. Failure to maintain a quality data base shows up in lower customer service and inventory turnover as well as decreased user confidence in the system.

• *Develop an item analysis checkoff list.* It is not good enough to concentrate on just one or two of the major item analysis tasks. Nor is it OK to complete item analysis only when it is convenient. Develop a formal checklist of item analysis tasks for DRP users to complete. Be specific on the required timing of the tasks, indicating whether they are weekly, monthly, quarterly or annual tasks. A suggested list of item analysis tasks includes:

Frequency	Task
Weekly	Maintain open purchase orders with valid promised delivery dates.
	Purge customer orders from the system that have been canceled.
	Resolve all data integrity problems which surface in weekly DRP review.
Monthly	Balance inventory through warehouse transfers.
	Review items in transition (recently added or flagged for deletion).
Quarterly	Evaluate supplier lead times and update the item data base as required.
	Analyze safety stock strategies and adjust as needed.
Annually	Review item costs and prices.
	Review standard pack sizes, item weight and cube.
	Analyze inventory deployment.

If We Knew Then...—Sales Forecasting

The issue of sales forecasting was the most controversial of our DRP system implementation. "DRP will not work without a good forecast" was a common statement made by our Inventory Planners once they began working with DRP. Developing an appropriate response to the sales forecasting issue proved to be the most difficult situation we had to overcome in attempting to improve our inventory management performance.

The issue of forecast accuracy divided our department into two camps. The Inventory Planners, who work DRP, contended that the only way that they could improve their inventory performance was if the forecasts were better. The Forecast Analysts contended that the forecasts are always wrong, and the key was to use DRP's planning capabilities to help deal with the inevitable forecast error. There was little room for negotiation between the two camps. Both felt that they were right and the other group was wrong.

During the early days of our DRP operations, there was a great tendency on everyone's part to override the system. The Forecast Analysts "tweaked" the sales forecasts to make them appear more believable to the Inventory Planners. They spent time smoothing out monthly forecasts for individual products. For example, if the system forecasted sales of Widget A of 100, 0, and 100 units for the next three months, the Forecast Analyst would smooth the forecast to be 67, 67, and 66 units for those months. Also, the Inventory Planner's often would override the planned order quantities generated by DRP because "they didn't look right."

In both cases, it began to be difficult to determine how well the system was performing because of the volume of system overrides.

Fortunately, the favorite pastime of overriding the system has been significantly curtailed. Our experience shows that, in general, overriding the sales forecast is a waste of a Forecast Analyst's and Inventory Planner's time. Our rule of thumb is: only override the sales forecast when you know something that the system does not. An Inventory Planner's knowledge of an upcoming sales promotion is a situation where the Inventory Planner knows something that the system cannot predict using past sales history alone. However, overrides based on "it doesn't look right" should be avoided.

It is important to constantly measure forecast accuracy. This measurement lets you know if your forecasts are getting better over time. Also, the system should measure which forecast is better, the system generated forecast or the manual override. This key statistic tells you whether time spent overriding the sales forecast is a valuable use of your time. We measure forecast accuracy by determining the percentage of items with monthly and quarterly forecast error within a range of + or - 40%. Items with forecast error outside of that 40% range are targets for closer scrutiny to determine if the forecasts can be improved or different forecasting techniques and equations should be utilized.

...What We Know Now—Sales Forecasting

We have had a difficult time resolving the sales forecasting issue. It seems, however, that putting all of the inventory improvement opportunities into the lap of the Forecast Analysts will only keep it constantly searching for better Forecast Analysts and a better forecasting system. The ones we have must not be very good since they are always wrong.

However, if we could start over at Day 1 in our DRP project, here are things we would do differently in the area of sales forecasting:

- *Educate Inventory Planners on Forecasting Techniques.* We should provide our Inventory Planners with a better understanding of the forecasting techniques employed in the monthly forecasting process. This includes training on the basic capabilities and formulas utilized by the forecasting system. Inventory Planners should not feel that the forecasting system is a "black box" which generates forecasts using mysterious mathematical equations which do not apply to our particular business.
- *Research Forecasts Errors More Systematically.* Basically, we wait until a stock-out occurs and then try to research what went wrong. Instead, we should be more proactive in identifying items with consistently high forecast errors in order to take corrective action before a stock-out situation occurs. Our Forecast Analysts and Inventory Planners need to work more closely to research the causes behind stock-outs in order to prevent them in the future.
- *Educate Users How DRP Helps Overcome Forecast Error.* Our DRP users are convinced that only through improvements in the forecast will we be able to improve customer service and inventory turns. We need continued basic DRP education in how the related areas such as safety stock management, lead time reductions and supplier scheduling help to overcome the inherent uncertainty associated with the sales forecasting function.
- *Cross-train Inventory Planners and Forecast Analysts.* We have recently implemented a program where one of our Inventory Planners and one of our Forecast Analysts switched jobs for a six-month period. This method will foster a better appreciation of the problems which each position encounters in day-to-day operations. This should help resolve some of the finger pointing between the two groups that we have experienced since our system went into production.

If We Knew Then...—Disciplined DRP Procedures

Since our new DRP system was PC based, the existing mainframe purchasing and order point system remained in place. At first, the EOP/EOQ system was used to second guess DRP for ordering purposes. Slowly, the use of EOP/EOQ was put aside in favor of DRP.

Step by step operating procedures were published but not as a cohesive operating manual. Application of these working procedures varied by Inventory Planner. When subsequent excess inventories and backorders occurred, it was difficult to diagnose the source of the problem when procedures were practiced inconsistently.

We knew all the "right things" to do from the software training, but each user was pretty much on his own to operate the system. As time marched on, some Inventory Planners were more successful than others. We began to research the key things that made some of our users more successful than others.

...What We Know Now—Disciplined DRP Procedures

Procedures development and execution always seem to take a back seat when installing new systems. However, we could have operated our new system much more effectively with consistent and disciplined DRP operating procedures in place. Some of these areas include:

- *Develop standard DRP operating procedures.* During the pilot process, written procedures should be refined and established as routine. Consistent procedures substantially reduce the number of variables in problem investigation and usually nets better overall performance.

• *Work DRP action messages.* DRP generates three primary action messages for an item: 1) release planned order; 2) expedite open purchase order; and 3) de-expedite (delay receipt) open purchase order. There is a temptation to only act on the release planned order action messages in order to create new purchase orders. However, all action messages must be worked in order to take full advantage of the tools which DRP offers. Using DRP simply to generate new purchase orders reduces DRP to a simple reorder point system, and the resulting performance measures will be disappointing.

• *Maximize forecasting system output.* Consistent operating procedures are just as important to the sales forecasting function as they are to DRP. Set up routines which provide exception information to the Forecast Analyst. On a regular monthly basis, perform an analysis of factors which impact the quality of the sales forecast. While the forecasting system will not always be right, it does not even have a chance if the quality of the data being fed to it is invalid. Pay special attention to the following situations:

– Items with negative quantities in monthly sales history buckets.

– Items flagged for deletion from the data base.

– New items.

– Forecasts with manual overrides.

– Unexplained demand spikes.

– Specific forecast equations which cause lower forecast accuracy.

Rather than review each forecasted item, find ways to summarize and report the likely problem areas for manual review.

• *Item analysis.* Periodic execution of Item Analysis tasks is necessary to keep the DRP running smoothly. Over time, item parameters such as standard pack size, lead time and safety stock change. Item Analysis must be a regular procedure to keep DRP planning schedules valid.

If We Knew Then...—Performance Measures

DRP is a system designed to help improve the four basic performance measures of a distribution company. The four key measures are: Customer Service, Inventory Turnover, Gross Margin and Productivity. It is important to constantly measure your performance in these measures against your company's business plan objectives. Only through tracking the measures against the business plan can you determine if the system is providing the benefits expected.

During our DRP implementation project, we placed a lot of emphasis on the four key measures. Our Director of Product Management constructed a large 5' x 8' bulletin board to post our monthly performance in several areas. Suddenly, everyone's performance in Line Fill Rate and inventory turnover was published for everyone in the company to see.

The four key DRP success measures are:

• *Customer Service Rate.* This measure indicates whether you have the right product in the right place at the right time. Out Line Fill Rate measures the percentage of customer sales order lines we can fill complete from the customer's assigned warehouse. We measure our Line Fill Rate, by Inventory Planner, on a daily basis.

• *Inventory Turnover.* This measure relates how effectively you are managing your inventory investment. Monitoring inventory turns prevents "buying" extra customer service rates by increasing inventory levels above company objectives. We measure inventory turns, by Inventory Planner, on a monthly basis.

• *Gross Margin.* A key benefit of DRP and supplier scheduling should be to improve gross margin. Improved customer service performance should result in higher sales, providing increased gross margin dollars. Increased volume and long-term relationships created through supplier scheduling should result in additional discounts from the supplier. We measure gross margin by major product line on a monthly basis.

• *Productivity.* DRP improves productivity through reduced expediting of customer backorders and past due purchase orders. DRP works to eliminate paperwork and non-productive activities. Measuring productivity is important to balance improvements in customer service and turns with the work required to accomplish them. Appropriate productivity measures vary by company, but may include such things as the number of P.O. lines and receipts, the number of backorder lines, or the number of expedites/de-expedites processed. We measure the number of backorder lines, by Inventory Planner, on a monthly basis.

During our first year of DRP operations, we found it especially difficult to manage the trade-offs between Line Fill Rate and inventory turns. The Line Fill Rate measure became a visible statistic which became tied to our company bonus plan which everyone participated in. We had set a goal of achieving a 92% Line Fill Rate, and we reached that goal with room to spare. Our mind-set was that improvements in customer service could only come with increasing inventory. Given the choice between the two measures, upper management directed Line Fill Rate was more important than inventory turns. As a result, our total invenotry increased by 34% over the same period 12 months earlier.

...What We Know Now—Performance Measures

Here are the major lessons that we have learned that would make monitoring performance measures more effective:

• *Manage Trade-off Between Customer Service and Turns*. We should have worked harder at managing the trade-off between line fill rate and inventory turns. While DRP helped us to exceed our line fill rate target, our total inventory slowly climbed during the year. We measured turns on a monthly basis, but we conceded our turn goal in order to achieve our customer service goal. Our focus should be to use the tools of DRP to improve both customer service and turns at the same time.

• *Work at Improving Turns by Specific Product Line*. While we became pretty good at forecasting total company inventory levels on a monthly basis, we were not able to effectively plan inventory levels for individual product lines. Our Inventory Planners found it difficult to impact inventory turns for each of their product lines. That fact contributed to the focused attention on improving the forecasts as the only means for reducing inventory. We continued to use the DRP system as an order launching system rather than an inventory planning system.We needed to provide more attention to using DRP's planning capabilities to help improve the inventory turns for individual product lines.

• *Initiate Supplier Scheduling*. Supplier scheduling is the process of providing suppliers with the time-phased requirements plan generated by DRP. The Inventory Planner works directly with the supplier on a weekly basis to implement the DRP schedule. Supplier scheduling is an effective tool for improving customer service, inventory turns and gross margin. We have been slow to initiate supplier scheduling since our system conversion. This process should begin during the first 12 months of DRP operations.

• *Seek Out Productivity Improvement Opportunities*. Our department's productivity has improved since we now have fewer backorders to expedite. However, we still generate too much paper in our daily inventory planning functions. We should examine all working procedures of Forecast Analysts, Inventory Planners and Expediters to seek out additional productivity improvement opportunities.

Conclusion

Our first year of DRP operations provided both positive and not so positive results. We achieved steady improvements in customer service, which led us to add even more products to our stocking catalog. At the same time, we did not realize the inventory reductions originally expected from the system. However, we learned these lessons from the best possible teacher, that being experience. Certainly, there are some things we would have done differently if we knew then what we know now.

About the Authors

Fred Tolbert, CPIM, is Inventory Planning Manager for Contel Material Management Company, the warehousing and distribution division of Contel Corporation. In his position, he has been instrumental in implementing DRP, Sales Forecasting and Electronic Data Interchange programs.

His career in materials management began as a Systems Consultant with Arthur Andersen & Company. There he specialized in the design and implementation of inventory control and accounting systems for the public utility industry. He moved to Contel Material Management Company as Systems Development Manager involved in implementing an integrated Distribution Management System. He has BBA and MBA degrees from the University of Georgia and is an active member of the Atlanta APICS chapter.

Clark Driscoll, CPIM, is the Inventory Planning Supervisor at Contel Material Management Company. His focus has been DRP and DRP II implementation and management. In his position, he completes analysis and "What If" simulations for various logistics models and decisions.

He holds a BA in Business Administration from Oklahoma Baptist University. He has worked in finance and quality for an aircraft manufacturer and served six years in the U.S. Navy Supply Corps primarily in material and logistics. He is an active member of APICS and a commander in the U.S. Navy Reserve.

Reprinted from the 1989 APICS *Conference Proceedings.*

Implementing DRP II: How to Do It Right

Mary Lou Fox

During the past few years, many companies have implemented distribution resource planning, DRP II, systems. Many more companies are projected to implement DRP II in the 1990s. The experience that has been gained from the companies already using these systems offers guidance to new companies traveling down the same implementation path.

From my experience, no two companies have the exact same experiences implementing DRP II; but there are many similarities which provide useful information to some things that are essential and some thinks that often prove detrimental. The purpose of this paper is to discuss the issues involved in implementing DRP II.

What Is DRP II?

DRP II is a comprehensive system for the management of finished goods inventory. Traditionally, finished goods inventory has been managed by many people in a company and involves several areas— planning inventory levels, anticipating inventory usage, providing input to manufacturing of the quantities of product needed for distribution, and distributing inventory to warehouses.

Often these tasks have been done by different people, and without a lot of computer support.

DRP II is an integrated computer system which supports the decision making for the management of finished goods inventory. The first area that is included in DRP II is forecasting for each product at each stocking location (warehouses, distribution center, plant warehouse). This SKU forecast is developed using a statistical method to produce an estimate of usage based on the past demand history. Then forecasters can override this forecast to accommodate information about the market such a promotions or price changes.

Another area of finished goods management included in DRP II is inventory planning, which means establishing safety stock levels, determining how often the inventory should be replenished, and determining coverage levels. DRP II systems have various rules and parameters to calculate an inventory plan for each individual SKU.

Distribution requirements planning, DRP, compares forecasts and inventory levels for each SKU and determines when replenishment shipments must arrive at the location. These shipments are calculated for several weeks out into a planning horizon—often a year or so into the future. Then these shipments are offset in time by the leadtime required to get them from their sources and are shown as demand on the source. The source inventory is managed in a similar fashion except that the input is not a forecast of demand but the schedule of DRP shipments that need to be made to replenish warehouses. The result of these DRP calculations are a series of shipment schedules for all the items in the distribution network.

At each plant, the DRP plan represents what product will be needed by distribution in each week for each product to meet shipment schedules.

Many companies have manufacturing operations with large amounts of capital equipment that incur lengthy and expensive changeovers. Often each item cannot be produced each week so there is inevitably the need to produce items before they are really needed by distribution. Because of this, the DRP requirements are used by master schedulers to plan production schedules sufficiently far in advance to balance manufacturing efficiencies with inventory buildups to achieve the optimum cost for the corporation. So DRP II systems include a master scheduling capability so that feasible schedules can be calculated based on the DRP requirements for each product at each plant.

The actual deployment of finished goods is a daily, operational task that is managed within a DRP II system. Planners decide to release DRP shipments after determining that there is adequate source inventory to deploy and there are enough other products to fill a vehicle.

DRP II provides better tools to inventory planners to make the daily decisions that are necessary to effectively run the distribution operations of a company.

Profile of a Typical Company Using DRP II

A company which finds DRP II useful to manage its finished goods inventory usually has one or more of the following characteristics.

1. Make to Stock

This means that the company must produce and inventory the finished products in one or more stocking locations in advance of real customer orders.

DRP II offers the solution that a forecast of demand drives all the planning and scheduling of shipments so that product is available when needed.

2. Deployment of Stock is a Costly and/or High Volume Operation

The sheer volume of finished goods inventory being moved through the distribution network is high. Daily decision making to determine what products to ship is a large task.

DRP II drives daily deployment decisions based on the current inventory level and forecast usage of each SKU. In addition, DRP II provides tools to manage vehicle loads.

3. Complex Distribution Networks

Many companies have multiple stocking locations for their items and the movement of products from their producing locations to the final customers involves multiple movements.

Some companies have a three echelon network with product moving from plant to regional distribution centers and then to local warehouses. Other companies move product from one plant to another plant before moving it out to a warehouse. In other cases, companies produce the same product in multiple locations and need to bring the DRP requirements to the proper producing locations for each warehouse.

The necessity to plan product flows through these networks is a large task which is managed easily with a DRP II system.

4. Production Schedule Changeovers are very Costly and/or Time Consuming

It is typical in many process and high volume repetitive industries, that changeovers to the production lines are costly to do and require a lot of time. The necessity to minimize unnecessary changeovers to avert impending stockouts is key to reducing costs and improving throughput.

DRP II provides a much better input of demand to the master scheduler so that stable schedules can be created.

5. Extensive Promotion and Deals

Many make-to-stock companies, especially with consumer products, sell a large percentage of their annual volume on some type of deal or promotion. The promotions represent a large bulge of product moving through the operations of the company during a short time interval. Most companies cannot produce and distribute the promoted volume during the promotion period, but must plan an inventory buildup, often weeks in advance. They need adequate visibility into the volumes to be produced and distributed in order for plans to be made. Otherwise, premium freight might be needed or overtime costs incurred.

DRP II provides visibility into the forecast volumes and to the shipment schedule required to produce and move products through the distribution network.

Implementing DRP II—The Issues

When a company installs a new general ledger, accounts payable, or an accounts receivable system, the implementation process will go through several predictable stages. The company must define their requirements to determine the features of the new system which are essential to incorporate their existing practices.

They consider the data processing issues to be sure that the system is installed, data are gathered correctly, and adequate hardware and user terminals are available. Training the users on the new system is also key to a successful implementation so that the users learn how to do the transactions needed for those systems.

Typical computer system implementations deal with the following issues:

- What are our requirements?
- What software meets our requirements?
- What hardware is needed to run our new software?
- How do we train the users?
- How do we migrate our data to the new system?
- What new procedures do we need to use to make the new system work?
- How do we verify that the new system is giving the same answers?
- How and when shall we cutover to the new system?
- How do we document what we have done so that we can keep the new system going even if there are personnel changeovers?

The system that is being implemented has new features, reports, and a user interface. The company must learn new procedure for accomplishing the necessary transactions. But the basic system has not changed the function that is being automated. Accounts receivable are still being calculated and recorded according to generally accepted accounting principles. There is just a new computer system which must be learned to do a routine accounting task.

Implementing DRP II requires the company to address all the same issues discussed above.

The key difference between implementing a DRP II system and implementing an accounting system is that DRP II represents a different approach to the business function for managing finished goods inventory. One method of doing a task is not being replaced with a more fully featured version of the same method. The tasks that are being automated are being replaced with a different method for doing the same task.

For example, if a reorder point system is being used, an inventory level triggers an order to replenish an item at the warehouse. In DRP II, the combination of a forecast, an inventory level and current intransit shipments are used to plan replenishment shipments for several weeks. This means that the quantity and timing of a replenishment shipment calculated by the DRP II will be different from the old system. The distribution requirements given to manufacturing will be different under DRP II. So implementing DRP II is not as simple as verifying that the "numbers are the same." The numbers will not be the same, but will be better.

There must be a recognition of this fact up front, because it implies that the project team implementing DRP II must do additional tasks in order to implement the system successfully. These include:

- Understand how the existing system works. This means how the company forecasts, plans inventory levels, decides what quantities are needed to be manufactured, decides how much inventory should be sent to a warehouse, decides when to transship from one warehouse to another.
- Figure out which of the existing system methods will remain under DRP II and which will change. Just because a task, report or calculation has been done before, does not mean that it makes sense in a DRP II system. There must be "zero based analysis."
- Figure out where the data to drive DRP II will come from. To drive forecasts, the company needs monthly demand (sales volumes) for each product at each stocking location facing independent demand. To drive the DRP II calculations, the company needs current stock on hand for each SKU as well as the shipments in transit to each location. Getting this data may be an issue for the company.
- Decide how often a forecast should be calculated. The typical decisions are weekly, monthly, or every 4 weeks. There is a tradeoff between the volume of data required for weekly forecasting and the time to review the data weekly, and the added benefits of control at a weekly level.
- Decide how overrides to the forecast will be done. This involves getting the proper input from marketing and sales as to what to expect for future sales. From experience, getting a proper forecasting process set up is a large job that is absolutely essential to getting desired results from DRP II.
- Another forecasting issue is what to do about demand within the forecast period. At the beginning of the month, the SKU forecast is the company's best prediction as to what will be sold during the coming month. During the month, some demand has already occurred. So the issue becomes how much of the forecast to predict for the remainder of the period. Another issue is how to use known information such as open customer orders. Modern DRP II systems provide multiple methods for blending the forecast with known demand during a period.
- Decide inventory stocking policies for each SKU such as its safety stock inventory level, its customer service objective, and how frequently and in what quantities it should be replenished. Is this data available somewhere already in the company data files? For many companies, this information is not readily available. Most companies need to review existing policies and decide what makes sense in a DRP II environment.
- DRP is inherently a wish list—it calculates what stock is necessary at each stocking location for each product to meet demand. DRP does not scale back its wish for replenishments based on the availability of stock at a source. So when there is inadequate stock available to meet DRP demand, an inventory manager must decide how the existing stock will be deployed. How this is done in the system, who does it, how and when it is communicated to the destinations (especially important is multi-national DRP II environments) are all typical issues that must be addressed as the company meshes DRP data with the master schedule data.
- Another key issue is how frequently to replan. For many companies, visibility into the daily changes in stock levels and open customer orders is important. Others are driven by a desire to move product in a Just-in-Time environment. For these companies, daily replanning is a necessity. Others can plan in cycles of 2 to 3 times a week or only once a week. The key issues are how volatile are the data, how short are the lead times, and how able is the company to review data daily.

These are a sample of the issues that must be addressed in the course of implementing a DRP II system. Often companies have not fully confronted them before, so the implementation process requires discussion to determine the best solutions.

Typical Implementation Plan

To ensure that DRP II is implemented successfully, companies need to approach the process in an organized way. There are several methodologies which can be successful. This paper outlines the one that STSC uses with its DRP II implementations.

The implementation process must consist of these stages:

1. Project organization
2. Project Management
3. Education and Training

Project Organization

To carry out the implementation, a project team needs to be formed which consists of key people from each area which will be impacted by the new system. Typical members of the team come from the areas of distribution, inventory planning, production scheduling, marketing, finance, and data processing. The members of the team must be decision makers who can decide how the new system will be implemented, and have the authority to carry out the decisions. The members do not need to be high level managers, but do need to be respected members of the organization with the vision to see beyond the present structures to plan the environment for the new system. The team also has a key user or two who can reflect how the system and the tasks are done today.

There is also a steering committee of high level managers of each functional area who will meet regularly with the team, review their progress, and resolve issues that are brought to them. It is inherent in the process that new ways of dealing with the business will arise. Hopefully, the project team can sort these out. Those that cannot are brought to the steering committee for resolution so that the implementation can proceed in a timely fashion.

The organization needs to free up team members from their regular work so that they can do their DRP II learning. One area that is absolutely critical for companies to be successful is the necessity to let the project team have the time to learn the software well and to sort out the issues so that the implementation will reflect the way the company needs to do business using DRP II.

The team also needs to keep a log of issues that arise during the meetings, publish the log, and resolve the issues as soon as possible.

Project Management

To properly manage a project, certain things are usually required. The first is a statement of what the project is supposed to do. This clearly delineates timing, purpose, and expected results.

The key to success is upper management involvement to clearly define goals, make necessary resources available, and to communicate expectations.

Then a project plan establishes the tasks that need to be done, the responsible person, and the due date. This is an essential step to plan the total project, to keep track of progress, and to communicate that progress to management.

The plan also details the milestones that the project will achieve and the completion dates. For example, the milestones might include having forecast training classes, completion of a forecast pilot, and going production with forecasting.

The last key factor in managing a project successfully is accountability. The team must be empowered to make decisions and be held accountable to getting the system successfully installed.

Companies that use a pilot approach are the most successful. In a pilot, the users learn to use and apply the software on a small segment of the business. The learning process is iterative and the issues that arise during this stage are important. As the team understands the system, they will plan how to best manage the business. Then they can test their decisions to see if they work for the business.

When the pilot is operational, then additional groups of products are added to the system and the implementation proceeds.

Education and Software Training

There is a difference between education and software training. Software training is short-focused courses to teach how to use the system and how the system works. Each course should be designed around a single module of the software. Both beginner and advanced courses should be available. After each course, the team members practice what they have learned so that they can decide which parts or the software to implement.

When the rollout of the system to end users is done, their software training is focused on the tasks that they need to do daily.

An initial high level course that focuses on an overview of the software and the issues that need to be addressed is an excellent way to begin a project.

Education focuses on the "why" not the "how" of the new system. It explains the theory and concepts behind DRP II and inventory management. Most important, it helps users understand "what's in it for me"?

Education is key to a successful implementation because DRP II represents a new way of managing the finished goods inventory and people need to understand what it is, why it is a better approach for the company, and what their role is.

Education needs to be given to each member of the project team and to the users. What gets taught and how long the classes last depend on the group. The most successful education classes have a mix of different functional areas in the room. It is very effective to teach a group of marketing, distribution, and production planners why forecasting is important and the benefits of better inventory management. Properly done, the interaction between the people in the room facilitates the communication of perspectives and functional needs that must be understood to make the system successful.

Benefits

Companies that have successfully implemented DRP II achieve multiple benefits.

For some companies, inventory can be reduced. Simply having the visibility into the real needs for inventory for products allows high stock levels to be reduced.

For other companies, inventory reduction is not as important as the velocity of the inventory—how quickly it moves through the distribution network to the customer. DRP II has a positive effect on this as well since DRP anticipates usage and schedules shipments to arrive when they are needed. By reviewing planned schedules daily, the shipments can be sent as needed.

Many companies experience a dramatic reduction in transportation costs when DRP II is implemented. Many companies respond to stockouts with the shipment of the product using premium freight such as LTL, or truck when rail was the least costly. Or they make shipments from alternate sources and incur added cost due to longer distances. Or they transship from one warehouse to another thus adding an extra movement of the product. DRP II reduces transportation costs by giving visibility to planned demand needs so that replenishments can be anticipated and sent in time.

Customer service is very important with companies today, and DRP II helps companies maintain a targeted level of service by SKU. This lets the company evaluate the cost of maintaining a level of service for each item. For some companies, this results in a deliberate policy of high service for high volume, high profit items, and a lower service policy for less important items.

For most companies, the biggest benefit is the increased communication within the organization due to the fact that the different functional areas are using a common database of planning information to drive the business.

Summary

Implementing DRP II can be done successfully if a company follows the approach outlined above. The key ingredients include (1) use an organized approach to the process, (2) recognize that the business is going to do things differently when DRP II is implemented and establish a process to make the appropriate business decisions to achieve this change, and (3) provide the resources and the commitment to see the process through to the finish.

About the author

Mary Lou Fox is Director of Professional Services for STSC, Inc. She has several years experience helping companies implement integrated logistics software. Currently she manages the consulting, education, and technical services at STSC.

Ms. Fox is a member of the Council of Logistics Management and the Metro Washington, DC, chapter of APICS. She is a graduate of Boston College with a B.S. in Mathematics and a graduate of the Polytechnic Institute of New York with a M.S. in Computer Science.

*Ms. Fox has an extensive background in the development of software products. As development manager at STSC, she was responsible for the development of LOGISTICS*PLUS, an integrated logistics planning system that combines forecasting, DRP II and MRPII.*

Reprinted from *APICS—The Performance Advantage,* December 1995.

Gaining an Edge with Supply Chain Management

M. Eric Johnson and Tom Davis

Like greenhorn cowboys struggling to control a stampede, self-reliant managers in many companies are finding themselves overwhelmed in the fight to head off market demands for responsive order fulfillment. As with quality in the 1980s, order fulfillment is rapidly evolving into a non-negotiable dimension of operational competitiveness. In the past, companies wishing to score highly with customers on delivery responsiveness allowed inventories to bloat. Today, the costs of holding inventory, especially in rapidly changing markets, prohibit that behavior. Companies must now provide good service while maintaining low inventories. This requires careful supply chain management, which, like driving cattle, is a team sport.

For years, companies have worked to master parts of the puzzle. Some companies concentrated on the manufacturing process by implementing quality programs and adopting Just-in-Time philosophies while others reengineered the new product generation process, cutting precious time from product development. In the end, many poignant examples have shown that excellence in product design or manufacturing alone does not guarantee order fulfillment success. IBM learned this lesson with its hot line of Thinkpad PCs. An instant hit from its introduction, the Thinkpad was dogged for years with delivery problems, pushing customers to the competitors. Such high-profile examples can be found in nearly every industry—from Motorola's cellular phones to Sara Lee's cleavage-building brassieres and Nabisco's low-fat cookies.

In some industries, such as carbonated beverages and apparel, supply chain management has always been an important dimension of competition. For example, companies like Pepsi and VF (maker of Lee and Wrangler jeans) have survived for years in industries where superior logistics strategies translate directly into profits and growth. Today, few industries are immune from customer demands for delivery. Hewlett-Packard, for example, succeeded for 50 years in the electronic instrument market where customers ordered equipment through a field representative and waited patiently for delivery. Not so today: Slow deliveries disgruntle customers in every market HP competes in from multi-user workstations to gas chromatographs. Moreover, successful order fulfillment requires much more from managers than the traditional view that logistics implied—managing warehouses and trucks. It requires integrated supply chain management, which includes everything from product design and vendor selection through final distribution.

For those who survived the gush of Japanese improvement programs only to be mired in the quality wars, supply chain management may seem little more than another fad—it's not. Supply chain management is the inevitable consequence of geographically dispersed suppliers and markets. When companies were vertically integrated and served regional markets, managing the supply chain was easy. However, as companies began to roam the globe in search of low-cost suppliers and new markets for products, the coordination challenges of managing supply chain links grew. Supply chain management is about managing the links in the product chain—links between suppliers and manufacturers, links between divisions and departments, links between marketing and manufacturing, links between product development, manufacturing and distribution. The goal is low-cost order fulfillment—to make supply meet demand.

Measuring Supply Chain Performance

As with any management endeavor, a prerequisite to success is measurement. While there are many important measurements of corporate health, supply chain metrics must capture two important, sometimes conflicting objectives—supply chain costs and order fulfillment. In a sense, one can think of the supply chain as an engine that converts assets into fulfilled customers. The goal is to produce happy customers at the lowest possible cost. Order fulfillment means reliably delivering a defect-free order. The fulfillment process includes almost all contact with the customer including order entry, confirmation, delivery and after-sale service. For our discussion, we concentrate on delivery. This facet of order fulfillment is often measured using fill rates that describe the percentage of items shipped on time (see sidebar). The costs associated with providing order fulfillment are many. However, a good surrogate measure of supply chain cost is inventory that can be measured in several ways, including inventory dollars or weeks of supply.

In their efforts to measure supply chain performance, Hewlett-Packard has adopted a reporting scheme that combines these two measurements. This satisfies two important constituencies—marketing, which is concerned with

 © APICS

satisfying the customer, and finance, which is concerned with asset performance. Using this reporting scheme, actual supply chain performance can be compared across product lines. Generally speaking, it should be easy to provide good service with lots of inventory. The challenge is to produce high levels of delivery service with low levels of inventory, and it is this challenge that HP has presented its product line managers. For the supply chains of some product lines, this may mean a simple adjustment in inventory deployment. For others, radical improvement or supply chain redesign may be required.

Supply chain theory suggests that the efficient trade-off of inventory and delivery service follows a curve. The shape of the curves is dictated by the physics of the individual supply chain—for example, the vendor lead times and reliability, manufacturing lead times and reliability, distribution channel structure and demand variability. With effective management of information and inventory, the performance of a product line should fall on the curve. Of course, a poorly managed supply chain would operate off the curve.

Improvements in delivery service can be obtained by increasing supply chain inventories. This naturally allows for a service/inventory trade-off. The consequences are played out daily in many companies. When delivery service dips, marketing often takes initiatives to increase inventories and improve service. However, when inventories are high, finance will often push to reduce them and improve asset performance—at the expense of customer service. In the end, many companies swing back and forth on the curve, but never improve the supply chain.

Improving Supply Chain Performance

The goal of supply chain management is not simply to optimize the tradeoff of inventory and delivery service—moving on the curve—but rather to improve the physics of the supply chain. There are many ways to improve supply chain performance, from radical redesign of the supply chain itself to process improvements throughout the chain.

Most supply chains can be broken into four major operational processes: forecast, supply, transformation and distribution. Improvement in any one of these processes will result in some improvement in the overall supply chain. However, the level of overall improvement varies for different supply chains. For example, in the fad-sensitive apparel industry, improvements in the forecasting process may net large supply chain improvements. Sport Obermeyer, a leading manufacturer of ski wear, dramatically improved its forecasting process by capturing leading indicators of demand from early sales. The improved forecast translated directly into profits by reducing excess inventories of products that must be liquidated through deep price markdowns. In other industries with more stable demand, improvements in the forecasting process may have a much smaller overall effect. For them, building reliable supplier relationships or

Metrics for Order Fulfillment

Simply put, you can't satisfy a customer without delivering the product on time. In study after study, delivery performance ranked high in customers' minds, often just below the product's attributes. And it's not just delivery speed that is important. In fact, in many cases, reliability ranks ahead of speed when achieving order fulfillment success. This should come as no surprise. Federal Express would not have made its fortune without first convincing customers that overnight delivery really meant overnight.

Companies hoping to increase customer satisfaction through better order fulfillment must use appropriate metrics to establish the right performance objectives. In our research of common service metrics, we found two principal shortcomings. First, few metrics are truly driven by the customer. Second, most metrics ignore variability. Naturally, we prefer metrics that capture these attributes without sacrificing the appeal of more traditional measures like fill rates. One group of metrics that we find to be increasingly relevant to today's order-driven systems are what we call order windows. This set of metrics is derived from the concept of an order aging curve. The aging curve shows the cumulative percentage of orders filled over the time horizon. For example, the aging curve might show that 20 percent of the orders were shipped on time or early, 60 percent within one day, and 95 percent within two days.

The curves themselves present a wealth of information—much more than a single fill rate number. Since they are based on complete customer orders, they better relate performance as perceived by the customer than item, dollar or line fill rates. They also help a manager ascertain the system's variability. For example, the performance of two different companies can be plotted. It may show that both companies fill about half of their orders immediately. However, the aging curve may show that company A is more reliable, with nearly all of its orders shipped within one day whereas only three-quarters of the orders are filled in that window by company B. Moreover, it may also show that company A is less likely to ship the product too early, which can be as undesirable as late shipment for many customers.

Metrics based on time windows capture the most important aspect of the delivery process—reliability. As many have noted in the world of quality management, reliability is the key to process control. Taguchi has argued this point best. He notes that the mean *of a process is often not difficult to change; reducing the* variability *is the first and most difficult problem. As we noted earlier, customers expect and require reliability.*

improving the transformation (manufacturing) process may be the key to substantial supply chain improvements.

While process improvements are important, the largest supply chain improvements can often be made by changing the supply chain network itself. These changes typically involve the number and physical location of nodes in the supply chain—the suppliers, manufacturing plants and distribution centers. For example, a decision to source a key component locally with shorter and more reliable supply lead times changes the network and may produce large supply chain dividends. On the other side of the network, proximity to the customers is the key driver for supply chain success in some industries. For example, Pepsi is constantly analyzing its network of bottling facilities, looking for locations near demographic hot spots.

HP learned that changes in product design can subtly change the role of nodes in supply chain, netting big improvements (see sidebar). They redesigned the popular LaserJet and DeskJet printers to allow for product customization at distribution centers scattered throughout the world. The role of the distribution center changed from simply shipping products to including a light manufacturing process to customize the printer. The change allowed HP to make option mix decisions much later in the distribution channel where more customer information was available. The HP case illustrates possibilities for supply chain improvements when functional barriers are lowered and the role of different nodes in the supply chain can be challenged.

Wal-Mart challenged the traditional role of the suppliers and distributors in building its superb supply chain. Working directly with their best individual manufacturers, Wal-Mart surrendered responsibility for managing warehouse inventories of their stockkeeping units. In exchange, it exacted a promise of near-perfect order fulfillment. The concept, termed vendor managed inventory, is now sweeping diverse industries from retailing to health care. Wal-Mart also challenged the accepted turnover practices at its distribution centers to speed product movement. Using a cross-docking strategy, many outbound trucks are directly loaded from inbound trucks. The products never touch the floor.

From product design to stocking store shelves, successful supply chain management requires rethinking many traditional business processes. But that is not all. For years, managers have been improving and reengineering their own processes but ignoring their function's impact on supply chain performance. Supply chain management requires a systems perspective, managing across the nodes of the supply chain while also considering the links between the processes. The lone ranger mentality will not suffice. Armed with powerful information systems and empowered to cross-functional boundaries, today's managers are being presented with enormous opportunities for radical order fulfillment improvements by managing the supply chain.

About the Authors

M. Eric Johnson is assistant professor of operations management at Vanderbilt University. Tom Davis is employed in the Home Products Division of Hewlett-Packard Co.

Design for Postponement—How HP Improved Its Supply Chain

In the late 1980s, Hewlett-Packard pioneered use of thermal inkjet technology for personal convenience printers. At that time, the personal printer market was segmented into two primary classes: dot matrix printers, which were inexpensive, and laser printers, which were more expensive but provided much higher print quality. Inkjet printers offered near-laser print quality at a near-dot matrix price. At first the inkjet printers stumbled in the market. Early printers required special paper and the ink would sometimes smear if touched before it dried. However, by 1990 these problems were solved and HP faced a new enviable problem—demand skyrocketed.

As demand increased, HP's printer inventories throughout the world also grew rapidly, yet delivery service declined. It seemed that HP never had the right inventory. For example, when sales of the French unit were selling fast, the German unit languished on the shelf. While the basic printer was the same throughout the world, DeskJets for each country had to be specialized at the factory in Washington state. This involved assembling the printer with the correct power supply (110 or 220 volts), power cord (plug), and a manual written in the appropriate language. Even though distribution centers in some countries would be bulging with inventory, printers could not be shipped to another country where demand was strong.

While HP had designed the printer for low-cost manufacturing, the supply chain costs were high. To solve the supply chain problems, HP redesigned the DeskJet and its packaging to allow for last-minute customization. The printer's power supply was moved out of the printer itself, making it part of the power cord. The packaging was modified so that the correct power supply and documentation could be added at the final distribution center. The printers themselves were generic. This concept effectively postponed the product differentiation until final distribution. Thus, rather than holding inventories of many "different" products, HP could hold inventories of the generic printer and deploy them quickly to countries where demand was strong. This risk pooling strategy allowed HP to substantially reduce its inventory investment while improving customer service—a shift in the supply chain curve.

 © APICS

Reprinted from the *APICS 1992 Conference Proceedings.*

The Planning Cycle—DRP to MRP

John W. Martini

It is easy to simplify manufacturing to two issues: Planning and Execution. Planning deals with: what to make, when to make it, and how much to make. Execution deals with: how to make it, the processes involved, the quality program and the whole JIT philosophy. This paper will narrow its focus to the planning tools for the manufacturing/distribution pipeline. The manufacturing/distribution pipeline starts with the raw materials and purchased parts required by the manufacturing plant. At the manufacturing level, you add in the fabricated components, subassemblies and assemblies to produce the finished goods inventory. At the distribution level, you have primarily finished goods. There are three separate but similar proven planning tools—Material Requirements Planning (MRP), Master Production Scheduling (MPS) and Distribution Requirements Planning (DRP). MRP functions as the planning tool to schedule the inside factory (what the factory produces) and the outside factory (what is purchased from its suppliers). MPS is the scheduling tool for the finished goods inventory at the factory level. DRP plans the inventory at a distribution center. While the underlying logic is very similar for each of these tools, there are subtle and not so subtle factors which can dramatically impact the inventory plan at each point in the manufacturing/distribution pipeline. This paper will look at the logic of each tool, the factors which can have impact on the inventory levels, and where the opportunities are for reducing the planning cycle and total cumulative lead time (see **Figure 1**).

Andre' Martin, in his second edition of his book on Distribution Resource Planning uses the following diagram to illustrate the situation (see **Figure 2**).

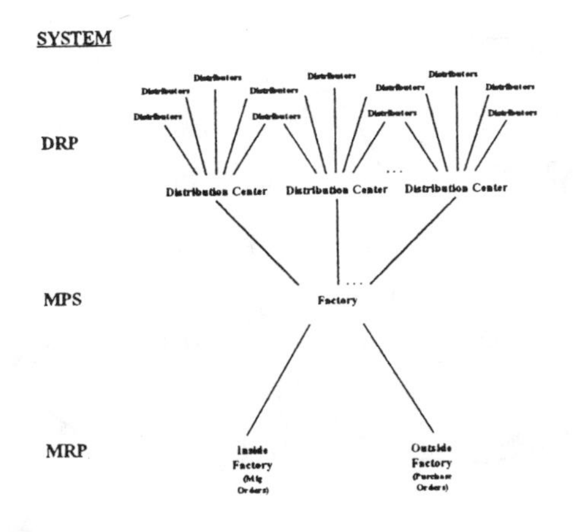

Figure 1.

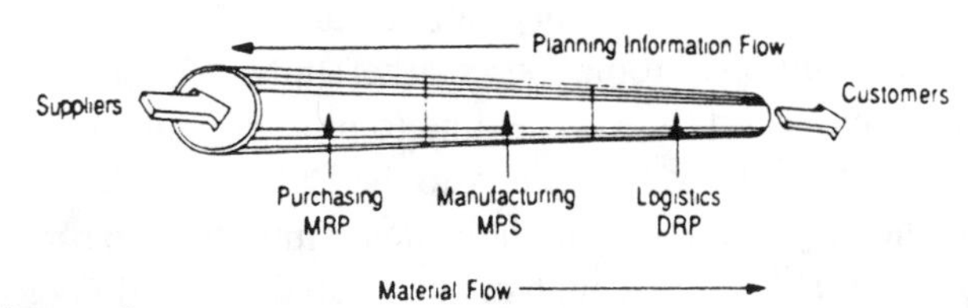

Figure 2.

The flow of material is from suppliers to manufacturers to the distribution channel. The flow of information is from the customer to the distribution center to the manufacturer to the suppliers. This can be looked upon as a timeline and the time to flow material forward is just as important as the flow of information from the customer back to the supplier. There are opportunities to reduce many of these time elements. Time is one of the major factors which influences inventory at the different levels.

Distribution Requirements Planning is the first tool I will discuss (see **Figure 3**).

DRP is part of the demand management function and basically plans

- What product at this DC
- How much of each product at the DC
- How much to order
- When to order.

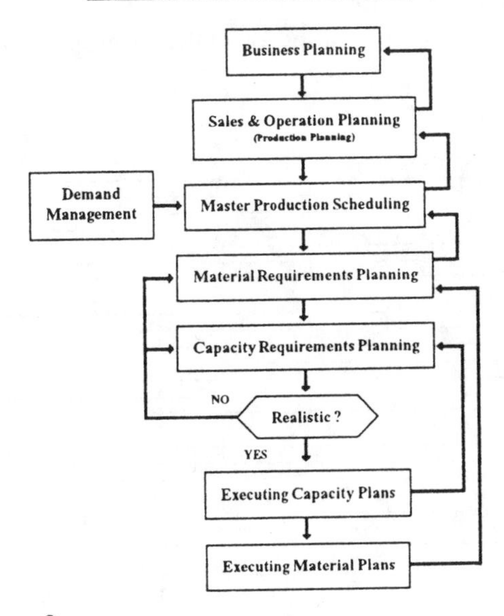

Figure 3.

The factors which influence the DRP plan are

- Forecast (and sales history)
- Lead time
- Safety stock.

The forecast is an estimate of what the distributors (customers) will ask you to deliver over your planning horizon and is based on sales history, internal and external factors, market conditions, promotions, market strategy, pricing conditions, etc. Lead time is the time to process, ship, and receive an order from the factory to the DC.

Generally, the total cumulative lead time (time to obtain raw material, etc., thorough manufactured finished goods) is not involved at the DRP level except when there is an unusual demand not reflected in the forecast.

Safety stock is the amount of inventory at this DC to achieve the required customer service level. This could be a one to six weeks or more supply, based on the forecast.

The forecast, derived from the sales history records, is generally some type of average which may not accurately reflect the real need. The forecast should reflect trends, seasonality, etc. Even geography and regional differences can have an influence. Note that the closer you get to the end user, the more difficult it is to forecast. The law of larger numbers favors a national forecast.

Sometimes you see safety time instead of safety stock. Safety time is simply safety stock translated into weeks of demand based on the forecast.

DRP will drive the inventory to the safety stock level. Safety stock is required due to

- lack of information (planned future sales)
- timeliness of information (distributor, DC, manufacturing plant
- lead time—DC and manufacturing
- demand fluctuation

The following is an example of a DRP printout (see **Figure 4**).

WEEK	PAST DUE	1	2	3	4	5	6
FORECAST		10	10	10	10	10	10
SCH. REC.							
ON HAND	130	120	110	100	90	80	70
F. PL. ORD.							
PL. ORD.					80		

WEEK	7	8	9	10	11	12	13
FORECAST	10	10	10	10	10	10	10
SCH. REC.		80					
ON HAND	60	50	120	110	110	90	80
F. PL. ORD.							
PL. ORD.						80	

WEEK	14	15	16	17	18	19	20
FORECAST	10	10	10	10	10	10	10
SCH. REC.			80				
ON HAND	70	60	50	120	110	100	90
F. PL. ORD.							
PL. ORD.							

Figure 4.

The projected available balance line is a simple arithmetic calculation (i.e., on hand—forecasts/orders + scheduled receipts). Note that the inventory level is driven to the safety stock level. These calculations, with the planned orders, are done for each part number for each DC. In the specific situation that I am familiar with, there are:

- 25 DC's
- 400 SKUs (not necessarily the same for each DC)
- 10,000 individual DC/part number combinations.

Therefore, there are 10,000 recommendations for planned orders being funneled down to the Master Production Schedule. This integration process is why Andre Martin states that DRP is the solution to the problem of:

"how to get a system that is integrated with manufacturing—one that will not only distribute the product in the best way, but will also make sure that the product is available for distribution."

Now that DRP generates the planned orders, this demand is then processed by the Master Production Schedule System. The Master Production Schedule is somewhat more complicated because of additional logic, calculations, time fences, and possible multiple levels. The MPS is the anticipated build schedule for end items or finished goods.

MPS takes the bill of material, forecasts (for DRP, the planned orders), customer orders (make to order), on-hand inventory balance, safety stock, lead time, time fences, and MPS orders and generates planned MPS orders with lower level gross requirements cascading down through the bill of material.

Safety stock at the MPS level also drives the level of finished goods inventory at the factory. Most companies have not only make to stock items, but also make to order items. Some of the items can be sold to OEM and thorough the distribution channel (see **Figure 5**).

Because of this, multilevel MPS is needed where the demand at the highest level is the wholesale product (fore-

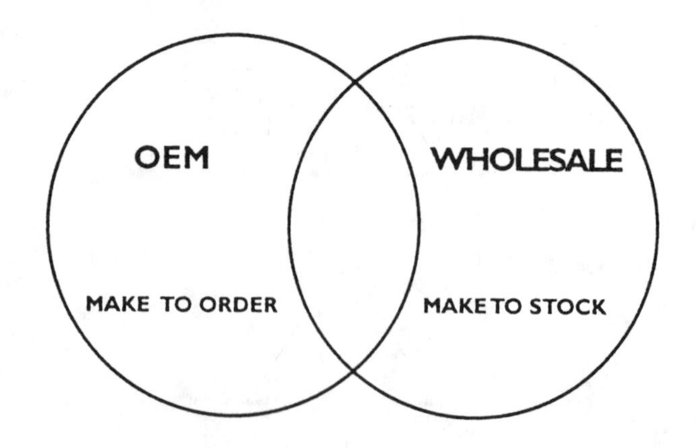

Figure 5.

Level	End Product	System	Demand	Enviroment
0	TA-250W	MPS	Sales Forecast	Make-To-Stock
1	TA-250A	MPS	Sales Orders & Level 0 MSO	Make-To-Order
Lower Levels	Components, Purchased Parts	MRP	Net Requirements Based On MSO (Dependent Demand)	

Figure 6.

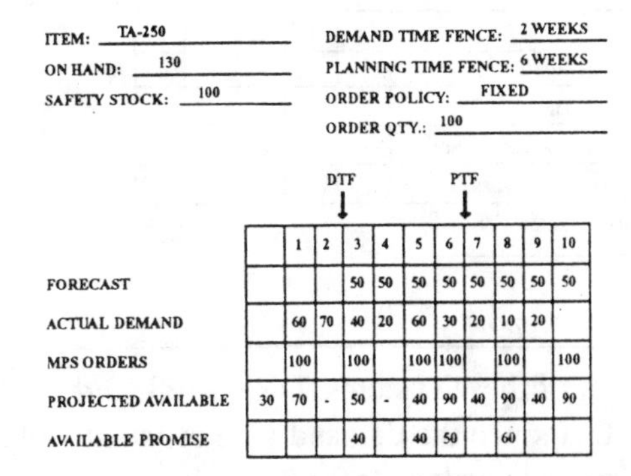

ITEM: TA-250
ON HAND: 130
SAFETY STOCK: 100
DEMAND TIME FENCE: 2 WEEKS
PLANNING TIME FENCE: 6 WEEKS
ORDER POLICY: FIXED
ORDER QTY.: 100

DTF (after period 2) PTF (after period 6)

		1	2	3	4	5	6	7	8	9	10
FORECAST				50	50	50	50	50	50	50	50
ACTUAL DEMAND		60	70	40	20	60	30	20	10	20	
MPS ORDERS		100		100		100	100		100		100
PROJECTED AVAILABLE	30	70	-	50	-	40	90	40	90	40	90
AVAILABLE PROMISE				40		40	50		60		

Figure 8.

cast or DRP planned orders) and the next level down is the make-to-order demand coming from OEM sales. The total demand from the top level (Distribution) and the next level (OEM) cascades down to the next level which is MRP (see **Figure 6**).

The Bill of Material is the Goes-Into's—the What-Does-It-Take-To-Make-This-Item. The forecast at the top MPS level (Distribution level) is generally replaced by the planned DRP replenishment orders. True forecasting is done at the DC level or forced down from the top (National forecast) based on historical ratios or future projections based on prior sales to the individual DC's. At the second level (OEM), there can be a legitimate forecast, if you forecast OEM items. Safety stock is needed if your lead time is not zero weeks and want to maintain the customer service level required by the marketplace. Safety stock here would be the lead time times the weekly demand based on the planned DRP orders. Lead time at this level is the time it takes to make the item at this level in the Bill of Material.

Time fences are two: Demand Time Fence (DTF) and Planning Time Fence (PTF). Demand Time Fence is generally the time to assemble the end item. The Planning Time Fence is the total cumulative lead time (see **Figure 7**).

The projected available balance (PAB) uses the time fences for its calculations. Inside the demand time fence, actual demand is used for the PAB. Between the DTF and the PTF, the greater of the two (forecasts or demand) is used to calculate the PAB. Beyond the PTF, the forecasts are used for the PAB, but if DRP is used, then the planned DRP orders are used. MPS orders are generated based upon the PAB being maintained at the safety stock level. These

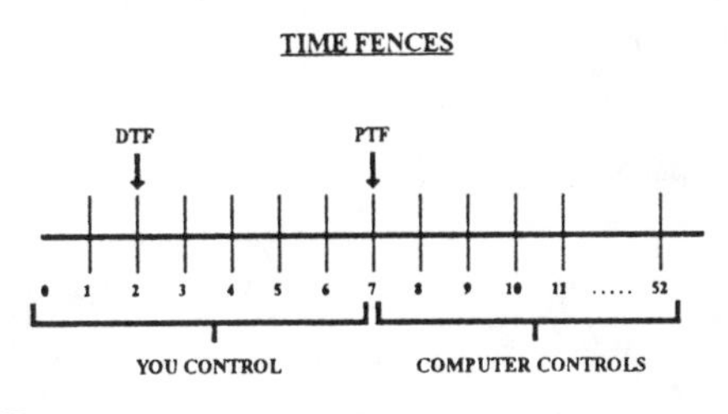

Figure 7.

MPS orders then generate gross requirements for the next level in the Bill of Material (MRP). The most misunderstood calculation at the Master Production Schedule is the available to promise calculation. Simply put, it is the unsold portion of the Master Schedule Order (MSO). The calculation is the MSO quantity minus what has been sold up to the time period of the next MSO. For the sales and order promising department, this calculation and pegging data empowers them to give good delivery dates on incoming orders and gives them the data from which negotiations can begin if an oversold condition exists (see **Figure 8**).

Oliver Wight, in the foreword to the classic volume on Master Production Scheduling by Berry, Vollman, and Whybark, states that MPS is "the most critical management challenge in running an MRP system." It is even more critical with DRP driving the distribution demand.

MPS gives the gross requirements to Material Requirements Planning. On hand inventory balance, gross requirements, lead time, released orders, planned orders and safety stock (if required) are used to calculate the projected available balance. MRP looks at dependent demand coming from MPS, which looks at independent demand. The gross to net calculation and the subsequent released and planning orders is the logic of MRP. MRP is generating recommendations for the inside factory (factory production orders) and for the outside factory (purchase orders). MPS drives MRP. At the MRP level(s), production is required to satisfy demand coming from higher level(s). Generally speaking, there are no forecasts at the MRP level(s). Economic Order Quantity may be a factor. However, with the emphasis on reducing setup time, the EOQ decreases since setup is part of the EOQ calculation. Lead time is a significant factor. Long lead times for factory production orders generally increase work-in-process inventory. Short cycle times can dramatically reduce work in process. Long lead times for purchase product increase raw material and purchase parts inventory. The MRP printout centers on the projected available balance with demand being the gross requirements and the supply side is the planned orders (see **Figure 9**).

PERIOD		1	2	3	4	5
GROSS REQUIREMENTS			10		40	10
SCHEDULE RECEIPTS		50				
PROJECTED AVAILABLE BALANCE	4	54	44	44	4	44
PLANNED ORDER RELEASES					50	
LEAD TIME = 1 PERIOD LOT SIZE = 50						

Figure 9. *MRP report*

The power of these systems (DRP, MPS, and MRP) lies in the fact that since the demand side constantly changes, these systems can recalculate the data reflecting the changes and generate action messages indicating where there are problems so that action can be taken. But it is not only the demand side that can change. Within manufacturing, there can be routing changes, capacity changes, equipment and tooling changes, etc., that can affect the priorities and due dates. These systems can effectively handle these changes and replan accordingly.

From my perspective, there are many opportunities to improve. First is the lead time reduction. There is raw material/purchased part lead time (purchase order to receipt). There is manufacturing/assembly lead time (production order to In-Stock-Status). There is distribution lead time (replenishment order to on-hand-inventory). There is information lead time (time to process shipment from DC to customer to decrease on-hand inventory).

Purchasing can look at high volume items and see if the vendors are willing to stack them. Blanket orders could be used with weekly or monthly releases subject to negotiated rules. You can look at buying capacity at the vendor and thereby reduce the lead time. Vendor scheduling is another alternative which can effectively reduce supplier lead time.

With manufacturing lead time, the JIT philosophy can effectively reduce them by smaller lot sizes, flexible equipment and tooling, cellular manufacturing, preventative maintenance, flexible workforce, etc. Timeliness of data can have a dramatic effect on safety stock at the DC. How long does it take once an order is shipped from a DC to a customer for the inventory at the DC to be decreased? EDI can reduce the time it takes if your current system relies on the U.S. Postal Service. EDI is even improvement over fax technology since the data doesn't have to be rekeyed. Suppose you have the following lead times:

RAW—4 Weeks
MFG—8 Weeks
DIST—4 Weeks
—
16 weeks

If you reduce the RAW to 3 weeks, MFG to 6 weeks and DIST to 3 weeks, you have reduced the total lead time from 16 weeks to 12 weeks—a 25% reduction. That 25% reduction in lead time reduces safety stock, WIP and raw material and purchased parts inventories by more than 25% because of the compounding effect down the pipeline.

You begin by chipping away, little by little, high volume items first. The results will follow. If lead times are shorter, then safety stock can be reduced. Reducing manufacturing lead time reduces the work-in-process inventory. The journey will only end when you can ship tomorrow what you produce today because you sold it yesterday.

Additional Reading

Martin, A.J., *DRP—Distribution Requirements Planning,* Oliver Wight Limited Publications, Inc., Essex Junction, VT, 1990.

Wallace, T.F., *MRP II: Making It Happen,* Oliver Wight Limited Publications, Inc., Essex Junction, VT, 1985.

Schorr, J.E., Wallace, T.F., *High Performance Purchasing,* Oliver Wight Limited Publications, Inc. Essex Junction, VT, 1986.

Berry, W.E., Vollman, T.E., Whybark, D.C., *Manufacturing Planning and Control Systems,* Richard D. Irwin, Inc, Homewood, IL, 1992.

Berry, W.E., Vollman, T.E., Whybark, D.C., *Master Production Scheduling—Principles and Practice*, APICS, Washington, D.C., 1979.

About the Author

John Martini is currently the Materials Manager for the Ilsco Division of the Bardes Corporation. John is a past president of the Cincinnati, Ohio Chapter of APICS and has made presentations at APICS International Conferences, national and regional seminars, and chapter meetings. He is also a member of NAPM and participated in their research symposium at Michigan State University. Mr. Martini is a part-time instructor at Xavier University teaching a graduate course in Materials Management. He has a BA in philosophy from the Athenaeum of Ohio, M. Ed. from Xavier University and a M.A. in mathematics from Western Michigan University.

Reprinted from APICS 1989 *Conference Proceedings.*

Closing the Transportation Loop

Susan L. Oaks and Stephen M. Closs

Introduction

Even though transportation is as old as the first man walking on earth, we still have problems scheduling and providing efficient transportation. In fact, we have more problems today than ever before. The complexity of life in the twentieth century has made the once simple concept of merely moving truckloads of goods from one place to another much more difficult. Now it is necessary to move goods in small quantities, at specified times, and at reasonable cost. At times this can seem like an impossible task.

One objective of this presentation is to consider the requirements of transportation in a Just-in-Time environment. A second objective is to describe some of the computer-aided vehicle routing tools available. The third objective is to explore some methods for helping to solve at least part of the new transportation dilemma through the application of these tools to help dispatch orders for today's more demanding and sophisticated customers while keeping costs at a reasonable level. An example of a vehicle routing system is demonstrated to illustrate the concepts discussed throughout the presentation.

Vehicle Routing Tools

One of the many types of tools available to assist in effective transportation management is a computer-aided vehicle routing and scheduling system. These systems can identify areas for substantial savings in the transportation area, and have been used in routing private fleet vehicles for a number of years.

Computer-aided vehicle routing systems operate by developing a path through a network of customers, constrained by whatever limitations exist for vehicles, drivers, roadways, in order to deliver (and/or pick up) customer orders. Normally the solution algorithm involved in the system is designed to optimize vehicle usage or minimize mileage. Figure 1 illustrates the inputs and outputs of a typical vehicle routing system.

Some of the benefits that can be realized include a reduction in the number of vehicles utilized, a reduction in the total miles traveled, a reduction in the number of hours spent by drivers on the road, and a reduction in the amount of time that a transportation manager spends trying to reduce costs in these areas while trying to provide a high level of customer service. A computer-aided vehicle routing system allows a transportation manager enough flexibility to look at the trade-offs between customer service and transportation costs in a timely manner.

As with most opportunities to realize efficiencies, there are costs associated with the use of a computer-aided vehicle routing system. Although the actual costs vary depending on the actual system and the extent of automation in the implementation of the routing system, the basic cost components remain the same. Initially, there is the cost of the actual vehicle routing system. This can range anywhere from $2,000 to $150,000 depending on the features desired. Often, the computer required to operate this system is not included in the price, so the hardware costs must be considered. There are direct and indirect costs associated with training transportation personnel to use the routing system. The vehicle routing system will need to have access to the customer lists, so there is a cost of converting this data either electronically or manually. In addition to the initial purchase or license fee, there are some on-going maintenance costs and there may be annual license fees with some of the systems. Since technology changes rapidly, it is advisable to have an annual support agreement with the vendor to provide continuing help and support, as well as information about updates or enhancements.

There are two types of vehicle routing systems, and the major difference is the method in which they are implemented. These two methods are strategic and operational. We'll discuss each one in turn.

The first method is the strategic type of vehicle routing system. Strategic routing systems develop routes under the assumption that demand is at a near constant level during the routing period. Strategic routing is usually performed on a periodic basis where the time between development of routes is dependent on the frequency of demand variations. This type of system provides a basis for developing fixed routes for deliveries. Strategic routing is the faster and less costly path to computer-aided vehicle routing of the two methods. The cost reduction found in strategic routing will not be as large as that found in operational routing due to the fact that the vehicle utilization will be lower. Strategic routing provides customers with a known and fixed delivery time, and will generally be favored by customers.

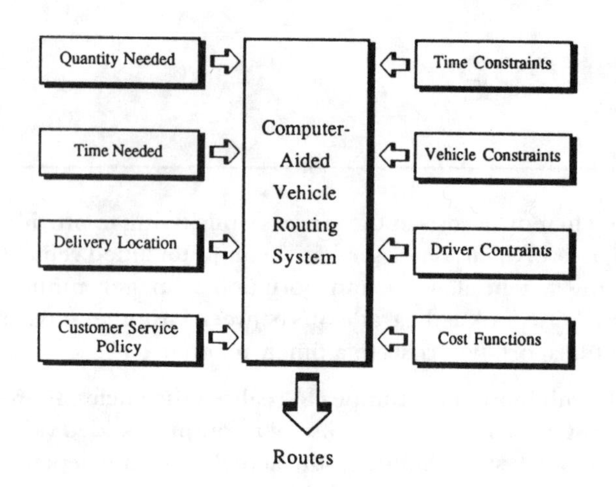

Figure 1

The second method of computer-aided routing is operational or daily vehicle routing. As is implied by the name, operational routing is performed with the actual demand for the period. An operational routing system routes vehicles based on the actual orders to be delivered. This method provides better vehicle utilization, thus lower transportation costs. Since this method must normally be integrated with other computer systems in order to be a feasible solution, daily vehicle routing can be more complex and more expensive to operationalize.

Regardless of the type of vehicle routing system that is implemented, there are a number of features that are available. Very few packages have all features available in one system, so it is required that the most important features for each specific application are identified. Some of the features which generally need to be considered are:

Delivery time windows

Delivery time windows define when you can and cannot make a delivery. It is critical to have the capability to consider delivery time windows if operational vehicle routing in a Just-in-Time environment is planned.

Pickups and deliveries

Pickups and deliveries refers to the ability of the system to route both types of movements on the same vehicle. This will provide more transportation efficiencies by integrating inbound materials, both from suppliers or material returning from customers, with outbound distribution.

Interfaces with other systems

The capability of a routing system to interface with other systems is an important feature to consider before implementation. When determining whether a strategic or an operational vehicle routing system best suits the problem, the ease of interfacing with other systems becomes a critical issue. It is normally essential for an operational vehicle routing system to interface with other systems, such as order management or warehouse picking systems.

Manual over-ride capability

Manual over-ride capability allows changes to be made to the computer-generated routes based upon extenuating circumstances, or a dispatcher's special knowledge of a situation. The complexity of the customer requirements influences the importance of this capability.

"What if" capability

"What if" capability refers to the ability of the system to analyze numerous scenarios and compare the results. This allows the development of cost/service trade offs. Customer service levels can be varied while the system determines the cost of the solution. Normally this capability is desired for both strategic and operational implementations of vehicle routing systems.

Graphics

There are varying levels of graphic capabilities in routing systems. These range from no associated graphics to graphics containing street level detail. A large portion of the cost of a vehicle routing system is tied to the extent of the graphics capabilities.

In general, the more features that are identified as necessary or desirable, the more expensive the vehicle routing system. Larger, more complex systems also tend to require more computer resources both during initial implementation as well as during normal operations.

Transportation Requirements under Just-in-Time

There are three primary requirements for transportation under a Just-in-Time environment that increase the challenge for a supplier to that type of customer. These requirements are:

Short order lead times

Frequent, smaller quantity orders

Scheduled delivery times.

We'll consider each of these aspects separately before considering how we can use computer-aided vehicle routing to assist in fulfilling these requirements.

Short Order Lead Times

The concept of Just-in-Time taken literally makes this requirement self-explanatory. Because manufacturers do not want large inventories of raw materials, but are operating in dynamic environments (particularly true in make to order), the time between placement of the actual order and the scheduled delivery time is often quite short. The more the lead time can be effectively decreased, the more accurate can be the forecast of what the manufacturer needs.

Frequent, Smaller Quantity Orders

Again, this requirement is driven by the desire to reduce raw material inventories. Smaller, more frequent orders allow for more precision in ordering, and less space to store the order upon arrival of the goods. Consider for instance deliveries to the point of use on the production line where there is only space for a few hours of raw materials.

Scheduled Delivery Times

Just-in-Time environments require that deliveries be scheduled to occur at the same time each day or each week, or that the delivery time be scheduled on a variable time basis with a fairly accurate prediction of the time that delivery will take place. This requirement is caused by the need to control deliveries from many suppliers through a limited number of docks. To choreograph this effectively, there must be some control exercised over the participants.

Using A Vehicle Routing Tool Under Just-in-Time

Now let's examine how a computer-aided routing tool can help accomplish the objectives and requirements of Just-in-Time without increasing the cost of transportation to unacceptable levels. Each of the requirements outlined above will be addressed in turn.

Short Order Lead Times

Computer-aided routing can accomplish a task in minutes that would take hours by manual methods. This makes it the perfect tool to use in situations where short lead times are a fact of life. Only minutes after all candidate orders are received, planned routes are available for review. The technology of electronic data interchange makes it possible to receive orders directly into the system that will feed the routing system. It also provides the opportunity to communicate the estimated time of arrival of the delivery.

Frequent, Smaller Quantity Orders

The implication that more frequent, smaller quantity orders has on transportation is that serving the same customers the same volume over a period of a year requires many more trips to those customers, thereby increasing the cost of transportation. It therefore becomes critical to accomplish these deliveries as efficiently as possible. Computer-aided routing assists in this effort by optimizing the path between customers and by trying to effectively use all of the space on the vehicle. This is a task that is much more difficult to do manually when there are many small orders to route as opposed to a few large orders.

Scheduled Delivery Times

There are two approaches to this requirement that can be taken by implementation of computer-aided vehicle routing. One is to use a tool to develop routes which will essentially remain fixed in the short term. An advantage to this approach is that it allows customers to depend on a fixed delivery time and day and adjust their orders accordingly. While this may meet the requirements of many customers, there are also several disadvantages to this approach. The major drawback of fixed routing is that it does not take advantage of the opportunity to completely fill a vehicle to its maximum capacity, thereby losing transportation efficiencies. A second related disadvantage is that in order to preserve the fixed route under fluctuating volumes, it is necessary to deliberately plan for the vehicle to be under capacity in normal circumstances so that it will not go over capacity on a day with a high volume swing.

Another approach to solving the requirement of rigid time schedules is to develop routes on an operational basis. This refers to routing the orders that are ready to be dispatched based upon their time of need, their physical size, and the customer's location, among the other constraints which are considered in the routing problem. In this approach, the time that the customer needs the material becomes a key determinant of the sequence of deliveries which will be made by the delivery vehicle. The time frame that is acceptable to the customer around the required time is referred to as a time window. Restrictive time windows reduce the flexibility in the solution, causing a less optimal routing configuration. One method for maintaining flexibility is to take steps to ensure that the time windows are only as restrictive as is absolutely necessary for the customer's requirements. This requires that communication take place between the supplier and customer to avoid artificially restrictive constraints.

Demonstration

The features, data requirements, constraints, and applications discussed above are demonstrated through examination of a personal computer-based vehicle routing system.

Conclusion

The unique requirements placed on inbound transportation to the Just-in-Time environment make routing and scheduling vehicles more difficult than ever before. This task can be made easier through application of computer-aided vehicle routing. Computer-aided routing allows the constraints of Just-in-Time to be met while costs are kept from dramatically increasing by developing efficient routes under these constraints. The use of this technology allows the constraints to be met in a much shorter time than manual methods would allow, while considering many more alternatives than would ever be possible to evaluate manually.

About the authors

SUSAN L. OAKS serves as the Director, Logistics Practice, Dialog Systems Division of A. T. Kearney. During the past five years she has worked with many client firms in the application of decision support models to logistics problems. Ms. Oaks is certified by APICS and presented "Artificial Intelligence Applications in Inventory Control" at the 1987 International APICS meeting. She received her formal training at Michigan State University where she earned an MBA in Materials and Logistics Management She is also a member of the Council of Logistics Management where she is currently serving as an officer of the Grand Rapids Roundtable.

STEPHEN M. CLOSS is the Director, Decision Support Systems, Dialog Systems Division of A. T. Kearney. He has been instrumental in the development and application of vehicle routing systems with a variety of clients. Mr. Closs has presented at national conferences of the Council of Logistics Management. He completed his education at Michigan State University where he earned a BS in Electrical Engineering. He is also a member of the Association for Systems Management and The Institute of Management Science's College on Simulation.

Reprinted from the *APICS 1996 International Conference Proceedings.*

Using Distribution Resource Planning to Manage Inventories in Multiple Locations

Bernard T. Smith

This paper covers the following material about DRP:

- Goals
- Performance measurement
- Term definitions
- DRP networks
- Differences between DRP and MRP
- Similarities between DRP and MRP
- Benefits
- Action to Take

Goals

The author has worked in over 400 DRP start ups in different parts of the world. The first thing is to set DRP goals before starting a project. Generally, goals tell why you are going to use DRP in the first place.

- To improve customer service, fill rate, in stock position
- To increase inventory turnover or reduce days of supply
- To improve profit usually lost because of inventory excess write downs
- To reduce cost of operation handling items and setting up orders
- To reduce freight costs by using truck load and car load shipments
- To reduce inventory management expense at remote locations

It's worthwhile to actually start managing a portion of the company inventory with the DRP procedure to measure the impact on these goals. The portion of the inventory should be substantial enough to get the department's attention. It should be from 20 to 30 percent of the business. It should be a problem area now so that even the pilot can get some good results. Don't parallel the test with the old inventory management procedures. It's too easy to fall back into using the old ways of doing things. If you run in parallel, it's hard to tell how much improvement came from DRP and how much just came from focusing attention on the area.

If the DRP procedure will operate in a multilevel distribution network, start at the top level. In other words, there may be regional warehouses shipping to distribution centers who are in turn shipping to customers. Start the DRP inventory management at the regional level. If goods are not available at the regional level, it's a problem to improve performance at the distribution center level.

Performance Measurement

The performance measures should fall in line with the goals of the DRP procedure. The measures should be quite complete so as not to confuse improvement with simple trade-offs from one area to another. For example it's possible:

- To improve fill rate but decrease inventory turnover by increasing safety stock.
- To improve turnover but reduce profit by discounting and dumping inventory excesses.
- To improve profit but decrease turnover by ordering large time supplies for discounts.
- To increase turnover but run up the cost of handle and freight by frequent orders.

The performance measure should be summary performance measures of overall progress. It gets confusing when a company shows A item fill rates are up, B items are down, and C items are about the same. The bottom line is what has happened to fill rates overall up or down?

The performance measures should show progress against last time, last month, and the same time last year. Comparing to other companies even in the same industry is difficult because companies have different personalities. Certainly a full line distributor with high profit will have lower turnover and customer service than a distributor who carries only fast movers at a lower profit.

Avoid having more than one measure of the same goal. If you measure dollar service level, don't measure line fill rate as well. Pick one measure of customer service and make it happen.

Term Definitions

DRP, Distribution Resource Planning, uses many of the same terms as MRP, Manufacturing Resource Planning. Both always show information period by period out into the future.

- Gross requirements

—The forecast whether generated by a computer or by people.

—Real customer orders by delivery date.

—Planned orders from a DRP system at a lower level.

—Exploded requirements from a higher level like an assortment.

- Scheduled receipts

—Open purchase orders by delivery date.

—Open production orders by delivery date.

—Open transfers pending from another location.

- Projected on hand

—The projected inventory balance adding future in bound and subtracting future outbound.

- Planned orders

—The quantity DRP would like to order to satisfy the parameters the company is using in the DRP procedure.

- Firm planned orders

—The overrides the planner or buyer has made to the DRP planned orders.

DRP Networks

The simplest DRP network follows the physical flow of goods from a factory to a distribution center.

More involved networks include:

- Multiple factories shipping to multiple warehouse locations.
- Multiple factories and outside suppliers shipping to multiple warehouses.
- Multiple factory/warehouses shipping selected products to each other.
- Multiple suppliers shipping to a regional warehouse which breaks bulk to other warehouses.
- Dummy consolidation center warehouses that receive and break bulk to other warehouses in the system.
- Retail stores that receive some goods direct and some through the warehouse.
- Factories that use allocation schemes to distribute to multiple warehouses.
- Import order distribution when goods arrive at a domestic port.

The DRP procedure should always follow the physical flow of goods. There should be no make believe. If goods are stocked in five separate warehouse locations, the DRP procedure should treat each location uniquely. Sum up the resultant time-phased planned orders for manufacturing planning. Forecast by individual warehouse location.

The consolidation center should be an expression of the immediate source of the product. The vendor should be an expression of the ultimate source of the product. So an item can be purchased from Whirlpool but flow through the Chicago warehouse to the Seattle warehouse. Seattle would show Chicago as the consolidation center but Whirlpool as the vendor.

Sometimes a consolidation center for a low level distribution point will become a regular warehouse at a higher level. For example, Aleutian Islands warehouse may use Anchorage as their consolidation warehouse source of supply. Anchorage warehouse however may be using Seattle warehouse as its consolidation center source of supply.

All goods should have a primary source of supply. Goods that are consistently rerouted from one source to another have not been planned properly. Goods can come from a secondary source but it should be an exception. If it seems that one source cannot handle the total volume, then the item distribution should be segmented either by sizing, packaging, or location. For example, ship all the 4-foot ladders from Chicago. Ship all the 6 and 8 footers from New York. Or ship the West Coast ladders from Chicago and the East Coast from New York.

Differences Between DRP and MRP

Multiplant Multiwarehouse

MRP generally concerns itself with a total company forecast of an item. It considers things such as capacity and raw material availability. DRP uses forecasts at multiple levels of distribution for an item such as plants, distribution centers, and retail outlets. Rather than using total forecasts of a product's sales in a company, DRP looks at forecasts in individual stocking locations versus current inventory in those locations. It sums up the planned replenishments of those locations to calculate the total company need.

Allocations

MRP is generally involved in allocating plant and material resources to the production of individual items. DRP concerns itself with the proper distribution of the product to multiple geographic locations as the product is received from the vendor or as the product comes off the manufacturing line.

Joint Replenishment

MRP usually is looking at the right quantity of an item to manufacture. DRP is generally looking at a group of items to purchase or move from one site to another, for example: a mix of products to fill up a container, truck load, car load, or minimum vendor restriction.

Finished Goods

MRP is concerned with the production of finished goods from raw materials and manufacturing resources. DRP is concerned with the inventory management of finished goods and repair parts...

- ordering
- expediting
- delaying
- allocating
- measuring performance
- identifying service problems
- identifying inventory excesses
- building economical transportation loads
- tying in with key customers

Schedule to Planned Orders

MRP generally uses company-wide forecasts to determine manufacturing requirements. In many cases these same companies use reorder point procedures to distribute the resultant production. DRP sums the time phased replenishment orders throughout the network to come up with the production needs in the future. DRP determines where the goods should go as they come off the manufacturing line.

Large Number of SKUs

Because DRP operates at the lower levels of distribution there are a great many more stock keeping units to deal with than with MRP. For example a plant that manufacturers 1000 items may distribute to ten distribution centers. DRP would be involved with 10,000 SKU's in this company.

Automated Forecast Input

Because DRP is operating with so many more SKU's than MRP it must have computer generated forecast input. Using ratios of forecast distribution of a company forecast is not an acceptable substitute.

Identifies and Redistributes Excess

DRP can look at the past distribution of production in relation to sales in the form of on-hand balances. Where it sees an imbalance in the distribution of inventory it can redistribute the excess and eliminate the need for additional production.

Links to Nonmanufacturing Customers

MRP for many years has allowed manufacturing companies to link to their raw material suppliers. Now DRP allows nonmanufacturing companies and purchasers-for-resale to link to their suppliers.

Similarities Between DRP and MRP

Bill of Material Explosion

DRP needs time-phased bill of material explosions to handle assortment, pallet load mixes, and kit requirement. MRP uses bill of materials for raw material determination.

Paperless Purchasing

Both MRP and DRP are such busy displays of time-phased requirements that both demand paperless processing.

Action Messages

Both MRP and DRP use the three basic action messages

1. Order some now
2. Expedite what was ordered before
3. Delay or cancel what was ordered before

Other Similarities

Both are powerful scheduling tools. Both require summary measures of performance. And both use the logic for ordering originally designed for MRP.

Benefits

For over 14 years I used a reorder point system in Servistar Corporation where I was Vice President Inventory Control up until August of 1986. Nobody, including Andre Martin, could talk me into switching over all of my inventory to DRP. Since then, however, my successor, Joan Trach, the new Vice President of Inventory Control, has converted all of the items to DRP with outstanding improvements in inventory turnover and fill rate.

With my own eyes I've witnessed quantum jumps in company performance through the use of this simple concept in hundreds of companies around the world.

Action to Take

For so many years, we consultants have told our clients that computers only present information and that people must make decisions. We've created a class of people who spend their lives making routine decisions the computer can make better. It's time now to move on. It's time we start giving our computer systems guidelines for decision making and then use the decision the computer makes. It's time that either our automatic systems work or we rebel and throw them out.

DRP is an excellent example of a procedure that should work as automatically as the heating system in our home. Whether we grow the system in-house or purchase it from outside it should be an automatic system. Visit a company that is using DRP properly to see the dramatic impact on inventory management.

About the Author

Bernard Smith's clients read like Who's Who in Business—*Thomas J. Lipton, Northern Telecom, Eveready Battery, Whirlpool Corporation, Pepsi, McDonnell Douglas,*

Imperial Chemical Industries, Apple Computer, Digital Computing, Servistar Corporation, Stanley Tools, General Electric, Osram Sylvania, Nestle's, and many other fine companies.

Early in his career, Bernie managed a data processing, systems, and programming staff of 75 people and two IBM mainframe computers for Warnaco. Later, Bernie became Vice President Inventory Control and Long Range Planning for Servistar Corporation.

In 1986 he formed his own company, B.T. Smith and Associates, programming and selling computer software for marketing and inventory management. During those years he had the chance to see firsthand the interaction between data processing, systems, and programming departments and users in more than 400 companies worldwide.

Bernie received his B.A. and M.B.A. degrees from the University of Bridgeport in Connecticut. He taught in the graduate studies program—managerial accounting, long range planning, and information systems. In his role as consultant and teacher he has presented to thousands of people—APICS, NPMA, NRMA, Council of Logistics Management, NWHA, NTMA, FIT, ATA, PMI, and many others. He's a past board member of the Red Cross, associate of the Carnegie Mellon management decision games, and past President of the Chamber of Commerce.

Reprinted from APICS 1996 *Conference Proceedings*

Integrating Vendor-Managed Inventory into Supply Chain Decision Making

Mary Lou Fox, CPIM

What Is VMI?

Effective use of vendor-managed inventory, or VMI, leverages advanced technology and trading-partner relationships to enable the flow of information and inventory throughout the entire supply chain. It provides visibility into demand at the trading-partner level—often where the consumer or purchases is—to improve the flow of products, eliminate inefficiencies, and lower costs. When done well, VMI improves customer service by eliminating stockouts, decreasing inventory, and ensuring that the right products are in the right place at the right time based on consumer demand.

VMI is also known by several other acronyms: CRP (Continuous Replenishment Program), QR (Quick Response), and ECR (Efficient Consumer Response). Traditionally, these programs have been designed by large retailers who have required their vendors to participate, although ECR was jointly developed by grocery distributors and manufacturers.

The following benefits of a rapid replenishment program to a retailer, distributor, and manufacturer are clear and will be explained in further detail:

1. Improved service to stores, which reduces store out-of-stocks and leads to higher sales.
2. Reduced distribution center (DC) inventories.
3. Reduced administrative costs, as more transactions are handled electronically.
4. Reduced operating costs.

Some manufacturers feel they do not benefit from replenishment programs, because they are forced to incur the additional costs of managing the retailer's replenishment simply to retain the retailer's business. Under pressure to "get something going" to satisfy the immediate needs, the manufacturer passes up the opportunity to reap significant rewards from the program.

How Does It Work?

VMI incorporates demand planning and distribution planning to provide integrated, enterprise-wide answers to problems in the supply chain. A consumer-driven forecast for demand is compared to inventory on hand and in transit, and this determines the net requirements at the customer DCs. Then, shipment amounts can be determined, as well as grouped into specific orders. An efficient VMI system should work with traditional transaction systems already in place. The transaction system will feed data into the VMI system, providing actual demand for a specific forecast period and additional inventory information. By using an inventory plan in this manner, the user can generate a replenishment order, which becomes a purchase order for a trading partner.

At Johnson & Johnson, for example, a Customer Support Center was founded in 1991 with the challenge of meeting the demands of all its customers—mass merchandisers and grocery and drug retailers. Today, by using an integrated supply chain management system with a robust VMI module, Johnson & Johnson supplies more than 15 external customers, and is expected to double that number within 12 months.

Black & Decker implemented an advanced demand planning solution as part of its VMI program and obtained outstanding results. Customer-service levels to one of the company's largest retail customers reached 98 percent, and returned goods from that same customer decreased from $1 million to $75,000.

Schering-Plough implemented a VMI program to meet standards set down by one of its largest customers: Kmart. Schering-Plough received a Top 10 vendor performance award in its first year in the giant retailer's Partners in Merchandize Flow program. Through its use of an advanced supply chain system that includes VMI, Schering-Plough has since increased service levels to nearly 99 percent and reduced inventory levels at its Memphis facility by 25 percent.

How Manufacturers Benefit from VMI

A manufacturer analyzing rapid replenishment programs must assess the value of these programs to future success and the need to take a comprehensive approach to their implementation. In the grocery, consumer products, apparel, and automotive manufacturing industries, these programs are a competitive necessity.

From an operations perspective, the customer information used for ordering in the rapid replenishment program is integrated with information used for planning inventory and production in the manufacturer's planning processes, providing a single supply chain view into demand and supply.

There Are Four Key Benefits to the Manufacturer:

- Improved Customer Service. The obvious area of improvement comes from the ability to respond quickly to the needs of retailers' distribution centers. A more substantial improvement results when the manufacturer integrates the retailer's information throughout its replenishment planning process. Then, the manufacturer is more efficient at moving products out to the retailer and at stocking the right products in its own DCs, so they will be available when the retailer's orders materialize.
- Reduced Demand Uncertainty. A common occurrence for every manufacturer is the large, unexpected customer order. Demand is uncertain under most circumstances, but the lack of visibility beyond current, open customer orders increases the need for DC buffer stock and necessitates expediting when the unexpected occurs. A rapid replenishment program based on time-phased planning uses forecasts at customers' DCs to provide needed visibility to future customer orders and allows the manufacturer to plan and to have inventory to meet the demand when it occurs.
- Reduced Inventory. When the manufacturer succeeds in using the demand information provided by the retailer in its planning process, the manufacturer can use the forward visibility inherent in the demand information to position inventories in the supply chain when needed and to reduce excess stocks used to buffer uncertainty. Essentially, the manufacturer trades information for inventory.
- Reduced Costs. Adding the rapid replenishment ordering process to the existing customer service function typically increases the level of effort committed to a customer. The way for the manufacturer to achieve cost reductions is to use replenishment programs as an opportunity to reengineer the customer demand fulfillment process to include both fulfilling customers' orders and replenishing DCs as a single business process, rather than as the isolated work of two departments.

VMI's Importance in the Supply Chain

The increasingly competitive environment in many industries is requiring companies to implement interenterprise processes, such as VMI. Collaborative processes like VMI are the future of trading relationships across the supply chain, which means that any demand- and supply-planning processes must be modified to account for these collaborative efforts. A company's role in the supply chain as a carrier, retailer, wholesaler, or manufacturer then becomes another factor that adds complexity to demand and supply.

A manufacturer, for example, would want to establish VMI relationships with its large customers. Some customers will simply provide a forecast of orders and will ask to ensure delivery of those orders. Other customers may provide daily shipment data expecting replenishment based on the data. Still others may provide point-of-sale (POS) movement data across stores, asking that the manufacturer use this data when planning replenishments. Finally, some may actually provide store-level, accounting-quality POS movement data and not only ask to replenish to this demand stream, but accept payment of goods based on it as well.

These increasing complexities are requiring that companies take a new look at planning supply and demand to meet their customers' needs and to rise above the competition.

The computerized planning tools currently used to manage the supply chain tend to fall into two categories: point solutions and conventional supply chain solutions. Point solutions are planning tools that address one particular business function, such as forecasting, manufacturing planning, or load building. These solutions are often feature-rich, but address a limited scope of business processes.

The integration limitations of point solutions are overcome by conventional supply chain management systems. These systems are built by the vendor from the ground up, with the aim of enabling a comprehensive supply chain management process that includes and integrates demand planning, distribution planning, manufacturing planning, and transportation planning. For example, if a planner is looking at a supply planning screen and sees a shortage, he can do a few quick clicks to "peg" into a demand planning screen. The planner can evaluate whether the demand is caused by forecast or customer orders, whether it is an estimated or statistical forecast, whether the forecast is consistent with history, and whether an event such as a promotion is causing the demand. This information is crucial to a supply planner trying to determine whether expediting is justified to relieve a projected shortage.

This type of pegging is not possible without an integrated system. Users of interfaced point solutions must go through a cumbersome process of opening two applications and selecting the same data twice, rather than simply pegging up the planning chain within an integrated database.

Current supply chain solutions also give a planner the ability to integrate the supply chain across enterprises. Users of supply chain systems employ techniques like POS data and VMI to integrate their vendors and customers into a holistic supply chain model.

By giving the replenishment program demand information to all planners—up and down the supply chain—more planning can be performed more effectively. The resulting reductions in expediting premium freight and transshipments are significant.

With the number of rapid replenishment initiatives increasing, it is important to create a vision of how these programs are best implemented instead of rushing to "get something going." The best and most cost-effective approach is to take the long-term view, which is the integrated supply chain approach.

If the manufacturer incorporates the replenishment program into its customer service, fulfillment, forecasting, and distribution functions, and uses the information passed through Electronic Data Interchange (EDI) for planning as well as order fulfillment, it can achieve maximum benefit while still implementing individual programs in a timely fashion.

Customer Case Study

In its 106-year history, Johnson & Johnson has never posted a loss. And there's good reason. As the world's leading healthcare products maker, the company is renowned for its product lines—including TYLENOL® Acetaminophen, MONISTAT® Cream, and BAND-AID® Brand Adhesive Bandages—and for quickly adapting to the many market changes of the past century.

Consistent with this reputation, Johnson & Johnson is proving to be a leader in continuous replenishment—a process that has been lauded as the way of the future for effectively managing the transfer of products between manufacturers and retailers. Continuous replenishment improves customer service by eliminating stockouts, decreasing inventory, and ensuring that the right products are in the right place at the right time based on consumer demand.

Johnson & Johnson's continuous replenishment efforts were initiated in 1991. Responding to the market's increasing emphasis on customer service, the company set up a unique organizational structure focused on a new type of "Customer Support Center." Designed to provide customer service for all of Johnson & Johnson's Consumer Sector operating companies—including Johnson & Johnson Consumer Products, Inc., McNeil Consumer Products Company, and Advanced Care Products—the Johnson & Johnson Consumer Sector Customer Support Center is a separate company within the organization. It handles order management, distribution, and accounts receivable functions while offering the added benefits of a totally committed project team and a single point of contact for all customer service activities—including inventory replenishment requests.

It wasn't long before the Customer Support Center's continuous replenishment capabilities were put to the test. By the end of 1991, QR requests were knocking loudly on Johnson & Johnson's door, prompting the Customer Support Center to quickly develop an approach to continuous replenishment that could meet the demands of all its customers—including mass merchandisers and grocery and drug retailers.

To help support the onslaught of Quick Response requests coming from some of the company's largest customers, Johnson & Johnson selected Manugistics, an integrated set of supply chain management applications. Using information from EDI transmissions, Manugistics links the Customer Support Center with Johnson & Johnson's customers and distribution centers. The system is tied directly to the company's order management system—which includes order processing, transportation load building, and sales reporting systems. Information from these systems is fed downstream to each of the separate operating units to provide decision support throughout the organization.

It took less than three months for Johnson & Johnson to implement Manugistics and begin running multiple QR programs for each of the organization's operating companies. Today, Johnson & Johnson is supplying more than 15 external customers using what is now referred to as the "Efficient Consumer Response" project.

To accommodate its customers, Johnson & Johnson had to develop one standard method for managing its continuous replenishment processes in-house. "We've had to accommodate more than 15 different interpretations of the same inventory replenishment model," said Joe Bakunas, manager of logistics and replenishment for the Customer Support Center. This exposure has provided the project team with an in-depth understanding of diverse customer needs. Bakunas believes this knowledge has enabled them to roll out the program to new customers at a very quick rate. "Manugistics is a very flexible system, allowing us to quickly recreate information every day based on the latest piece of data we get from the customer," he explains. "We're rewriting our own book in terms of how we do logistics with our customers."

Jeffrey Gora, replenishment planner for the Customer Support Center, stresses that although rolling out a replenishment program to one customer is a large accomplishment, "If you don't have the flexibility to roll it out to others, the method can't accomplish enough. It's a nice gold star, but you're extremely limited in what you're really able to do. The larger your program, the larger your benefits."

Johnson & Johnson can certainly testify to the benefits. According to Gora, Johnson & Johnson now has a very thorough way to generate customer requirements based on warehouse withdrawal. "That puts us one step, maybe two steps closer to the end consumer. And the flexibility we have with Manugistics gives us the capability to look further down the pipeline and mange demand."

In the future, Johnson & Johnson plans to add as many customers as possible to the program. "We see this as a strategic advantage for Johnson & Johnson," says Gora, "because it is significantly increasing our ability to supply products to our customers." To continue the forward momentum, the company is steering toward the client/server version of Manugistics and further improving processes to provide even better continuous replenishment to its customers.

Because its customers are holding the reins on the future, Johnson & Johnson has no way of knowing what's around the next bend. What it does know for sure is that two and a half years ago the company found itself at the entrance to a new way of doing business and in eight weeks had built a strategic method for continuous replenishment. With a record like that, there is little doubt that Johnson & Johnson will remain at the top of its industry—whatever the future holds.

About the Author

Mary Lou Fox, CPIM, is senior vice president of professional services for Manugistics, Inc., Rockville, MD. Her expertise is in helping companies implement integrated logistics software in the areas of demand, distribution, manufacturing, and transportation planning.

Reprinted from APICS 1998 *Conference Proceedings*

Making Consignment and Vendor-Managed Inventory Work for You

Mark Williams, CFPIM

Introduction

As manager of a manufacturing or distribution operation, you've just been notified by two of your largest customers that they want to purchase goods on consignment. A third very large customer wants to emulate Wal-Mart and begin a Vendor-Managed Inventory (VMI) program - with you as the chosen vendor.

You're beginning to see the pattern: your customers want to increase their profits at your expense. Instead of paying for product within 30 days of delivery, the two who want a consignment program want to delay payment until after using or selling your product. The third wants to go one step further - they want *you* to plan *their* inventory!

It's obvious how these moves will benefit your customers, but is there any benefit for you? We'll examine these issues in a moment, but first, let's define terms.

Consignment & VMI Defined

The APICS Dictionary[1] defines consignment as "The process of a supplier placing goods at a customer location *without receiving payment until after the goods are used or sold*" (author's emphasis). This is very different from traditional practice whereby a customer pays for goods within a set time period after receiving them (often 30 days). Under consignment, it makes no difference whether product sits in the customer's warehouse or shelves for two days or two years; the supplier receives nothing until it is used or sold. This could result in a serious cash flow problem for the supplier if goods continue to be produced but money is not collected.

Vendor-Managed Inventory (VMI) is a planning and management system that is not directly tied to inventory ownership. Under VMI, instead of the customer monitoring its sales and inventory for the purpose of triggering replenishment orders, the vendor assumes responsibility for these activities. In the past, many suppliers operated vendor-stocking programs where a representative visited a customer a few times a month and restocked their supplies to an agreed-upon level. Popularized by Wal-Mart, VMI replaces these visits with information gathered from cash registers and transmitted directly to a supplier's computer system via Electronic Data Interchange (EDI). Now, suppliers can monitor sales of their products and decide when to initiate the resupply procedure. This is not an inexpensive proposition for suppliers. Investments must be made in new systems, software, and employee training. Which brings us back to the question: Is there a payoff?

Benefits of VMI

In the article "Integrating Vendor-Managed Inventory into Supply Chain Decision Making," Mary Lou Fox [2] outlines four advantages of VMI:

1. Improved customer service. By receiving timely information directly from cash registers, suppliers can better respond to customers' inventory needs in terms of both quantity and location.
2. Reduced demand uncertainty. By constantly monitoring customers' inventory and demand stream, the number of large, unexpected customer orders will dwindle, or disappear altogether.
3. Reduced inventory requirements. By knowing exactly how much inventory the customer is carrying, a supplier's own inventory requirements are reduced since the need for excess stock to buffer against uncertainty is reduced or eliminated.
4. Reduced costs. To mitigate the up-front costs that VMI demands, Fox suggests that manufacturers reduce costs by reengineering and merging their order fulfillment and Distribution Center replenishment activities.

While these are all potential benefits of VMI, the most important ones were not cited.

- Improved customer retention. Once a VMI system is developed and installed, it becomes extremely difficult and costly for a customer to change suppliers.
- Reduced reliance on forecasting. With customers for whom a supplier runs VMI programs, the need to forecast their demand is eliminated.

VMI-Binding Customers to Suppliers

Once a VMI system is established, a customer has effectively outsourced its material management function to its supplier. After a period of time, the customer will no longer have the resources to perform this role in-house, making him more dependent upon the supplier. In addition, developing a VMI system entails major costs to the customer. His information services department has to spend time ensuring a smooth transfer of data to the supplier. And his materials management organization has to spend a significant amount of time making sure that the chosen supplier will perform, and beyond that, ironing out a myriad of details ranging from what will trigger a reorder to how returns will be handled. Once all this work is done, nothing short of a major breach in a supplier's performance will prompt the customer to search for a new supplier. With VMI, customer/supplier partnerships are not only encouraged, they are cemented.

Sidestepping the shortcomings of forecasting

Traditionally, most manufacturing and distribution operations determine what to sell and how much to sell by way of forecast. Countless hours are spent developing, massaging, and tweaking forecasts – only to have them turn out to be dead wrong. Why? Because a forecast is nothing more than "an estimate of future demand" (APICS Dictionary). And, unlike Nostradamus, most of us cannot predict the future! Under VMI, instead of a supplier forecasting what customers will buy - which means guessing at 1) what customers are selling, 2) their inventory positions, and 3) their inventory strategies – a supplier works with real sales and inventory data first hand. Because the supplier is effectively handling their customers' materials management function, customer inventory strategies are revealed. Soon, the supplier finds that it can provide input on the timing of promotions and safety stock strategies such that it can easily accommodate changes in demand. This reduction in demand uncertainty enables suppliers to operate at higher service levels with lower inventories. Clearly, these are benefits coveted by any and all suppliers.

Benefits of Consignment

Such are the benefits of VMI - what about consignment? Isn't that the same as giving a customer an interest-free loan? Maybe. Before passing judgement, let's take a look at how most companies do business and examine the components of inventory carrying cost.

Most manufacturing and distribution companies, with the exception of make-to-order firms like Boeing, hold inventory for customers in the form of finished goods. This buffers manufacturers against fluctuations in demand. However, this stock of finished goods doesn't come free. As Ross indicates below[3], annual inventory carrying costs for most companies range from 20 to 36 percent.

Cost of Capital	10 – 15%
Storage & Warehouse Space	2 – 5%
Obsolescence & Shrinkage	4 – 6%
Insurance	1 – 5%
Material Handling	1 – 2%
Taxes	2 – 3%
Total Annual Inventory Carrying Costs	20 – 36%

Let's examine the impact of consignment on two businesses that both have annual carrying costs of 36 percent. Company A holds finished goods inventory and Company B has just decided to provide it on consignment. Company A is responsible for capital, storage, handling, and all other costs listed above. Company B is responsible for providing the capital, and as owner of the goods, is responsible for paying taxes on what isn't sold. However, under consignment, Company B is no longer responsible for storage or material handling. In addition, as with most consignment agreements, Company B's customers now have responsibility for any damage or disappearance of goods on their properties. Thus, Company B has transferred its cost of insurance and "shrinkage." Finally, by closely tracking the use of product and acting swiftly on slow-moving items, Company B can minimize or completely eliminate product obsolescence.

A quick review of cost components demonstrates that by implementing a consignment program, Company B can reduce its annual inventory carrying costs from 36 percent to 18 percent (cost of capital + taxes) in a consignment program, a reduction of 50 percent! However, if too many dollars are put into customers' warehouses on consignment, the negative impact on cash flow could leave a supplier asset rich and cash poor, a condition that could lead to bankruptcy. The solution: a well-designed consignment agreement.

Keys Points in Any Consignment Agreement

When negotiating a consignment agreement, it is critical to consider the elements of cost, responsibility, and time. The key elements are as follows:

• Level of consigned inventory. A customer would prefer to hold a large amount of consigned inventory, viewing it as a cheap way of buffering against demand uncertainty. The supplier, however, must determine the level at which it can provide goods profitably. Negotiating a set number of weeks of supply will meet the needs of both parties. If the customer sells/uses $5.2 million dollars a year and the agreement calls for ten weeks of supply, both parties know that $520,000 is the consigned level. The supplier can now budget for the capital required and the potential taxes involved in supporting the inventory. Adjustments can also be made in its cash flow projections. This arrangement also provides the customer with an incentive for increasing sales of the suppliers' products since an increase in sales translates into an increase in consigned inventory.

- Responsibility for slow-moving inventory. Another key element in a successful consignment relationship is to keep the inventory moving. Developing inventory turn goals, by individual product or by product group, can uncover slow-moving items that are inappropriate for consignment. During negotiations, it is important to determine which party will monitor inventory turnover and how slow moving goods will be handled, whether they will be returned to the supplier or purchased by the customer and removed from the consigned inventory.
- Responsibility for damaged or lost inventory. Another critical factor to address during negotiations is the disposition of stolen or damaged inventory. It is customary for the customer to assume complete responsibility for all consigned inventories - lost, stolen, or damaged - on its premises. A periodic physical inventory needs to be established to account for all consigned inventories.

By following these guidelines, a successful–and profitable–consignment relationship can be established that benefits both parties.

Conclusions

We have examined some of the benefits of VMI and consignment from a supplier's perspective. Indeed, there are benefits to both approaches, as well as costs and risks. By understanding and managing the costs, and controlling the risks through careful negotiations, one can make both consignment and VMI work not only for the customer, but for the supplier as well.

References

1. APICS Dictionary, 8th Edition
2. Fox, Mary Lou, *Integrating Vendor-Managed Inventory into Supply Chain Decision Making*, APICS 39th International Conference Proceedings, 1996
3. Ross, David Frederick, *Distribution Planning and Control*, Chapman & Hall, 1996

About the Author

Mark K. Williams, CFPIM, is currently Consulting Manager with The North Highland Company, an Atlanta, Ga. based firm specializing in Supply Chain Management Consulting. Prior to this Mark spent two years at Georgia-Pacific as Senior Manager of Materials and Manager of Logistics, and over twelve years in manufacturing and materials management in various positions for the Vermont American corporation including Operations Manager, Distribution Manager, Materials Manager, Production Control Manager and Corporate Internal Auditor.

Mark received a BA in Political Science from the University of Louisville. He is an APICS Certified Fellow in Production and Inventory Management (CFPIM). He has taught many APICS certification review courses and spoken to both APICS Chapter and Region Meetings on a variety of topics. Mark has presented at three APICS International Conferences.

Mark is Past-President of the Falls Cities Chapter (Louisville, Ky.) of APICS. Currently, Mark is a member of the Inventory Management Committee of the Curricula and Certification Council. In addition, he is also Director of Education of APICS Region IV that includes Georgia, Florida, Alabama, Mississippi and Puerto Rico.